UNMAKING NORTH AND SOUTH

JOHN M. WILLIS

Unmaking North and South

Cartographies of the Yemeni Past, 1857–1934

Columbia University Press
New York

Columbia University Press
Publishers Since 1893
New York
cup.columbia.edu
© John M. Willis, 2012
All rights reserved

Library of Congress Cataloging-in-Publication Data

Willis, John M. (John Matthew), 1971–
  Unmaking north and south : cartographies of the Yemeni past, 1857–1934 / John M. Willis.
       p. cm.
  Includes bibliographical references and index.
  ISBN 978-0-231-70131-0 (alk. paper)
  1. Yemen, South—History. 2. Yemen, North—History. 3. Aden (Yemen)—History. 4. Yemen, South—Foreign relations—Great Britain. 5. Great Britain—Foreign relations—Yemen, South. I. Title.

DS247.Y45W56 2012
953.3'04—dc23

                                  2012029083

Columbia University Press books are printed on permanent and durable acid-free paper. This book is printed on paper with recycled content.
Printed in India

c 10 9 8 7 6 5 4 3 2 1

References to Internet Web sites (URLs) were accurate at the time of writing. Neither the author nor Columbia University Press is responsible for URLs that may have expired or changed since the manuscript was prepared.

CONTENTS

Acknowledgments vii
List of Figures and Maps xi
List of Abbreviations xiii
Notes on Transliteration and Translation xv

Introduction 1
1. Defining Authority on the Indian Frontier 17
2. Masterless Men 45
3. A Landscape of Uncertainty 73
4. Disorder and the Domain of Obedience 105
5. The Centre of Renewal and Reform 137
6. The Return of Indeterminacy 169
Conclusion: Unmaking North and South 197

Notes 207
Bibliography 249
Index 265

ACKNOWLEDGMENTS

This book began as a dissertation at New York University, under the direction of Zachary Lockman, Michael Gilsenan and Bernard Haykel and, later, Brinkely Messick and Lisa Wedeen as outside readers. Individually and collectively, they brought to bear on the project their vast knowledge, critical engagement, and unceasing encouragement. It is largely due to the open and collegial intellectual environment that Zach and Michael worked so hard to cultivate in the Department of Middle Eastern and Islamic Studies at NYU that this book is possible. I would also like to thank Michael Dwyer of Hurst Publishers and the editorial board of the Hurst series "Society and History in the Indian Ocean": Anne K. Bang, Kai Kresse, Scott S. Reese, and Edward Simpson. Scott, in particular, deserves special thanks for inviting me to submit my manuscript to the series and working with me closely to ensure that it was actually completed. In the mountain west, London and India, he has been both comrade and taskmaster.

My research was conducted in Yemen, the United Kingdom, and the Netherlands over several years. I was funded at various times by grants and fellowships from the Social Science Research Council Program in the Near and Middle East, the Fulbright IEE program, the American Institute for Yemeni Studies, the Department of Middle Eastern and Islamic Studies at New York University, and the University of Colorado Innovative Seed Grant Program. I could not have conducted research in Yemen without the aid of several institutions and people. I would like to thank the American Institute for Yemeni Studies and especially Marta Colburn and Christopher Edens, both of whom acted as resident directors in Sanaa while I was there. The Yemeni Center for Studies and Research sponsored my residency in Yemen and arranged for my research permits each time I visited. At the Dar

ACKNOWLEDGMENTS

al-Makhtutat, the General Director of the Western Library, 'Abd al-Malik al-Maqhafi, made access to the collection exceedingly easy, and Ahmad Haza', the Head of the Department of Reproductions, put much effort into microfilming manuscripts for me, often at short notice. 'Abdullah al-Washali, the Director of the Eastern Library on behalf of the Ministry of Awqaf, allowed me access to the collection there and personally photocopied materials for me. At the Say'un branch of al-Markaz al-Watani li-l-Watha'iq, 'Abd al-Rahman al-Saqqaf, the Director of the Say'un Museum, and Muhammad 'Abd al-Qadir al-Sabban, the Head of the Department of Documentation, allowed me to peruse the collection there and make numerous copies. 'Abd al-Salam al-Wajih and Ahmad 'Abbas Ishaq of the Imam Zayd b. 'Ali Cultural Foundation provided extensive manuscript lists, digitized manuscripts on CD, and invaluable assistance in interpreting local accounting symbols. N. al-Mutahhar has my immense gratitude for generously sharing with me select documents from the collection of Imam Yahya's chief notary, Qadi 'Abd al-Karim al-Mutahhar. In London and Kew, the staffs of the Oriental and India Office Library in the British Library and the British National Archives were always helpful. J.A.N. Frankhuizen of the University of Leiden Library Special Collections made access to the newspaper collection there extraordinarily easy and productive.

The production of the book was financed by a University of Colorado Kayden award. Maps were hand-drawn by Molly Holmberg of Mollymaps. Parts of Chapter 1 appeared earlier as "Making Yemen Indian: Rewriting the Boundaries of Imperial Arabia," *IJMES* 41 (2009) and are reprinted here with the permission of Cambridge University Press.

I would like to thank colleagues in the field of Middle East studies who have contributed to or supported my work in one way or another, though in naming them it is not my intention to slight those I may have overlooked: Sabri Ateş, Nathan Citino, Jim Jankowski, Thomas Kühn, Geoffrey Porter, Paul Sedra, Joshua Schreier, Shelagh Weir, Jessica Winegar, and Carole Woodall. At the University of Colorado I would like to thank Peter Boag and Susan Kent for providing a supportive environment for junior faculty and especially for those of us working on the non-West. My colleagues in the History Department, Lucy Chester, Sanjay Gautam, Kwangmin Kim, Miriam Kingsberg, Marjorie McIntosh, Mithi Mukherjee, Myles Osborne and Richard Reitan, have read and commented on various chapters of the manuscript. Carla Jones and Ruth Mas, as Directors of the "Transnational Discourses of Islamic Community" project, provided a

ACKNOWLEDGMENTS

context in which I could substantially rethink parts of my overall argument. They and the other participants in the working group, Najeeb Jan, Nabil Echchaibi, and Dennis McGilvray, have my thanks.

I would like to thank my immediate and extended family for their unwavering support as I transitioned from graduate student to Assistant Professor. My parents, Travis and Virgie Willis, and my brother and sister-in-law, Andrew and Mary Willis, have my sincerest gratitude. More recently, it has been my great honour and good fortune to have been welcomed as family by Harigovinda and Roswitha Jagtiani; I could not ask for better in-laws. Finally, none of this would have been possible without the patient care and boundless love of my wife Nina. Only Ghalib's words can do justice to my love for her and to her I dedicate this book:

حال دل نہیں معلوم، لیکن اس قدر یعنی
ہم نے بار ہا ڈھونڈھا، تم نے بار ہا پایا

The condition of the heart is unknown, but for this:
Many times have I searched for it, many times have you found it

LIST OF FIGURES AND MAPS

Figures

Figure 1. 22 May Memorial, Aden (photo: J. Willis) 3
Figure 2. Ship of State: Roundabout in Crater (photo: J. Willis) 4
Figure 3. Reproduction of Hunter and Sealey's genealogy of the 'Abdali Sultans (source: Hunter and Sealey, *Arab Tribes* (1909), 325) 27
Figure 4. Sir Ahmad b. Fadl, KCSI, Sultan of Lahj (source: Jacob, *Kings of Arabia*, 141) 38
Figure 5. Subayhi notables in receipt of British payments, c. 1907 (source: IOR R/20/A/4874) 64
Figure 6. Palace of the Amir of Dali', engraving based on sketch by Harris (source: Harris, *A Journey through the Yemen*, 195) 83
Figure 7. Wahab's map of Amiri Boundary, showing lines drawn by the British commission, the India Office, and the Ottoman commission (source: IOR R/20/E/234) 89
Figure 8. Imam Yahya's royal procession, escorted by troops of the regular army (source: Volta, *La Corte Di Re Yahia*, 80) 125
Figure 9. Imam Yahya's "piercing gaze" (source: Rihani, *Arabian Peak and Desert*, frontspiece) 145

Maps

Map 1. Yemen and the Nine Tribes of the Aden Protectorate xvi
Map 2. Subayhi Country, Showing Main Trade Route 62

LIST OF ABBREVIATIONS

BNA	British National Archives
CO	Colonial Office
EL	Eastern Library
FO	Foreign Office
GAT	Gazetteer of Arabian Tribes
HA	Handbook of Arabia
IOR	India Office Records
MRAP	Military Report on the Aden Protectorate
ROY	Records of Yemen
SM	Say'un Museum
WL	Western Library

NOTE ON TRANSLITERATION AND TRANSLATION

Arabic words are transliterated according to a simplified version of the format used by the *International Journal of Middle Eastern Studies*, in which I have chosen to omit diacritical marks. I have used or dropped the definite article "al-" for ease of reading, and I have elected to retain the British "Aden" rather than the Arabic "'Adan" and the less clumsy "Sanaa" instead of "San'a.'" For the spelling of places and tribal names I have found two works indispensable. For the North I have relied on Ibrahim Ahmad al-Maqhafi's *Mu'jam al-Buldan wa-l-Qaba'il al-Yamaniyya* (2002) and for the South I have, in turn, relied on Hamza 'Ali Luqman's *Tarikh al-Qaba'il al-Yamaniyya* (1985).

When working with Arabic documents in the British archives, I was confronted with the decision of whether to rely on the originals (when intact) or the English translations. Unless otherwise indicated, I have quoted from the translations for the very reason that the English texts were inevitably those on which the Aden government relied in forming policy. Similarly, it was the English translations that were sent on to Bombay, Delhi and London. In cases where the original Arabic text was intact, I have compared the translation with the original, and when quoting in the chapters that follow, I have inserted the Arabic in transliteration when I felt that reference to the original might clarify the translation or suggest alternative translations. Otherwise, all translations are my own.

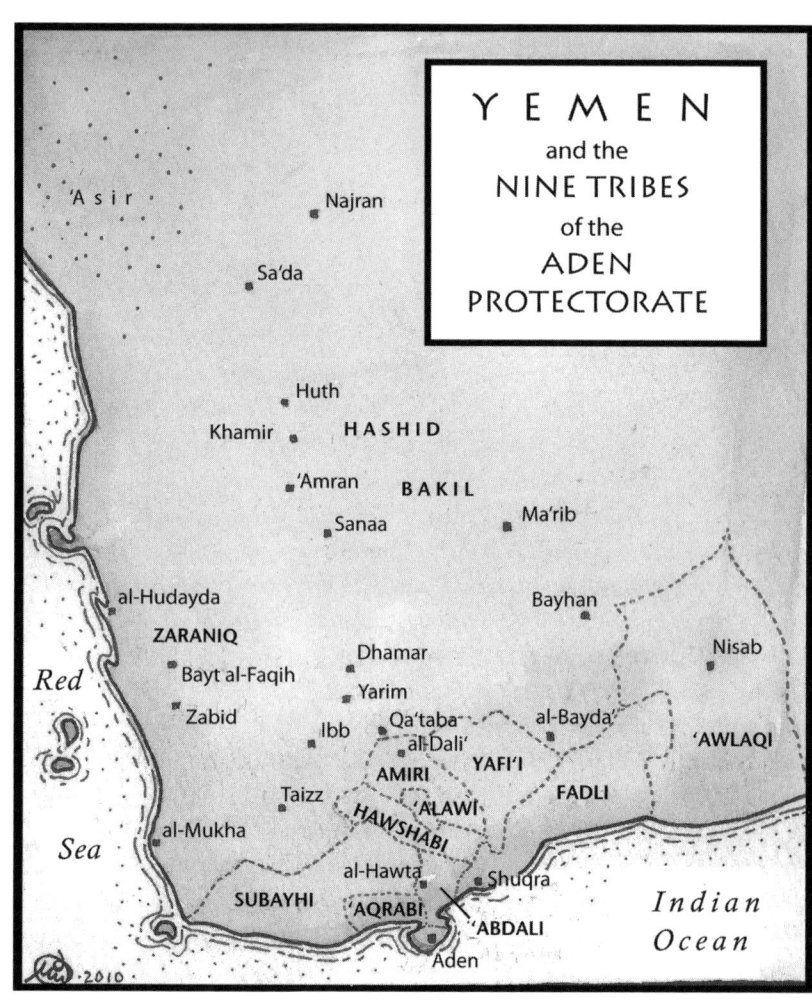

Map 1: Yemen and the Nine Tribes.

INTRODUCTION

A whole history remains to be written of spaces—which would at the same time be the history of powers (both of these terms in the plural)—from the great strategies of geopolitics to the little tactics of the habitat, institutional architecture from the classroom to the design of hospitals, passing via economic and political installations.

Michel Foucault[1]

The fragmentary past of unified Yemen

In June 2006, sixteen years after the countries of North and South Yemen were unified, the journalist Yahya 'Abd al-Raqib al-Jubayhi was quoted as saying, "Every Yemeni who now is ignorant of the meaning of South and North is a product of the achievement. Since 22 May, each Yemeni chants whether it is overtly, silently, in pleasure or in misery, in poverty, in sickness or good health, they repeat no more South and North."[2] This hopeful, indeed joyful, assessment of Yemen's political present came just six years after the Arab Republic of Yemen celebrated the tenth anniversary of the unification of the separate nations of North and South Yemen on 22 May 2000. The event in May 2000 was meant to commemorate the end of the separate regimes of the republican North and the communist South and the fulfillment of a national destiny that had been left incomplete by years of division since the twin revolutions of 1962 and 1967.

The event was the occasion for unprecedented mobilization of the state. Signs and billboards appeared, celebrating a decade of unity, public trash receptacles were installed, seemingly overnight, on the major thoroughfares of Sanaa, and the city for once seemed relatively tidy. On the day of the celebrations, minor representatives from the leadership of the Arab world were there to witness the events and to sit with President 'Ali 'Abdullah Salih as he presided over the grand military parade, including a fly-past of fighter aircraft, in front of the presidential palace. They were joined by nearly 100,000 participants, many bussed in by the government, to watch a series of floats and folklore performances celebrating the cultures of the various regions of Yemen, cast here as national culture, followed by a military display. The subtext was fairly clear: the Yemeni union, though comprising regional difference, was ultimately held together by force of arms. The whole affair cost some twenty to fifty billion Yemeni *riyals* in a country in which an estimated 42 per cent of the population live below the poverty line.

As Lisa Wedeen has argued, the celebration was very much an "exemplary event" that displayed the state's ability to muster its resources, both civilian and military, and provide, even if only for a moment, the basic services that many assumed it could only wish that it could. It was a moment in which the state under the rule of 'Ali 'Abdullah Salih could enact, through a highly choreographed performance of competency, Yemen's unity and the modernity of the state.[3] I would like, however, to turn to the commemoration in the southern city of Aden, the former capital of the communist People's Democratic Republic of Yemen. The festivities were reenacted there a few days later but were much more subdued. The dignitaries of the Arab states did not make their way south for the occasion. Nor was the exaggerated display of the state's military power repeated there: no air shows, no paratroopers, and no marching infantry escorted by armored cars and tanks. There were speeches, however, in the Khur Maksar neighborhood, across from the British Consulate where the road had been repaved and public seating installed. There was also the monument: a somewhat unimpressive piece of public sculpture that had been produced for the occasion (fig. 1). At the base was the image of a Yemeni fortified gate, perhaps based on the southern gate of the city of Sanaa, the capital of unified Yemen. At the upper corners of the image were the numbers "14" and "26" enclosed in circles. Respectively, these numbers commemorate the beginnings of armed resistance against British colonial rule in the South on 14 October 1963 and the military coup against the Zaydi Imamate in the North on 26 September 1962. Rising from the base of the sculpture was a pillar at the top of which was inscribed the number "22," in reference to the unification of North and South on 22 May 1990.

INTRODUCTION

While an otherwise unremarkable piece of public art, the sculpture was a monument to the power of a nationalist narrative that posed Yemeni unification, or reunification as it was often called, as an inevitable and logical historical development. In its representation of the two revolutions of North and South as the base from which sprang the 1990 union, the sculpture suggested the irrelevance of the historical or geographical specificities of each revolution and the ambivalences in the nationalist movements that led to the foundation of two very different regimes. There was no mention, for example, of the highly uneven union that took place in 1990, in which the Southern political elite and its President 'Ali Salim al-Bid were subordinate to the North. Nor was the brutal civil war of 1994 mentioned, in which the Northern military defeated a secessionist movement in the South and occupied the city of Aden. Both revolutions have been understood in nationalist

Figure 1: 22 May Memorial, Aden

literature as movements meant to correct what were otherwise historical anomalies: the British occupation of Aden and Southern Yemen from 1839 to 1967 and the Islamic Zaydi kingdom which had reigned in Northern Yemen under the Hamid al-Din Imams from 1904 to 1962. The independent states that were formed after the revolutions of '62 and '67—in both republican and communist forms—have similarly been treated as mere temporary arrangements that awaited national unity. Unified Yemen was, in effect, simply waiting to happen and the individual revolutions of North and South were initial steps towards the fulfillment of an historical destiny.

In contrast to the 22 May memorial, I would like to suggest a more ambivalent reading of the nationalist narrative based on two other memorial sites. Contrary to the 22 May memorial's obvious historicism, both of these sites suggest that the geographical imagination is just as important as the historical imagination. At nearly the same time as the celebration of

Figure 2: Ship of State: Roundabout in Crater

INTRODUCTION

unification in 2000, a piece of public sculpture in the roundabout of the Tawila market, the principal square of Aden, was in the process of being constructed (fig. 2). From a concrete base, a pole extended upward, at the top of which was a replica of an Arab dhow, the local wooden sailing ship that used to ply the waters of the Arabian Sea and the Indian Ocean. The sail of the replica featured a portrait of the President, in profile, staring proudly into the distance. If the symbolism of the President at the helm of the metaphorical ship of state seems a bit too obvious, it was not necessarily so for the residents of Aden. Indeed, while the replica of the dhow as a symbol of the port's mercantile past, and hopefully future, was further clarified by an informational placard at the base of the sculpture, one question remained: *whose* commercial past was represented—was it Adenese or British, was it national or was it colonial, was it Southern or somehow representative of a unified "Yemeni" history? Despite the attempt to reaffirm the place of Aden in post-unification Yemen, and the authority of President Salih over the South, the sculpture's message remained ambiguous. Most tellingly, it was said locally that many people assumed the dhow represented the ship of Betteworth Haines, the British Captain who oversaw the occupation of Aden in 1839, leading to over one hundred years of colonial rule in the Yemeni South.

I encountered a similarly ambiguous attitude towards the country's past in a small cemetery, not far from Liberation Square in Sanaa. A young activist from the Zaydi legal school of Islam that once dominated Northern Yemen had taken me there so that I could see the grave of Imam Yahya Hamid al-Din (r. 1904–1948) whose family had ruled North Yemen until the republican revolution of 1962. It was a small graveyard, tucked away from the traffic of the street. The young man guided me through the graves, each indistinguishable from the next, until we reached one that was adorned with a small vase of flowers, now wilting in the sun. Perhaps whoever had placed them there had not heard that in unified Yemen, the Imam was considered the antithesis of everything the 1962 revolution stood for: the end of a narrow, religious domination, the abolition of social hierarchy, and the beginnings of progress and development; that is, the beginning of political modernity. As we stood silently looking at the modest grave, the caretaker approached us and asked what we were doing. When we replied that we had come to pay our respects to the former Imam, he began to tell as a familiar story of the Imam's justice. Every day, the man explained, the Imam sat under a tree in the courtyard of his palace, hearing the petitions of his subjects and dispensing justice on the spot. Despite the post-revolutionary vilification of Yemen's previous rulers, the man still saw in Imam Yahya the model of an Islamic ruler, rooted not in doctrine but in everyday acts of justice. For this man, and perhaps the anonymous person who brought flowers, the Imam was not a despot, but an embodiment of virtue, piety, and the law.

As Prasenjit Duara has noted, "national history secures for the contested and contingent nation the false unity of a self-same, national subject evolving through time."[4] If the narrative of the Yemeni nation has achieved a hegemonic coherence as the subject of history, these sites (or perhaps counter-sites is a better term) suggest that it continues to be haunted by the specters of its past. Neither colonial rule nor the Zaydi Imamate have been expunged from the national narrative; they remain just below the surface ready to shatter the fragile appearance of Yemeni unity and the expectations of the better future it promised. North and South, despite al-Jubayhi's assertion, have not disappeared, but linger on. It is my aim in this book to question the inevitability and naturalness of a unified Yemen by engaging in the type of history of *spaces/powers* to which Foucault was referring in the above quote. I do so not by analyzing the historical processes that made the imagination of a bounded Yemeni nation possible, but by looking anew at the history of colonialism in the South and the history of the Zaydi Imamate in the North. The principal question that animates the study is: how were both North and South Yemen made possible as bounded political, social, and moral spaces? And how do we write the histories of spaces that were themselves inextricably rooted in local and trans-local histories of economy, empire, state formation, religious thought, and resistance?

In the chapters that follow, I will argue that the Yemeni North and South as specific political, cultural and moral geographies were the product of a contingent and multi-layered history of interaction and possibility of which the nation was only one possible outcome. The two case studies that form the core of the work are the British Aden Protectorate in the Yemeni South and the Zaydi Imamate of the Hamid al-Din family in the Yemeni North in the period between 1857 and 1934. It is my contention that their formation must be situated at the intersection of three major political, social and ideological currents present in the Middle East and the Indian Ocean, which mediated between local and trans-local histories. The first is the post-1857 transfer of India to the British Crown and the subsequent institution of a policy of non-interference with what were considered Indian

INTRODUCTION

native "customs" and polities outside British rule. This was the beginning of what Barbara and Thomas Metcalf have called the "durbar" form of rule, which marked the end of colonial liberalism and ushered in a period of collaboration between the British Raj and the semi-independent princely states that lasted until independence in 1947.[5] The second trend is the expansion of the post-Tanzimat Ottoman state into the Arabian Peninsula and Yemen with the occupation of the Yemeni North in 1872. The creation of an Ottoman province of Yemen meant also the introduction of a program of state centralization and modernization that was new to the region. Finally, the third trend is the inter-war movement for Islamic unity, or Pan-Islamism, in the period after the dissolution of the Ottoman Empire, with its insistence on the linkages between moral reform, communal solidarity, and anti-imperialism.

By locating Yemen's North and South in structures, discourses and ideologies of local and trans-local import, it is my intention to intervene in a field on which the nation form and the associated narrative of progress (whether liberal or Marxist) has weighed heavily. Historians writing before 1990, for example, took the history of either North or South as their subjects, with the underlying assumption that the modern states of the Yemen Arab Republic or the People's Democratic Republic of Yemen were the natural agents of history.[6] With few exceptions, histories written in the period after 1990 have suddenly encompassed the whole of geographical Yemen as if the legal-political identity of a particular space was the driving force in its history or histories.[7] In these narratives British colonialism (which, it must be reiterated, lasted over a century) and the Hamid al-Din Imamate are treated as stages of historical development that merely paved the way for the movements of national liberation—whether those of the Free Officers, the National Liberation Front, or the Movement of Arab Nationalists—and the formation of the modern states. They represent little more than the history of the nation deferred, the history of aberrations in the inexorable movement towards the formation of the modern state, in whatever form it took, and authentic nationhood.[8]

Indeed, the field, with few exceptions, has been written in the form of what Paul Carter has referred to in his *The Road to Botany Bay* as "imperial history."[9] In a poetic account of the relationship between the practice of exploration and the formation of Australia as a national space, Carter argued that imperial history assumes that the nation as it is embodied in geographical space exists beyond histories of local politics and practice,

7

until it is discovered by the West. It is the history of European hegemony and the intellectual fields and practices through which it operated: global capitalism, empire, nation, and the tactical fields they deployed such as the census, cartography, and ethnography—all of which involved for Carter the taxonomic processes of naming as a form of power. In many ways the imperial history of unified Yemen and its Northern and Southern precedents as bounded, national spaces have yet to be dismantled. Bound to the state as they are, the histories and spaces that constitute the North and South have been inextricably tied to the Zaydi Imamate of the Hamid al-Din dynasty, the British colonial state, and the nation states that followed in their wake. Like Michel de Certeau's oft-cited metaphor of the view of Manhattan from the top of the World Trade Center, this view of Yemen's history has effaced the complex and fractured past of spaces, both North and South, constructed through their interaction with the forces of global capitalism, imperialism, Islamic reformism, and the multiple discursive fields that engaged in and against them.[10]

Spatial histories of modern Yemen

My understanding of Yemen's modern history begins with Fred Halliday's assessment of Yemen's formation as an historical space, in which he asserts that "there was nothing inevitable in 'national' Yemen either comprising or excluding the territory that it did."[11] As with Halliday, my guiding assumption is that there was nothing in these histories that suggested the formation of anything that could be called a "unified Yemen" in the nationalist sense. By writing the history of the spaces at contention in the history of modern Yemen, it is my intention to destabilize the historicism of modernity and its agents, whether the colonial state, the capitalist world economy, or the nation form itself. What a history of space, or a spatialized history, makes possible, as Doreen Massey suggests, is that it "enables an understanding of its positionality, its geographical embeddedness; an understanding of the spatiality of the production of knowledge itself."[12] It is history not of teleology, but of contingency. In thinking through what a spatial history of Yemen would entail, I turn once again to Paul Carter.

Against the tyranny of imperial history, as the history of the modern nation, Carter suggested the concept and method of what he termed "spatial history." Spatial history is embodied not in the map as a graphic representation of space, but in the act of exploration and the contingent

INTRODUCTION

operation of conquest, with its false starts, absence of paths, local resistance, and often fatal conclusions. It is not the presumption of a space already in existence but the production of space by engagement with geography at the level of practice. For Henri Lefebvre, this is space as it is enacted through everyday practice, but also through the imagination and dreams of spaces yet to be. This notion is akin to de Certeau's concept of "tactics" or, to continue with his metaphor of Manhattan, the act of walking through the streets of the city as opposed to watching them from above.[13] As the concept is employed in this book, however, spatial history necessitates charting the complex interaction between seemingly stable languages and representations of space and the multitude of daily practices of which these representations were ultimately an effect; these include not only the work of explorers as in Carter's formulation, but the discourses, forms of knowledge, and governing practices deployed by states, colonial or otherwise.

Already, a number of historians have raised questions about the production of colonial and national geographies, noting the relationship between the geographical imagination and the practices of colonial governance and the forces of global capitalism.[14] Much of this work has dealt with the cartographic practices of the colonial state, showing how much the act of mapping was a highly contested practice despite its incorporation into the larger field of the scientific disciplines and its claim to represent an unmediated reality.[15] Moreover, they show that geographical knowledge in the colonial context, no different from other forms of knowledge, always engaged contingent, localized histories, grounded in indigenous knowledges and practices. Spatial history, by definition and contrary to imperial history, is the yet undetermined, the contingent, and the improvised. It is, in essence, fragmentary. In this sense my approach to the spatial history of modern Yemen is inspired by Gyan Pandey's work on the fragment as a means to critique the nation form. "Part of the importance of the 'fragmentary' point of view," he writes, "lies in that it resists the drive for a shallow homogenization and struggles for other, potentially richer definitions of the "nation" and the future political community."[16] In the remainder of the introduction, I would like to map out how I intend to write such a history.

A spatial history of the Yemeni North and South, as I envision it, requires tracing the paths of the three intellectual currents I mentioned previously and the forms of institutional power they informed across two discrete spatial and temporal horizons. The first is the network of institutions, discourses, ideologies and practices centered in and emanating from Britain's

Indian empire after the assumption of Crown rule after the 1857 Great Revolt.[17] Aden's occupation in 1839 by the Indian Navy and its attachment to the Bombay Presidency assured its administrative and economic connection to what Robert Blythe has called the "Empire of the Raj," which spanned the Indian Ocean and connected India with East Africa, the Persian Gulf, and the Malay Peninsula in a common structure of imperial rule.[18] James Onley has painstakingly outlined the administrative relationship between the Persian Gulf states, Bahrain in particular, and the Indian informal empire, organized under the residency system, to make the argument that British India extended far beyond South Asia and included parts of what the modern paradigm of Area Studies has demarcated as the Middle East and the Arab World.[19] Indeed, defining India as the Interpretation Act of 1889 did as "any territories of any Native Prince or Chief under the suzerainty of His Majesty," we come to the conclusion that Aden and what became the Aden Protectorate were indeed part of the Indian Empire.[20]

As I have suggested, the Indian history of the Yemeni South cannot be reduced to an administrative relationship or the strategic needs of a commercial empire. Aden was also incorporated into the cultural project of empire that was characterized by the production, institutionalization, and dissemination of a body of knowledge about India's history, society, and culture, which then informed the governing practices of the officials sent to Aden. Queen Victoria's 1858 proclamation to the "Princes, Chiefs and People of India" declared the end of colonial liberalism by its adoption of a policy of non-interference in the lives of its subjects and the affairs of the semi-independent princely states, elevating the British monarchy to an imperial monarchy. The Queen's acceptance of the title "Empress of India" in the 1877 Imperial Assemblage reinforced the idea that the British monarchy had assumed the place of the now deposed Mughal emperor in the governance of what was assumed to be an endlessly diverse and hopelessly fragmented landscape of castes, tribes, and feudal princedoms. It was an imperial moment, as Sugata Bose argues, that indicated the rise of European notions of "unitary sovereignty, which replaced the concept of layered and shared sovereignty that had characterized Indian and Indian Ocean polities of the precolonial era."[21] The historical and ethnographic imagination that informed the post-1858 empire saw the states of princely India as embodying local traditions of monarchy, understood analogically through Britain's mediaeval past, that would act as subordinate partners to the British government and provide a political counterweight to the middle class nationalism of the Indian National Congress, formed in 1885.[22]

INTRODUCTION

The port city of Aden, occupied in 1839 as a coaling station and later a commercial entrepôt connecting the Red Sea to the Indian Ocean, was the first colonial acquisition of the Victorian period. It was governed directly as part of the Bombay Presidency, under the jurisdiction of Indian civil and criminal procedure and a British Resident. A cosmopolitan population of Somalis, Indians and Arabs was encouraged to settle in the town as laborers, craftsmen and small-scale merchants, while international firms from Europe and India took advantage of the port's brisk trade. The largely tribal hinterland of Aden was governed, by contrast, as a series of native states on the model of princely India. That is, the colonial administrators who arrived in Aden with years of experience in Afghanistan, Sind and the Punjab understood the local tribes as local aristocracies, founded in history and enjoying political legitimacy based on local traditions of hierarchical rule. The Aden Protectorate, formed at the turn of the century as a community of native chiefs allied with the British through treaty alliances, was imagined as part of princely India and incorporated into the state rituals that were meant to inculcate in the governed sincere loyalty to the British state rituals—the state assemblages and imperial durbars of the early twentieth century—that were meant to inculcate in the governed sincere loyalty to the British.

The second and third trends shift our attention to the Yemeni North in the late Ottoman and inter-war period, and deal specifically with the legacy of the Ottoman modernizing project, the Tanzimat, and the simultaneous development of the trans-local movement of Sunni Islamic reform. The Ottoman occupation of Yemen (1872–1918) brought the country into the empire-wide program of reform with the goal of modernizing its government, developing its resources, and cultivating a new modern political subjectivity in its people that emphasized Ottoman national identity. In this process, the state largely marginalized the already weakened Zaydi-Shi'i Imamate that had ruled much of the Yemeni North since the tenth century, and was understood in the context of Ottoman reform as a symbol of the province's backwardness. The eventual revolt of the Hamid al-Din Imams, initiated by Imam al-Mansur in 1898 and continued by his son Imam al-Mutawakkil Yahya in 1904, was directed at the Ottoman state and the Tanzimat as forces of irreligion and tyranny that had displaced the moral injunctions of Islam. Their ultimate reconciliation in 1911 was embodied in a treaty that recognized the Zaydi Imamate's inherent suitability to the religious dispositions of the country's inhabitants. Like the British in Aden, the Ottoman state had adopted a form of colonial indirect rule.

The threshold moment in the production of the Yemeni North, as I understand, is the collapse of the Ottoman state in 1918 following the First World War and the rise of Imam Yahya Hamid al-Din at the head of the Zaydi polity. A descendant of the Prophet and a scholar of Islam, Imam Yahya transformed an otherwise marginal Shi'i spiritual and temporal institution into a powerful state that challenged British rule in the South and made claims to lead the entire Islamic world. He did so in two ways: first, he adopted the modern military organization of the Ottoman Tanzimat state, under the command of former Ottoman officers, and created a powerful army with which he conquered the majority of the Yemeni North; second, he effectively adopted and mobilized the reformist ideology and anti-imperialism of the Sunni Salafi movement that had arisen in the Middle East and moved to the rest of the Islamic world via the Pan-Islamic press.[23] Activists of the Salafi movement, foremost among them Jamal al-Din al-Afghani, Muhammad 'Abduh and later Muhammad Rashid Rida, argued the necessity of reasserting Islamic orthodoxy as embodied in the Quranic revelation and the normative model of the Prophet Muhammad (through the practice of *ijtihad* or rational inquiry) as a means of both strengthening the moral community of Muslims and encouraging Islamic unity in the face of European empire.[24] It is from within this discursive tradition with its dual insistence on moral reform and anti-imperial activism that Imam Yahya was able to enter into a trans-local debate about the future of the community, the necessity of resisting empire, and the potential role of the Yemeni Imamate, even though it came from the Zaydi school, in reviving the moral community in the absence of the Ottoman Empire.[25]

In light of what has been discussed so far, it should be clear that one of my working assumptions is that Yemen's modern history, whether North or South, cannot be seen as self-originating, but was always embedded in discourses, institutions, and governing structures of trans-local, even global import. It is therefore difficult in hindsight to accept the view of the American diplomat and Arabist Charles R. Crane who, upon visiting Sanaa in 1928, wrote that "the Yaman … is absolutely shut in—no part of the world is more so."[26] Crane's view of Yemen as located out of place and time is illustrative of what David Harvey argues is typical of Enlightenment thought, which "perceived 'the other' as necessarily having (and sometimes 'keeping to') a specific *place* in a spatial order that was ethnocentrically conceived to have homogenous and absolute qualities."[27] What Harvey has pinpointed is the spatial equivalent of what Johannes Fabian referred to as

INTRODUCTION

the "denial of coevalness" in anthropological thought: the assumption that the "other" resides not only in another space, but in another time as well.[28]

Indeed, the Yemeni South was very much part of the Indian Ocean world as mediated by Britain's empire in India. While the formation of the Aden Protectorate had as its expressed goal the preservation of local political systems among what the British would call the "nine tribes" of the Aden hinterland, its very incorporation into the systems of knowledge and state rituals (for example the imperial durbars of 1903 and 1911) ensured that the political life of the South was inextricably entwined with India. Indeed, it was assumed by the Durbar of 1903, which commemorated the coronation of King Edward VII, that the native chiefs of the Protectorate, as they were known, were members of a trans-regional native aristocracy that spanned the breadth of the empire, bound to the British Crown and acting as conservative partners in the imperial project. Similarly, Imam Yahya, who in his lifetime never set his eyes on the sea, was part of a much larger ideological and political world than has been previously assumed. By engaging in a Sunni-dominated Islamic public sphere, on the basis of the Islamic discursive tradition of reform, Imam Yahya join a common field of debate that linked Sanaa to cosmopolitan centers such as Cairo, Beirut and Bombay, regardless of his leadership of a minority Shi'i community. In this sense, we could place the Hamid al-Din Imamate's inter-war participation in the movement for Islamic unity or Pan-Islamism alongside other reformist movements, such as the Irshad movement and its 'Alawi counterparts in Hadramawt and Java, the Indian Khilafat movement, and even the Jadidist movement in Central Asia.[29] Like these movements, Imam Yahya's engagement with Islamic reformism had to contend with the ideal of a universal ethical community and the growing reality of modern politics rooted in territorial belonging. In his anti-imperialism, which took as its point of departure a critique of the divisive nature of ethnic nationalism and the European state system, he was interacting with a complex field of inter-war political debate. Although it is seductive to argue, as Erez Manela does, that many inter-war nationalist movements were inspired by the "Wilsonian Moment" represented by Wilson's "Fourteen Points" and its emphasis on self-determination, one should also keep in mind that there were other models of association beyond the nation that were circulating in this period, such as socialist internationalism, Pan-Asianism, forms of international humanism, and Pan-Islamism—all of which shared rejection of the post-Westphalian order in one way or another.[30]

Sources and book overview

It should be made clear from the outset that this book does not present a narrative history in the conventional sense, not does it make the claim of total history. These chapters, whether read serially or independently, are meant to evoke possible histories rather than a single and hegemonic history. I have organized each chapter around a specific problem in the constitution of both the Aden Protectorate and the Hamid al-Din Imamate as it has arisen in the archives, both colonial and Zaydi. For the South, I have been guided by the ethnographic categories that the colonial state itself generated in its encounter with the Aden hinterland: the concept of the tribal ruling houses or "native chiefs," the martial tribesmen they commanded, and the landscape they inhabited. For the North, the guiding theme has been the language of moral reform and the constitution of legitimate Islamic authority in the absence of the Ottoman state. My goal has been to reveal the highly fractured process by which these spaces came into being through the complicated interplay between discourses, representations, and the institutions and practices that they inform. It is my hope that the reader will be acutely aware of the extent to which forms of hegemonic space, whether imperial or Islamic, also generated their own potential for resistance.

The first half of the book analyzes the British occupation of Aden in 1839 and the creation of the Aden Protectorate in the years that followed. It highlights the incorporation of the Southern Yemeni hinterland into the Indian system of semi-independent princely states not only in terms of administrative organization, but also in terms of state ritual and the production of historical, ethnographic and cartographic knowledge. The first chapter looks at the process by which the "nine tribes" of the Protectorate were elevated to the status of native chiefs. Looking at the example of the 'Abdali sultans, I suggest that this was accomplished by the elaboration of a pre-colonial history of native sovereignty that was institutionalized in the colonial period through agreements of protection, colonial largesse, and ultimately their incorporation into empire-wide ritual. Chapter 2 looks at the figure of the martial tribesman as it informed notions of chiefly authority. British knowledge of the tribes was informed by the Indian understanding that certain populations had inherently martial, criminal, or loyal natures; in the Aden Protectorate the Sabayha, one of the "nine tribes," was deemed criminal because its lack of a central political figure and its itinerant nature confounded notions of tribal sovereignty and colonial geography. Chapter 3 takes as its point of departure the problem of colonial sovereignty

INTRODUCTION

in its relation to geography and landscape. Looking at travel literature, the practice of cartography, and tribal administration, I suggest that the British understanding of chiefly sovereignty bore little resemblance to the multilayered, contested, and ever negotiable forms of sovereignty that they encountered outside Aden.

The second half of the book explores the formation of the Imamate of Yahya Hamid al-Din in the North, emphasizing the extent to which it drew its administrative apparatus from the post-Tanzimat Ottoman Empire and its ideology from the inter-war Salafi movement. Chapter 4 argues that although the Hamid al-Din Imams rose in the late nineteenth century in opposition to the modernizing reforms of the Ottoman administration in Yemen, after the end of the First World War Imam Yahya quickly adopted the forms of coercive power used by the Ottoman state and initiated a military campaign that put him in control of the Yemeni North by the end of the 1920s. This new form of military power, however, was deployed in the service of an older notion of Islamic authority that saw obedience to the Imam as incumbent on believers and reinforced a social hierarchy based on noble descent and religious knowledge. The next chapter looks at the ways in which Imam Yahya's state was formed in the context of inter-war movements of Islamic reform and anti-imperialism. Yemen's political independence and Imam Yahya's program of religious reform were presented in the Muslim public sphere as signs of the country's special place in the post-Ottoman order: a place of pristine religious practice and anti-imperial activism. Imam Yahya's attempt to position Yemen at the forefront of a resurgent Islamic community, however, sat in contradiction to his simultaneous move to establish the dynastic rule of his own family and to negotiate bilateral treaties with European nations as a state like any other. The final chapter brings together the two halves of the book in an examination of the decade-long war between Imam Yahya and the tribes of the Aden Protectorate. The clash between two geographies of state rule—the universal order of Islamic authority and imperial sovereignty—created a situation in which the inhabitants of the hinterland were forced to navigate between two largely incompatible political spaces. The conflict ended in 1934 with the signing of the Anglo-Yemeni Treaty, which recognized the political status quo and the boundary between North and South.

Like many historians of empire, I was confronted with an embarrassment of archival riches on the history of the Aden Protectorate in the British National Archives and the India Office Library. However, owing to the

UNMAKING NORTH AND SOUTH

Indian government's avowed policy of non-interference in hinterland affairs, what we know is often framed by communications between the colonial administration and the native chiefs themselves and their shared interest in security and stability. The history of the Hamid al-Din Imamate presents problems of its own, namely the absence of a Yemeni state archive and the political sensitivity surrounding the pre-revolutionary regime. My principal sources for this period are the literary biographical chronicles (singular *sira*) that were written by Imam Yahya's supporters to commemorate and eulogize his rule, some published and some held in mosque libraries (the western and eastern libraries of the great mosque in Sanaa) in manuscript form. These were supported by articles from the state press, *al-Iman*, published and unpublished poetry, and miscellaneous correspondence, tax registers, petitions, and other documents held in the Say'un Museum in the Hadramawt and in the private collection of N. al-Mutahhar, a descendant of Imam Yahya's chief notary, Qadi 'Abd al-Karim al-Mutahhar. For both North and South, subaltern histories remain partial and fragmentary, but nonetheless important.

1

DEFINING AUTHORITY ON THE INDIAN FRONTIER

The political system of India is neither Feudalism nor Federation; it is embodied in no Constitution; it does not always rest upon Treaty; and it bears no resemblance to a League. It represents a series of relationships that have grown up between the Crown and the Indian Princes under widely differing historical conditions, but which in process of time have gradually conformed to a single type. The sovereignty of the Crown is everywhere unchallenged.

Lord Curzon, 1903[1]

Introduction

On 19 January 1839 the South Arabian port town of Aden was bombarded by ships of the Indian Navy and occupied by soldiers of the East India Company. It was the first British colonial acquisition of the Victorian period. Just a year before, Capt. S. B. Haines, the man who would later command the assault on Aden, had met Sultan Muhsin b. Fadl al-'Abdali of Lahj, who claimed the port as part of his territory. At that time the outright occupation of the town had yet to be considered, and the two men were discussing instead the possibility of leasing the town for the purpose of storing coal for the Royal Navy. After lengthy deliberations, the Sultan expressed his desire to come to some agreement. Haines later wrote an account of the meeting in a letter to the Superintendent of the Indian Navy in which he described Muhsin b. Fadl's overture: "At last he announced that he would rather have the English, but would they receive him as an ally, and protect his country from being molested; in fact receive him and country on the same terms as the Nabob of Surat."[2]

Whether intentional or not, the exchange says much about the political imagination in the western Indian Ocean in the early nineteenth century. That Sultan Muhsin so quickly invoked the East India Company's relationship with one of India's many autonomous regional rulers as a way of forecasting future relationships suggests the extent to which Britain's growing empire was by this time an ineluctable and increasingly hegemonic force in Arabia. To be sure, there was a longstanding commercial relationship between Yemen and India, via the ports of al-Mukha and Surat and the trade in coffee, but it was the framework of Britain's informal empire that provided the normative model for trans-regional political relationships.[3] By the time the conversation between Haines and Sultan Muhsin took place, the British had already established residencies in the territories of over forty "native princes," who accepted British advisers and a relationship of political subordination.[4] The 'Abdali Sultanate would shortly thereafter join the ranks of the Indian native princes as part of an imperial association of local rulers under British suzerainty, the local iteration of which was the Aden Protectorate, formed in the late nineteenth century.

This chapter begins mapping out the process by which the tribal polities of the Aden hinterland, the 'Abdali Sultanate in particular, became Indian native states in colonial policy, discourse and practice. It does so by focusing on the production of the "native chief" as a category of colonial governance and administration. The assumption that Aden's hinterland comprised numerous tribal chiefs was in part the legacy of a series of British administrators who brought their experience in the Bombay Presidency, the princely states of western India, and the Punjab to bear on frontier policy, beginning with the occupation in 1839. Informed by a historical and genealogical imagination that saw a country populated by a native aristocracy of great antiquity, the British elevated the Aden native chief as the natural leader of local society. In the period after the revolt of 1857 and Queen Victoria's subsequent proclamation of non-interference in the affairs of India's native states, Aden's chiefs and the 'Abdali sultans in particular were incorporated into the rituals of empire that constituted, celebrated and perpetuated the trans-regional association of native princes and imperial power.

In what follows I will trace the specifically Indian history of the Yemeni South and the Aden Protectorate, in particular in light of its administrative status as part of the residency system and its cultural production as an effect of the mundane state practices of ethnographic observation, historical inquiry, and state ritual. I first look at the process by which the "nine tribes" and their native chiefs were produced as objects of knowledge and colonial rule in the period after 1839. The second part of the chapter looks more specifically at the 'Abdali sultans and the British engagement with local history as a means of elevating the 'Abdali to the position of paramount chiefs in the Aden hinterland. The chapter concludes with an analysis of Aden's place in the 1903 Coronation Durbar that took place in Delhi under the administration of Lord Curzon. I argue that it was not only the structures of empire that united the Yemeni South and India, but also the assumption that both places were characterized by a condition of political and cultural fragmentation that could only be united by British imperial power. This ethnographic assumption was the basis for what Barbara Metcalf and Thomas Metcalf have called the "durbar" view of government by which the British ruled India in consultation with what were considered the "natural" leaders of local society.[5]

Indirect Rule in Imperial Arabia

Britain's Indian Empire by 1858 was divided roughly between those areas under direct rule and those areas that were considered, accurately or not, as "native states" or often "princely India." The native states had varied histories. Some were pre-Mughal polities such as the Rajput states in the west, while others like the Nizams' state of Hyderabad were founded by former Mughal provincial administrators who carved out independent political spheres with the contraction of the empire in the eighteenth century. The British dealt with these states through a policy of indirect rule that was developed on an ad hoc basis during the eighteenth and nineteenth centuries, often responding to the financial burden that direct rule would bring or the necessity of securing military alliances with more powerful native states. The relationship between the British and the princely states was embodied in a "treaty of friendship" and, in the case of the larger states, the establishment of a British Residency to represent imperial interests. These treaties often entailed the surrender of certain elements of sovereignty in exchange for British protection and support, hence the description of these relationships as a form of indirect rule.[6]

As in India, colonial rule in the Yemeni South after 1839 was based on the distinction between direct and indirect rule. The port town of Aden was to be ruled directly as a colony through the Aden Residency, and the tribal hinterland beyond was to be subject to the various agreements and treaties that were the substance of indirect rule. Although Aden was originally occupied to provide a coaling station for the Royal Navy, many of the political residents hoped that it would become a prosperous port in its own right. Aden was declared a free port in 1850, and local merchants from the once prosperous port of al-Mukha were encouraged to relocate to Aden. Land in the town was given to wealthy merchants who agreed to build houses and shops in stone. The development of the port as a settlement, commercial center and military base encouraged the growth of a cosmopolitan population of Europeans, East Africans, Arabs, Jews and South Asians. An 1864 act organized the town's legal system according to Indian civil and criminal procedure and decreed that the population would be subject to the Indian Penal Code, and ultimately to the High Court of Bombay.[7]

It was S.B. Haines, the Captain of the Indian Navy who commanded the occupation of Aden and acted as the settlement's first political agent until 1854, who oversaw Aden's early development as a commercial port. To ensure the safety of caravans into the port and the settlement's population he concluded a number of agreements with the population of the hinterland and monitored conditions in the countryside with a network of spies from the local merchant population. His relationships with the local notables who would come to represent the "nine tribes" of the Aden hinterland were governed by what he saw as an intuitive understanding of the Arab character, a vision into their interior life. He expressed as much in a letter to Bombay in 1854:

Long experience with the Arabs /upwards of 30 years/ has taught me that they must be defeated with their own weapons, by quietly letting them know you perceive their intentions before they are prepared to carry them out and let them feel you are their superiors in tact, intellect, judgment and activity of purpose that their Secret thoughts are known to you that your information is sure secret and correct and that you are prepared to counteract their designs.[8]

On the surface, Haines' claim suggests similarities to the Edwardian Orientalists discussed by Satia, who assumed that Arabia could only be grasped through personal intuition.[9] Rather, Haines was claiming mastery of local political culture, which was based, he thought, on the power of vision: the ability to read secret thoughts and intentions, or in an Islamic context, the ability to discern inner truths (*batin*) from outward appearances (*zahir*). By claiming this power, Haines assumed the mantle of the

DEFINING AUTHORITY ON THE INDIAN FRONTIER

'Abdali sultans as the first among many local Shaykhs within a common field of authority. As such, he assumed the payment of stipends to the surrounding tribes and took military action against other tribes that threatened the security and the commerce of the Aden settlement.[10] Haines was less the romantic Orientalist than an Indian nabob who assumed the role of local potentate, drawing the ire of the Indian government and the proponents of colonial liberalism in the process. It is no surprise then that like many a nabob, Haines was removed from his post in 1854 for financial malfeasance and replaced by career political officers who oversaw the bureaucratization of hinterland policy.[11]

In the period after Haines' removal, the Aden Residency was staffed primarily by men from the Indian Political Service, and the men appointed as political residents to Aden in the same period had very similar professional backgrounds and fields of experience.[12] All of the residents came from the ranks of the Bombay Army and after 1857, the Bombay branch of the Indian Army. Moreover, all of these men had campaign experience either in the Afghan wars of 1838–39 and 1879–80 or in the annexation and administration of Sind. The career of James Outram, who served as Resident in 1854, is instructive. Outram began in the Bombay Infantry, participating in the Afghan war of 1839 and later joining Charles Napier in the Sind campaign, which resulted in the establishment of the British Residency in Hyderabad. It was in this early period that Outram forged a reputation as a keen manager of "tribal politics" in the frontier marches of the Bombay Presidency, especially amongst the semi-nomadic Bhil peoples. In a policy that would later be replicated in the Aden Protectorate, Outram attempted to discipline what was considered to be a "predatory" tribe by creating an all-Bhil Army unit and encouraging settled agriculture amongst Bhil communities. Both were considered a success. Later, Outram was given the Residency of Baroda, the largest native state in western India, where he was viewed as a stern reformer and champion of administrative discipline.[13] The men who followed Outram in the position of Resident were well acquainted with the problem of managing tribal or itinerant populations along the western frontiers of imperial India, and Afghanistan, Sind and the Punjab provided, whether explicitly or implicitly, useful analogies for forming policy in the Aden Protectorate.

By the mid-nineteenth century, a bureaucratic apparatus for the administration of the tribal hinterland was slowly developed. The creation of an institutional and legal structure for colonial rule in the port of Aden was mirrored by the concurrent normalization of procedures by which information on the tribes would be collected, evaluated and deposited within the state archive for later collection and publication as the official body of knowledge on the inhabitants beyond Aden. Using practices similar to those earlier deployed in India, the Aden government embarked upon a number of projects meant to catalogue and record the territory and its population that lay beyond its own fortified refuge in the city. It is in this period that we begin to see the development of what Nicholas Dirks has called the "ethnographic state," a state that was dependent on the production of knowledge about the colonized and the institutionalization of cultural and political difference as a means of ruling colonized populations.[14] The result of this process was that the difference between the tribal hinterland and the port city of Aden was institutionalized, and with it, the importance of the native "chief" at the top of the local social and political hierarchy.

In 1858 the Aden government established an Arabic Translation Department, which was responsible for all correspondence with the hinterland and the collection of information on its inhabitants.[15] In 1869, the Arabic Guest House was created to host visiting notables from outside Aden. The Translation Department and its guest house quickly became the locus of the colonial production of knowledge on the tribal hinterland through its monopoly on the translation of correspondence and its elaboration of a hierarchy of tribes linked to Aden through stipends and rituals of rule, which I will discuss more fully below.[16] Whereas in the past state largesse had been dispensed to tribal chiefs according to rather arbitrary criteria, entertainment in the guest house was offered according to a carefully graded hierarchy which determined not only the allowance given to each chief but also the number of retainers they were allowed to bring with them, reflecting their importance to the colonial state.[17] After administration and staffing by local native informants in the early years, the rise of British interpreters in their stead pointed to an increase in the specialized knowledge of colonial administrators and, ironically, the rise of the power of the 'Abdali sultans as the principal intermediaries between the colonial state and the population beyond Aden.[18]

Once the institutional apparatus for dealing with tribal correspondence had been established, the Ottoman occupation of the northern highlands and the city of Sanaa in 1872, and the subsequent incorporation of the region into the Ottoman Empire provided the context in which the British formally recognized the tribes as constituting a British sphere of influence.

DEFINING AUTHORITY ON THE INDIAN FRONTIER

In a letter presented to the Sublime Porte in 1873 the British formally requested that the Ottoman government respect the independence of what were thenceforth referred to as the "nine tribes" (often referred to as the "nine cantons") of the Aden hinterland with which they had established treaty relations. These were the 'Abdali, 'Aqrabi, 'Alawi, Amiri, 'Awlaqi, Fadli, Hawshabi, Subayhi and Yafi'i tribes.[19] What is important to note at this point is that these were, with only slight variation, the local ruling houses and tribes that had rebelled against the Qasimi dynasty of the Zaydi-Shi'i Imams of Northern Yemen in the eighteenth century, so that the British quite consciously maintained the appearance of the previous political geography beyond the walls of Aden.

The formal recognition of the "nine tribes" as political and social entities necessitated greater knowledge of the land beyond Aden, and thereafter the British initiated several projects to map the area. Again with reference to the Indian frontier experience, a group of cavalry seconded from the Sind Horse was sent to the port in 1868 and renamed the Aden Troop. Encouraged as a means of monitoring frontier lands, the Aden Troop also became an essential tool in the production of geographical knowledge of the hinterland. During the 1870s the Aden Troop conducted a number of forays outside Aden, collecting topographical details on much of the neighboring territory.[20] A formal survey of the area was conducted in 1891–92 by a member of the Survey of India, Colonel R. A. Wahab, who had earlier been employed in the demarcation of the Russo-Afghan frontier. He was later named the chief British Commissioner for the more expansive and politically charged project of delimiting the Protectorate's northern boundary with the Ottomans. The joint Anglo-Ottoman Boundary Commission of 1902–05 took the British further into the area of the "nine tribes" than they had been to date, providing an opportunity to collect information on the inhabitants of the hinterland and to fix them permanently in geographical space through the state cartographic project.

The institutionalized accumulation of knowledge on the tribal hinterland was then codified in authoritative texts. In 1886 Hunter and Sealey's statistical and descriptive work, *An Account of the Arab Tribes in the Vicinity of Aden*, was published and quickly became the point of reference for those writing about or formulating policy for the Aden hinterland;[21] a compendium of genealogies, treaties and historical narratives for each of the "nine tribes", the work was closer to Aberigh-Mackay's *The Native Chiefs and their States* (1877) than the monumental ethnographic work of Kaye's *People of*

India (1868–75). During the period of the Anglo-Ottoman Boundary Commission a new series of memoranda were written on the "nine tribes," which, although they included far more detail than previous reports, generally reproduced the account of Hunter and Sealey (which was updated and reissued in 1909).[22] The tribe as it was constituted through the field of state ethnography and historiography was less a community organized according to common patrilineal descent than a complex of ruling houses, the men they ruled, and the geographical space they inhabited.

The "nine tribes" named in the 1873 memorandum were, in fact, a group of notable families that shared a history of opposition to the Northern Zaydi Imamate in the eighteenth century. These families ruled over populations of martial tribesmen, left anonymous in British accounts, characterized only by their proclivity for warfare or brigandage. Indeed, Aden's colonial administrators brought with them from India an ethnographic language of "martial" and "criminal" races that was intuitively applied to the Aden hinterland. The Yafi'i and 'Awlaqi tribes of the eastern mountains, for example, were thought to be natural warriors, often compared with the Pathans of the North-West Frontier or the Gurkhas of Nepal.[23] Similarly, the Sabayha, who resided in the plains and valleys along the Red Sea coast were constructed as natural criminals and brigands in colonial ethnographic thought, owing primarily to the absence of both settled agriculture and hereditary leadership among them (see Chapter 2).

The institutionalization of the "nine tribes" as a social, political, and historical construct ensured that when the British signed treaties of protection with them in the period between 1888 and 1904, it assumed that they had done so with the natural leaders of the Yemeni South.[24] What is perhaps most surprising about the institution of the protectorate system at the turn of the century, however, is that the 'Abdali Sultanate of Lahj was absent from the list of signatories who collectively represented the "nine tribes" and the protectorate chiefs. Its exclusion was no accident; it was an expression of the extent to which the 'Abdali sultans were tied to the colonial presence of the British in Aden and their continued political and economic hegemony in the region. From the occupation of Aden and the signing of the first treaty with the British in 1839, the 'Abdali sultans were able to capitalize on their proximity to Aden and their own claims to preeminence in the hinterland in order to effect a near hegemonic position, economically, politically and even conceptually, within the protectorate system. It was they who benefited most from the economic and political realignment of the hinterland, and no treaty was necessary to bind them to the British. But their position was rationalized not only in terms of their service to the colonial state and their relatively long history of friendly relations with the British but also in terms of an older history of rebellion, independence and state formation which justified their importance past and present.

The colonial history of a native prince

The reason why the 'Abdali sultans of Lahj were recognized as the preeminent native chiefs within the "nine tribes" had much to do with Aden's first administrators' understanding of the political history of the Yemeni South in the eighteenth century. Not long after the occupation of Aden, S.B. Haines attempted to write a basic historical narrative of the Aden hinterland, which centered on the 'Abdali Sultanate of Lahj. He included his narrative in an 1845 memo, to which he affixed the title "History of the Present Family of Lahej." On the basis of the ruling family's own dynastic chronicle or *da'ira*, Haines recreated the history of the 'Abdali dynasty. His introduction to this text is worth quoting in full:

> I have thus, in brief manner, collected a few historical traditions relative to the early Government of Yemen and Aden but I labor under considerable difficulty in connecting the chain of events between the years 1043 and 1141 A.H. when the "Deira" or Doomsday Book of Lahidge first appears. This period may be assumed as the Commencement of the Dynasty of the present reigning family at Lahidge, who then threw off all yoke, declaring Aden and Lahidge free, and who, strange to say, never until August 1844 had any demand for tribute made upon them.[25]

This introduction is important for the colonial historiography of Lahj for two reasons. First, the description of the 'Abdali *da'ira* as the "Doomsday Book" of Lahj suggests implicitly a similarity between the dynasty and Britain's own mediaeval past, and therefore a place for the 'Abdalis on a course of linear civilizational development that would ultimately result in some form of the modern state. Second, and more important to the overall production of the protectorate order within the framework of the Indian native states, is the reference to the date 1141 AH (1728 CE) with which the *da'ira* began. As Haines wrote, 1728 marked the "commencement" of the dynasty after declaring its independence from the Qasimi state in the Yemeni North that had conquered much of the South in the seventeenth century. The pivotal events of the year 1728 would come to frame the basic British understanding of the polities of the Yemeni South and their inclusion in the construct of the "nine tribes."

Haines begins with an account of the various dynasties which ruled Yemen, giving special attention to the Zaydi Imamate. It is from the history of the Qasimi state that Haines attempts to construct a transition to the local history of the Yemeni South and the 'Abdali Sultanate. From the high literary chronicles of the Imamate, he moves to the dynastic chronicle of the 'Abdali family from which he extracts its history, a history which in turn legitimates the authority of the Sultanate. The 'Abdali *da'ira*, according to Prideaux's 1872 account of the hinterland tribes, recorded not only historical events connected to the ruling family, but also the specifics of what he called the "permanent settlement" of land tenure that was supposedly concluded between the Sultanate and its subjects after 1728. While the British were seemingly more concerned with the historical outline it provided, so much that Prideaux could emphasize that it was "not only the territorial but the historical archives of the Arab States," the *da'ira* constituted the administrative and dynastic identity of the Sultanate.[26] Prideaux's allusion to the permanent settlement in Bengal (1793) points to the very different conception of colonial rule as it was envisioned outside Aden. Unlike in India, there was no interest on the part of the new rulers of Aden in securing a system of private property, nor interest in taxation at any level. Nor did the British presence in the Aden hinterland resemble colonial rule in Nigeria some years later, in which indirect rule was still a means by which tax revenue was gathered. The *da'ira* as a record of land tenure and settlement was of less interest to Haines than the historical narrative he could cull from it, and this regardless of the local importance of land ownership as a basis of power. Indeed, the importance of the document derived from its status as the historical memory of a local political dynasty on which the basis of indirect rule could be founded. The emphasis on history as the basis of authority is in clear contrast with colonial rule in the Punjab, as Gilmartin describes it or even East Africa according to Lugard's writings, in which tribal authority in the colonial imagination was directly related to land ownership and taxation.[27]

The reference to the Domesday Book is more than accidental, then, insofar as it suggests an analogy between the 'Abadil and Britain's own mediaeval past and, therefore, to the origins of the British state itself. The allusion to origins is mirrored in the reference to the "Commencement of the Dynasty" and its own efforts to record its presence in the *da'ira* in 1141 (1728), when the 'Abdali family was supposed to have declared its independence from Qasimi rule. From 1728, Haines gives a chronological

DEFINING AUTHORITY ON THE INDIAN FRONTIER

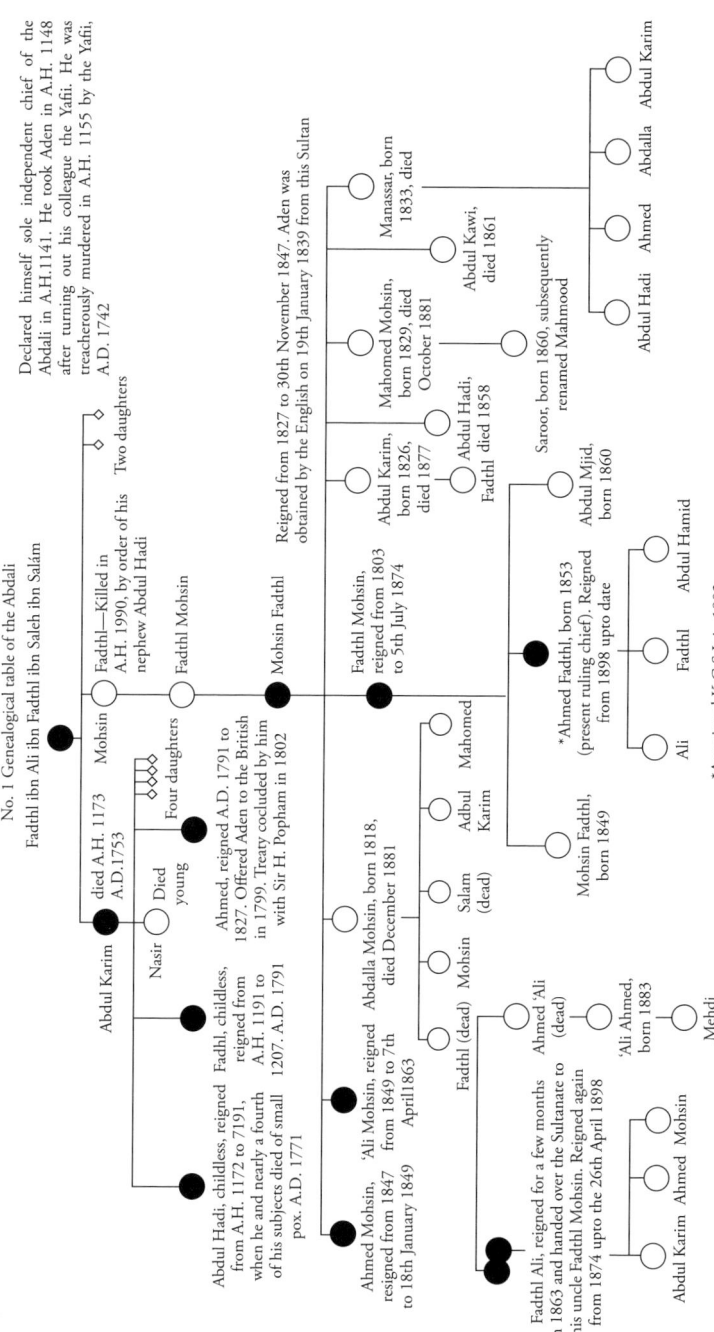

Figure 3: Reproduction of Hunter and Sealey's genealogy of the 'Abdali Sultans.

account of the rulers of Lahj based on the *da'ira* until the year 1800, at which point the account becomes a narrative of the British occupation of Aden and the foundation of the colonial government. That is, the local history of a local authority undergoes a smooth and, to some extent, faultless transition into the history of the colonial state itself. Although on the one hand this transition is portrayed as natural and certainly positive, the "rapid downfall" of Aden being traced to the early years of 'Abdali independence, on the other hand it creates a hierarchy of local authority, the British merely placing themselves in Aden as a paramount power rather than replacing the 'Abadil. The history of the sultans of Lahj, and therefore their authority, is left intact, if ultimately subordinate.

Haines' attempt to historicize the dynasty should not be underestimated. Playfair reproduced his account nearly word for word in his official history of Yemen in 1859, which was dedicated to and printed by the Government of Bombay.[28] The narrative of Lahj's independence was preserved without question until the end of British rule in 1967, reproduced most notably in Hunter and Sealey's handbook. While the handbook's historical narrative closely follows Playfair's text, it further memorializes the origins of the independent Sultanate by including a genealogical table of Lahj's ruling family, beginning with the reign of Fadl b. 'Ali b. Fadl b. Salih b. Salam, the ruler who dissociated himself from the Imamate in 1728 (fig. 3).[29] In fact, this historical moment of resistance and independence, under the direction of the ruling family of Lahj, provided the basis for the authority of all the ruling families of the Protectorate (by association and participation) and the colonial claim for a historically separate Yemeni South.[30] Yet the date of 1728 and the assumptions it carried with it were based on a particular reading of history that projected a late nineteenth-century 'Abdali hegemony back to the eighteenth century.[31]

"Silences are inherent in history," Trouillot writes, and the British reading of the later years of Qasimi rule was selective and ultimately strategically effective in the reorientation of the South toward Lahj and Aden.[32] The primary Zaydi chronicle from this period, however, suggests that the importance placed on the year 1728 by the British was of more recent provenance. The reign of Imam al-Mansur Husayn b. Qasim (r. 1727–48) was chronicled by Husayn b. Husayn al-Rusi in a work entitled *al-Barahin al-Mudi'a fi al-Sira al-Mansuriyya*.[33] Rusi's history is of some importance for it deals with the Qasimi state in a period of contraction. This period was characterized in part by the fragmentation of state power in which a number of

DEFINING AUTHORITY ON THE INDIAN FRONTIER

regions in the Shafi'i south broke away from Qasimi rule after nearly two hundred years.[34] It is in the context of this contraction that 'Abdali independence and the significance of the year 1728 should be understood, although in al-Rusi's text neither bears the traces of momentousness which they are accorded in the colonial narrative.

The first year of al-Mansur's reign (1140 AH, roughly 1727) in al-Rusi's narrative is significant in so far as the Imam realized his need to know the condition of the peasantry and ordered those in administrative positions to "discover for him what the country contains, in the most complete form" (*yaktashifu lahu 'an ma fi al-bilad 'ala atamma al-kamal*). This prescient expression of the state's desire to possess, through the collection of information on the country and its inhabitants, preceded the series of campaigns in the North and South that followed. As for the year 1141 (1728), however, it begins with the army's march in the direction of Lahj and Aden, but the rebellion of the 'Abdali Shaykh (and the use of "Shaykh" rather than "Sultan" is telling) is given little importance. Rusi merely notes that the Shaykh rushed to surrender and declare his obedience to the Imam. Imam al-Mansur then appointed a governor who brought order to the place. The profession of one's obedience and the appointment of a Zaydi governor was, of course, a common trope used to indicate submission to the Imam in the chronicle literature.[35]

In al-Rusi's treatment of the following years, the Imam continued his campaigns in the South, not against the 'Abadil, but against the Bani Qasid sultans of Jabal Yafi' and their tribal followings, who repeatedly engaged the Imamate's troops and threatened their tenuous hold outside of the highlands. The full significance of this emphasis requires some explanation of the role of Yafi' in the Qasimi state in the latter years of the dynasty. Jabal Yafi' was divided politically into Upper and Lower sections (*al-'ulya* and *al-sufla*); the latter was under the authority of the Bani Qasid sultans (the Al 'Afif) and the former under the Shaykhs of the Al Harhara, who derived their political and religious authority from a close relationship with the family of Shaykh Bu Bakr b. Salim, the *mansab* (representative of a religious lineage and administrator of its shrine) of the village of 'Inat in Hadramawt. These two polities commanded the allegiance, in various forms, of the tribes of the surrounding area, which were mostly engaged in small-scale agriculture along the terraced mountains.[36] Although Zaydi rule was established by the mid-seventeenth century, Qasimi authority was short-lived. By the reign of Imam al-Mu'ayyad Muhammad (r. 1681–1686), Jabal Yafi' was allied with the Amir of Kharafa (Daliʿ), the Rassasi Sultan (Baydaʾ), the Fadli Sultan, the ʿAwlaqi Sultan and their tribes in a revolt against the Imamate. The lines of the alliance that would later be associated with ʿAbdali independence (and the colonial concept of the "nine tribes") had already taken shape by the late seventeenth century and Lahj was notably absent from it. The power of the Yafiʿi sultans and their tribes became more important during the reign of Imam al-Mahdi Muhammad (Sahib al-Mawahib, r. 1686–1721) when prominent Yafiʿis were appointed Governors of the Hujariyya, Aden, Lahj and Abyan, while the sultans gained the rights of taxation in the port of Aden.[37]

By the time Imam al-Mansur came to power in 1727, then, the Yafiʿi Sultanates were arguably the most powerful polities in the South, and it was they (and not the ʿAbadil of Lahj) who presented the most significant obstacle to the reclamation of the region in the name of the Qasimi dynasty.[38] It was only in 1731, according to al-Rusi, that the ʿAbdali Shaykh assassinated the Zaydi Governor of Lahj, pushing the Imam to order the reoccupation of the place in the following year. An order that the ʿAbdali Shaykh should pay a fine of 15,000 riyals to the Imam's representative and the realization that he might well be murdered for his earlier act pushed him to call upon Sultan Sayf b. Qahtan al-ʿAfifi and present him with slaughter beasts (plural *aqaʾir*) in the market.[39] With the aid of Yafiʿi tribesmen, the ʿAbdali Shaykh was able to oust the Zaydi garrisons from Lahj and Aden, and in return the Yafiʿi Sultan was given the rights to the port's income.[40]

Haines referred to the Yafiʿ as "the most powerful tribe in Yemen" in 1845, an opinion expressed by the traveller Niehbur years earlier during the latter years of the Qasimi dynasty.[41] The Yafiʿ was recognized as a tribe far older than the ʿAbadil; its name could be found in pre-Islamic inscriptions and was mentioned by Hamdani. But even in terms of the formation of political centers, by which the British implicitly gauged the history of South Arabia, the Bani Qasid Sultanate was older than that of the ʿAbdalis, its foundation by Muʿawwada b. Muhammad al-ʿAfif dating to 1069 AH (c. 1658).[42] But the fact that the tribe's power was based in the southern highlands left it outside the scope of the colonial state in Aden, at least in the years prior to the Anglo-Ottoman Boundary Commission. When Haines wrote at the beginning of his historical summary that he had difficulties making connections between the history of the Imamate and that of Lahj, it was not merely a historical lapse due to the absence of texts, but an investment in a view of local history that drove a wedge between the history of the Zaydi North (and any claims the Imamate might have on the South) and the surrounding polities, such as Yafi'. It was a view of history that saw Aden as the source of all power, political and economic, in the South and therefore the 'Abadil as the inheritors of this power. Implicit in this view was the sense that the British, by virtue of their occupation of Aden and treaty with Lahj, were themselves the legal heirs of 'Abdali power, displacing Lahj yet drawing on the history of Lahj to justify their own presence. In this refashioning of history, Lahj was to rise to a prominence it had not historically enjoyed, until it was in fact displaced by the colonial state.

Lahj was located on the plain of the fertile Wadi Tuban in which most of the major trade routes converged. Although only two-fifths of the land was cultivable, a largely agricultural population was able to grow both red and white sorghum in the summer and winter seasons, often producing up to three harvests each. A small number of people were engaged in the production and dyeing of cotton cloth, and a similarly small group of Jewish craftsmen was settled there. Caravans carrying agricultural products from the Hujariyya, the highlands and the eastern provinces descended along the dry stream beds through Subayhi country, Dali', 'Alawi, Hawshabi country and Abyan to meet in Lahj where they were registered and billed at the Sultan's customs house.[43] From their palace in al-Hawta, the ruling family of Lahj collected enough from taxes on land, customs and monopolies to maintain a standing army of around four hundred slaves; they also regularly deployed mercenaries from the nearby Subayhi region and Jabal Yafi'.[44] The relative agricultural and commercial wealth of the Sultanate, combined with its largely settled population of between four and ten thousand peasants and tribesmen, earned the place a reputation for peace, security, and productivity.[45]

By its geographical proximity alone, Lahj was bound to profit from the British presence in Aden, especially after Haines declared the city a free port in 1850.[46] In 1849, Haines entered into a treaty with the Sultanate by which the customs duties on all inland trade were set at two per cent, but this was only part of a broader program of economic cooperation between Aden and Lahj. The same treaty called for Lahj to encourage the cultivation of European vegetables for the city, of which the Sultan became the sole provider.[47] In the same year, the naval department leased the wells at the village of Hiswa from the Sultan for the supply of water.[48] In 1867 the British and the 'Abadil constructed an aqueduct from Shaykh 'Uthman, outside Aden, to the town, for which Lahj received half the proceeds from the sale of water. Moreover, merchants from Lahj acted as brokers for the sale of cattle from the Somali coast and as labor contractors, while the sultans themselves held monopolies on the sale of salt from Hiswa and on the supply to the Lahji population of all manner of goods imported from Aden.[49] By the reign of Sultan Fadl b. Muhsin (r. 1863–74), two-thirds of the Sultanate's income was derived not from revenue generated from agricultural land in the Wadi Tuban, but from business associated with the port of Aden.[50] Under his successor, Sultan Fadl b. 'Ali (r. 1874–98), the British purchased the village of Shaykh 'Uthman for the resettlement of Aden's growing working class; as a reward the Sultan's annual stipend was increased from 6,492 to 19,692 dollars.

Underlying the economic and, to a certain extent, political integration of Lahj into Aden was the concurrent political expansion of the Sultanate into the territories of the other "nine tribes." As already mentioned, the Sultanate had already aligned itself politically and economically with the British by the end of Haines' tenure as political agent. In the 1850s Haines supported 'Abdali military campaigns against both the 'Aqrabi and the Fadli which were meant not only to protect the trade routes but also to crush resistance to the diversion of trade away from the small regional ports of Bir Ahmad and Shuqra to the free port of Aden. By definition, then, the security of Aden meant the security of Lahj. Notwithstanding these developments, the growing relationship between Lahj and Aden did not immediately translate into 'Abdali power throughout the hinterland. As Gavin noted, the Sultan, at this time, was little more than "a political *primus inter pares*" among the rest of the "nine tribes."[51] This was to change, however, during the reign of Sultan Fadl b. Muhsin.

The growing economic relationship between Lahj and Aden also fostered a climate of greater political cooperation from which Fadl b. Muhsin profited greatly. Through the careful cultivation of relations with William Merewether, the Political Resident at the time (1863–67), he was able to accrue enough political capital in the Aden government to support a series of attacks on the surrounding chiefs. In 1864, he suspended payments of a subsidy to the Fadli Sultan. When the Fadli, allied with the 'Awlaqi, attacked Lahj, Merewether authorized the use of British forces and gunboats to attack Fadli territory, in 1865 and 1866, occupying parts of Fadli country for eleven days.[52] Next, in 1868, soldiers from Lahj occupied the village of Zayida which contained the main water source for the Lahji irrigation system. An agreement with the British for the extension of the

Shaykh 'Uthman aqueduct to the village ensured that 'Abdali claims to the land would thereafter be supported. By 1870 Fadl b. Muhsin was raising money and troops for the conquest of Ta'izz and the whole of the Hujariyya province with an eye towards exploiting its rich agricultural lands and potential revenue. While the scheme was never implemented it is an indication of the power the 'Abdali Sultanate began to wield in the latter part of the nineteenth century.

Under his successor Fadl b. 'Ali (r. 1874–98), this early policy of extended influence in the hinterland became a policy of local domination, especially in light of what was considered Ottoman interference in the British (and 'Abdali) sphere of influence after 1872. In two telling episodes, the 'Abdali Sultanate effectively annexed two of the "nine tribes" to its own domains, therefore reducing the number of native chiefs, on whose historical legitimacy British claims to suzerainty rested, to seven. From 1881 to 1886 the 'Abdali Sultan was given complete authority over the Sabayha and treated as their "Chief" in a move to control a growing arms trade and to secure the trade routes to the Hujariyya (see Chapter 2). In 1894, with the aid of Subayhi, 'Awlaqi and Yafi'i mercenaries, Fadl b. 'Ali drove the Hawshabi Sultan from his territory in response to his alliance with the Ottoman regime in the North.[53] He was then elected Sultan of the Hawashib, much to the annoyance of the Aden government, a situation which continued for the rest of the year. The Hawshabi Sultan was later reinstated, but thereafter his election was to be approved by Lahj and the 'Abdali Sultan was given the right to dispose of their customs duties, which were now collected in al-Hawta.[54]

By the time Ahmad b. Fadl (r. 1898–1913) came to power as Sultan the 'Abadil were truly second only to Aden in the amount of influence they wielded in the hinterland. Harold Jacob suggested the prevalence of this attitude in Aden when he wrote after the First World War: "The Sultans of Lahej have said to me, 'You are the Government; we look to you,' and in turn I have ever associated the Lahej House with Aden, and included him in the category of Government."[55] Indeed, in the time of Sultan Ahmad, Lahj and its ruling family were the paramount native power in the hinterland, the Sultan himself being referred to as "our father" (*abuna*) by the other ruling families in their correspondence with the British. This was no mere pleasantry, for the Sultan was Aden's main informant (outside the Translation Department) on local politics and was heavily depended upon for the resolution of all local conflicts. He was the local face of the government in many respects, involving himself in protectorate affairs in ways impossible to the British by virtue of their policy of non-intervention and the always incomplete nature of colonial knowledge of the tribes. Yet underlying this convergence of interests was the maintenance of 'Abdali difference as the paramount native chief. While I have suggested that the position of the 'Abdali sultans within the colonial hierarchy of tribes was based on a particular colonial reading of history, this position was reproduced through a series of state rituals which acted to bind the local polities and their populations to the colonial state while incorporating them symbolically into the Indian Empire at the global level.

The Durbar Model and the Indianization of the Protectorate

> *Rustum Beg of Kolazai—slightly backward Native State—*
> *Lusted for a C.S.I.—so began to sanitate.*
> *Built a Gaol and Hospital—nearly built a City drain—*
> *Till his faithful subjects all thought their ruler was insane*
>
> Rudyard Kipling[56]

By the time Ahmad b. Fadl came to power in 1898 the British had established a form of indirect rule based on the figure of the ruling Chief, with a direct lineage going back to a pre-colonial history of resistance and independence. If the 'Abdali dynasty of Lahj was defined as the paramount "native chief" in the Yemeni South through its status as preeminent successor state to the Zaydi Imamate in the South and its subsequent position in British political and economic strategy, its incorporation into the wider Indian Empire was accomplished through its placement in a symbolic and ritual order that was decidedly imperial rather than local. The context for this elevation of the role of the 'Abdali Sultanate from local British ally to participant in the imperial arena was the ostensible transformation of British policy in India in the period after the 1857 revolt. In an attempt to address the causes of the revolt, Queen Victoria addressed India in a proclamation that ended the rule of the East India Company and transferred sovereignty to the British Crown. Moreover, the proclamation promised "to respect the Rights, Dignity, and Honor of Native Princes as Our own," while confirming a future policy of non-interference in local "custom" in the rest of India.[57] In the remainder of this chapter I will analyze the role of the Aden Protectorate chiefs, and especially the 'Abdali sultans, in this post-1857 order, with specific reference to their participation in the Delhi Durbar of 1903.

DEFINING AUTHORITY ON THE INDIAN FRONTIER

The post-revolt policy of non-interference in local custom and the increased interest in maintaining certain forms of what could be called traditional authority encouraged the elaboration of hierarchies of importance to the colonial state and related schedules of honorifics by which the native princes could be recognized. In 1861, a knighthood specific to the Indian Empire (the Order of the Star of India) and comprising three classes was created to honor service to the colonial state, on the part of both the native princes and British civilian and military officers. In 1865 the *alqabnama* register was compiled, listing all of the native princes, their specific forms of address, and their associated privileges from the colonial state. And by 1867, the use of gun salutes as a mark of honor had been organized according to the hierarchy established in the *alqabnama*.[58] This was the elaboration of what Metcalf and Metcalf have called the "durbar" form of government. The term "*darbar*" ("durbar" in British usage) was taken from Indo-Persian political practice, roughly translated as "royal court" or "royal audience."[59] The durbar model of colonial governance was based on the assumption that India comprised separate and autonomous communities of castes, tribes, and religious communities that could only be ruled by their natural leaders through a process of consultation with the imperial state.[60] It was a vision of Indian political society, as Partha Chatterjee has argued, based in the notion of immutable difference and inherent incapacity for democratic government.[61]

In the Aden Protectorate, the Arabic Guest House and Translation Department were responsible for the creation of a tribal hierarchy that, by the early twentieth century, also entailed a rigid system of honors and protocol. Tribes were divided into four classes, corresponding to their size, wealth, and general importance to British policy. Each class determined the number of gun salutes a chief received, the type of reception he was given upon his arrival in Aden, his access to the office of the Political Resident, the number of retainers he was allowed to bring on official visits, and his ability to recommend followers for individual access to government officials and state hospitality at the guest house. The 'Abdali, Fadli and Qu'ayti sultans, as well as the rarely seen Sultan of Qishn and Socotra, were ranked in Class I, and received the commensurate benefits.[62] The most sought after of these benefits was the personal meeting with the Political Resident, which was itself governed by strict protocol, especially regarding seating arrangements, as a means of depicting spatialized relationships of dominance and subordination.[63]

Although official visits by Class I native chiefs occurred generally no more than once per year, visits by those recommended by these chiefs were

35

more frequent.⁶⁴ Although they lacked the element of public spectacle, the lesser meetings were nonetheless important enactments of state ritual, and for the practical purposes of colonial rule, an indispensable source of information on affairs beyond Aden. The basic points of contact between the Aden government, then, were often informal visits at which the British distributed payments to influential tribesmen through an official "darbar fund," often euphemistically referred to as "gifts." As Bernard Cohn has argued in the Indian context the idiom of durbar, in British usage, came to connote a ritualized meeting between British officials and local "notables" at which honors, titles and presents were granted or exchanged. What had been previously a ritual act of incorporation between the royal person of the Mughal emperor and his feudatories, Cohn argues, was transformed by the British into a contractual agreement based on an economic exchange.⁶⁵ That the durbar in Aden came to connote not only the individual meetings between colonial officers and the native chiefs but also the fund from which largesse was distributed is an indication that this understanding was maintained in Arabia as well.⁶⁶ Harold Jacob, one of Aden's more experienced administrators, noted as much in his description of a typical meeting with a local tribal Shaykh:

'Respect' means money. An Arab will visit you and say he has longed for this interview with the longing of a camel for her young. 'I wanted a munazara (interview); and a muzawara (the same thing); and a mukabila (ditto); and a mushahada (only a synonym); and a muwajhaha (Oh, how monotonous it all is, but the poor fellow will put off the real motif as long as possible!). He then pauses for a breather and watches your face intently to divine, perchance, the largesse for which solely he came.⁶⁷

It is a testament to the power of the Raj as a normative model of colonial governance that by the time the idiom of durbar was transplanted to South Arabia, the Mughal state ritual of royal incorporation had already been transformed into a ritual enactment of a contract relationship that, at least to the British, centered in part on an economic exchange. As far as I have been able to ascertain, no British official suggested the potential difficulties of applying a ritual idiom rooted in the Indo-Persian state practices of the Mughals to the Yemeni South. Nor did anyone recognize that these rituals had no basis in a South Arabian past, whether real or imagined. Indeed, in the Aden Protectorate the durbar was reinvented by the Aden Residency and its administrators, certainly in effect if not by intent, as a uniquely colonial creation, defined by its relationship to British power. It was through the institution of durbar in the Aden Protectorate that a group of tribal polities defined by their history of resistance to the Zaydi Imamate in the eighteenth century was re-contextualized in a modern history of empire whose core lay far beyond the boundaries of Arabia. If this was only suggested by the localized idiom of durbar, it was made evident by the invitation of the native chiefs of the Protectorate to the Coronation Durbar in Delhi in 1903.

The purpose of the Durbar as envisioned by the Viceroy of India, Lord Curzon, was to commemorate the coronation of King Edward VII and to simultaneously provide a performative instance of the durbar model of government. For Curzon, the 1857 revolt was long past. He was less concerned with rewarding those Indian princes who had remained loyal than with institutionalizing in state ritual the idea of an associational, as opposed to a representative, government. In the face of the rising middle class nationalism of the Indian National Congress, formed in 1885, the durbar model of government offered the continued paternalism of British rule in consultation with India's native aristocracy, the native princes. In this sense, Curzon's Durbar was the public announcement and demonstration of a new alliance against the agitation of a nascent nationalist movement and the introduction of the native princes to an Indian and British audience as a political force, if ultimately a conservative one, for measured reform.

The Durbar was by necessity based on the imagination of a diverse though coherent society of native princes, organized at the level of something called "India." The assumption that Indian society was composed of numerous castes, tribes and religious sects was essential to Curzon's political vision, which understood the British monarchy and the framework of empire as the only unifying forces in an otherwise fragmented society. These sentiments were made clear in a speech delivered to the Legislative Council in Simla in late 1902 in which he defended the institution of durbar as an authentically "eastern" practice that unified subject and sovereign in a shared expression of solemnity. Moreover, he argued, it served the British Empire and his project for a unified princely India, noting that "the life and vigor of a nation are summed up before the world in the person of its sovereign:"

Here, in India, it is for the first time under the British Crown that this unity has been attained, and that the entire Continent has acknowledged a single ruler. The political forces and the moral grandeur of the nation are indisputably increased by this form of cohesion, and both are raised in the estimation of the world by a demonstration of its reality. There is another point of view from which I regard such a display as having far more than superficial value. In all our various divisions in this country—divisions of race and class and custom and creed—the one thing that holds us together, and subordinates the things that make for separation to the compelling force of union, is loyalty to a common head, membership of the same body politic, fellow-citizenship of the same Empire.⁶⁸

Long after the Mughal empire had effectively been replaced by the British Empire and its sovereign, Curzon was attempting to institute a new form of imperial culture in which India's native aristocracy were not just subjects, but participants in their own governance, even if in a subordinate position.

Around one hundred native princes accepted invitations to the 1903 Durbar. Invitees came not only from India "proper," but also from the Per-

Figure 4: Sir Ahmad b. Fadl, KCSI, Sultan of Lahj.

sian Gulf, Afghanistan, and Burma. Invitations were also sent to the courts of Persia, Siam, and Japan, in addition to representatives from South Africa and Australia. Three of Aden's "native chiefs" were invited to the Delhi Durbar: the Sultan of Lahj, Ahmad b. Fadl al-'Abdali, Sultan 'Awad b. 'Umar al-Qu'ayti of Shihr and Mukalla in the eastern Hadramawt region, and the Amir Shayif b. Sayf of Dali'. All three accepted the invitation, and the Aden government planned a simultaneous celebration in the port city itself.

It was the specifically South Arabian political context, however, that led to their invitation. The Anglo-Ottoman Boundary Commission had begun its work in 1902, and the protectorate signatories along the proposed border were the most vulnerable to the highly contested process of boundary delimitation. In particular, the authority of the Amir of Dali', Shayif b. Sayf, was continually questioned by the Ottoman Commission, and the mere presence of Ottoman soldiers along the proposed border created a political space in which many of the Amir's erstwhile subjects or clients pushed for autonomy or even outright independence from the emirate. In light of the ongoing dispute with the Ottoman government and the perceived fragility of Amir Shayif's position, it was decided that the Amir's attendance at the Durbar would bolster his standing with his own people and send a message to the Ottoman government that he was now an established member of Britain's empire.[69] For the Sultans of Lahj and Shihr and Mukalla, the case was somewhat different. Sultan 'Awad b. 'Umar's invitation was part of a general effort to secure good relations with the easternmost part of the Yemeni South in which British influence was still nominal, and the Qu'ayti Sultan, although having signed a treaty of friendship in 1888, was not yet considered part of the Aden Protectorate. As for Sultan Ahmad b. Fadl al-Abdali, he was invited in recognition of his preeminent place in the colonial tribal order and his history of service to the colonial state.

Once Aden's native chiefs arrived in Delhi, they were removed from the regional hierarchy of the Protectorate and re-situated within an imperial hierarchy that governed and indeed constituted the entire event. In Aden, the 'Abdali Sultan sat at the head of the protectorate order, not only in terms of wealth and political power, but also in terms of his place in the symbolic order. As a Class I chief, he received a salute of nine guns upon entry into the port of Aden. Only Sultan 'Awad b. 'Umar received a salute of twelve guns, and this was a personal rather than a dynastic salute, which would cease at his death. In India, however, Sultan Ahmad b. Fadl and his fellow chiefs were of much less importance and were placed in a much lower position in an empire-wide ranking. Curzon had decided early on to avoid any possible clash over precedence amongst India's native princes, and it was determined, therefore, that princes would be organized according to the Presidency or region with which they were associated according to local rules of precedence.[70] The chiefs of the Aden Protectorate were grouped with the other native states associated with the Bombay Presidency. Of the over three hundred princes recognized by the British in that administrative unit (many of whom were merely large landlords), twenty (including those from Aden) attended the Durbar. At the top of the Bombay hierarchy were states such as Kolhapur, Cutch, and Khairpur whose rulers enjoyed salutes of either seventeen or fifteen guns. The Aden chiefs with salutes of nine guns (excluding the Qu'ayti Sultan's personal salute of twelve) sat at the middle of the Bombay Presidency's hierarchy in terms of their perceived political importance, although no chiefs had salutes of less than nine guns.[71] In comparison with the princes of major states beyond Bombay such as Hyderabad, Mysore and Baroda, those from Aden were even more marginal.

The camps of the Viceroy's guests, all of which were situated around Curzon's main camp, were laid out according to the same hierarchies in a spatial enactment of the durbar model of government. Each guest was allotted a plot of land the size of which was relative to the number of salutes to which he was entitled. The number of guests and retainers each chief was allowed to invite was also dependent on their official status, so that the Nizam of Hyderabad, with a salute of twenty-one guns, brought five hundred guests, while the Sultan of Lahj, with nine, brought two hundred people. The camps themselves, then, reinforced the colonial conceit of aristocratic India—endlessly diverse, hierarchically organized, and united by the framework of British power. This sentiment was echoed by the official historian of the Durbar who described the camps as a microcosm of empire, noting that they represented "peoples of every race and religion, more diverse than those of Europe itself."[72] The guests from the Aden Protectorate, encamped with the other Bombay chiefs some miles south of the viceroy's camp, prompted the remark that their presence "helped to recall the fact that the political boundaries of the Indian Empire extend across the seas beyond the confines of the great peninsula."[73]

In the Durbar ceremony that followed, two moments stand out as significant statements of the Raj's policy toward its native princes. The first was Curzon's address, which reiterated the necessity of imperial paternalism, for it was only Britain that could master India's inherently fragmented nature.

DEFINING AUTHORITY ON THE INDIAN FRONTIER

In a closing statement, both reassuring and threatening, he made clear that there was no future without the Raj, arguing that, "under no other conditions can this future be realized than the unchallenged supremacy of the paramount power, and under no other controlling authority is this capable of being maintained, than that of the British Crown."[74] The second was the point at which the native princes were to ascend the dais and personally greet and congratulate the Viceroy and his guests. This act of obeisance ultimately demonstrated that the durbar form of government allowed the participation of India's native aristocracy only insofar as it was subordinate to the King-Emperor and his Viceroy.

The protectorate chiefs were among those who offered their congratulations to their hosts. The official history notes that Sultan Ahmad b. Fadl of Lahj and Amir Shayif b. Sayf of Dali' approached the dais and offered brief words of congratulations to the Viceroy. Sultan 'Awad b. 'Umar of Shihr and Mukalla took the opportunity to recite a lengthy ode, extolling the virtues of the newly crowned King Edward and the British Empire.[75] Following the official ceremony, there were nine more days of related ceremonies and exhibitions, one of which featured Sultan Ahmad b. Fadl (fig. 4). In the audience chamber of the Mughal Emperor Shah Jahan, nearly two thousand spectators arrived to observe the official procession of the Indian Orders (the Star of India and the Indian Empire), of which Curzon was the Grand Master. As the various ranks passed in pairs through the hall, Sultan Ahmad, newly honored as Knight Commander of the Order of the Star of India, was among them. His position at the pinnacle of the Aden Protectorate order had now been recognized at the level of the Indian Empire.[76]

Conclusion

As he began the organization of the 1903 Durbar, Curzon wrote that "A Durbar is a peculiarly Indian and not a colonial, function. It is attended by forms and ceremonies immemorially consecrated in Asia, but entirely unknown in the New World. In the colonies it would be an anachronism and an absurdity; in India it is a feature of a hallowed system."[77] Curzon's comment, whether intentionally or not, postulates the existence of two separate cultural and political spheres—the British and the Indian—on which the durbar model of governance was founded in the period after 1857. Indian princely society as represented in the Durbar, and indeed constituted by the Durbar, was however not limited to South Asia but was a trans-regional aristocracy whose members were united under British suzerainty. It was the role of the British to unite them.

As I have argued, what united the Aden Protectorate chiefs and the native princes of South Asia in this ritual order was the overarching framework of imperial India, which was based not only upon their legal identity as "native chiefs" within the Indian residency system, but also upon the assumption that India comprised infinitely fragmented societies, divided by tribe, caste and confession. This vision of society, of which the Yemeni South was an integral part, was itself an effect of an epistemological project, which produced knowledge about India's political past and ethnographic present and institutionalized it in the normalizing procedures of the state. In the Aden Protectorate, administrators with experience on India's northwestern frontiers brought with them an ethnographic imagination that saw the Yemeni countryside as populated by a number of tribes led by families of "native chiefs." Uniting this diverse landscape of tribes was an historical narrative of opposition led by the 'Abdali sultans of Lahj to the Zaydi Imamate of the Yemeni highlands. The body of knowledge that resulted from Aden's ethnographic state ultimately justified the promotion of the 'Abdali sultans as the natural leaders of the Yemeni South after Aden's occupation in 1839 and as Britain's closest ally in the region thereafter. This vision of Aden's history fitted neatly into India's post-1857 political order and found expression through the elaboration of a carefully graded hierarchy of tribes, reproduced by various state rituals, such as the local durbars and Curzon's Delhi Durbar in 1903. The Delhi Durbar's importance in this order was that it made explicit Aden's place in greater India as a political and a cultural construct.

But the Aden Protectorate chiefs played a very different role in imperial policy from the more significant native princes in the Indian Subcontinent. Curzon had hoped that the native princes would provide a stable and conservative native ally in the face of growing middle class nationalism. However, as Thomas Metcalf argues, the durbar model rested on a contradiction: the native princes were to represent "traditional" authority while pushed by the Raj to adopt "liberal" reforms. Even then, the native princes were constrained in what they could accomplish by British limits on their authority—their authority to wage war, initiate policy, and indeed to govern.[78] They were, in the words of Nicholas Dirks, "hollow crowns."[79] By contrast, there was no nationalist movement in Aden until the 1940s, and the policy of the British in the hinterland was to empower the native chiefs as a bulwark against the Ottomans across the frontier, a guardian of free trade in the countryside, and a civilizing influence on the tribal population. Indeed, their invitation to the Delhi Durbar was meant to increase their prestige (always a palpable concern to the colonial authorities) by association with the British or *al-dawla al-'uzma*, the exalted state.

It was not until the beginning of the "forward policy" of Sir Bernard Reilly in the 1930s that the Aden government began to intervene more directly in the area of the Protectorate with the intention of creating stable, conservative states on the basis of local authority. To these ends, a school for the education of the "sons of Shaykhs" was founded in 1937 to instruct the countryside's young notables in modern principles, obviously emulating the Mayo College founded for the education of native princes in India. Until that time, however, the British were fully committed to the native chiefs, not as a force for benign and moderate reform, but as a form of traditional authority, rooted in history, that could guarantee stability and security. It was the maintenance of this authority in both material and symbolic terms that proved most difficult for the colonial state. In the chapters that follow, I will look at the remaining constituent elements of the "tribe" in the colonial imagination—the martial tribesman and the landscape—with continuing reference to the problem of authority.

2

MASTERLESS MEN

The other of the modern state is the no-man's or contested land: the under- or over-definition, the demon of ambiguity. Since the sovereignty of the modern state is the power to define and to make the definitions stick—everything that self-defines or eludes the power-assisted definition is subversive. The other of this sovereignty is no-go areas, unrest and disobedience, collapse of law and order.

Zygmunt Bauman[1]

Introduction

Conflict erupted quite unexpectedly in the Arabic Guest House in the center of Aden in 1904. At the time, a group of Subayhi (plural Sabayha) tribesmen and a numerically larger group of 'Awlaqi (plural 'Awaliq) tribesmen were enjoying the entertainment accorded them by their treaties of protection and were in residence at the house. As the Swedish linguist Carlo Landberg's local informant narrates the event, the conflict had to do with the assignment and quality of rooms; the 'Awlaqi group, by virtue of their greater number, and one assumes their own assessment of their importance, were not satisfied with the comparative size and quality of their accommodation. In order to rectify the slight, the 'Awaliq decided to remove the Subayhi men by force, and the Sabayha, in turn, refused to be removed. All too willing to fight to uphold honor, the Sabayha also noted that they were armed with "French rifles" (*riyafil fransawiyya*) that they had obtained in Djibouti. Lest the disagreement get seriously out of hand, which it was indeed threatening to do, the Extra Assistant Resident G. Wyman Bury was contacted and came to the guest house in an attempt to calm down both parties. Failing to do that, the Aden Resident was forced to call in Indian troops to expel the 'Awlaqi, who ultimately took the blame for an armed conflict in the middle of town.[2]

Although in this case the 'Awaliq were considered the aggressors, the incident reveals a much greater tension in the creation of the Protectorate. In this case, the problem was not merely that the 'Awaliq had instigated a fight in a government building in the middle of town, but that it so easily got out of hand, nearly erupting into a form of armed conflict that was decidedly new in the hinterland. The Subayhi reference to French rifles alludes to the flooding of the region with relatively cheap, precision arms at the turn of the century, and their rapid adoption by the tribes of the Protectorate. This in itself was new, but it became a problem precisely because the power of the martial tribesmen had increased exponentially, and it was therefore all the more necessary to see that they could be controlled by the "ruling chiefs."

The durbar model of rule was dependent on the ability of the native sovereigns to, at the very least, control their subjects, but the clash at the guest house revealed the potential fault lines in the colonial understanding of local authority. In particular, the incident involved two tribes which were quite different in the British ethnographic and political imagination. The 'Awaliq were from the eastern mountains, with a long-established Sultanate, and a history of participation in the revolt against Qasimi rule in the eighteenth century; they were part of the established narrative of the formation of the "nine tribes." By contrast, the Sabayha fell outside the colonial understanding of tribe on which the Protectorate was based, and proved to be the type of anomaly that threatened the very order on which colonial rule in the hinterland and the durbar model itself were founded; that is, they did not have a single chief. Without a singular, recognizable authority over them, the martial prowess of the Subayhi tribe was recast as a natural tendency toward brigandage and predation. Through the latter part of the nineteenth century, the tribe was slowly criminalized by the colonial state, but what was first seen as a mere disposition towards criminality was, by the turn of the century, understood as a threat to the colonial order.

This chapter looks at the production of the martial tribesman as an object of colonial rule and a constitutive element in the mapping of the space of the Protectorate. Taking the Sabayha as a case study, I argue that the production of the colonial typology of tribe, with its emphasis on the "ruling chief," inadvertently produced the Sabayha as its antithesis—as a martial tribe without leadership. The growing body of colonial knowledge did not remedy the situation, but in fact made even clearer the inadequacy of the "nine tribes" in representing the population of the Aden hinterland. But while the absence of a recognizable leadership amongst the Sabayha exacerbated their already criminal nature, the appearance of the tribe at the intersection of a growing trans-regional trade in contraband arms, and a series of conflicts over economic rights on the caravan routes, effectively placed the Sabayha beyond the pale. No longer part of the warrior class of "martial tribes," they were now brigands and predators, or in Beier's terms "masterless men."[3] Yet rather than adjust their understanding of local social and political forms, the British attempted to create a master for those who had none. This chapter begins by placing the origins of the category of the martial/criminal tribes in a larger imperial context. It then moves to the creation of the "Sabayha" tribe as a criminal tribe in the late nineteenth century and looks more closely at its role in the arms trade and the ensuing conflicts along the trade routes in the westernmost part of the Protectorate.

Martial/criminal tribes

The concept of the martial races had its origins in the reorganization of the Indian Army in the years after the revolt of 1857. Prior to the revolt, the various armies of the East India Company put little emphasis on racial characteristics, and intermixed recruits without reference to caste or religion. Although the Bengal Army, for example, recruited greater numbers of the higher castes, Brahmins and Rajputs, this was done with little reference to their military abilities. After 1857, the regiments that had taken up arms against the British were disbanded, and the bases for recruitment were reconsidered. The Peel Commission of 1859 made a number of recommendations pertaining directly to the military and designed to prevent any recurrence of the events of 1857. Most notable was the suggestion that the army should be composed of recruits of different "nationalities and castes" mixed throughout each regiment to prevent their mobilization along ethnic or religious lines. However, the Punjab Committee argued that regiments should be composed of companies that recruited on the lines of single caste and ethnic groups, as part of a policy of "divide and rule."[4] The Eden Commission of 1879 ultimately called for the reorganization of the army according to regional commands, which in turn would recruit from outside these regions into military units which were now "racially" or "ethnically" homogeneous. Pride of place in the new army, especially by the 1880s, was given to those groups supposed to excel in military endeavors (as opposed to the "effeminate" Bengalis), particularly Punjabis, most of whom were Sikhs. By the turn of the century, the theory of the martial races had been codified in the recruiting handbooks for the Indian Army.[5]

As Thomas Metcalf has argued, "the notion of 'martial races' drew sustenance from a variety of elements in the cultural baggage of late Victorian England."[6] It was assumed that those races descended from the Aryans who conquered northern India, such as the Dogras, maintained superior racial characteristics. For others, the geographical and environmental conditions in which they lived made them especially "hardy"; this was said to be true of the Gurkhas in Nepal, for example. Just as important as their natural military proclivities, however, was their natural discipline and respect for authority, proven, in British eyes, by the loyalty of the Sikhs during and after 1857. The effect was the creation of a sociology of the martial races which was represented and codified not only in a nascent colonial ethnography, but in the practices of the Indian Army.[7]

But while it was believed that particular races were naturally inclined towards military pursuits, it was also believed that some were inherently disposed to crime and disorder. As Sanjay Nigam has written, the notion of the criminal caste emerged in the 1830s with the campaign against the Thags and the Buddhuks. While the Thags had engaged in ritual murders and the Buddhuks acted as itinerant mercenaries, the notion of habitual criminality slowly began to be associated with mobility, itinerancy, and modes of living other than settled agriculture. The parallels with the bourgeois fear of the "habitual criminal" in Britain noted by some historians are justified, and the colonial response ran parallel to measures such as the Habitual Criminals Act of 1869.[8] Although a number of measures meant to register and monitor the so-called criminal tribes were initiated much earlier in the Punjab and North-West Province, the post-revolt period saw an India-wide effort to control all itinerant and supposedly predatory groups. The 1871 Criminal Tribes Act listed four tribes (out of the original twenty-nine requested by the police) as inherently criminal.[9] According to the terms of the Act, their members were registered and forced to remain in their native areas of residence through a system of passes, while others were forcibly resettled in agricultural villages and compelled to engage in small-scale farming.[10] Colonial ethnography in this case, just as in the case of the martial races, defined criminality as well as martial loyalty in terms of race, caste and tribe.

The nature of early indirect rule in South Arabia meant that there was little chance that a military force would be raised on the basis of recruitment of locals, but martial race theory found its way into the colonial understanding of the tribe nonetheless. As was discussed in Chapter 1, a tribe in the colonial imagination and practice was organized according to a number of ruling chiefs with a shared genealogy connecting them to the revolt against Zaydi rule in the eighteenth century. These chiefs ruled, to a greater or lesser degree, populations of armed tribesmen (the British did not collect statistics on women or children). Unlike in India, the fact that tribesmen in the Aden hinterland were arms-bearing, and therefore all martial tribes according to colonial typologies, meant that there were no easy distinctions between those with military potential and those with criminal tendencies. Indeed, as a 1915 report on the Protectorate attested, "most tribes may be described as fighting races."[11] Geography, as in India, provided one indicator as to the criminal or martial dispositions of the tribes. The tribes residing in the eastern mountains of the Protectorate, for example, such as the Yafi'i or 'Awlaqi, were regarded as natural warriors because they were supposed to have hardy dispositions and be accustomed to warfare in the rugged terrain of the hills. In fact, the same report compares the "Arab of the hills" favorably with the Pathan, "though less formidable, and without the dash of the latter."[12] Yet, despite their martial inclinations, they were not known to be predatory, and in fact played a similar role to that of the Sikhs in the colonial military during the years of the forward policy in Aden in the 1930s.[13] Residing in the desert plains and valleys of the westernmost part of the Protectorate and at the other end of the spectrum of martial tribes was the Subayhi tribe, which was continually labeled as inherently predatory. Geography certainly played its part in the imagining of the martial and criminal tribes, but it did not lie at the heart of the issue. So what did distinguish the martial from the criminal tribes?

The crucial distinction for the colonial state was whether or not the tribes were deemed to be naturally amenable to authority. Dirks has suggested that in the Indian case this was a primary concern for the colonial state: the fact that "there was an intimate relationship between martiality and criminality, the two attributes distinguished in the end only by the mysterious question of loyalty to British rule, was an issue that for the British was the most crucial one of all."[14] Loyalty to British rule in the Aden context was generally associated with loyalty to the protectorate chiefs and their states. The Yafi'i, as I discussed in the previous chapter, were ruled by two established sultanates founded in the seventeenth century. Not only did their sultans wield a measure of real authority, their tribesmen could also largely be directed or administered by the British through their local leadership. This was especially so when the Yafi'i were in the employ of the 'Abdali Sultan, who provided the paradigm for hinterland authority. As for the tribesmen of the 'Abadil themselves, they were popularly considered inferior as fighters, and as a people were said to be "the most civilized and least warlike."[15] They were simply *too* settled, and their leadership *too* civilized to engage in martial pursuits, hence their reliance on mercenaries from the mountains. The mountain tribes, by contrast, were small landowners who cultivated sorghum along terraced fields: they were neither nomadic Bedouin nor effete landlords.[16] They provided the perfect balance, in colonial terms, of local authority, between a settled lifestyle and martial prowess. For some British observers, the mountain tribesman represented an Arabian version of the English yeoman farmer, both small landowner and warrior, as Bury noted wistfully when he compared him to those who "strewed the flower of Europe's chivalry in struggling heaps along their harassed front on Crispin's day."[17] Moreover, unlike many of the inhabitants of the Aden hinterland, the British generally evinced a degree of respect for these tribes. These distinctions were crucial, and were characteristics seemingly absent in the Subayhi tribe.

The colonial invention of the Sabayha

The Sabayha inhabited the south-western portion of the country, bordering the sea from the Bab al-Mandab to the small port of Ras 'Imran, and on the north the territory of the Maqtari, Sharjabi and Athwari tribes. In the western part of the country a chain of mountains, following the coast of the Red Sea and extending inland some ten miles, divided the arid plains of the Sabayha from the fertile lands of the Hujariyya to the north. Moving inland, there were the important ranges of Jabals Habwa, Rasin and the longer range of Jurdud. To the east of these hills were the Zurayki and Qubati ranges. These hills were largely rugged and devoid of vegetation. They were, however, cut by numerous valleys (*wadi* plural *awdiya*), which made a certain level of cultivation possible, mostly seasonal and rainfed, and acted as roads connecting the Hujariyya with the coast and, ultimately, the port of Aden. The Sabayha were spread out in these *wadi*s and along the coast in small villages, organized loosely according to clans. The Barhimi and 'Atifi tribes resided along the arid coastline stretching from Ras al-Kaw' to Shaykh Sa'id, bordering what would become Ottoman Yemen. The majority of the population, however, inhabited the valleys, especially the Wadis Ma'adin and Ma'baq. The Mansuri, Makhdumi, and Rija'i tribes were settled there, as were the Dubayni and Julaydi tribes and the Wahhasha confederation.[18]

The British had encountered the Sabayha shortly before the occupation of Aden in 1839. In his survey of the coast of southwest Arabia Haines described them as "kind and communicative" and suggested that "they are governed by their principal chiefs, who are absolute."[19] While one would assume that in hindsight this description must have seemed over-optimistic, it does point to the rather significant fact that the Sabayha were not always considered to be a criminal tribe, but were in fact "criminalized" through the course of development of colonial rule in the nineteenth and early twentieth centuries and the inability of the colonial state to incorporate them into their classificatory schema.

Their criminalization followed the expansion of British trade in the Aden hinterland, especially after 1850. In 1839 Haines entered into a number of agreements with the inhabitants of what later would be termed Subayhi territory with the goal of securing the caravan routes to Aden.[20] The security of the trade routes framed the next major report on the tribes of the hinterland, written by Haines' successor James Outram in 1854. Certainly Outram's report evinced greater knowledge of the population beyond Aden, but the Sabayha were deemed insignificant in comparison with the 'Abdali, Fadli and 'Aqrabi with whom the Aden administration was still at odds. Nonetheless, Outram repeated what was already fast becoming the general view of the Sabayha in Aden: namely, that they were predisposed toward criminal pursuits. For Outram, the Sabayha were considered Bedouin by the surrounding population. Although they engaged in agriculture and marketed their produce in Aden, they were predominantly nomadic and were "notoriously addicted to plunder." Moreover, the tribe was characterized by social fragmentation, comprising numerous "clans" and "as many different Sheikhs." While Haines had entered into agreements with a few, it was Outram's belief that no agreements with them would be respected in view of their "unsettled" nature.[21] That is, despite their criminal nature, they were not yet a problem for colonial rule.

It is safe to say that the Sabayha only became the object of the colonial production of knowledge when they began to threaten the interests of Aden near the latter part of the nineteenth century. As trade with the hinterland grew in the years following Aden's transformation into a free port in 1850, knowledge about the tribe became more crucial to the colonial government as its officials attempted to secure trade through various treaties. The agreements entered into with the Sabayha in the following years indicate increasing concern with the possible threat the tribe posed to the growing commerce with the interior and the need to control it.[22] In 1871 a series of treaties were signed with various sections, which were meant to protect a number of commercial concerns by tying them to the Aden government. The 'Atifi signed an agreement by which they promised to protect British subjects shipwrecked along their shores. More important, however, representatives of the Mansuri, the Khalifi section of the Barhimi, the 'Atawi section of the Jurabi, the Makhdumi and the Rija'i signed treaties by which they agreed to protect the trade routes and relinquish all transit dues in return for a monthly stipend of twenty-five dollars. These signatories in no way represented the totality of tribes and sections located near the major trade routes, but the treaties did point to the direction that Aden would later take by attempting to assign territorial responsibility to particular sections along the roads. The colonial state was primarily interested in assigning a master to those who had none. This was accomplished ten years later in response to continued depredations on the caravan routes.

On 5 May 1881 the 'Abdali Sultan signed a treaty with the Aden government in which he was recognized as "exercising sovereign authority over the territory occupied by all the tribes of the Subaihi, and including the Mansuri, Makhdumi, Rujai, and Dubaini, which three former are at present stipendiaries of the British Government, but excluding such as at present acknowledge Turkish supremacy."[23] By this treaty, he took responsibility for all the territory recognized as Subayhi, including the protection of its roads, abstention from collecting taxes and the control of smuggling. In turn, the British paid all of the Subayhi stipends directly to the 'Abdali Sultan and would not authorize any Subayhi Shaykhs to visit the Residency without a letter of recommendation from the Sultan. The Subayhi tribe, for the purposes of colonial administration, no longer existed. Underlying this agreement was the type of local politics the British had studiously avoided. In order to effectively police the Sabayha, the 'Abdali Sultanate was forced to build and man a series of small forts across Subayhi territory and to pay out stipends to all of the major Shaykhs.[24]

Hunter and Sealey's statistical *Account of the Tribes* (1886) memorialized the Sabayha's subordinate position to the 'Abdali in what was to become the foundational ethnographic and historical text on the protectorate tribes. The authors reserved mention of the Sabayha until the section on the 'Abdali Sultanate, its income and general population being included with those of the 'Abadil. More important, in a collection in which the major figures of authority were listed by name, the Sabayha were only listed by section and the number of "fighting men" they could muster. They were recognized not by their native chief (which they did not seem to have), but by the threat they posed to the Aden Colony.[25] It is no surprise, then, that the authors also memorialized the criminal character of the tribe, much of which was simply reproduced in later handbooks. The Sabayha are the nearest to the "typical Bedawin in character," we are told: "True 'Children of the Dawn,' as their name may be held to imply, they by preference select that hour for their attacks on wayfarers."[26] They devote little attention to agriculture, even less to commerce and subsist on a sparse diet of sorghum, and they are wracked by poverty. Their lack of authority, lack of permanent habitation and of agricultural settlement have engrained in them a tendency toward treachery and banditry. As demonstrated by Hunter and Sealey, the Sabayha were a tribe characterized by absences: they had no genealogy, no history, no fixed abodes, no economy, and no culture.

In the same year that the *Account* was in press, sections of the Sabayha who opposed 'Abdali suzerainty over the region attacked the Sultan's garrisons which had to be extricated with the assistance of fifty cavalrymen from Aden. The 1886 agreement was officially rescinded.[27] What followed was an attempt to bring the Sabayha into the series of treaties that would place them under British protection. But although the Sabayha had been named as one of the "nine tribes" within the British sphere in the 1873 memorandum to the Ottoman government, their institutionalization within the protectorate system was a far more difficult matter. In a system based on the recognition of a single native chief whose authority was rooted in history and genealogy, the Sabayha once again proved problematic. When they officially became part of the Protectorate in 1889, it was not on the basis of a single treaty of protection, nor was the entire area recognized as Subayhi included in the treaties. Rather, only the 'Atifi and Barhimi sections could be induced to sign treaties, effectively covering the coastal area, but not along the inland valleys in which the trade routes were located. But even to suggest that these sections acted as corporate bodies under single authorities is more than a little inaccurate. While it had long been recognized that the Sabayha had no paramount "chief," the treaties with the Barhimi and 'Atifi revealed that even at the level of what the British called the "sub-tribe" there were no single authorities with which they could deal. The treaties were not negotiated with a single Shaykh or headman, but a cross-section of local men of influence, not one of whom could be considered more authoritative than the other.[28]

As the British were drawn into closer relations with the Sabayha, the reports on the tribe betray a hint of anxiety as it became clearer that they did not fit the typology of the native state elaborated years earlier. A 1903 "Memorandum on the Subehi Tribe" was written by Generals Maitland and Warneford as part of the Anglo-Ottoman Boundary Commission's work, along with similar memoranda on the other "nine tribes."[29] The report professed that the most important sections of the tribe were "those whose districts are in the proximity to the frontier line," and included a general chronology of events that had taken place in all of the Subayhi territory since 1839. More important for the production of knowledge on the Sabayha, the authors, for the first time, recognized that the tribe had no single chief and decided that it should not be treated as a single political unit: "each section has therefore been regarded for political purposes as a separate tribe, and has been dealt with apart from others." This statement applied mainly to a brief discussion of the Maqtari and Athwari tribes along the boundary claimed by the Ottoman government; neither of those tribes was in treaty relations with the Aden government, and both claimed to be independent of the Ottomans. The memo dealt little with the sections of the Sabayha with whom the British had been dealing for some time: except for a list of those sections who had submitted to 'Abdali authority in 1882, they were absent from the memo. Again, the sections of the Sabayha amounted to little outside a larger corporate body with a recognizable figure of authority. Instead, after the narrative account of tribes in proximity to the border claimed by the Ottomans, there was appended a list of over fifty Subayhi villages, their headmen, and number of inhabitants.

As Zygmunt Bauman suggests, "ambivalence is a side-product of the labor of classification; and it calls for yet more classifying effort."[30] This was certainly the case with the Sabayha. Indeed, the increasing amount of information in the form of endless lists of sections, Shaykhs, villages and local *'aqils* did not necessarily add to the security of the colony. Rather, as the number of independent headmen and villages multiplied within the body of knowledge on the tribe, so did the difficulties in formulating any clear policy on the basis of the Subayhi tribe. The large number of potential figures of authority emptied the concept of the protectorate "chief" of any meaning in this context and confirmed the colonial fears that the Sabayha were nothing more than a population of martial tribesmen with no authority over them at all. Thus, the more fully the Sabayha were brought into the protectorate order, the more closely the British followed their every move. The more closely they were watched, the more likely their actions would be read into the growing narrative of colonial anxiety. Indeed, it is at this moment, in which the colonial apparatus for dealing with the tribes was most developed, that the Sabayha were most clearly constituted as problems in the colonial archive. By the turn of the century, it is difficult to find any reference to the tribe except as a problem to be solved, a potential threat to the security of the city and its commercial interests. When it appeared as a historical subject in the files of the Aden Residency it was in connection with the trade in precision firearms and their use in the tribal conflicts, which took place on the caravan routes through Subayhi country.

The Sabayha and the arms trade

> *Adieu! Oh spear and matchlock!*
> *No longer do men carry you:*
> *I shoulder the French (Le Gras) and Martini-Henry,*
> *And the changed conditions put to flight the milk-livered.*[31]

By the end of the nineteenth century, South Arabia had begun to import in great quantities breech-loading rifles from the French colonies in East Africa, especially Djibouti. Not only were these new weapons of far more deadly accuracy than the matchlocks previously used by the tribes of the hinterland, but their relatively low prices put them within the reach of a far greater number of people. For R.J. Gavin, this sudden increase in the number of precision firearms in the Aden hinterland led to a noticeable increase in the occurrence of tribal feuds, which resulted in greater casualties and, in consequence, an escalation in retaliation. By the turn of the century, he argues, South Arabia was locked in a cycle of local feuds, the overall effect of which was social and political chaos outside of Aden.[32] The rate at which these changes occurred is suggested by Bury, reflecting on his service in the eastern part of the Aden hinterland at the turn of the century:

UNMAKING NORTH AND SOUTH

When I first entered the country twelve years ago I got to know every rifle by sight—in Upper Aulaki—and could have counted them on fingers and toes, but you would need to be a Briareus to do that now. There have been no intermediate stages, as in most other barbaric states, where the match-lock gives place to the flint-lock, and it to the M.L. percussion musket, which is replaced by the breech-loading weapon of early pattern. No,—there was a direct leap from the old 'bindok' to carbines and rifles of Le Gras, M.H., and Snider patterns (this latter has never been popular owing to its limited range and high trajectory). In the hands of most members of a ruling house you will now find high velocity small-bores and smokeless ammunition.[33]

Although one would be wise to doubt the accuracy of Bury's memory, especially in view of his reputation for self-promotion, that these weapons were adopted rapidly is not at issue. Even so, as Dresch notes, "tribes were far from slaves of weaponry," and he suggests that local populations generally adapted the social norms of retaliation to fit new developments in weaponry.[34] Building on Dresch's observation, I suggest that rather than relate the traffic in arms and the proliferation of new forms of weaponry to an increase in violent conflict in terms of simple causality, we should instead consider why these developments were brought so suddenly within the gaze of the colonial state at this particular time and place.

The trade in weapons of precision in the Red Sea region was a result of the re-equipping of European armies in the late nineteenth century. The Prussian army adopted the breech-loading "needle gun" in 1866, and by 1878 all major European armies were armed with breech-loaders such as the Chassepot, Snider and Martini Henry rifles with metallic cartridges and steel muzzles. While these developments put more obsolete weapons onto the international market, especially in Africa, it was the second major development in small arms technology that brought more advanced weapons into the Arabian Peninsula. By the late 1880s Germany had already reequipped its army with repeating rifles; France followed in 1885 with the Lebel, Austria in 1886 with the Mannlicher and Britain in 1888 with the Lee Metford. Smokeless powder was uniformly adopted, pushing large quantities of black powder onto the international market as well.[35]

The division of East Africa into British and German spheres of influence by the Agreement of 1886 brought this part of the continent under the control of the German East Africa Company and the Imperial British East Africa Company. Armed resistance to their presence pushed both powers to take measures to control the indiscriminate trade in firearms. The more important initiative was the Brussels Treaty of 1890, which was meant to curb both the East African slave trade and the traffic in firearms. Nonetheless, a bustling trade in firearms continued in the Red Sea, and the French port of Djibouti was quickly becoming the hub of the Red Sea arms trade. While the port itself was the ideal point of entry for arms heading towards King Menelik in Shoa, and by 1898 the forces of the "Mad Mullah" in Italian-ruled Somaliland, there was growing demand for the weapons throughout the region. This pattern of trade, R.W. Beachey notes, often involved small merchants dealing in a variety of goods. Merchants from Muscat might carry a cargo of dates from Basra in Iraq to Aden and northern ports in Somalia and then proceed to Djibouti where they would purchase arms with the proceeds from the sale of dates. These arms could then be sold down the Benadir coast before a return to the Persian Gulf with the southwest monsoon. Others went from Djibouti to the Somali coast during the northeast monsoon, making it easier to proceed first to Aden. Still others went to Mukha, Mukalla or Ras al-'Ara (Subayhi country) with weapons to be shipped back to the Mijertain coast or to be sold to the local populations. The level of this trade was considerable and involved any number of nationalities.

By the turn of the century it had become clear that inhabitants of the Aden hinterland and beyond were actively participating in this trade, not only as customers but as merchants as well. The already heavy dhow traffic between the coast of South Arabia and the ports of East Africa provided more than adequate cover for a local trade based on relatively small purchases, marketed individually in Yemen and beyond. An incident recorded in the archives serves as an illustration of the market. After hearing that tribesmen from the Protectorate had travelled to Djibouti for the purchase of arms, the Political Resident Ernest DeBrath sent a translator from the Arabic Department in 1907 to the port to inquire into the matter. In the report filed on his return, he noted that there were several shops owned by Greek, Armenian and French merchants dealing in small arms. He entered just one of these shops in which there were several men from the Yemeni South purchasing small quantities of French rifles and ammunition to be transported to the port of Ras al-'Ara on the Gulf of Aden in Subayhi country. The men themselves were not all Sabayha, but from several different areas in the Aden Protectorate and Ottoman Yemen.[36]

While the presence of a cosmopolitan merchant class, the seemingly public nature of the transactions, and the complicity of the French customs authorities in the trade were enough to alarm the British in Aden, the pattern of purchases were a more immediate challenge to colonial policing efforts. The fact that most purchases were for individual use, often single rifles and cases of ammunition, made the detection of contraband arms extremely difficult if not impossible beyond Djibouti. Moreover, as the tribal names of the purchasers in the incident cited above indicated (Humaydi, Maʻmai, ʻAqrabi), they came not only from Subayhi country (the Maʻmai) but also from several regions along the coast within the Aden Protectorate (ʻAqrabi) and Ottoman Yemen (Humaydi). As will be shown below, the trans-local nature of the trade prevented a purely local solution to the problem, regardless of attempts by the colonial state to define it as such.

If the scene described can be at all considered the typical pattern of arms purchases in Djibouti, the next step was to ship them back to South Arabia. In light of the relatively small individual purchases, the shipping of arms was always conducted by the smaller wooden dhows used in the Red Sea and Indian Ocean, most of them individually owned and operated. The authorities at Aden had by 1907 compiled a list of the boats, their owners and pilots who were engaged in the arms trade as it affected Aden. Nineteen dhows were listed as the principal transports used in the trade; their owners included residents of Tajura, Djibouti, the village of Khawkha in the Tihama, and Aden. Moreover there were several merchants of the Zaraniq tribe in the Tihama who regularly hired these boats on their behalf.[37] Again, the participants came from various East African ports, ports in Ottoman Yemen and those within Aden and the Protectorate.[38]

Once a boat was hired and the weapons carefully hidden inside, the consignment was taken to any number of small ports in the Gulf of Aden or on Yemen's Red Sea coast, depending on the purchaser and variables of security and weather. Along the Red Sea coast, arms were unloaded at Khawkha, Midi and other small ports and villages, all of which were inside Ottoman territory. More important to the British, however, were the increasing arms shipments to ports in the Gulf of Aden. Arms were landed at a series of small villages, most of which were in Subayhi territory. From there weapons were loaded onto camels and carried to the markets in the towns of Lahj and Daliʻ where a larger regional trade was conducted.[39] It was even noted at one point that weapons were openly sold at the Friday market and other weekly markets in Lahj, despite the ʻAbdali Sultan's attempts to curb the trade in his territory.[40] In fact, it was rumored that the Sultan made a tidy profit from the arms trade, an accusation he firmly denied.[41] Nonetheless, the trade extended from Lahj far into the territory of the Protectorate and beyond. Weapons were said to be moving from Lahj into Hawra country and into 'Awlaqi country in the easternmost part of the Protectorate from Balhaf.[42] It was even found that a regular supply of ammunition was making its way into the city of Aden by a number of merchants from the Somali coast who operated within the Protectorate. Given passes by the 'Abdali Sultan to enter the port town, they concealed ammunition in the baskets used to carry their wares and would meet at the "Mosque of the Dervishes" in Ma'alla, which was referred to as the "center of distribution to Somaliland."[43]

The weapon most frequently in demand was the French Le Gras rifle. The Le Gras, which was referred to locally as the *fransawi*, was considered superior to other weapons for a number of reasons. It was apparently of a convenient size and pattern, suitable for those riding camels. Its cartridges were more durable than those of the English Martini-Henry rifles and could be reloaded several times.[44] But most important, the *fransawi* was readily available in significant numbers and was comparatively cheap. Although reports differ, the Le Gras rifle was sold within the Protectorate for between ten and fourteen dollars while the Martini-Henry, or *harti* as it was called, was generally sold for around thirty to forty.[45] The ubiquity of the weapon led Harold Jacob to remark, "[t]he Le Gras carbine is the favorite weapon in Al Yemen, and its bullet is as deadly as that of the old Snider arm. The Arabs would be very skeptical of the stopping powers of my 0.303, and as derisive of the carriers of the fusil [matchlock]."[46] Indeed, the new rifles were used throughout the hinterland and had been incorporated into local culture, as the verse which opened this section indicates, yet the Sabayha were seen as the principal agents in its trade.

Although the trade was so fluid as to make any talk of a "center" of the commerce in firearms ridiculous, the authorities at Aden directed their attention to the Sabayha. It was certain that a large number of weapons were entering the Protectorate through the strip of coast theoretically under their authority, but it was much more difficult to relate responsibility for the trade to tribe and section. While it could be said that the Barhimis brought in arms through al-Judhir, al-Maliha, al-Kaw' and Fuqum and that 'Atifis brought in arms through Ras al-'Ara and Shaykh Sa'id, neither the trade nor the geography of the trade corresponded to the social and political divisions understood by the British as Subayhi. A report revealed, for example, that members of the Ma'mai and Julaydi sections were active participants in the weapons trade in Ras al-'Ara, as were members of the eastern tribe of the 'Awlaqi.⁴⁷ None of these men were 'Atifi. Rather, they were from the Wadi Ma'adin, some distance from the coast, or from 'Awlaqi country in the far east of the hinterland. The number of such incidents could easily be multiplied, but what is clear is that the importation of arms into Subayhi territory was conducted by a number of private merchants, dealing in small numbers, connected only by their general geographical proximity to the Red Sea. The question is why the British blamed the Sabayha.

By 1906, the Aden authorities began to threaten both the Barhimi and 'Atifi Shaykhs with military action. Shaykh Sa'id Ba 'Ali al-'Atifi was warned that if the trade did not stop, the 'Abdali Sultan would be given authority over him, to which he responded with assertions of his innocence. He wrote that "we have never gone abroad nor have we been trading in them." Instead, he suggested that he had fulfilled his obligations in curbing the trade but the monthly stipend he received from the 'Abdali Sultan had been withheld. He then admitted that he had allowed Subayhi arms merchants to travel through his territory with weapons for which he "received its customary dues." The issue, then, for the 'Atifi Shaykh was that he had only agreed to stay out of the trade, but not to hinder his main source of income, which was the collection of customs dues.[48] Moreover, the 'Atifi Shaykh admitted that he did not exercise control over the inland section of his own tribe, nor was he at all inclined to extend his influence to all sections of his tribe. His influence was restricted to the coast.[49] But what was really at issue was the meaning of authority and its relationship to territory. While the British assumed, or at least wanted to assume, a complete and homogeneous sovereignty over an abstract space which could be considered 'Atifi, the meaning of 'Atifi limits (plural *hudud*) was more complex. As we shall see in Chapter 3, the authority of any one amir or sultan was based on a variety of arrangements negotiated through time and space with different segments of the population, which brought with them different rights and responsibilities. In no way could any protectorate chief exercise a uniform sovereignty over the whole of his territory. This proved problematic for the British time and time again, yet the colonial equation of sovereignty with space was never challenged.

In the end, however, the inhabitants of the Protectorate were already well armed and the Aden authorities could do little to prevent the trade. It was suggested, for example, that the tribes should be made more amenable to government authority through a number of ways. Proposals to introduce the Martini-Henry rifle into the hinterland assumed that the tribes would be dependent on Aden's largesse for supplies of weapons and ammunition, thus allowing them to control the numbers released among the population.[50] Even if they were supplied to the more important chiefs and their armies, it was deemed impracticable, if only because of the great expense that would be incurred. Moreover, few chiefs other than the 'Abdali Sultan actually had standing bodies of soldiers or police, which meant that the weapons would need to be released to the general male population. The preferred option of disarmament of the "petty" tribes (which normally meant the Sabayha) was deemed too difficult and expensive for practical application. Preventing the importation of weapons was deemed no easier, and would require the cooperation of the British, Italian, French and Ottoman governments.[51]

Not surprisingly, the authority of the 'Abdali Sultan was again seen as the solution. Despite the fact that the Sultan had not been responsible for the Sabayha since the 1881 agreement had fallen into abeyance in 1886, it was still assumed that the authority of Lahj would be able to put an end to the arms trade. However, the 'Abdali Sultan had little confidence in the Aden Government's proposal to take control of weapons distribution in the Protectorate. The distribution of Martini-Henry rifles to the Sabayha would not make them any more dependent on the British or any less dangerous to the Sultan. Sultan Ahmad pointed out that there were already as many as 30,000 of these rifles present in the country and that blacksmiths were able to alter their chambers to accommodate the much cheaper and more abundant French ammunition. Ultimately, he argued, the practicalities of controlling a trade that encompassed the entire hinterland were beyond his abilities, and he wrote, "You know that the coast extends from Maidi to beyond Balhaf, and in many of the ports the fire-arms and ammunition are imported in all directions, how could it be possible, therefore, for us to thoroughly extirpate them, and our tribesmen numbering over 3,000 are bound by necessity to be armed by the same guns and in the same such arms are adopted in all directions in our vicinity and others?"[52] In light of the rapid diffusion of the arms within the hinterland, he advised several times that if the British truly wanted to control the trade, they should curb the sale of arms at Djibouti.

Security and the roads

If the Sabayha proved difficult to deal with as the principal agents of the trade in firearms, they were especially so in the years just prior to and following the Brussels conference. While the major difficulties encountered by the colonial authorities in assigning responsibility for control of the trade in arms to the Sabayha stemmed from its trans-local nature and diffusion throughout the hinterland, the threat posed by the Sabayha on the roads was directly related to the absence of a paramount authority within the tribe. Between the years 1908 and 1919, a series of files were compiled on the Sabayha's interference on the trade routes, constituting a narrative of insecurity—a narrative that could only be resolved by the designation of a paramount authority over the Sabayha.[53]

Caravans travelling from the Hujariyya region in Ottoman Yemen to Aden moved along one of three sub-routes that followed dry *wadi* beds: the Wadi Sha'b and the more heavily travelled Wadi Ma'baq and Wadi Ma'adin. All of these routes crossed the territories of various Subayhi sections: sections of the Dubayni resided in the Wadi Sha'b, sections of the Dubayni, Jurabi, Sumati and Mansuri resided in the Wadi Ma'baq, and in the Wadi Ma'adin there were several sections of the Jurabi ('Atawi, 'Ayyari, Shukri, Bughayli, Masfari, and Makmahi) and the Juraywi section of the Dubayni.[54] The length of the trade routes and the fact that they passed through the territory of so many sections of the major Subayhi tribes were matters not

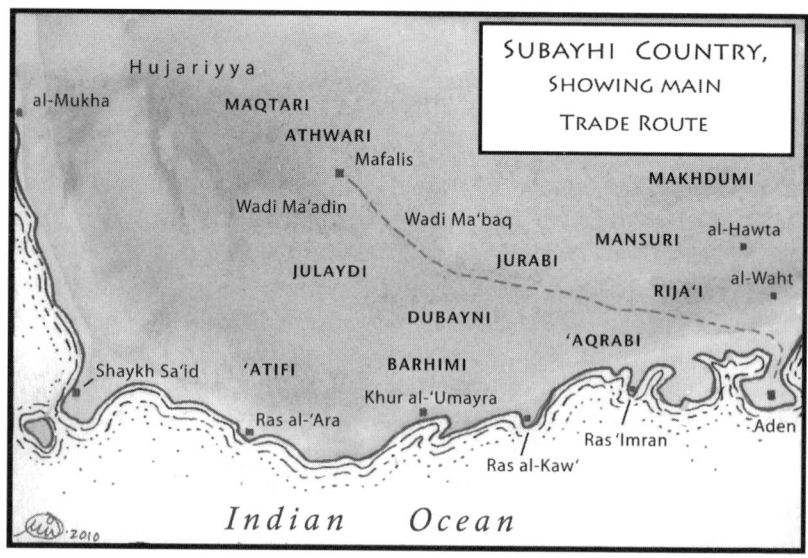

Map 2: Subayhi Coutry, showing main trade route.

lost on the Aden authorities who found that the original agreements with the "Sabayha" were of little use in protecting trade. While the British had long paid out a number of stipends beyond the 'Atifi and Barhimi Shaykhs who had signed treaties of protection, by the time the Anglo-Ottoman Boundary Commission had completed its task in 1905 it was clear that the policy of stipends was not providing the desired results. Through the course of delimitation of the boundary a whole cast of local notables were brought into relations with the British. Although no new stipends were authorized, the number of notables in receipt of "presents" (*masruf*) increased dramatically, as indicated in the table below (fig. 5).

On the one hand, the number of local Shaykhs brought into the colonial gift economy seems to have indicated an attempt to bring any person of influence under the control of the Aden government; on the other hand, the specific arrangement of payments corresponded closely to the most important inland trade routes. Shaykh Sa'id al-Jurabi, for example, resided in Judran in a fortified house commanding the Wadi al-Ma'adin route.[55] Sa'id Muhammad Ya'qub al-Masfari and Shaykh 'Ali al-Bughayli both resided at al-Ghariqa along the same route. Shaykh Hasan al-Juraywi resided at Tafih, and all of the 'Atawi Shaykhs lived in fortified houses along the Wadi Hayh through which the route passed. The situation was similar on the other two routes, and it is therefore not surprising to see that the majority of those in receipt of colonial largesse were from the Jurabi, Wahhasha and Dubayni tribes settled along the course of the Wadi Ma'adin. The proliferation of these payments to the notables along the trade routes was not merely a recognition of the limitations of the authority of the interior Shaykhs; the fact that the 'Atifi Shaykhs could not control the territory they claimed as their own, for example, did not result in the extension of payments to infinitely smaller sections. Rather, the principle behind making these payments was "to confine presents and stipends to those actually on the main roads and to emphasize their territorial responsibility for all offences committed on the roads in their limits, and to as far as possible ignore the petty tribes not situated on the main roads."[56]

The value of trade carried along these roads should not be underestimated, for it engaged a good part of the local population in one way or another. While dates, grain and produce made their way to Aden from Subayhi country, especially the Wadis Ma'baq and Ma'adin, the caravan traffic was based on the export of agricultural products of the much richer lands of the Hujariyya in the southern highlands. Fruit, grains and pulses were sent to Aden, but these products were dwarfed in value by the export of coffee and Maqtari *qat*. The value of coffee alone reached 323,000 Rs. by 1870, comprising one third of Aden's landward imports.[57] But while coffee was sold in Aden to be exported, *qat* was strictly for consumption within the town. Chewed daily for its stimulant effect, the green leaf of the plant was integral to social life in Aden and the rest of Yemen. The plants were highly perishable, meaning that the caravans arrived daily with new supplies to feed the habits of the growing urban population. The Maqtari *qat* was not of the highest quality but it was by far the cheapest and was therefore consumed in greater quantities by the working classes of the city. From the British point of view, the trade was extremely profitable, for it generated a significant income in duties placed on its importation, all of which were credited to the city's municipal fund.[58]

Tribe	*Notables in Receipt of Payments*
'Atifi	Sa'id Ba 'Ali al-'Atifi
Mansuri	Shahir b. Sayf al-Mansuri and Nu'man Ahmad al-Shujayfi
Makhdumi	Murshid Ba Nasr al-Makhdumi
Rija'i	Salim Ba 'Abdullah
Barhimi	Ali b. Ahmad am-Tummi, Salim Thabit al-'Utiri, Salih Ba Jirja al-Bushbushi, Janad b. Husayn al-Musafi, and 'Ali Muhammad and Munassar al-Khulayfi
Dubayni	Hasan 'Imad al-Juraywi, Darwish Battash al-Juraywi, Haza' Qasim Muqbil al-Mashaqi, Sayf Dhiban al-Dhuyaybi, Ahmad al-Daghir al-Tahiri, and Salim 'Abdullah Murshid al-Suwaylimi
Jurabi	Sa'id al-Jurabi al-'Ayyari, 'Ali al-Bughayli, Sa'id Muhammad Ya'qub al-Masfari, Salih Ba Haydara al-'Atawi, Sa'id Zayd Hawwash al-'Atawi, 'Abd al-Kurayh al-'Atawi, 'Ali 'Imad al-'Atawi, 'Abdullah Suwayhar al-Maflahi, and Sayyid Qadri Yasin on behalf of the other sections
Wahhasha	Sa'id Ja'far al-Ma'mai, Ahmad am-Basus al-Ma'mai, 'Imad b. Ahmad al-Julaydi, Fadl Ahmad al-Sumati, Hizam Ba Suwayd al-Sumati, Ahmad Sa'd al-Sumati
Buraymi	'Alawi b. 'Ali
Sha'bi	'Abd al-Qawi
Zaydi	Muhammad al-Masri and Muhammad al-Rabh

Figure 5: Subayhi notables in receipt of British payments, c. 1907.

The caravan trade was organized by a group of intermediaries called *muqaddims*. It was the *muqaddim*'s role to oversee the transport of commodities from their place of origin to the market, organizing the caravan itself and arranging for its protection if necessary. Eight *muqaddims* were recognized from Subayhi territory, seven of whom belonged to various sections of the Dubayni tribe, although none was especially prominent. The other *muqaddim* was Shaykh Saʻid al-Jurabi from the ʻAyyari section, who was recognized by the British as the "most important of the caravan Mukadams" and "perhaps the most enlightened of the Subehi Shaikhs."[59] Just as important as Saʻid al-Jurabi was the Humaydi Shaykh, Muhammad ʻAli Muqbil from the Ottoman side of the border. The caravan trade was dominated by these two men: Muqbil dealt with the majority of the trade in *qat* while Saʻid al-Jurabi handled the majority of the trade in coffee and other agricultural products. The profitability of the position was considerable; the Political Resident at the time wrote prosaically, "this mukadamship is a paying business."[60]

The British were soon to realize, however, that the security of the roads and local disputes were always intimately related. At the beginning of 1908, what began as a feud between the Julaydi section of the Wahhasha and the Humaydi tribe over a murder some time before came to engulf the entire Wadi Maʻadin and nearly brought the caravan trade to a halt. But what the colonial archive framed as merely a problem of trade and security, the local actors conceived as a question of community right concerning the proper division of the *muqaddim*ship, of water distribution, and of restitution for wrongs committed. What the British attempted to control through the formation of contractual relationships and the extension of largesse, the local population attempted to mediate through their arbiters, the *mansab*s and descendants of the Prophet Muhammad or *sayyid*s, and the attempt to reestablish what were seen as traditional rights and customs.

The Julaydi section of the Wahhasha had maintained an ongoing feud with the Humaydi on the Ottoman side of the border concerning a murder some time before. But they also began to question the monopoly of Saʻid al-Jurabi over his part of the *muqaddim*ship. ʻImad b. Ahmad al-Julaydi claimed that he had rights to part of the fees collected by Jurabi. When this was refused the Julaydis attacked a Jurabi-led caravan. Not long afterwards the Masfari Shaykh, Saʻid Muhammad Yaʻqub made a similar claim, which was also rejected. In response, the Masfaris refused to pay the dues owed to the Zaʻwari, another Jurabi section, for their allocation of local *ghayl* or floodwater for irrigation. The Zaʻwari, who controlled the allocation of water, cut off the Masfari fields. Saʻid al-Jurabi then turned to the Humayda for assistance. Their position as monopolists on the roads made them natural allies and they attacked the Masfari, who had enlisted the aid of the other Jurabi sections against the ʻAyyari and the Zaʻwari. Once a Dubayni was killed in the ensuing skirmishes, a number of their sections joined against the ʻAyyari and Humaydi as well.

Saʻid al-Jurabi began to build a fortified tower overlooking a number of watercourses used to irrigate Jurabi fields with the intention of cutting their water in retaliation.[61] Likewise, the opposing Jurabis and Dubaynis began building one at a critical crossroads along the Wadi Maʻadin in order to facilitate their blockade of caravan traffic.[62] The alliance of Jurabi, Dubayni and Julaydi sections succeeded in intercepting most or all of the *qat* and coffee caravans travelling along the *wadi*, confiscating their merchandise, money and weapons and often the camels. By the beginning of May trade had been halted to the extent that the agent of the *qat* merchants in Aden began complaining to the British Resident. It was their habit to pay the landowners in advance for consignments of *qat* through a single agent, and with the interruption in trade, they had lost their investment. They invoked their position as subjects of the British government and asked for protection and restitution, as "we are poor family men and have sustained great loss and have no other sort of means except selling Kat." More particularly, they pointed to the importation of arms from Djibouti as the principle cause of the increase in robbery on the caravan route.[63] Not only did Aden's merchant community begin to agitate for a resolution of the conflict in the hinterland, but commercial interests in the Hujariyya on the Ottoman side of the boundary began to complain as well.[64]

As the conflict intensified and commerce in the Wadi Maʻadin was brought to a standstill, it had the effect of momentarily breaking the monopoly of Muhammad ʻAli Muqbil and Saʻid al-Jurabi and allowing other sections to take over the task of escorting caravans. The Mansuris, for example, took charge of a number of caravans since they could not be attacked lest they be brought into the feud, and on at least one occasion they handed a caravan over to the *mansab* of Shaghit who, as the custodian of a local religious shrine, was considered protected or *muhajjar*.[65] But trade was also redirected to another route protected by the Bushbushi, a section of the Buraymi. The trade had already improved to the extent that an ʻAqrabi Shaykh could write to the Political Resident, complimenting the

British on their excellent work looking after the safety of the road. On his part, the ʿAbdali Sultan offered to escort caravans into Hawshabi country where local *muqaddim*s would take over.⁶⁶ The Sumatis even declared that the road would henceforth be considered a public road—literally "God's road" (*al-tariq sabil allah*)—and therefore beyond tribal jurisdiction.

Almost as soon as the conflict broke out, a number of the Subayhi country's notables were mobilized to effect an arbitration of the dispute. Sultan Ahmad called in the traditional arbiters of conflicts: Sayyid Ahmad Saʿid, the administrator of a local religious shrine in Jurabi country, and Sayyid Qadri Yasin would both play the role of mediators since they were descendants of the prophet Muhammad and therefore belonged to no tribe.⁶⁷ The more important figures, however, were several Shaykhs from tribes residing beyond the Wadi Maʿadin, whose efforts to conclude a temporary truce were foiled by the reluctance of all parties to offer hostages as a guarantee for good behavior. Other Shaykhs from outside the disputing tribes also attempted to intervene. The news that the Jurabi-Julaydi-Dubayni alliance had agreed to blockade the roads leading to Aden at the end of the truce negotiations made the issue of forcing arbitration that much more urgent.⁶⁸ While Saʿid al-Jurabi and Muhammad ʿAli Muqbil had agreed to arbitration by the ʿAbdali Sultan, the others had refused. The Residency then sent a series of letters to the Shaykhs of the sections involved, condemning the pursuit of their feud on the roads, which the British considered little more than "the acts of a robber," and calling on them to "cease from these evil deeds and to appear before us at once that we may take steps to bring about a permanent settlement of your disputes."⁶⁹

The invitation to Aden and the explicit warning to those accused of interrupting the roads was met by a clear response. A number of Shaykhs representing the Jurabi-Julaydi-Dubayni alliance against the two *muqaddim*s wrote to the Aden Resident declaring their innocence, not of attacking Humaydi and ʿAyyari caravans in itself, but of committing the more serious crime of highway robbery (*qatʿ al-tariq*). Rather, they were taking socially sanctioned action in light of what they presented as an infringement of traditional rights:

> The sons of Ali Mokbil have by force and might deprived us of, and usurped our established rights, which we are now determined to reassert and recover in a similar manner. God has now willed that we should regain our privileges and establish ourselves in them, in like manner as the sons of Ali Mokbil had possessed themselves of them.

UNMAKING NORTH AND SOUTH

We inform you that the disorder has gained footing (*waqa'a al-rabsha*) since Saleh bin Ahmed the Mansuri, Mahomed Ali the Humaidi and Saeed al Jorabi entered into alliance. If we acquire our usual rights and every person regains his position the status quo will be maintained, and the routes will be considered sacred for the sake of God and Government. There shall be security to the travellers and we shall come to you.[70]

Conflict on the roads would continue, they declared, "until we obtain our claims in respect to the stream mokadamship and our other privileges detailed above." The rights they claimed through "continued practice" were also claimed to be supported by what Shaykh 'Imad b. Ahmad earlier referred to as "documentary rights" (*waridat*). Although the documents never found their way into the colonial archive, it was an attempt to establish a claim based on custom and usage over time, based on the sanctity of past agreements recorded in writing. Moreover, their actions, they argued on several occasions, were directed only at those with whom they were engaged in a feud; the road had continued to be safe for those classified as socially "weak" (*du'afa' wa-masakin*, a designation used for those who did not belong to one of the armed tribes). The same was true of the Maqtaris who could continue to export their *qat* so long as it was not under the protection of Muhammad 'Ali Muqbil or Sa'id al-Jurabi. For the British, however, the central concern was the security of the roads and commerce, not traditional rights, and they continually pressed the parties involved to agree to a temporary truce.

In the end it was Sultan Ahmad b. Fadl who brought an end to the feud. He ordered the payment of compensation to different members of the Julaydis and Jurabis, but he would not recognize former rights to fees on the caravan routes, but "those which the parties hitherto enjoy."[71] That is, he recognized the status quo. Hostages were then handed over by Shaykh 'Imad b. Ahmad and Muhammad 'Ali Muqbil as surety for the maintenance of safety on the roads and for any claims they might hold against each other. They both signed an agreement by which the safety of travellers, merchants and goods on the roads was assured. In an agreement typical of South Arabian tribal society, they placed the road under a form of collective tribal protection known as *hijra* (*fa in al-tariq muhajjar*), by which all the signatories took responsibility for any deeds committed against those travelling its length "within their known limits" (*fi hududina al-ma'rufa*).[72] The road was declared inviolate, and the shame of any infringement of the agreement, as well as its defense, would be theoretically shared by all signatories equally.

There are a number of details missing in the records. Although there is discussion of compensation and the distribution of payments is listed, it is difficult to make sense of what determined how much was paid and to whom. The act of mediation, which implies negotiation between the parties, is nowhere to be seen. The records include only a bare outline of the proceedings and the texts of the final agreements, suggesting unwillingness on the part of the Aden authorities to involve themselves in the politics of the hinterland. It was the result of arbitration that interested Aden and not the act itself, which was increasingly left to the 'Abdali Sultan.

We should not be surprised, however, that the colonial archive is so vague about the mediation efforts, or that ultimately the status quo was upheld. The logic of indirect rule in the hinterland did not confer importance on the dynamics of local politics outside the port of Aden, so long as security was maintained. If the above account seemed confusing (and it is hardly clearer in the documents) it is because the series of files opens with a crisis which had already erupted. Although the mediation efforts and truce might have seemed to conclude the Subayhi threat to security, the records continue to list a series of conflicts—a seemingly endless cycle of crisis and mediation.[73] For the British, the events themselves and their local political importance were not as significant as finding a lasting resolution, not only to this episode, but to all problems emanating from the territory of the Sabayha. It was left to Sultan Ahmad b. Fadl to restate the central problem of the colonial order with his usual candor and precision:

> The chief cause of their not being amenable to order (*'adam dibat*) is because they are not subordinate to a single chief and none of their leaders possess actual power or influence (*kalima nafidha*) over them. On several occasions you asked us about their leaders and we find it difficult to inform you correctly about their leaders and we find it difficult to inform you correctly about them owing to their unsteady disposition (*thaqlat halatihim*). If one chief has some influence today, the next day he will be totally deprived of any power and his words are never respected.[74]

Confronted once again with the fact that the Sabayha did not have a native chief, the Aden government responded in a most predictable fashion: it decided, as in 1881, to assign the tribe a figure of authority.

At the end of the First World War, when the new 'Abdali Sultan 'Abd al-Karim b. Fadl b. 'Ali was again resident in Lahj after the wartime Ottoman occupation of Lahj, the issue of the Sabayha was raised. The road was again unsafe, and incidents were likely to become more frequent than before since so many Subayhi Shaykhs had been unable to collect stipends during the war. The almost immediate movement of Imam Yahya Hamid al-Din's troops towards the borders of the Protectorate made it much more urgent to the British to rein in the Sabayha. On 27 February 1919, the 'Abdali Sultan entered into a new agreement for the control of the Sabayha. The Sultan agreed to "settle all transgressions perpetrated by the Subaihis against merchants and others traveling on the trade route."[75] In return, the government again made the Sultan the mediator of all relations between the Sabayha and Aden. All stipends were paid through him, and invitations to visit the Residency came only from him. He was allowed both to dismiss troublesome Shaykhs and to punish anyone found interrupting trade, albeit after consultation with Aden. A master was finally found for the masterless.

Conclusion: fighting indeterminacy

In his study of the colonization of Australia, Paul Carter has suggested that the British encounter with the aboriginal population was in part framed by anxiety over its mobility or the inability to locate it in a distinct space. For the British, the local population was a threat to the colonial state because it was itself stateless in the Western sense. Carter argues however that "their wandering did indeed constitute a 'state'—a form of social and political organization. But this was expressed, not as a power over past and future—the pet obsession of the usurping historical culture—but as a power over space."[76] The British experience with the Sabayha shared the same preoccupation with mobility and the transgression of political and social borders that this entailed. Phrased differently, the Sabayha refused to confine themselves to the space which the colonial concept of the "nine tribes" had allotted to them. If the "nine tribes" as a political and social space were defined by a historical and genealogical imagination linking ruling houses to the revolt against Qasimi rule, the Sabayha were the antithesis of this order. In the absence of a ruling chief (and therefore a history and genealogy) the Sabayha were by nature instigators of chaos and disorder and were treated by the British as a criminal class.

In their failure to fulfill the basic assumptions of what constituted the tribe in the colonial imagination, the Sabayha became a specter of indeterminacy that haunted the colonial project through the turn of the century. They appear in the archival records at moments of crisis, when the edifice of the protectorate order was seemingly under threat. Subayhi involvement in the arms trade, for example, suggested the extent to which the local population was active in trans-regional networks of commerce, crossing both tribal boundaries and spheres of imperial influence. The fluid movement of merchants, money and weapons threatened not so much British rule as the security regime that the concept of the "nine tribes" and the durbar model were supposed to ensure. In the cases of the arms trade and conflict on the roads that attended it, however, it was the peculiar, acephalous nature of Subayhi society that was seen as the cause of its predisposition to criminality. The British response was consonant with Bauman's understanding of the modern state's desire "to exterminate ambivalence."[77] For the Sabayha, this meant effectively ending their anomalous position in the Protectorate by assigning them a native chief.

Since the British policy of non-interference in the Protectorate effectively saw the hinterland as a space of security rather than the law, the Sabayha were never subjected to the disciplinary and rehabilitating power of the state as the criminal castes were in India. Administrators in India (such as a later Aden Resident, James Outram) had attempted to instill in some criminal tribes a sense of loyalty and respectability through military recruitment; a Bhil Corps was raised in 1841, for example, which performed with distinction in defense of British rule in 1857, and over 2,000 recruits from the criminal tribes of the Punjab served in the First World War as well.[78] Similarly, state settlement projects aimed to eradicate the very mobility that fostered predatory tendencies.[79] The Sabayha were treated with a great deal more pessimism. G. Wyman Bury, who appeared first in this chapter as the official forced to deal with the incident at the guest house in Aden, suggested that they could be of great use to the British in native military units, but saw their "fierce intractable disposition" as an impediment to loyal military service.[80]

In 1918, the British established the Yemen Light Infantry on the basis of local recruits. Although it was disbanded at the end of the First World War, many of its recruits found places in the Aden Protectorate Levies, which were established in 1928 as part of Aden's post-war defense scheme in which local troops would be supported by the Royal Air Force. Their mission would be to police the northern border of the Protectorate with the support of air power. The Levies did not, however, recruit among the Sabayha. Rather, the new Levies, like the Yemen Light Infantry before, were recruited from the tribes of the eastern mountains, or the "more prosperous" tribes in Bury's terms, particularly from the 'Awlaqi, 'Awdhilli and Yafi'i.[81] That is, the British deferred to the Yemeni "martial races." Indeed, as the then Political Resident,

Major General Stewart, wrote in 1927, "[the] best fighting material in the Protectorate is in the mountain tribes."[82] The first armed police force in the city of Aden also recruited its first officers from the ranks of the Levies, so that the dominance of the martial tribes was reproduced within the Colony. The martial tribesman would dominate the city as he did the countryside.

The situation was quite different for the Sabayha, however. Although by 1928 it was reported in Aden that "since gun-running from French Somaliland ceased many years ago, the protectorate tribes are practically entirely dependent on us for their supply of ammunition," the Sabayha never ceased to be a problem to be solved for the British.[83] The agreement with the 'Abdali Sultan in 1919 may have shifted the responsibility for the tribe, but they continued to practice their own form of politics on the roads with regularity. In the period after the First World War, Imam Yahya made the same complaints as the Ottoman government and the local population before him.[84] However, with the 1919 treaty the Sabayha became a problem not for the colonial state but for the 'Abdali Sultanate, not a crisis for colonial rule but for local rule.

3

A LANDSCAPE OF UNCERTAINTY

This metaphorical way of speaking is a pointer to the way spatial history must interpret its sources. It also indicates, concisely and poetically, the cultural place where spatial history begins: not in a particular year, nor in a particular place, but in the act of naming. For by the act of place-naming, space is transformed symbolically into a place, that is, a space with a history.

Paul Carter[1]

Introduction

"Who has not stood at times in front of some old picture, and imagined himself walking into the artificial stillness of its landscape?" Freya Stark asks rhetorically while recounting her arrival in Daliʻ where she was to spend Christmas 1939 as a guest of the Amir. And she continues:

It comes to life as he advances into imaginary distance; the donkey trots with panniers in the foreground, the little boy with stick perpetually lifted brings it down with a whack. Fresh dust is on the ruts of that track that winds into the background by towns perched there on small and naked hills. The painter has put them in clearly, one by one, diminishing as the track winds in smaller perspective; in his faithful rendering you can see specks of people—men with sashes and rifles, teams of oxen ploughing in the fields. You can see the Emir descending from his castle, by a steep path that cuts diagonally to the small town below; the chestnut pony whisks its long tail, his bodyguard are running all about him. Smoke rises; the tiny whitewashed windows look out like eyes of owls from their dark walls; sparse trees are dotted in the fields.

"Something is always happening in this landscape," she notes and continues to describe the scene of kites in flight, the shrillness of their calls, and the general din of life ascending from the town, "for the fact is that it is not a painting at all, but the everyday, incredible landscape of Dhala [Daliʿ]."[2]

Writing after South Yemen's independence in 1967, Donald Foster, a former government minister in Aden and the Federation of South Arabia and an amateur landscape artist, wrote a book in which he attempted to "draw a picture" of the area as he knew it. He makes clear his preference for the landscape form, noting, "[t]here is perhaps more scenery than there are people, more mountains than Mohammeds, but that is because I share with Rose Macaulay a preference for places over people."[3]

Like Stark, he describes in great detail the journey from Aden to Daliʿ, following the Hardaba road to the Khurayba Pass, the last obstacle before the plateau. His narrative is punctuated not only by descriptions of the landscape but also by an indication of the relationship between place and local authority. Beyond the Khurayba Pass lie not only the Emirate of Daliʿ but the Shaʿiri and Qutaybi peoples as well. Also like Stark, he notes that Daliʿ "is a miniature landscape: the eye fastens on the plateau, punctuated with little conical towers, each capped with a fortified house, tall, angular; on small fields between meandering foot paths, where oxen are ploughing; on a movement of dark figurines, women in black at a well-head." But Foster's account is somewhat more menacing. Listing the number of political officers murdered in the Emirate, he amends Stark's romantic account, noting instead that "things tend to happen at Dhala—things mostly disagreeable."[4]

On the surface these two accounts have much in common. They both view Daliʿ through the aesthetic of the landscape, reducing the Emirate and its inhabitants to a pleasing prospect to be consumed by the Western reader. Both authors claim to represent Daliʿ as a natural, unmediated space and, in doing so, pass over the problematic nature of this landscape as an effect of the colonial project in the Yemeni South. Art historians have long noted that the landscape form as a way of seeing was intimately related to the rise of capitalism and the modern state, and more recently scholars have argued that the conventions of the landscape and the picturesque were integral to the aesthetic appropriation of the colonial world as well.[5] The descriptions of Stark and Foster are engaged at some level in this appropriation, but the landscapes they claim to represent are not necessarily the same. The two narratives, one by a renowned traveller and the other by a former colonial official, suggest an ambivalence in the way that Daliʿ and, by association,

A LANDSCAPE OF UNCERTAINTY

the Aden Protectorate were brought into the British Empire. Stark's description of the place employs the very familiar aesthetic of the picturesque; that is, Daliʻ looks like an artistic representation of the land and its people. It is a pastoral image of security, prosperity, and abundance. Foster, while restating Stark's description, goes further in that he invokes not only the tribes that live in the region, but their history of violent resistance to British colonial rule. His is an unsettled vision of the tribal landscape, which suggests both the pastoral Daliʻ allied with the British and the turbulent world of the tribes beyond the plateau. Between these two views, those of Stark and Foster, the landscape is very much part of the "dreamwork" of imperialism as the critic W.J.T. Mitchell suggests, "unfolding its own movement in time and space from a central point of origin and folding back on itself to disclose both utopian fantasies of the perfected imperial prospect and fractured images of unresolved ambivalence and unsuppressed resistance."[6]

This chapter investigates the interplay between the "perfected imperial prospect" and the "unsuppressed resistance" that characterized the British experience of the protectorate landscape. The durbar model of association had suggested the possibility of a colonial pastoral, of a tranquil countryside in which ancient ruling houses governed obedient subjects. This historical and sociological imagination was all the more powerful because it was made real through a number of state practices that made both the "protectorate chiefs" and their tribal subjects objects of rule. Yet, the encounter with the hinterland population at the level of the everyday practices of colonial administration suggested an uncertain landscape in which every hill was fortified by recalcitrant tribes, subordinate to none and hostile to all. This was especially the case by the end of the nineteenth century, as the government in Aden began to realize that the protectorate chiefs were anything but the models of benevolent authoritarian rule that they had hoped. The anxiety produced by this gulf between the landscape as produced by colonial knowledge and the landscape as a place of everyday practice pointed to the general instability that characterized the whole colonial project in South Arabia by the turn of the century.

Daliʻ, in particular, was the site in which this anxiety was manifested because it was one of the few places in the Protectorate where the British maintained a prolonged presence in the late nineteenth and early twentieth centuries. This was in part due to Daliʻ's location astride the most important trade routes to the Yemeni highlands, marking the effective limits of the British protectorate. Its strategic importance was dramatically reinforced in 1872 with the Ottoman occupation of the Yemeni North and the establishment of an Ottoman administrative presence in the town of Qaʻtaba just north of Daliʻ. The alarming new political environment revealed both the limits of the policy of non-interference practiced up to that time and the inadequacy of knowledge about the Emirate of Daliʻ and its inhabitants, often referred to as the "Amiri" tribe in reference to the Amirs who ruled the area. What followed soon afterwards was an increased colonial presence in the hinterland whose object was to describe, map, and administer the Emirate in a manner consistent with practices in India, but new in the Yemeni South.

In what follows, I will look at three modes of visualizing the "Amiri" landscape in this period and the itineraries of the men who employed them. The first is the 1892 travelogue of the journalist and fellow of the Royal Geographical Society Walter Harris, which narrated his 1892 journey from Aden to Sanaa and included the only descriptive account of Daliʻ from this period. The second is the Anglo-Ottoman Boundary Commission (1902–05), directed by R.A. Wahab of the Survey of India, which had the goal of delimiting the boundary between the Aden Protectorate and Ottoman Yemen. The third is the short-lived Daliʻ Agency (1902–07) under Col. Harold Jacob, which was set the ill-defined task of managing tribal relations in the territory of the Amir of Daliʻ in the period during and after the Boundary Commission. These three modes of appropriating and representing the landscape—the descriptive, cartographic, and administrative—aimed at making the social and political space of the tribal hinterland legible, whether through the genre of the travel narrative, the map, or the practice of colonial governance. Essential to the goal of producing a landscape that could be read, as Paul Carter has so convincingly argued in the Australian context, was the act of naming, of taking local spaces and giving them meaning within the framework of imperial power. It was in the process of naming the Amiri landscape, framed at the outset by the British construct of the "nine tribes," that the colonial state and its agents most acutely discovered the limits of colonial knowledge and, ultimately, of the durbar model of governance that had so readily been applied in the Yemeni South.

Writing the Amiri landscape

In an article published in 1937, Harold Ingrams, a political officer based in the Hadramawt, wrote a general survey of the exploration of the area of the

A LANDSCAPE OF UNCERTAINTY

Aden Protectorate, beginning with the nineteenth century. Reflecting on the history of colonial rule in Aden and the hinterland, he wrote: "It is a curious fact that most of this vast territory came under British protection without the penetration and exploration that usually precede the establishment of Western influence in a primitive country."[7] Indeed, the exploration of South Arabia in the period directly before and some time after the occupation of Aden proceeded slowly; the interior of the Protectorate outside Lahj, the seat of the 'Abdali Sultanate, and especially Dali', had rarely been visited until the end of the nineteenth century.

Even so, there was very little sense of conquering *terra incognita* outside Aden. Contrary to a spate of recent works that have argued on the basis of the Australian example that non-Western landscapes were brought into being in the colonial imagination by the very process of exploration and the practice of naming, South Arabia was somewhat different.[8] The Protectorate order was founded on an historical imagination that assumed a country populated by a local aristocracy, united by a political genealogy that led back to the eighteenth-century uprising against the Zaydi Imamate in the North. This sense of history framed the colonial encounter with the Amiri landscape; indeed, the British were faced with a place constituted by a history that preceded them. It was generally understood that the Dali' plateau had been ruled until the sixteenth century by a *sayyid* house subject to the Zaydi Imamate. They were then overthrown by descendants of *muwallad* or mixed-race slaves, and from them the Amirs of Dali' were descended. In the period under discussion, the Emirate was ruled by 'Ali b. Muqbil and Shayif b. Sayf. For the British, the historicity of the Dali', as with the 'Abdali Sultanate, was taken for granted.

At the level of everyday practice this historicity was evident in the movement of commerce, which was itself etched into the landscape. The Aden hinterland was crossed with a long-established network of roads, connecting the Yemeni South to the ports of the Red Sea and the western Indian Ocean. Hunter's 1877 account of the settlement in Aden, for example, noted the presence of the major routes, through which tribal territories they passed, and specified which types of commodities passed along them. The Dali' road was particularly important, for it carried the majority of the highland trade to the markets in the south, and Aden in particular. Coffee, wax, *ghee*, grain, fruits and madder, in short, every product from the agricultural lands of the Yemeni highlands was transported along this road. More important, he pointed out that it passed through the territories of the

Amiri, 'Alawi, Hawshabi and 'Abdali tribes; that is, it crossed the territories of more tribes than any other route.⁹ The first treaty signed with the Amirs in 1880 stipulated that they must guarantee the security of the roads and must be answerable for any outrages committed by the tribes under their authority.¹⁰ Later agreements were signed in 1888 with the other tribes along the route, codifying the customs duties each was allowed to levy on particular commodities.¹¹ The ordering of the roads, in fact, took greater precedence than establishing a permanent relationship with the Amirs, but that was to change shortly thereafter.

The fact that the British signed no agreements with the Amirs of Dali' until the 1880s was very much because there was little interest in the further reaches of the hinterland until the Ottoman occupation of Sanaa in 1872 and the subsequent extension of Turkish administrative authority to the Southern town of Qa'taba. By 1873, the Ottoman authorities had forced Amir 'Ali Muqbil (d. 1886) to accept one of their administrators and to pay upwards of 800 Maria Theresa dollars a year to the government in Sanaa. When he sought assistance from the British in Aden, he was imprisoned and replaced by his uncle as Amir. While he had regained his position by 1878, he had lost considerable influence in his territory owing to the number of local headmen who had sought independent agreements with the Ottoman state. It was at this point that the British began to take a greater interest in Dali'. The Amir was given artillery, and the Aden Troop conducted what was referred to as a *"promenade militaire"* through the Amir's territory in 1880 as a show of force and a way of gathering intelligence. Nonetheless, from their base in Qa'taba, Ottoman forces continued to gather taxes from villages subject to the Amir of Dali', robbing him of revenue and undermining his authority with surrounding tribes, many of which began to make greater demands on the proceeds from the caravan trade.

In spite of this contested past, the entry on Dali' in Hunter and Sealey's 1886 handbook on the "nine tribes" presents a picture of the Emirate's landscape that, while framed as an empirical account of the region and its inhabitants, suggests the ideal vision of one of Aden's native chiefdoms. Compared with other regions in the Protectorate, Dali' was agriculturally rich: the authors described the variety of crops cultivated, the robust health of the domestic animals raised by the peasantry, and the abundance of rainfall and sweet water wells. As for the Emirate's residents, the majority "are land-owners, and assist in tilling their own soil." Although there were few merchants or craftsmen, the account notes that "none, except the Jews,

A LANDSCAPE OF UNCERTAINTY

appear very impoverished, and the general bearing of the people is far from warlike."[12] This general scene of comparative prosperity and tranquility was, it is implied, due largely to the benevolent rule of the Amir, who oversaw security and the application of the law with a fair, if heavy, hand.[13] The overall picture of harmony and seemingly absolute rule portrayed in the handbook—a positive phenomenon in the language of indirect rule—also led the German explorer von Maltzen in an earlier moment to declare confidently: "politically, this is the best administered State of all South Arabia."[14] It is difficult not to think that this reassuring portrait of the Daliʻ Emirate was possible, at least to a certain extent, because it says little about the contested process by which geographical knowledge on the Emirate was generated. Hunter and Sealey excluded from this passage the movement of the Aden Troop, the reports of informants, and the work of earlier cartographers. Indeed, the work of empire itself was absent from their account. Instead, Daliʻ as a pleasing prospect was divorced from both history and context. Not so with the literature of the explorer, for which we turn to Walter Harris.

In 1892 Walter Harris, a correspondent for *The Times* who had spent a number of years travelling and reporting on events in Morocco, embarked on a journey from Aden to Sanaa, following the Daliʻ road. While his stated goal was to report on the ongoing war between Imam al-Mansur and the Ottoman state (see Chapter 4), he left a detailed account of his trip northward. His journey was novel in this period; most travellers avoided the dangerous northward journey through the inland borderlands and instead set out from the Red Sea port of Ottoman Hudayda. Interestingly, his trip also coincided with the first major effort by the British to map the Aden Protectorate as part of the Indian Survey in 1891–92. For our purposes, his text is interesting as an example of the way in which the landscape aesthetic not only functioned as a tool of the imperial project in the Yemeni South but also suggested the deep anxieties that accompanied the creation of the Protectorate.

After a short spell in Aden, Harris began his journey from Lahj, where he had bought provisions and hired camels and escorts. The first few miles of the trip took him along the course of the Wadi Tuban, which he described as "rich cultivated land, watered by a careful system of irrigation, and gorgeous in its verdure."[15] As his party exited the lush valley basin, which marked the end of ʻAbdali territory, his description of the landscape changed appreciably. "Wild and depressing the scene was," Harris wrote, noting wistfully the absence of peasants returning from their fields, of shepherds with their flocks, and of wild songs sung by the "sons of the desert." Indeed, nearing the end of Lahj proper, they followed the course of a stream thought by the local population to be especially poisonous and effectively marking the boundary between the 'Abdali Sultanate and the tribal wilds beyond. Crossing from 'Abdali to Hawshabi territory, a nebulous border guarded by frontier forts, he presented a letter from the Aden Residency to the Hawshabi Sultan requesting safe passage. That his passage into Hawshabi territory and away from urban life and the settled countryside represented by Aden and Lahj was mediated by the colonial state was further indication that the landscape was distinctly more menacing the further he travelled. Once in Hawshabi territory he had crossed into the mountainous terrain of the interior, devoid of habitation and crossed by wandering Bedouin. "The scene," he wrote, "looked sepulchral and gloomy."[16]

While his description of the landscape beyond Lahj is in most places evocatively dour, in others the land is so distinctly different as to escape his ability to capture it in a narrative language of any kind. At several points, Harris' power of description simply falters in the face of phenomena too utterly foreign to his aesthetic sensibility. After his party reached the green fields of the Wadi Tuban, the setting of the sun produced a "night which fails all description." The next morning, as the party set off across the frontier between 'Abdali and Hawshabi territory, a sandstorm struck, which again had a singular quality that defied past experience. But as Harris and his party approached the Dali' plateau, they encountered a place at which not only his descriptive talents but his knowledge of the historical Yemeni South—by which I mean his understanding of the "nine tribes" as historically constituted princely states—were entirely inadequate:

Before daylight we were on our road again, following for a little way the course of the river Sailet el-Melh. The country here had become more mountainous, one flat-topped peak being particularly noticeable. The natives call it Dhu-biyat, but I can find no mention of this name elsewhere. On the summit is a tomb, that of a certain Seyed Hasan, about whom there seemed to be traditions of his having possessed remarkable powers, but as to whose history apparent ignorance prevailed, nor can I find any records of any powerful Imam having been buried on this spot.[17]

Later observers would confirm that indeed there was a *wali* Hasan buried there, but this fact is less interesting than what this moment said about the limits of colonial knowledge.[18] Not only, it seems, did the landscape resist the aesthetic conventions of descriptive travel writing, it also challenged a

A LANDSCAPE OF UNCERTAINTY

colonial order that was founded on a historical narrative—the rebellion of the "nine tribes" in the eighteenth century and their subsequent independence as autonomous political and social formations—that proved inadequate in explaining the political and cultural realities of the Protectorate. While the "natives" had informed him that the hill was called Jabal Dubayyat and that it was rightly known as the resting place of the holy man Sayyid Hasan, for Harris the place stood outside history, certainly outside the type of textual history he expected, and its status as true geographical knowledge, because it was rooted in indigenous knowledge, sat on dubious foundations. In fact, this failure of the native to properly translate the landscape into a language comprehensible to the colonial state was a theme that would recur in the context of the Boundary Commission and the Daliʿ Agency afterwards.

In spite of the visceral unease Harris felt as he moved further away from Aden, his narrative suggests a surprising clarity regarding his place in geopolitical space. The territory he crosses is marked by the frontier posts of the ʿAbdali and Hawshabi sultans, just as his progress along the roads is punctuated by the presentation of letters of recommendation from the Aden Residency. After passing Jabal Dubayyat, his party entered the territory of the Ahl Ajʿud, which he notes was on "the border of the Aloui tribe [ʿAlawi]" and where he presented his credentials once again to the local Shaykh. His complete awareness of the political borders he is crossing, as much as the letters from the colonial government he carries, indicate the extent to which his topographical descriptions were already framed by a tribal geography of British making. Indeed, while the roads and the borders travelled by Harris are those claimed by the tribes themselves, based on local knowledge and practice, the presentation of British letters of passage changes the condition of the passage through these territories, re-contextualizing it as part and parcel of the web of agreements and treaties signed between the tribes and the colonial state.[19]

The extent to which the landscape, even at this early date, had been colonized becomes even more apparent as he describes his approach to the Emirate of Daliʿ. As Harris and his team ascended the mountain road to the Daliʿ plateau, the tone of his narrative changes remarkably. "Dawn changed to sunset, and the world became alive again," he wrote, and he continues to describe the vast differences in the landscape along the Wadi Khurayba as he met its upper reaches. While the valley was still surrounded on either side by the vast rock walls of the mountains that had earlier appeared to him as "sepulchral," the banks of the running stream provide an altogether more appealing scene:

> The valley itself was green and fresh, and the banks of the stream, which appeared in places tumbling and dancing over the rocks, again to disappear below the surface, were covered with a thick jungle of dense tropical vegetation, the trees hung with garlands of creepers. Birds chirruped and hopped from bough to bough; great painted butterflies sailed by, rivaling the sunrise in gorgeousness; and monkeys and apes chattered and grunted on the steep mountain-sides. After the journey of desert and rock, the change was a delightful one.[20]

Shortly after encountering this changed landscape, Harris met a group of Bedouin encamped close by. They, like the land itself, received him kindly and he spent a short time enjoying their hospitality. He and his group then continued on, following the course of the Khurayba river "dancing and rippling over its pebbly bed, for all the world like some Highland trout-stream." The idyllic nature of the scene and the ease with which the analogy to the Scottish Highlands was made are telling and point to his method of taming what, up to that point, had been a hostile landscape. As they continued along the river, "about half a mile distant, and perched on the summit of a high rock, loomed the frontier fort of the Amir of Dhala, a square tower surrounded by some lower buildings. The place looked a regular acropolis, and seemed impregnable." An approaching Shaykh greeted Harris and accepted his letter of introduction from the Aden Residency, and though he warned the party of the "turbulent state" of the mountain tribes beyond, they were not to be found among the civilized dwellings on the plateau. "The fact that we had now entered the land of fixed abodes became every hour more apparent," he wrote, and the observations that followed point to what the presence of fixed settlements meant. By the end of the day's travel, he and his party had set up camp and were lazing by the river, while "not a breath of wind was stirring." Indeed, in contrast to the previous days' journey, the arrival on the Dali' plateau and the entrance into the domain of the Amir offered a final rest in a place very much in the process of being colonized, even though indirectly, before the arrival at the Ottoman border. Numerous villages of stone houses, skilled works of irrigation and the surrounding "green fields and mimosa trees" suggested a thriving civilization the likes of which they had not seen since leaving Lahj. And for the first time since leaving Aden, he spies an old schoolmaster, directing a group of young students, all of whom were reading from Qurans printed in Beirut. "The whole scene," Harris wrote, "was one of perfect peace."

A LANDSCAPE OF UNCERTAINTY

The importance of this description is that Harris illustrated what Hunter and Sealey's handbook had merely implied. Whether intentionally or not, Harris was expressing the British predilection for places with a history, ruled by figures with legitimate and historical authority. Like Haines' reading of the 'Abdali *da'ira* discussed previously, the scene described by Harris was part of the greater process of aligning the Aden hinterland with Britain's own mediaeval past (and with the present of some of its "untamed" regions), in this case making "British" the landscape of Dali' through the use of analogy. In contrast to the landscapes Harris crossed after he left Lahj, Dali' was, as Carter wrote, a place "where language made sense."[21] Nor was this the peculiar response of a lone traveller. Indeed, the descriptions of what in the Arabian context was an Arcadia found a wide audience in the colonial government, for the mild climate and relative abundance of the Dali' plateau were central to the plan to create a hill-station there for the convalescence of troops weary from service in Aden. In terms of the conditions of camp life for Europeans, one official wrote, "it compares favorably with any

Figure 6: Palace of the Amir of Dali', engraving based on sketch by Harris.

station in India, hill or otherwise."²² Harris' own sketch of the scene is suggestive of the general colonial view of Daliʿ prior to the Anglo-Ottoman Boundary Commission: a distant fortress overlooks a verdant tropical landscape, replete with date palms and surrounded by a running stream (fig. 6). A lone and faceless Arab figure tends his camel in the foreground, no doubt in the service of Harris and his crew. That the picture is otherwise devoid of human life is not entirely surprising. As Raymond Williams wrote "a working country is hardly ever a landscape," and while Harris' narrative is replete with images of the local inhabitants, it is only meant to convey a sense of the peace and security prevalent in the Amir's territory and its potential for colonial exploitation.²³

Hunter and Sealey's representation of Daliʿ is remarkably free of the ambivalence present in Harris' account precisely because it effaced the contingent process of exploration in the collection of geographical knowledge. It is the act of following the roads, as Harris shows, that reveals the major sources of tension in the colonization of the Amiri landscape. Underlying the map of the "nine tribes" was a more contingent geography of rocky paths through a barren countryside, populated by tribes in what was thought to be a perpetual state of turbulence. Though the handbook refers in passing to the territory "actually ruled" by the Amirs, the full import of the statement is otherwise lost in the otherwise idyllic description of the Emirate. This does not mean, however, that the tension between the concept of the "nine tribes" and the local landscape was experienced only by the explorer or traveller.

Harris's narrative itself suggests the extent to which the explorer's experience of landscape intersected with that of the scientific surveyor. While he was encamped in the Khurayba valley one evening, Harris writes, "two Englishmen appeared in view, riding horses, and guarded by a considerable number of Indian troopers and a few of the Aden corps, and followed by a large train of baggage-animals."²⁴ He had encountered Captains Domville and R.A. Wahab with their surveying party, and was able to then spend the afternoon with them, dining in what he described as their "luxurious camp." The surveyors, he noted, had been successful up to this point but, he wrote in hindsight, they later met with difficulties "on the part of the natives," which ended in an exchange of gunfire. Harris ends his account of his meeting with Wahab quickly, but before returning to the narrative of his journey, notes that he obtained from Wahab the correction of his aneroid barometer, which he had yet to use, owing to his desire to avoid suspicion among his travelling companions. In this moment, the paths of the explorer and the surveyor intersect and reveal the extent to which their worlds overlapped, joined by an instrument of measurement and observation.

Yet, the projects in which the explorer and the scientific surveyor were engaged shared more than a passion for science and extended to the nature of their interaction with the landscape itself. Ryan writes that "the cartographic and aesthetic gazes both attempt to construct landscape as a text which may be read," but the process of this construction, and not merely the goal of a constructed landscape, was to a great extent shared as well.[25] The 1891–92 map created by Wahab was, in fact, no more stable a representation of the space of the "nine tribes" than Hunter and Sealey's handbook. This next section turns to the delimitation of the boundary between the Aden Protectorate and Ottoman Yemen between 1902 and 1905 as a means by which to reveal the contingent process of "naming" the tribal landscape through the cartographic project.

Mapping Dali': the Anglo-Ottoman Boundary Commission

Despite over twenty years of what the British considered blatant Ottoman interference in the affairs of the Protectorate, it was not until Shaykh Muhammad Nasir Muqbil of Mawiya erected a small fort at the village of al-Darayja in 1900 that the British decided to respond in a decisive manner. While the construction of forts along tribal boundaries or trade routes was a common move for local Shaykhs attempting to extend their influence, al-Darayja happened to be located in Hawshabi territory along a fairly important road. Muhammad Nasir Muqbil had been supported in his position by the Ottoman administration, but the move had to do with local more than imperial politics, involving as it did the rights to collect customs and to curtail the movement of smugglers into northern Yemen. In local political terms, the conflict was one between Lahj and Mawiya over the routes through Hawshabi territory and therefore over direct influence in the region. It just so happens that these events occurred when the Indian government under Curzon was very ready to agree to aggressive action on the part of the Aden authorities. Early in 1901, after repeated warnings, a force from Aden marched on al-Darayja, engaged the Ottoman troops who had taken up positions there, and razed the fort. With Ottoman and British forces facing off in Hawshabi country, both governments agreed to establish the Anglo-Ottoman Boundary Commission to delimit the boundary between their respective spheres of influence. While the great-power politics and imperial machinations that provided the political background for the commission's activities have been covered adequately elsewhere, little attention has been given to the process by which the British determined the limits of local authority and therefore the placement of the boundary.[26] As I shall show, the settlement of the boundary issue had much less to do with the science of cartography than with further explanation of the historical formation of local sovereignty and its territorialization.

In early 1902, the British commissioners met for the first time with their Ottoman counterparts in the town of Daliʻ. The British commission was led by Colonel R.A. Wahab of the Survey of India. Prior to the commission, he had assisted or led geographical surveys in the Punjab, Waziristan, and Afghanistan as well as conducting the first survey of the Aden Protectorate in 1891–92. The first order of business was to agree on the boundary between Qaʻtaba and the territory of the Amir of Daliʻ or what was often called the "Amiri" tribe. Much of the northern part of the Amir's territory was claimed by the Ottoman commissioners, including the whole of the Shaʻiri tribe and Jabals Maʻfar and Jahhaf, on the basis of imperial *firman*s and actual administrative practice in the period after 1872. Their argument was supported by their assertion of uninterrupted Ottoman sovereignty over the whole of South Arabia that dated back to the first occupation in the sixteenth century. Of the documentary evidence produced by the commission, nineteen documents dated to the seventeenth century, the latter period of the first occupation, while the rest were from the period after the second occupation of 1872. To take the example of the Shaʻiri tribe, the Ottoman case rested on two *firman*s (dated 1617 and 1621) appointing Shaykhs to the tribe and a series of receipts for money paid by a Shaʻiri Shaykh into the treasury in Qaʻtaba from the period between 1883 and 1889.[27] The rest of the Ottoman claims rested on similar documentation from the first occupation and the post-1872 period and were based on the assumption that Ottoman sovereignty had continued unabated since the seventeenth century.

Since a large part of the Ottoman case rested on current administrative practice within the boundary region, the government attempted to create facts on the ground through several means. Shortly after the formation of the joint commission, Ottoman soldiers descended on the strategic points of Jabal Jahhaf, Jabal Maʻfar and the village of al-Jalila, less than a mile away from the town of Daliʻ, along with several other villages in the Wadi Safiyya. Material signs of the Amir's sovereignty were erased from the landscape: his forts were razed in al-Jalila and other villages and their garrisons were expelled.[28] Local Shaykhs were put on the Ottoman payroll as official appointees or expelled. In the most conspicuous case, Jabal Jahhaf was renamed the "civil district of Jahhaf" and a member of the locally powerful Zindani family appointed Shaykh.[29] From these forward positions, Ottoman soldiers or their local proxies were sent forward to collect revenue, especially in the villages of the Wadi Safiyya which had been occupied at the start of the Boundary Commission's work.[30]

Nowhere were the basic differences between the British and Ottoman positions more evident than in the proposed mission statements for the Commission. According to Wahab's orders he was charged with delimiting the boundary "between the territory of the tribes in the vicinity of Aden having direct relations with His Majesty's Government and the dominions of His Majesty the Sultan." His Ottoman counterparts, however, objected to the reference to the Sultan's domains and preferred instead "between the territory of the "nine tribes" and the sanjak of Taiz."[31] As the British commissioners realized early on, the substitution of "nine tribes" for the reference to "direct relations" was an attempt to play upon this very ambiguous concept, and to open the possibility of excluding the eastern regions of Bayda' and Bayhan from the British Protectorate, since they were never included in the 1873 memorandum to the Sublime Porte. Without a doubt, the British put little stock in what one official referred to as "their mythical theory, that, in virtue of their *partial* occupation of the Yemen between 1520 A.D. and 1630 A.D., the whole country down to Aden is Ottoman territory."[32] Nonetheless, it was recognized with some alarm that the proposed title of the commission would put the burden of proof on the British. In particular, it put them in the position of explaining exactly what the "Amiri" tribe was.

H.M. Abud, a member of the British commission, wrote after the first meeting that in the case of tribes such as the Sha'iri, which were administered by the Amir but were not part of his "tribe," defining the mission in this way would put them at a severe disadvantage. In surprisingly blunt terms, he argued that the Ottoman position would "force us to prove that these tribes form part and parcel of one of the "nine tribes" and this it is doubtful if we can do."[33] Indeed, the prospect of defending the Amir's claim to the surrounding tribes was made even more difficult as the body of knowledge on Dali' grew with the extended presence of the British commissioners up-country. Although the commissioners had stressed the importance of drawing a boundary that included the territory ruled by the Amir at the time of Wahab's initial survey of 1891–92, it became clear that it would not represent the boundaries of a tribe so much as lines of allegiance to the ruling house of Daliʻ. In a memorandum by Abud in which he defended drawing the boundary in this way, he noted that what had been referred to as the "Amiri" tribe previously was, in fact, a confederation of tribes "banded together under the Amir of Dthala for mutual support and protection." In plainer terms, Abud stated that in light of the Amirs' purported *muwallad* (mixed race) descent, "[t]hey have thus no tribe and consequently there is no such tribe as the Amiri."[34]

Abud's admission that the Emirate of Daliʻ could better be understood as a series of political alliances rather than a tribe served to complicate a process already burdened by a heated intra-imperial debate concerning where the boundary should be placed and whether or not the existing maps were sufficient for the purpose. The British, quite naturally, took Wahab's map of 1891–92 as the reference point for the demarcation of the boundary, and this was also where the disagreement began (fig. 7). Gavin is right to suggest that the map itself was ambiguous, for it did not indicate the boundaries of the Amir's territory, but was instead merely suggestive of them.[35] The question then was, according to which criteria was the boundary to be drawn? Curzon's immediate frame of reference was the original 1873 memorandum which had set apart the "nine tribes" as the British sphere of influence. "Tribal rather than geographical considerations" were to be the guiding principle, and the boundary should include all of the Amir's possessions and all those groups paying his taxes.[36] This was the prevailing attitude among the commissioners as well. The line the Viceroy recommended to Aden and London represented the current lines of authority exercised by the Amir, based on "full enquiry into the actual circumstances and from documentary evidence."[37] As he saw it, the boundary began in the west on the Hawshabi border, followed the course of the Wadi Tuban north and arched north east to encompass the Humaydi and Ahmadi territories, which had not actually been surveyed in 1891–92. From there, the line continued east to include all of Jabal Jahhaf and the Wadi Safiyya, separating the British sphere from the Ottoman sphere just south of Qaʻtaba. For the India Office in London, however, the line was merely a political boundary and not a representation of tribal territory; it was to have meaning only at the level of international relations, as a barrier to foreign approaches to Aden.[38] The acquisition of

A LANDSCAPE OF UNCERTAINTY

Figure 7: Wahab's map of the Amiri boundary, roughly showing (from north to south) boundaries claimed by the British commission, the India Office, and the Ottoman commission. This map does not show the India Office's early exclusion of the Wadi Safiyya from Amiri territory.

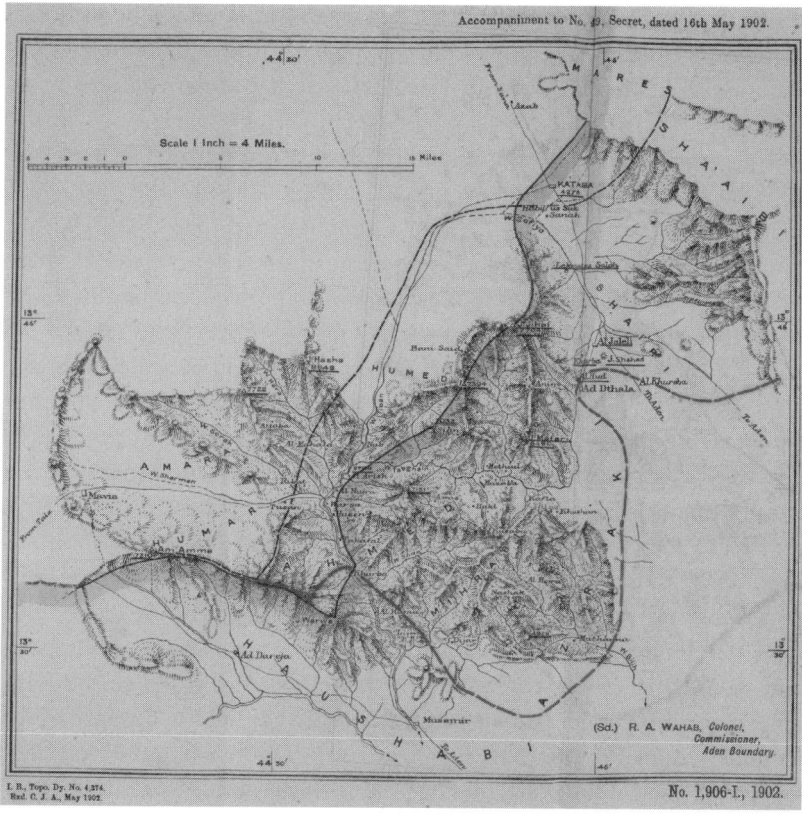

more territory, even territory under the authority of one of the "nine tribes," was antithetical to the India Office's proposed policy of non-interference. Conflict with the Ottoman Empire was to be avoided on this issue, and the boundary it recommended was that which represented the supposed "status quo" at the time of the 1891–92 survey. The problem, however, was that the "status quo" was based on an imperfect reading of the map. Since no boundary had ever been indicated on it, the India Office understood the "status quo" in terms of the limits of the actual shaded features on the map. That is,

89

the boundary began in the west and followed the course of the Wadi Tuban north, from whence it followed the course of the mountain ranges northeast to Jabal Jahhaf. From there, the line then descended south-east, thus including the unshaded Wadi Safiyya and its villages on the Ottoman side of the border, most of which were considered independent or under the authority of the Amir of Daliʿ. The India Office's boundary, true to its word, paid no attention to a "tribal" geography but merely followed the contours of all elevated points.

The conciliatory attitude embodied in this reading of the map was opposed both by the Aden government and by Curzon, who wrote in a telegram to the India Office, "had we contemplated that Your Lordship would interpret limits of Wahab's survey in this manner, we would never have recommended delimitation."[39] But Wahab pointed specifically to the way in which the India Office had read his map. Reiterating his support for the boundary he had earlier suggested, Wahab argued that the lines of the 1891–92 map had been seriously misinterpreted, as the shaded lines did not represent "a watershed or definite natural feature." Moreover, he contended, if it were at all practicable to lay down an "arbitrary" boundary on the ground that was related neither to natural features nor to tribal limits, it would exclude a number of Humaydi and Ahmadi villages (recognized as historically under the authority of the Amir) from the British sphere, and therefore constitute "a constant source of trouble in the future."[40] The line suggested by the India Office would not only remove both the Humaydi and the Ahmadi tribes from the British/Amiri side of the line, but also remove the majority of the Shaʿiri tribe in the Wadi Safiyya, on the basis of its understanding of the "status quo" in 1891–92. Wahab, moreover, challenged the issue of the status quo by producing new evidence that the Amir had never lost control of Shaʿiri territory. The Amir had recently handed over to Wahab the full accounts of his annual tax collecting forays for the years 1892–1902.[41] The documents showed that, contrary to the belief that the Ottomans had enjoyed full control of the Wadi Safiyya and Shaʿiri country, the Amir had been collecting revenue from all of the villages in the region but four. The "status quo" as Wahab saw it was indeed represented by the line he had first recommended to the Aden government.

But how exactly did Wahab decide on this particular line and what did it mean? The discourse of scientific geography had shown itself woefully inadequate in the formulation of an acceptable boundary. Even the map, that quintessential icon of abstract space, was in many ways useless to the

A LANDSCAPE OF UNCERTAINTY

British case, for it proved illegible at the level of colonial practice. In addition to the debate over the meaning of the lines on the map, whether the proposed boundary or even the cartographic practice of shading, parts of the territory within Wahab's boundary (particularly Humaydi country) had not even been surveyed in 1891–92 and remained "blanks" on the map. The illegibility of the map was compounded by the fact that the Ottoman commission did not even employ a trained surveyor, but opted for the creation of facts on the ground by occupying villages and enticing local leaders with stipends.[42] Numerous confrontations between Ottoman troops and British surveyors indicated the extent to which the Porte was opposed to the issue being determined on the grounds of cartography.[43] It was historical sovereignty, rather than maps, that mattered. It is little surprise, then, that at a later date Ibrahim Seifi, the head of the Ottoman commission, denied any knowledge of the 1891–92 map or that it was the basis of the British claim—it was simply irrelevant to the issue.[44] Clearly, the delimitation of the boundary was not to be the best forum for the science of geography, but to understand how the boundary was indeed drawn requires a closer look at the daily operations of the commission, which, I believe, reveal the fragile boundaries of the cartographic project as it was practiced in Aden.

Our knowledge of the commission's work relies in part on Wahab's diary, which itself became a daily record of the contingent process by which the boundaries of the "Amiri" tribe were slowly etched out.[45] Over several weeks in early 1902, the Amir began to approach Wahab with documents meant to prove his sovereignty over the surrounding region and its inhabitants. In particular, he produced documents pertaining to the Sha'iri tribe and the inhabitants of Jabals Ma'far and Jahhaf, the most contested localities in the early part of the commission's work. At roughly the same time, Wahab recorded that the commission conducted a number of interviews with Shaykhs from the areas in question. Although he included few details of these meetings, the information he did record is suggestive of the process by which he assembled the British case in support of the historical sovereignty of the Amir over the surrounding tribes. Many of the Shaykhs at these meetings came expressly to declare their loyalty and obedience to Amir Shayif b. Sayf. Others came at the commission's request to clarify their boundaries or number of villages and inhabitants. What is important to note for the moment is that the domain of the Dali' Emirate, which the British had long claimed as belonging to the "nine tribes," was actually constituted as a geographical space to be mapped or made the subject of

91

internationally recognized boundaries on the basis of a diverse assemblage of historical documents and encounters with the local population. The boundary was not so much created as a series of fixed geographical points based on latitudes and longitudes but was rather the cumulative effect of piles of documentation, the elaboration of limits (*hudud*) in local terms, and the recording of a number of assertions of loyalty and obedience from the more important tribal Shaykhs and village headmen.

In a sense, then, with the collection of this vast archive to be presented before the commission, the boundary itself was settled before the official survey was conducted. That is, Wahab was able to set the terms of the debate over how the landscape was to be named, and it was to be named through a framework of "Amiri," not Ottoman sovereignty. But what did this sovereignty mean? The documentary record produced by Amir Shayif, most of which has only survived in English translation, covered a period ranging from the late Qasimi period in the eighteenth century to the period of the Ottoman occupation in the late nineteenth.[46] The picture of Amiri authority that emerges from these documents, however, does not support the British contention that the Amirs had exercised a continuous and homogeneous sovereignty for nearly three hundred years. Rather, it would be more accurate to say that the Emirate as a political formation was continually reconstituted in space and time. The rights and obligations spelt out in the documents are not at all uniform. Documents originating from the Qasimi and Ottoman states recognized the Amirs' rights of revenue extraction over particular areas in return for their loyalty. In some cases, the Amirs of Dali' had acted as landlords, exercising varying degrees of authority over the population. In Jabal Ma'far, for example, the Amir was both landlord and head of the community, with a greater role in the legal, political, and economic affairs of the local population than he had in any other place outside the town of Dali'.[47] In other cases, as with the Azraqi, the Ahmadi and the Sha'iri, tribes were required to heed the summons of the Amir in times of war and rally around his standard in a relationship referred to, at least in the Yafi'i context, as "to hear and follow" (*sum'a wa-tub'a*).[48] Still others, such as the tribes of the Radfan mountains (the Ahl Aj'ud confederation and the Halimayn), owed the Amirs little more than a nominal and undefined allegiance.[49]

What the British did not or could not acknowledge was that the agreements, despite their language, were never meant to be in effect in perpetuity, or at least were not so in practice. While the presence of multiple

A LANDSCAPE OF UNCERTAINTY

versions of the same agreements, by virtue of their repetition, was invoked by the British to strengthen Amir Shayif's claims to authority, these documents more than likely pointed to a history of contestation between the Amirs and the surrounding population, reflecting a dynamic political environment in which alliances were continually negotiated and renegotiated. Thus, for example, the sale of Maʿfari lands and the rights these entailed under Amir Shaʿfal (in 1862 and 1874) was again recognized with the accession of Shayif b. Sayf to the Emirate of Daliʿ in 1886.[50] Of course, what is clearly missing from the documentary evidence is the local context, which might shed some light on the types of relationships being formed by these agreements.

Nowhere is the importance of context more apparent than in the later professions of allegiance heard by the members of the British commission. In this case, we have a much better sense of the circumstances in which these statements were made than in the earlier documents produced to support the Amir's historical sovereignty. The appearance of Ottoman soldiers in the vicinity of Daliʿ and the occupation of al-Jalila and other Shaʿiri villages at the beginning of the commission's work posed the threat of a more centralized form of state administration and the possibility of greater taxation and continued likely infringement on the independence of the smaller tribes and polities. Because of this, and the familiarity with the agreements already signed between the British and the "nine tribes," there was great incentive for local notables to side in as public a manner as possible both with the Amir and the British. Hence, in these performances of loyalty, not only did local Shaykhs profess their supposedly older allegiances to the Amir, but some also requested British protection, which was an entirely new phenomenon in the politics of the Daliʿ plateau.

These details point to the extreme variability and contextual specificity of the types of relationships formed between the Amirs of Daliʿ and the surrounding populations, tribal and non-tribal. The political arrangements described are in many ways reminiscent of what Winichakul has referred to as "multiple sovereignty" as it was exercised along what are now the borders of modern Thailand. Winichakul argues that the smaller kingdoms and chiefdoms on the Thai-Lao border were subject to several overlords or states at the same time, as part of a greater strategy of survival, each relationship entailing different rights and responsibilities. The elaboration of theories of territorial sovereignty associated with the creation of the "geo-body" of the nation entailed the effacement of these relationships.[51] In Daliʿ, the power of the Amir was based on the exercise of a form of multiple sovereignty, which established an elaborate complex of overlapping rights and obligations with the surrounding communities. By using these documented agreements as the basis for a modern boundary, an interface between two sovereign territorial powers, the commission imposed a meaning on them which they were never intended to convey. The implications of subordinating these local social and political arrangements to the exigencies of the map would not be fully clear until after the Boundary Commission's work was finished.

Daliʿ and the end of the Indian model

"When first we stepped into the Hinterland," Harold Jacob wrote in 1908, "we were naturally imbued largely with Indian ideals."[52] He was referring to the British assumption that single figures of authority could be used as the basis for the form of indirect rule on which the durbar model was based. It was, he confessed, a system that was not sustainable in the Yemeni South: "this is the "one man" system so repugnant to the Arab mind and which has, I fear, made shipwreck of our best plans in this Hinterland." He wrote these words the year after the Daliʿ Agency, an administrative office that operated from 1902 to 1907 in support of the Boundary Commission and later as an instrument of tribal administration, was disbanded as contrary to the British policy of non-intervention. Jacob, a Lieutenant Colonel in the Bombay Political Department and speaker of both Hindustani and Arabic, had spent his time as Political Agent (1904–07) promoting the role of the British government as a purveyor of justice along what were believed to be native lines. His mission is perhaps expressed best in his own words: "I mediated, at the instance of disputants, in their blood-feuds, appealing to Koranic *imprimatur*; toured throughout the district in my charge; mixed freely with the tribesmen, and kneaded-in, as unobtrusively as possible, the leaven of British influence."[53] That is, Jacob was less the Edwardian Arabist guided by poetic intuition described by Priya Satia than the older model of the colonial field officer, trained in local languages and sacred texts and intent on maintaining the goodwill of the local population through the benevolent hand of British power. By the time the agency was withdrawn from Daliʿ, however, he had begun to question the very foundation of the concept of the "nine tribes" and the durbar model as it had been applied to the Aden hinterland.

Throughout 1907 a protracted debate divided the Aden administration concerning the necessity of the Daliʿ Agency to the future security of the

A LANDSCAPE OF UNCERTAINTY

hinterland and, more immediately, to the standing of the Amir. With the conclusion of the Boundary Commission in 1905 there were no security-related reasons for the maintenance of the station up-country, and the ultimate rejection of the proposal to construct a sanitarium for British troops on the plateau meant that there was little else to warrant the expense. The Aden administration, however, continued to question Amir Shayif's ability to execute properly the obligations of his earlier treaties with the British. Specifically, the British wanted to be certain that the Amir actually could exercise throughout Dali' and the surrounding region the authority which they had so recently argued was effective and complete. In a monograph published a year later, Jacob answered this question in clear and, for the Aden government, potentially disturbing terms.

> I have always laid stress on the indubitable fact that this Hinterland comprises one vast system of democracy. Indian precedent encourages the grouping of many chieftainships under one responsible head. Imbued with Indian ideas and ignorant of local customs and aspirations, we have tried to establish the more convenient system of autocracy. This was in opposition to all established ideas and was moderately successful only so long as we remained in occupation. With our evacuation, the whole structure will collapse like a pack of cards, and demolition has indeed already begun.[54]

The import of this statement was twofold. First, it went against the claims of Wahab and the Boundary Commission that the Amirs of Dali' were actually the rulers of the land and peoples generally referred to as the "Amiri" tribe. Second, and this was perhaps more important for the colonial project in the Aden hinterland, it pointed to the fact that the durbar model of political association, which until then had provided the implicit and often explicit model for the protectorate system, was wholly inapplicable to the situation in South Arabia.

Despite his growing doubts over the Amir's ability to control his supposed subjects upon the withdrawal of the agency, and the apparent failure of the Indian system of indirect rule, Jacob's response was to exert all of his efforts to maintain the protectorate system of the ruling chiefs irrespective of its obvious lack of success in managing hinterland affairs. In one of many such statements, Jacob argued that it was not "a personal Amir we want to uphold, but the principle of the authority of His House."[55] The contradictions inherent in the maintenance of the "nine tribes" were nowhere more apparent than in the course of policy taken regarding the Qutaybi tribe of the Ahl Aj'ud confederation.

The Ahl Aj'ud inhabited the foothills of the Radfan mountain range to the east of Dali', numbering around 12,000 according to British estimates. The Qutaybi were one of seven tribes living there, together with the Ahl 'Abdullah, Hujayli, Mahla'i, Bakri, Da'iri, and the Dambari. While estimates of their population were uncertain, it was thought that they could field around 1,200 fighting men, more than any of the other six.[56] Along with the Halimayn tribe the Qutaybis were considered one of the "two pockets" (*jibayn*) of the Amirs—that is, one of the two tribes on whom the Amirs depended for military support—but the Qutaybi were the more powerful of the two. In fact, their preeminence among the Ahl Aj'ud earned them the sobriquet of the "spearhead" (*sinan*) of the confederation. While Hunter and Sealey had suggested that the Qutaybi were in fact part of an "Amiri" tribe and Warneford argued that the Qutaybi owed the Amirs some semblance of obedience, events at the turn of the century proved that this relationship was continually renegotiated if not utterly contested.

Throughout the 1880s and 1890s the Qutaybi asserted their control over the Wadi Hardaba, one of the major sections of the caravan road to Dali', and commenced levying dues on passing caravans. In 1884 the Qutaybi Shaykh, Muhammad Salih al-Akhram, had signed an agreement acknowledging the Amir's authority in return for the right to send recommendatory letters to the Aden Residency. This agreement was renewed in 1888 when the Qutaybi and other tribes of the Ahl Aj'ud once again declared their obedience to the Amir and took on the protection of the roads. Yet, the tribe continued to levy its own dues on caravans, and the Amir's soldiers were continually engaged in the attempt to secure the trade routes.[57] In fact, it proved so difficult for the Amir's forces to subdue the Qutaybi and provide a modicum of security on the roads that the Amir was compelled for a time to redirect trade from Hardaba to the Mashwara road beyond his territory. With his inability to bring them to heel, the question that arose was whether he actually was the functional and notional sovereign authority as was argued during the time of the commission.

For C.L. Merewether, the Dali' Agent from March to December 1904, the answer was emphatically in the negative. He argued that to support the Amir to the detriment of the Qutaybis had been a grave mistake which was undoubtedly the result of the difficulties of obtaining "accurate local knowledge." The Amir, he suggested, was "universally detested," and the prestige of the British in the hinterland was considerably lower because of their support for him.[58] As for the Qutaybis, Jacob noted repeatedly that they

A LANDSCAPE OF UNCERTAINTY

never should have been regarded as subject to the Amirs.[59] He asserted that they were tribes (*qabayil*) and not subjects (*ra'aya*), tribes whose disdain for authority could be compared easily with that of the Pathans on the Northwest Frontier. This was the sort of "democracy" to which he was referring in the passage quoted earlier: any one man claiming authority or a leadership role was still only one among equals, and his word carried only as much weight as his potential followers were willing to give it. Jacob's time in the Daliʿ Agency had forced him to come to the conclusion that "it was absolutely not correct to apply to the Hinterland cut and dried methods found suitable to India, or to stretch Arabia and India on one common Procrustean bed."[60] That is, the durbar model of association had to be amended in light of the political reality in the Aden hinterland. The practical ramifications of this change in thought were made explicit in his proposed policy for dealing with the Qutaybis.

Jacob's opinion was that the concept of the "nine tribes" should be amended in light of knowledge gathered on the ground in the period after the Boundary Commission. In short, he felt that the Qutaybi Shaykh, Muhammad Salih Akhram, should receive a stipend, a supply of rifles and ammunition as a gift, and all the honors and privileges bestowed on the "nine tribes," even though the Qutaybis were not among those first mentioned in the 1873 memorandum to the Ottoman government.[61] A draft text of an agreement, written in 1904, would have recognized the Qutaybis as a tribe on equal standing with the original "nine tribes." As in the other treaties, the Qutaybi Shaykh and his heirs or successors were taken as legal subjects and held responsible for maintaining security on the roads and discontinuing any new transit taxes. In return, the Qutaybi Shaykh was entitled to an annual stipend, gifts of weapons and ammunition and the honor of visiting Aden at the government's expense. However, the treaty differed in one very important way: it made all stipends payable through the Amir of Daliʿ. The need to justify a particular appearance of order based on the agreements with the "nine tribes" made it necessary to bestow these honors through the Amir of Daliʿ, who, despite all evidence to the contrary, was still considered to be the sovereign authority over the population of what were called the "Amiri lands." In effect, and contrary to Jacob's belief that they were an independent tribe, the Qutaybis were to be made subject to the Amir whether or not they could be said to be his subjects.[62]

The agreement was never signed, however, and with the possibility of the agency's evacuation rapidly approaching, it was necessary to come to some arrangements for the security of the trade route. It was generally accepted that responsibility would devolve to the ʿAbdali Sultanate for the road from Dar al-Amir to Nubat Dukaym, to the Hawshabi Sultanate from Nubat Dukaym to al-Milah, and to the ʿAlawi Sultan from there to al-Jimil. The final stretch of the road was to be protected by the Amir of Daliʿ. Nonetheless, the section of the road from al-Jimil into the Wadi Hardaba was contested by both the ʿAlawi and Qutaybi tribes. While this section of the road was not lengthy, it was subject to a number of overlapping claims based on property rights and claims of tribal limits (*hudud*). Jacob realized as much when considering how to apportion responsibility for its protection:

> Again, to whom should we hand over the custody of the road from Sulek to Hardaba? The Amir of Dthala claims it; so does the ʿAlawi Shaikh; so does the Saiyid of Dthubiyat, and so do the Kotaib. It is necessary first of all to discover the rightful claimant. Some say it is "Haqq Allah" (God's right) or "Had Allah" (God's ground) meaning by this that it is common to all, but also that the strongest will hold it.[63]

Effective claims to the road, however, were enforced by a series of small fortified houses at strategic points, as on the roads in Subayhi country discussed in Chapter 2. A fort at the village of Sulayk, some twenty-one miles from Daliʿ and within Qutaybi country, was held by British troops under the assumption that on evacuation, it would be handed over to Muhammad Salih al-Akhram, the Qutaybi Shaykh, under the auspices of the Amir. Only a mile and half away was the ʿAlawi fort of Dar al-Hamra (also known as Dar al-Qubtan after the late Capt. Warneford, the first Daliʿ Agent) which was just within Qutaybi country. It had originally been constructed with the assistance of the British for defense against Qutaybi attempts to collect excessive levies along the road, but with the possibility of reconciliation with the British, it was decided that the fort should be destroyed and rebuilt within ʿAlawi limits. Opposite this fort was a fort constructed by the Qutaybis on the Taʿizz hill (also called Dar al-Mayjar in honor of Jacob) from which they staged attacks against the ʿAlawis. This too was to be destroyed.

In September 1907, a conference was convened in Lahj to which the ʿAlawis, Hawshabis and Qutaybis were invited. The goal of the meeting was to conclude final and permanent arrangements for the security of the trade route before the withdrawal of the agency and the British troops garrisoning it. Under the auspices of Sultan Ahmad b. Fadl and a company of local *sayyid*s it was agreed that the fort at Sulayk would be destroyed by the British. Moreover, both the ʿAlawis and the Qutaybis agreed to dismantle Dar

A LANDSCAPE OF UNCERTAINTY

al-Qubtan and Dar Taʿizz adjacent to it. The draft agreements signed by both Shaykhs provided that no forts would be built to replace them, that all existing rights would continue to be recognized, and that all further conflict would be settled not on the roads, but by some form of mediation.[64]

By the end of September the Daliʿ Agency had been disbanded. Before removing themselves from the hinterland, however, British troops destroyed the forts at Hardaba and Sulayk. Enormous crowds of ʿAlawi and Qutaybi tribesmen and mercenaries had arrived to watch the spectacle. Jacob describes the event as heated with conflicts still smoldering, despite attempts at mediation and despite agreements signed. The occasion was one for tribal solidarity and venomous poetic exchanges between both parties. Jacob records a particular exchange of verses between Saʿid al-Duʿgri al-ʿAlawi and Muqbil ʿAbdullah al-Qutaybi in which the Qutaybi warned of future conflict:

Who gives myrrh to drink shall one day quaff a draught yet more bitter
You cried for help against the onslaught of but five of us
And have yet to oppose the full flood of our heroes and our Jinns as they rush down our Hills.
By God! If then present will ye cry out in your agony,
And down the slopes of Taiz shall ye rush headlong.[65]

Perhaps its inclusion by Jacob was somewhat apocryphal in light of later events, but without a doubt the conflict between the two tribes was no more settled than were the internal boundaries of the Emirate. In fact, just as the issue of sovereignty over the roads was decided and the agency was evacuated, the boundaries of local authority were on the verge of shifting again.

In January 1908 two sons of Muhammad Salih al-Akhram, the Qutaybi Shaykh, were shot by ʿAlawi tribesmen while attempting to scale the Taʿizz hill where the Qutaybis had so recently dismantled their fort. It was said locally that in response Shaykh Muhammad collected the *jambiyyas*—the curved daggers worn by tribesmen—of his dead sons, broke them into pieces, and sent them to the various sections of the Ahl Ajʿud and Halimayn tribes to rouse them against the ʿAlawis. Almost immediately Qutaybi tribesmen overran the Taʿizz hill and plundered several ʿAlawi villages. While local *sayyids* immediately interceded to effect a truce between both sides under the auspices of Amir Nasr b. Shayif, the conflict continued, and it was rumored that the Amir himself was supporting the Qutaybi.[66]

Yet in spite of the continuing conflict along the roads and the rapidly changing tribal geography, the Aden government decided to continue with its original plan of assigning responsibility for the security of the trade routes in written agreements, which were assumed to be effective in perpetuity. The arrangement which the British supported and which ultimately prevailed was based on "the general principle that responsibility should be primarily territorial."[67] This was reflected in the text of the agreement which was to be concluded between the 'Abdali Sultan, the Hawshabi Sultan, the Amir of Dali', the 'Alawi Sultan and the Qutaybi Shaykh. The document not only enshrined territorial sovereignty as the principal mode of recording tribal boundaries, it also made each chief responsible to the rest of the signatories for securing the road in his territory, all of whom ostensibly agreed to respond collectively against any offender. Moreover, in a much disputed clause, the signatory chiefs agreed to have their customs duties collected at a single point, the 'Abdali Sultan's customs house, Dar al-Amir. Tribal limits and the individualized agreements that had characterized political relationships in the past were to be supplanted by a single agreement, signed in the interest of the British, and assumed to be valid in perpetuity.[68]

At the same time that this agreement was being worked out in Aden, the Qutaybi offensive against the 'Alawi tribe continued with little sign that it would end quickly. Several 'Alawi villages were looted by Qutaybi tribesmen, including the village of al-Qash'a in which houses belonging to Shaykh 'Ali Nashir were demolished. A prominent *sayyid*, Fadl al-'Alawi, was appointed by Sultan Ahmad b. Fadl to mediate between the two parties on the basis of his status as a major landowner in the village of Saba, which ran down the middle of 'Alawi territory. He, however, proved less than impartial and was said to be enlisting the support of the Halimayn, the Ahl Aj'ud, and even the Azraqis in defense of Qutaybi interests.[69] The continuing expense of conflict combined with the loss of property, territory and customs on the trade route now occupied by the Qutaybis drove Shaykh 'Ali Nashir to write desperately to Aden for support in money and arms, noting at one point that the tribe had nothing left in its country but "men and stones" (*ma baqiya ila rijal wa-ahjar*).[70] Regardless of individual losses, however, the British took no position in the conflict so long as trade was not affected, and maintained throughout the dispute that the 'Alawi loss of customs was a "tribal matter."[71]

The conflict continued into 1909, as the Qutaybis occupied several more 'Alawi villages, including al-Dani, Sha'b al-Diwan, al-Ma'baja, al-Hawta, and al-Sawda. Moreover, they had established several new customs posts along the roads, including posts at Sulayk, Hardaba and Habilayn, and even

A LANDSCAPE OF UNCERTAINTY

within Azraqi country at Masnaʿa. It was not until they had established a position of dominance that they finally settled for arbitration, and this not until late in 1912. The accord that ended the conflict between the ʿAlawi and Qutaybi recognized this tribal realignment by ceding to the Qutaybis a considerable tract of formerly ʿAlawi land along the roads.[72] The agreement similarly ceded a tract of land to the ʿAbdali Sultan in compensation for the expense of mediating the truce over the course of the conflict. With this conflict settled, the Aden government was finally able to complete a series of treaties to stabilize the tribal landscape through delineation of authority and institutionalization of the customs dues. In 1914–15 the British signed new treaties with the ʿAlawis, Hawshabis, and Qutaybis for the protection of the trade routes. The loss of ʿAlawi territory was implicitly recognized by the treaty, which authorized the Shaykh to build a fort well within his own territory in the village of Maʿbaja. His customs fees were held at 12 annas per camel load and his stipend at a mere 25 dollars. By contrast, while the Qutaybis were only allowed ten annas per load, they were finally given the 50 dollar stipend that Harold Jacob had recommended previously. All customs were now to be levied and collected on behalf of the signatories to the agreement by the ʿAbdali Sultan in Lahj.[73] But the Qutaybi stipend was not to be paid by the Amir, but by the ʿAbdali Sultan. Once again, the ruling house of Lahj was seen as the preeminent native chief in the protectorate order. Despite Harold Jacob's misgivings, the durbar model endured.

Conclusion

Harold Jacob at one point in 1907 suggested that it would be best to pay the Qutaybi a stipend directly from the British government rather than from the Daliʿ Emirate. In such a case, he offered, "the Amir's suzerainty will remain, as ever, a convenient fiction."[74] His admission that a sovereign amir was indeed a figment of the colonial imagination should have been considered a startling revelation, for it raised serious questions about the "nine tribes" as an historical and administrative construct. If the Amir's sovereignty—his political authority over both his subjects and the territory they inhabited—was fiction, then so was the boundary delimited by Wahab's commission and accepted by the British and Ottoman governments as the legitimate border between their spheres of influence. The image of a pastoral Daliʿ, envisioned by Walter Harris and the colonial officers who imagined

101

the Emirate as the future site of a British hill-station, would be equally difficult to sustain if the hybrid form of authority exercised by the Amir was embodied in official policy. Despite the best efforts of British travellers, cartographers and colonial administrators, the tribal landscape of the Protectorate was no more legible that it had been in the late nineteenth century. Nor was the landscape any less ominous or characterized by less uncertainty—the map of Dali' was in many ways left unfinished.

Yet, in spite of Jacob's suggestion that the durbar model of association that had been adopted in post-revolt India and in the Yemeni South had failed, no one seems to have considered revising the particular form of indirect rule practiced outside of Aden. Committed to the colonial order of the "nine tribes" and their historical vision of native absolute authority, the British had little choice but to support the Amir Shayif b. Sayf and the notion that he ruled absolutely his emirate. The limits of this support became apparent with the onset of the First World War when the Ottoman army invaded and occupied the area of the Aden Protectorate for the duration of the conflict. Amir Shayif's successor, Amir Nasr b. Shayif, sided with the Ottomans in the absence of British military intervention to protect its protégés. Again, the carefully maintained vision of tribal order and chiefly authority that the Boundary Commission had etched into the land, and which the trade agreements had formalized in legal contract, fractured under the weight of an inter-imperial military conflict.

The introduction of the aeroplane seemingly changed the Amiri landscape. By 1928 the Air Ministry in Aden, which had assumed responsibility for Aden's protection the previous year, was producing precision aerial photographs not only of the Dali' plateau but of the towns of Qa'taba and Ta'izz as well, now part of the Imamate of Yahya Hamid al-Din. To all appearances, aerial photography had finally provided what seemed to be a representation of Dali' unmediated by the course of the roads, the rugged and imposing mountains, and the threat of the tribes surrounding the plateau. It achieved what even the map could not: the production of a uniquely "perspectiveless" view of Dali' that was fully legible, that relied not on the language of the traveller or the tools of the cartographer, but on the truth as captured on film. No longer constrained by the uncertainty of the landscape, the British were now able to enforce the Protectorate order through the use of punitive bombing, which had been introduced as a mode of colonial surveillance and repression in the Punjab and Iraq. In the Yemeni South, it was used first against the forces of Imam Yahya Hamid al-Din,

A LANDSCAPE OF UNCERTAINTY

who had invaded the Protectorate after the First World War (see Chapter 6), and later against what were considered recalcitrant tribes in support of the native chiefs.[75] It was the very myth of scientific objectivity represented by this new form of "perfected" knowledge that made possible later British claims that bombing unruly tribes was, on the whole, precise and therefore "humane."[76] The landscape had finally been conquered.

4

DISORDER AND THE DOMAIN OF OBEDIENCE

The Yemen has long awaited the advent of the Strong Man. He has arrived, and will bring order out of chaos.

Harold Jacob, 1923

Introduction

In 1927 the Syrian writer and Arab nationalist Nazih Mu'ayyad al-'Azm visited Yemen and was given permission to travel throughout the country and interview its inhabitants. After an initial meeting with Imam Yahya, he was visited by Qadi Muhammad Raghib Bey, one of a small number of Ottoman officers who had stayed behind after the First World War and taken employment with the Imam's government. Muhammad Raghib Bey now acted in the capacity of a Foreign Minister. In the course of their meeting, Nazih Mu'ayyad was able to ask the *qadi* various questions about the roads of Yemen and the Imam's plan to have them paved. He then moved on to the question of geography. Asked if there were any maps of Yemen, the *qadi* replied that there were not, although he had once come upon a map in the possession of some French engineers who were conducting a survey of the road from Hudayda for a future railway project. When asked if he had seen any of the maps of Yemen produced by the British military, he responded that he had not, although he had come across a British map before and found its use in Yemen impossible: "First, because it had serious mistakes and second, because the translation of place names from Arabic to

UNMAKING NORTH AND SOUTH

English distorted it and made reading impossible. So His Highness has expressed his regret that there is no map that will satisfy our needs." Asked if there were any books on Yemeni geography, the *qadi* simply responded, "No, not as such."[1]

Some time earlier, in 1923, another Arab traveller, the Syrian-American writer Ameen Rihani, had a meeting with Imam Yahya in his *diwan*. In the course of his interview, Rihani politely asked about the population of Yemen, to which the Imam responded, "five million." When Rihani followed by asking how many the Imam actually governed, he closed his hand and responded, "'A small number, very small." Although one of his Turkish ministers present that day (and it could quite well have been Muhammad Raghib Bey) insisted that all obeyed His Highness, the Imam reiterated that it was just a handful. Commenting on this encounter, Rihani wrote: "But when it comes to the boundary of Al-Yaman, the Imam recognizes only the ancient line which includes within it Oman, Hadhramout, and Aden. Coupling this with the gesture of just-a-handful, we get a clear idea of the extent of his political ambition."[2]

Taken together, these accounts seem to support the contentions of later historians that Imam Yahya Hamid al-Din was an historical artefact of an earlier age of Islamic absolutist rule. When the British naturalist Hugh Scott wrote of the Imam as "as absolute a monarch as any left in the world," he was drawing on a common trope of the Oriental despot, bound forever to the past and irredeemably out of place in the modern world.[3] Yet the episodes also evince Imam Yahya's and Muhammad Raghib Bey's keen sense of the problem of modern government and the technical capacities needed for administering the complex of territory, population, and resources that, at least in Michel Foucault's terms, constituted its object.[4] In his formulation, the art of government displaced an older form of "pastoral" power that had as its mode religion and its goal the cultivation of souls for the hereafter. Rooted in the Christian tradition, pastoral power targeted both the individual believer and the congregation, regulating everyday conduct through the institution of the church. In the modern formulation of government, it was security and the management of populations that guided states rather than the ultimate salvation of the pious. Its tools were the fields of statistics, economics, and the census.

Even if curious visitors to Imam Yahya's court overlooked it, the state's interest in population numbers and accurate cartographical knowledge suggested that a shift in the understanding of government was already underway in the Yemeni highlands by the first decades of the twentieth century. Imam al-Mansur (r. 1890–1904), who ushered in the rule of the Hamid al-Din family, called on Muslims in his summons to the Imamate to "command the greatest good and forbid that which is vile and wrong."[5] In terms of practical action, the Imam's goal was to enforce the *shari'a* and its rulings and to fight against unjust rule. This call to arms was manifested in 1898 in a general uprising against the Ottoman state that had occupied the Yemeni North in 1872 and incorporated it into the empire-wide project of state reform known as the Tanzimat. That is, the Imamate, not unlike pastoral power, was concerned with cultivating an ethical life among the believers, enforcing the law and their submission to it, and fighting injustice by word and deed.[6]

While Imam Yahya Hamid al-Din continued his father's uprising against the Ottoman state after his assumption of the Imamate in 1904 and in the same ideological terms as his father, his Imamate bore only passing resemblance to al-Mansur's. Although his *jihad* was still cast in the moral terms of commanding good and enforcing the *shari'a*, with the end of the First World War and the evacuation of the Sultan's administration, Imam Yahya drew freely and heavily from the Ottomans in his construction of the inter-war Imamate. With the assistance of former Ottoman officers and technicians, he adopted the modern instruments of communications and coercion—the telegraph and the modern military. This new army was then directed towards the conquest of geographical Yemen in a series of campaigns that lasted well into the 1930s. Underlying these campaigns was a new understanding of territory as a space to be mastered through its abstraction, delimitation, conquest, and ultimately management. The idea of space as an object of governance was mobilized, however, in the service of an older notion of sovereignty that equated obedience to the state with moral rectitude. In this view, the Imam, by virtue of his noble lineage, vast learning, and history of military resistance in the name of the *shari'a*, was duty-bound to "command good and forbid wrong" to a population that had fallen into political and moral chaos. Territory and population must not only be managed but realigned to conform to hierarchies of religious knowledge presided over by the benevolent gaze of Imam Yahya. It was an economy of moral and political power that was novel in its method and breadth.

This chapter traces the development of the inter-war Imamate in order to emphasize its dual genealogies. It begins by situating the rise of the Hamid al-Din Imamate in opposition to the Tanzimat program of state reform during Imam al-Mansur's reign. Although the uprising against the Sublime Porte continued under his son, Imam Yahya, it effectively ended with the Peace of Da"an in 1911, which ceded control of the Yemeni North to the Imamate. With the end of the Ottoman occupation at the end of the First World War, Imam Yahya laid the foundations for what later became the Mutawakkilite Kingdom of Yemen with the formation of a modern army that would support his claim to power, a claim rooted in older notions of religious authority. The chapter concludes with an account of the campaigns to subdue lower Yemen and the Zaraniq and Hashid tribal confederations in the 1920s. Their cessation, in the literature of the learned elite, marked both the return of just Islamic rule to the margins of state authority and the political unification of what was understood as a Yemeni homeland under threat from European empire.

Ottoman rule and the Hamid al-Din da'wa

In 1872 the Ottoman army under the command of Ahmad Mukhtar Pasha entered the city of Sanaa, completing the conquest of the Yemeni North that had begun just over twenty years previously. This was no mere occupation force, for a delegation of Sanaani notables had beseeched Ahmad Mukhtar Pasha to enter the city in order to restore some semblance of order to an otherwise chaotic political landscape. The return of the Sultan's army to the Yemeni highlands was of enough importance for Muhsin b. Ahmad al-Harazi, a contemporary chronicler of the period, to vividly record the triumphal approach of the soldiers as "they beat brass tambourines, drums, and [played] brass *mizmars*."[7] If his account is too celebratory it is because for Harazi, as a member of the Zaydi learned elite, the preceding decades had been characterized by an absence of political order and, therefore, by moral crisis.

In the several decades before the Ottoman occupation of Sanaa, the power of the Zaydi Imamate to rule beyond the highlands had long deteriorated. In the political vacuum that resulted a number of other social and political actors made claims to regional power on the basis of military might, command of religious knowledge, or control of economic resources. In the northern region of 'Asir, the Banu Mughayd tribe rose to dominate much of the Red Sea coast. Later it was the Sharif of the Abu 'Arish region who ruled the North with the support of the Egyptian army. The Egyptians had entered Yemen first under a renegade officer and later as an official

DISORDER AND THE DOMAIN OF OBEDIENCE

expeditionary force that took the Tihama and the port of Mukha as a means of monopolizing the export of coffee. In the South, the Sufi Shaykh Faqih Saʿid declared himself the long-awaited *mahdi* or rightly guided one and launched a war first on the British and then on the Imamate itself. There was even, it was said, a Jewish sorcerer in the highlands who carried weapons, despite his social status, and declared his right to rule as an heir of "al-Mansur al-Himyari."[8] For men such as al-Harazi, who were manifestly invested in the continuation of Zaydi rule, episodes such as these, like the occurrences of drought, scarcity, and inflation that he recorded with alarm, were portents of an age in which the social and moral order of the Imamate, an order based on the hierarchy of religious knowledge and noble descent, was increasingly under threat. In this situation the rule of the Ottoman Sultan was preferable to chaos.

With the return of nominal Ottoman authority to the Yemeni highlands and the formal creation of the Province of Yemen (*Yemen vilayeti*), the region was integrated into the Ottoman Empire and the project of state-directed reform known as the Tanzimat. The Tanzimat program had as its goal the structural reform of the empire in the areas of military modernization, fiscal centralization, and bureaucratic organization, as well as the cultivation of a new social contract between the state and its subjects, which would recast the dynasty of Osman as a multi-ethnic and multi-sectarian nation of citizens. State decrees such as the Hatt-ı Sharif of Gülhane (1839) and the Islahat Fermani (1856), as landmark statements of the ideology of reform, were just as important for their emphasis on the expansion and normalization of centralizing state power as they were for their espousal of ethnic and sectarian equality on the basis of an imperial national identity or Ottomanism. The movement culminated in the promulgation of the empire's first constitution and the convening of its first parliament.[9] Despite the rollback of many of these political reforms by Sultan Abdül Hamid II in 1878, the movement effectively redefined the Ottoman polity.

The Tanzimat vision of Ottoman modernity, as Ussama Makdisi has argued, was characterized by an understanding of progress adopted from European liberalism that distinguished between the modernity of the Ottoman elite in Istanbul, who had fully embraced the reformist project and its concurrent notions of political belonging, and the inhabitants of the provinces who had yet to do so.[10] In this vision of a geographically and temporally differentiated progress, it was the empire's internal "Others"—Arabs, Kurds, Bulgarians, Armenians, Shiʿis, Yazidis—who served as both the antithesis and the potential beneficiaries of an Ottoman modernity that was brought by the expansion of the state and its governing practices. What distinguished the ideology of "Ottoman orientalism," in Makdisi's terms, from its European incarnation was the dual move to assert, against Western conceptions of Oriental stasis, that the Ottomans were capable of progress while simultaneously singling out parts of the Empire that were ineluctably backward and in need of the civilizing presence of the state. Indeed, Ottoman Orientalism "posited an empire in 'decline' yet capable of an independent renaissance, Westernized but not Western, leader of a reinvigorated Orient but no longer of the 'Orient' represented by the West, nor that embodied in its unreformed subjects."[11]

The Province of Yemen was deemed one of those marginal places in need of uplift, and the form of governance practiced by the Ottomans in the highlands was guided by the assumption that Yemen and its inhabitants, while an integral part of the empire, had not reached the level of civilization that would enable them to participate in the Ottoman civic order. Only the incorporation of the country into the complex of institutions and practices associated with the Tanzimat state and—by the time of Abdül Hamid's reign with its emphasis on the empire's Islamic identity—the normative forms of a state-sponsored Sunni Islam would ensure Yemen's progress.[12] In practical terms, this meant that in the early years of the occupation the province's governors applied to Yemen at least some of the forms of administrative and fiscal reform that had earlier been applied elsewhere, even though they were limited by the government's chronic inability to collect taxes with any regularity and ensure a modicum of security.[13]

Almost immediately after the Ottoman occupation, Yemen was divided into sub-provinces along the lines of the 1864 law of provincial administration. Local administrators were appointed from the military and at the lower levels from local notables, attempts were made to regularize and collect taxes on villages and customs, and public works were initiated to benefit the local population and to serve as lasting symbols of Ottoman sovereignty.[14] A separate corps of Yemeni Hamidiye troops was organized to support the regular Ottoman troops and to cultivate the modern qualities of discipline and state loyalty.[15] Undergirding the reform of the fiscal, administrative and military apparatus was an effort to introduce new notions of knowledge and the law. Brinkley Messick has detailed, for example, the introduction of the *ruşdiye* preparatory schools, which gave instruction in what was understood to be "practical" knowledge (*ma'arif*) rather than religious knowledge (*'ilm*).¹⁶ In no field was this more apparent than in the introduction of the civil law code (the Mecelle), an attempt to rationalize and codify the *shari'a*, and the state *nizamiye* courts to the province.¹⁷ The success of the Tanzimat reforms in preparing the province and its inhabitants to join the Ottoman civic order, at least on the surface, could be gauged by the election of Yemeni representatives to the Parliament during the first and second constitutional periods.

Nonetheless, much of Ottoman policy in Yemen, according to Thomas Kühn, was guided by the assumption that Yemen had yet to attain the imperial center's level of civilizational development and therefore had to be ruled according to different principles.¹⁸ It was the Zaydi *madhhab* and the institution of the Zaydi Imamate in particular that distinguished Yemen from other provinces, a situation that pushed Ottoman administrators to craft new forms of governance that were more attuned to local "custom." That is, the Ottomans crafted a ruling ideology that was exclusionary in its principles and therefore not entirely distinct from the durbar model of rule practiced in the Yemeni South. Driven by the unrelenting resistance in the 1870s and 1880s of a number of the highland and coastal tribes, in addition to that of the Imams Muhsin and Sharaf al-Din, the Ottoman administration amended or chose not to apply key elements of the Tanzimat reforms in Yemen. Land reform was not implemented, the state *nizamiye* courts were shut down, and the Yemeni Hamidiye corps was ultimately disbanded. Instead, the Ottoman regime instituted a form of politics that targeted the Zayid religious establishment for cooptation, appointing its members to the lower levels of provincial government and state-administered *shari'a* courts. Yet, even as governors were appointed, dismissed and reappointed, and commissions were sent to investigate the causes of local opposition, the state remained wedded to a concept of development and progress, even if it rested on an assumption of Yemeni difference and the firm hand of the Ottoman military.¹⁹

It was in this context that the Imam al-Hadi Sharaf al-Din died in 1890, in the midst of an uprising against the Ottoman state. He was replaced, if reluctantly, by Muhammad b. Yahya Hamid al-Din who announced his summons to the Imamate in Ottoman Sanaa after being convinced to do so—we are told by his biographer—by a group of concerned Zaydi *'ulama'*. Muhammad b. Yahya was from the line of Qasim that had held the Imamate until the nineteenth century, and unlike many of the Imams of the early nineteenth century, he embodied the characteristics of an ideal Imam as elaborated by Zaydi doctrine. In particular, he was recognized as a scholar capable of independent judgment (*ijtihad*) and, soon after his summons, as a warrior in the name of the faith (*mujahid*). His call was answered by many of the Zaydi *'ulama'* and the northern tribes, in particular the Hashid confederation. The Imam al-Mansur, as he was now called, initiated an uprising against Ottoman rule that targeted the Tanzimat project as it manifested itself in Yemen. Quite the opposite of Tanyus Shahin's mobilization of the new discourse of Ottoman citizenship and religious equality in Lebanon, Imam al-Mansur's revolt was executed under the umbrella of a restoration of the *shari'a*, the rule of the Prophet's descendants, and the old order of social and religious hierarchy.[20] That is, the Imam invoked the very terms by which the Ottomans had institutionalized Yemeni difference and directed them against the state as an argument for the restoration of just Islamic rule.

As al-Mansur's biographer makes clear, the "days of corruption" had not ended with Yemen's return to the imperial fold for the old social and moral hierarchies embodied in the Zaydi Imamate had not been restored by the Sublime Porte. 'Ali b. 'Abdullah al-Iryani, a scholar and supporter of the Imam, began his chronicle of al-Mansur's reign with a lengthy defense of the normative status of the Imamate in the Qur'an and the Prophetic *hadith*. In doing so, he was challenging not only the legitimacy of Sultan Abdül Hamid, but that of the state itself. The proof texts were clear on the matter, he argued, and scholars were in agreement that the line of the Prophet had been selected by God to command good and forbid wrong. Even more so, al-Iryani suggested al-Mansur was the "renewer" (*mujaddid*) of the faith that the Prophet Muhammad had declared would arrive every hundred years, although the author amended the *hadith* so that it stipulated that the renewer would be from his genealogical line (*ahl al-bayt*).[21] What this meant for the community of Muslims in terms of practical politics was quite clear. "Following the summons of the Prophet's descendants," Iryani wrote, "is obligatory and an imperative command, and obedience to their summons and their sovereignty is a duty for all Muslims. He who deviates has taken an evil path."[22]

The rebellion that followed al-Mansur's accession to the Imamate, and rapidly challenged Ottoman rule in the Yemeni highlands, was defended by the Imam as an effort to restore the rule of the *shari'a* as executed by the legitimate heirs of the Prophet. Allied with the major northern tribes and wielding a message of reform and just rule, the Ottomans invoked the status of the Sultan as the rightful leader and guardian of the community, rather than the new discursive repertoire of the Tanzimat. Shortly after the rebellion began, a Syrian member of the Ottoman *'ulama'* castigated the Imam in a letter in which he asserted the legitimacy of the dynasty as the rightful successors of the 'Abbasids, ruling with the consent of the community in an unbroken line that extended to Sultan Abdül Hamid. Referring to al-Mansur as *sayyid* in recognition of his descent but not as Imam, he accused him of declaring the Ottomans apostates, encouraging the masses to rise against the government, and igniting the "fire of war among the Muslims." All of this, he wrote, "had necessitated the exalted Sultan's anger against you" and he warned of severe consequences if he continued to incite "the people of corruption and tyranny" against the state.[23]

Imam al-Mansur's response was equally rooted in the assertion of historical and religious legitimacy, but in his case the claim was based on the continuity of authority embodied by the Prophetic line. Responding to the Ottoman scholar's letter, the Imam accused the Sultan of failing to guard the *shari'a* in his capacity as the supposed head of the community. His officers in Yemen, the Imam wrote, had committed a multitude of sins. They had failed to uphold the law, made the illicit licit, raised the status of Jews and Christians above the Muslims, and insulted the descendants of the Prophet. In other words, the Ottomans had failed to respect a moral order and a vision of social hierarchy at the top of which were the *sayyid*s. Both of these, it was implied, were inextricably bound together. For this reason, the Imam wrote, he had initiated his uprising: "when we saw no choice but God's command, we asked for his aid, entrusted ourselves to him and exerted our efforts in jihad."[24] Ending with an implicit warning to the Ottoman state, the Imam wrote, "if the exalted Sultan knew the truth of the situation, he would rush to aid us, remove his administrators from Yemen, and order them to fight the infidel while forbidding them from fighting the pure line of the Prophet."[25]

Imam al-Mansur died in 1904 in the midst of his rebellion against Ottoman rule. His son Yahya b. Muhammad Hamid al-Din almost immediately announced his *da'wa* or summons to the Imamate in the village of Qaflat al-'Udhr in the territory of the Hashid tribal confederation. He then called the *'ulama'* to discuss his nomination. As the historian 'Abdullah b. 'Abd al-Karim al-Jirafi wrote some years later, "their word was entirely in agreement that no one could take the place of the Imam like his son, so they gave the oath of allegiance and he was called 'al-Mutawakkil 'ala Allah.'"[26] Afterwards, we are told, delegations from a number of great *sayyid* houses and from the major tribal confederations, Hashid and Bakil, came to give the oath of allegiance as well, all of whom "answered him [i.e. his summons] with obedience."[27]

In a later panegyric poem extolling the virtues of the Imam and 'Ali b. Abi Talib from whom he claimed descent, Qadi Yahya b. 'Ali al-Haddad referred to Imam Yahya as "al-Hashimi, al-Nabawi, al-Fatimi, al-'Alawi, al-Hasani, al-Qasimi."[28] This genealogy confirmed his descent not only from the Prophet through Fatima, but also from the ruling house of al-Qasim after whom the Qasimi dynasty was named. It was a genealogy of both innate virtue and political acumen and was embodied in his status as a scholar capable of independent judgment in matters of law (*mujtahid*) and as a warrior in the name of Islam (*mujahid*). His education began in Sanaa where he studied with a number of prominent Zaydi scholars. He later relocated with his father to Jabal Ahnum where he resumed his education and took *ijaza*s from a number of prominent scholars. In particular, he studied with Ahmad b. 'Abdullah al-Jindari (d. 1918), a prominent *sayyid* and scholar, who was also Yahya's first biographer. It was under al-Jindari's tutelage that Yahya began to study the standard works of *hadith* and eventually moved toward the Sunni legal tradition, as Bernard Haykel has chronicled. His father, the Imam al-Mansur, was said to have referred to his son with great disapproval as having "become like Jindari" (*tajandara*).[29] Yet Yahya was not the only person with such a distinguished pedigree, and his summons was not unchallenged.

Only six days after Yahya's *da'wa*, he was confronted with the summons of Sayyid Hasan b. Yahya al-Dahyani (d. 1924) in the *hijra* of Falala, near the northern town of Sa'da. The local tribes and notables responded to his summons, and like Yahya he declared himself Imam. Sayyid Hasan was equally qualified for the Imamate in terms of descent and education, and skirmishes quickly erupted between the two claimants. With the Zaydi prohibition on the presence of two Imams at the same time, however, the issue had to be decided.[30] Yahya's son, Ahmad, proposed that the two meet in the town of Sa'da with their supporters from the *'ulama'*. They would then engage in a debate in front of the scholars collected, in order to prove which claimant was more learned and therefore most qualified to lead the community. Whether in fear for his life or of being bested by Yahya, Sayyid Hasan did not show up, and the *'ulama'* declared Yahya the rightful Imam.[31] He was therefore not able to prove his intellectual qualifications for the position through a contest of wits with the Dahyani claimant; his was, to a certain extent, a position of default.

DISORDER AND THE DOMAIN OF OBEDIENCE

Nonetheless, the Imam derived a good deal of his social capital, if not from his proven knowledge, then from his opposition to the Ottoman occupation. While the cash-strapped Ottoman administration had attempted to incorporate Yemen into the post-Tanzimat program of reform and state centralization, it had faced organized rebellion since al-Mansur's call for *jihad* in 1898. This resistance was framed in largely Islamic terms, commensurate with the oppositional nature of Zaydism. Imam al-Mansur's *jihad* was justified as a means to protect the *shari'a* and the Muslim community from the irreligion of Ottoman rule, as was Imam Yahya's after the death of his father in 1904. In 1907, in the midst of his uprising, a delegation from Mecca arrived in Yemen at the request of the Sultan with the purpose of convincing the Imam to end his *jihad* against the Ottoman state. Detailing what he considered serious administrative abuses, including excessive taxation and rapacious officials seeking personal enrichment, the Imam framed the continued war in terms of restoring just Islamic governance. Like al-Mansur, he accused the Ottomans of ignoring the Ramadan fast and engaging in public intoxication, as well as supporting the heterodox Isma'ili community against the Imam's followers. "Is it wrong to fight those who neglect the bases of Islam?" he wrote, and it was this theme that was emphasized through the course of his continued efforts against the state.[32]

By 1908, the provincial Governor Hasan Tahsin Pasha was pushed to conclude a treaty with Imam Yahya, reinstating the *shari'a* as the legal system in the areas under the Imam's control.[33] When the Imam renewed the revolt in 1911, the government was compelled to sign a new, more comprehensive agreement. In the village of Da"an in the tribal territory of 'Iyyal Yazid the two sides signed a treaty recognizing Imam Yahya's religious and temporal authority over the Zaydi highlands in the north. In twenty articles, the agreement ended hostilities and renegotiated the Imam's relationship with the state, ceding to him the power to administer the *shari'a*, appoint governors and judges, and collect taxes with some degree of freedom.[34] The document did not allow for complete independence. The Ottoman state was entitled to a tenth of all taxes collected in the highlands, it had the right to appoint judges to deal with followers of the Shafi'i and Hanafi legal schools, and it retained the right to approve the application of penal judgments (*qisas*) in the Zaydi north. As Kühn has argued, the Da"an treaty was less the fulfillment of Imam Yahya's ambitions to be recognized as the legitimate leader of the Zaydi community than the enactment of an Ottoman state Orientalism which, guided by the assumption of insur-

115

mountable sectarian differences between Sunni and Shi'i populations, institutionalized them in a form of indirect rule modeled quite intentionally on European colonial models.[35]

Authority and obedience

From the conclusion of the Treaty of Da"an until the end of the First World War and the Ottoman withdrawal from Yemen, Imam Yahya was effectively a subordinate of the Sublime Porte. He was no longer the commander of the faithful, but a servant to the Sultan, and the Sultan's enemies were now his. This was particularly the case with Sayyid Muhammad al-Idrisi, the head of a Sufi order in the 'Asir region along the Red Sea coast of what are today Yemen and Saudi Arabia. During his uprising against the Ottomans, Imam Yahya and the Idrisi had made common cause against the state. Da"an had changed that, and the Idrisi was now his enemy. Even so, the demands of the Idrisi were remarkably similar to those of Imam Yahya prior to the treaty: he claimed spiritual and legal authority over 'Asir and a degree of independence from the government and its army. Moreover, he condemned the state's continued military actions against his Muslim followers at the same time as the Italians were attacking the country's coast as part of their war against Turkey (concentrated mainly in an assault on distant Libya) in 1911.[36] His fledgling state-building project was supported by Hashid and Bakil elements, including the paramount Shaykh of Hashid, Nasir Mabkhut al-Ahmar, who was angered by the Imam's treaty with the Ottomans, against whom he had so recently fought.[37]

As the Imam's forces joined the Ottoman army against the Idrisi, he attacked the Sufi Shaykh's religious credentials and his association with foreign powers. Although the Idrisi's religious legitimacy was denigrated by epithets such as "the one in error" (*dall*) or the "magician" (*mutahayil*), it was his attempt to forestall Ottoman and later Imam Yahya's hegemony in the region and his appeal to the West that caused the rift.[38] As the Imam noted in a number of announcements to the people of the region, the Idrisi had accepted arms and financial assistance from the Italians against the Ottoman Caliphate and therefore against the Islamic community. The Ottoman administration called for resistance to the Idrisi in language nearly identical to the Imam's. Supported by a series of *fatwa*s issued by a state mufti, the government stated that fighting Muslims who took cause with foreigners against the Caliph was permissible in Islamic law.[39] With the entry of the Ottoman Empire into the First World War, British support for the Idrisi supplanted Italian, and the Imam and the state formed an alliance on the basis of Islamic solidarity and support for the Sultan-Caliph.

Whatever the aim of the Da'an treaty, it did not stifle the Imam's claims to religious and temporal authority. His public proclamations against the Idrisi were less notable for his opposition to the Shaykh than for their increasingly frequent direction towards the "the people of Yemen, both Zaydi and Shafi'i" (*sukkan al-qutr al-yamani al-zaydi minhum wa-l-shafi'i*) rather than the narrowly defined Zaydi community over which the treaty had given him sovereignty.[40] Imam Yahya's markedly non-sectarian appeal to Yemeni Muslims indicated that, even though a client of the Ottoman state, he presumed the legitimacy of his own claim to leadership far beyond the Zaydi highlands. But it also intimated the extent to which his reign signaled the transformation of the Yemeni state away from earlier models of the Zaydi Imamate, a process that had begun in the late Qasimi dynasty in the eighteenth century.

Bernard Haykel has argued that the accession of a number of Qasimi Imams who did not fit the requirements of scholarly probity necessitated by Zaydi law created the conditions for the rise in stature of the scholar and jurist Muhammad 'Ali al-Shawkani (d. 1835). Although a Zaydi, Shawkani asserted the prominence of the traditions of the Prophet (*sunna*) as a source of law above the writings of the Zaydi Imams. Shawkani's appointment as the Chief Judge of the Qasimi state gave him access to the Imams as well as the power to appoint his students to positions of influence. Of greater consequence, he reinterpreted the juridical bases of the Imamate itself. Drawing on Prophetic *hadith*, he rejected the summons (*da'wa*) as the necessary path to the Imamate, arguing that one could be designated as such by the sitting Imam or by the oath of loyalty of the *ulama*. Furthermore, he rejected the conditions that the Imam must both be a *mujtahid* and trace his descent to 'Ali b. Abi Talib, arguing along Sunni lines that he need only belong to the Prophet's tribe of the Quraysh and appoint knowledgeable scholars to advise him. Finally, and contrary to the Zaydi notion of just rule, he argued that it was impermissible to rebel against the Imam unless he had committed a public act of unbelief.[41] The Imamate described by Shawkani was, in effect, what the Qasimi dynasty had become: a hereditary monarchy aided by an alliance with Sunna-oriented scholars.

The political formation that resulted from the alliance of state power and religious learning was animated by an imagined moral geography that situated its inhabitants in a landscape defined by their knowledge of and adherence to the tenets and practices of Islam. It was a hierarchical view of society that located piety and knowledge in the state and allied members of the *ulama*. In the face of the Saʿudi-Wahhabi alliance to the north, for example, Shawkani bemoaned the religious ignorance of the Imam's subjects (*raʿaya*), the tribes of the northeast and the residents of the cities, who, he believed, made Yemen vulnerable. It was the role of the Imam to appoint competent administrators and educated members of the religious establishment to instruct his reluctant subjects in their religious duties, all of which required the expansion of state authority and obedience to it. In short, it was a view of society that assumed, as Haykel notes, "that only those who have yielded to the authority of the state can be good Muslims," and the political vision it espoused was one in which the boundaries of a moral, religious and social order were coterminous with those of the state itself.[42]

When the Ottoman administration withdrew from lower Yemen in 1918, Imam Yahya asserted his authority to rule Yemen as the legitimate Imam of the Muslim community and initiated a military campaign to bring the rest of the country under his rule. The history of these campaigns is narrated in a series of biographical (*sira*) works that were written about Imam Yahya by his supporters among the learned elite in the 1920s and 1930s. These works appealed both to the universal, in their record of the expansion of the domain of the *shariʿa* under the guidance of the Prophet's descendant, and to the singular, in the specific Yemeni social and political context in which they unfolded. But what is important for our purposes is that these works also narrated the production of a new state space which was organized according to hierarchies of religious knowledge, inscribed in geography and united under the leadership and guidance of the Imam.

Indeed this new state space as a whole was subsumed under the concept of obedience (*taʿa*) and sometimes referred to in the historical literature by the spatialized metaphor of "the domain of obedience" (*hazirat al-taʿa*). In these texts, the domain of obedience was synonymous with the rule of the Imam, the application of the *shariʿa*, and the maintenance of a political and social order that preserved the rule of those with religious knowledge. Beyond the limits of obedience was a landscape of corruption (*fasad*), dissension (*fitna*) and chaos (*fawda*). The narrative thrust of these biographical works, then, is the slow but steady extension of the domain of obedience over the whole of the Yemen. If we turn to the chronicle written by Imam Yahya's chief secretary (*katib*), Qadi ʿAbd al-Karim al-Mutahhar, the extent

DISORDER AND THE DOMAIN OF OBEDIENCE

to which obedience informed a particular kind of geographical imagination becomes apparent. The author began his chronicle with an account of the year 1337/1918, the year the Ottoman administration began to evacuate Yemen, in which he demarcated the boundaries of obedience:

The Imam was residing in al-Rawda. The following lands were obedient to and under the order of our lord the Imam: Saʿda, and all areas to the edge of Bani Jumaʿa and Razih, all of the places in the far north (*qibli*), and al-Ahnum, Hajur al-Sham, Sharafayn, al-Suda, Kuhlan Taj al-Din, and ʿAffar. All of the middle regions to the edges of Yarim and al-ʿAwd were held jointly by him and the Ottoman state.[43]

Thereafter, al-Mutahhar continues to frame the passing of years with the expansion of the domain of obedience under the victorious armies of the Imamate. This space, however, was not like that of the Aden Protectorate as the British envisioned it, embedded in the nature of chiefly authority, the tribe, and the scientific discourse of geography. Rather, the borders of the domain of obedience as represented in the *sira* literature were ever expanding with the movement of the Imam's armies and his commanders—who were members of the learned elite—and the extension of his rule. That is, as we shall see below, these histories were chronological accounts which listed the places and peoples conquered, region by region. The narration of these movements is what Michel de Certeau would have called *spatial stories*. Unlike the map, which he argued "slowly disengaged itself from the itineraries that were the condition of its possibility," the spatial story is a log of movement, of place enacted through a sequential account of movement through space.[44] Nor was the view that of the perspective-less map as we saw in Chapter 3; rather it was Imam Yahya's "piercing gaze" (*nazar thaqib*) which saw beyond the outer world of appearances and uncovered hidden truths.

While the concept of obedience had a firm foundation in Shawkani's reinterpretation of the Imamate, the biographical literature suggests the maintenance and protection of a particular symbolic and practical order. As Makdisi has suggested in the context of Ottoman state discourse in Lebanon, the domain of obedience "encompassed politics and religion, public and private—all that contributed to a stable and tranquil social order."[45] In the biographical literature, opposition to the state was generally framed in a moral language, often indicated by phrases such as "the fires of dissension ignited" (*inshaʿalat niran al-fitna*), which indicated a collapse of just Islamic governance. Words such as dissension (*fitna*) and chaos (*fawda*) were more often than not linguistic codes for the disruption of religious and political hierarchies which were necessary for a stable, just, and moral order. This was not attributed to the behavior of the Imam's subjects (*ra'aya*), who are almost never accused of opposing the state. Rather, it was most always blamed on the local notables, Shaykhs and headmen who don the "garb of the state" (*ziyy al-dawla*) and exploit the socially and politically weak (*du'afa' wa-masakin*).[46]

The extension of this domain, then, was concerned with establishing proper hierarchies of authority and knowledge. The return to this state was marked by the arrival of the Imam's soldiers or "army of truth" (*jund al-haqq*), led by prominent *sayyid*s, who in turn, acted as embodiments of the Imam himself. The appointment of a governor (*'amil*) and *shari'a* judge (*hakim*) indicated the return of just rule, the application of the law, and the reform (*islah*) or "ordering" (*tartib*) of the affairs of the land. Obedience was embodied in a very specific set of practices which, in turn, distinguished obedient Muslims from the "people of corruption" (*ahl al-fasad*). First and foremost the entrance into obedience meant application of the *shari'a* and abolition of non-Islamic legal practices. What this meant in terms of practice was the performance of unspecified religious duties (*ada' al-wajibat*), which itself was a thinly veiled reference to the payment of the canonical tithes (*zakat*). Other practices that had no basis in Islam but had long histories in Yemen were necessary to the enactment of obedience as well. The taking of hostages as a guarantee for submission was recast as the taking of "hostages of obedience" (*raha'in al-ta'a*), just as the slaughtering of bulls as a ritual act of appeasement was referred to as offering "bulls of obedience" (*'aqa'ir al-ta'a*). What is important to note here is that obedience as a form of practice was only visible in relation to the state. The state itself, however, was changing dramatically.

New visions of order

Imam Yahya's Imamate was the inheritor of the Qasimi state legacy and the legal thought of Shawkani, which had elevated Sunni traditionalist thought to the realm of state power, especially in his defense of dynastic rule. Much of this influence was visible in the outward appearances of state practice. As Haykel has shown, the Imam adopted a number of state rituals from the earlier dynasty, such as the Friday royal procession and the use of the *mazalla* or royal canopy, a symbol of political sovereignty.[47] It was similarly

DISORDER AND THE DOMAIN OF OBEDIENCE

evident in Imam Yahya's elevation of traditionalist scholars to positions of importance in his fledgling administration and his own reference to Sunni interpretations of particular legal issues in his personal legal decisions (*ikhtiyarat*), which were issued as guides to his court appointees.⁴⁸

To assume that Yahya was solely influenced by the Qasimi model, however, would be misleading. Often overlooked is the extent to which he was inspired by and drew on the Ottoman administration that he had so recently opposed. Even though the Hamid al-Din revolt initiated by Imam al-Mansur had targeted the Tanzimat project of state centralization, Imam Yahya was quick to adopt elements of this project himself. While some have noted continuities between the Ottoman regime and the later Mutawakkilite Kingdom in areas such as education and the law, the most immediate impact of the Ottoman legacy was in the organization of the instruments of coercive power.⁴⁹ Indeed, perhaps the greatest innovation of the Imam's reign was the novel application of modern forms of military organization and communications as a means of commanding space and incorporating it into the political and moral order that was the domain of obedience.

The revolutionary nature of this development is captured in al-Mutahhar's chronicle, which, in effect, narrates the foundation of this new moral and political order. It begins appropriately enough with Imam Yahya's return to the town of Rawda, outside Sanaa, in 1918. There he was greeted by delegations from the city, representatives of the surrounding tribes, and Ottoman officers, and even the representatives of the Jewish community (*ahl al-dhimma*). In a display of the blessings his presence brought, the Imam exorcised a jinn from the daughter of a prominent *sayyid*, after it declared that it could only be removed at his command.⁵⁰ He then moved to Sanaa, accompanied by members of the major tribes of the highlands. After performing the afternoon prayer at the Great Mosque, he proceeded to the garden district, Bir al-'Azab, where he met the city's notables and members of the former Ottoman administration, including the most prominent local notables from the formerly Ottoman south.⁵¹ The image is one of the pious, just ruler, bringing together the tribes, notables, and the People of the Book in a stylized vision of the Islamic community.

After the account of his triumphant return to Sanaa, al-Mutahhar turns to what could be the pivotal moment in the transformation of the space of the modern Imamate. According to his narrative, Imam Yahya realized the necessity of reorganizing his military, especially in the face of what was referred to as the greed of the British in Aden. This moment, framed as a near epiphany by al-Mutahhar, was the effect of his realization that the power of the European nations derived from "their attention to the organization and education of their soldiers so that they only feared other organized soldiers."[52] The Imam then issued an official order that established the "victorious army" (*jaysh muzaffari*).

Like many Imams before him, Yahya summoned 2,000 men from the northern tribes of Sanhan, Bilad al-Bustan, Bani al-Harith and Bani Hushaysh. They were not to be used as temporary tribal levies, but trained as a standing army. Housed in the barracks built by the Ottoman government across from the Bab al-Yaman, the city's southern gate, the new recruits were placed under the command of 'Abdullah b. Muhammad al-Dumayn, a *sharif* from al-Jawf who had also held the rank of *bikbashi* in the Ottoman army in Yemen. Some two hundred Ottoman commanders and soldiers who chose to remain after the First World War were assigned positions as officers and instructors throughout the new army. The Ottoman parade ground behind the barracks, known as *al-'urdi*, was selected as the site for the new army's exercises, and the new recruits were quickly organized and trained along Ottoman lines by a former Ottoman officer named Kanan Bey.

The new military was organized into the regular army (*al-jaysh al-nizami*), the militia (*al-jaysh al-difa'i*), the artillery, cavalry, and tribal levies. The men in the regular army were recruited from the northern tribes and from the men who had served in the Ottoman gendarmerie. Each soldier was represented by a guarantor from his area or tribe who agreed to reimburse the state for the cost of uniforms and rifles in the event the soldier absconded. Service in the regular army was for life, except in the event that the recruit found a replacement for his position. For the paltry pay of five Maria Theresa dollars per month and four loaves a day, the regular army was to be the professional backbone of the new military, and its ranks reached anywhere from 15,000 to 20,000 men by the end of the 1930s. The militia was meant to provide the majority of the male population with a modicum of military training. At any one time, up to twenty-five per cent of the population of a given province or *liwa'* was to be in training in the capital; by the 1940s scholars have estimated that anywhere between 15,000 and 100,000 men were in the ranks of the militia.[53]

Supporting the new army was a series of small-scale factories producing munitions and equipment and a number of new educational institutions. A munitions factory was opened under the direction of an Ottoman Hungarian, Jurji Bey, and was soon producing cartridges at a rate of 4,000 per day. Moreover, new workshops were opened which were dedicated to the repair of rifles and cannon inherited from the Ottoman army and the production of war material. Craftsmen were organized by trade and were set to work building wood carriages for cannon, making bridles and saddles for horses, and various other tasks. The apparent newness of this sort of centralized production inspired al-Mutahhar to comment how "each group had its own proscribed space and specific task."[54] At the same time, the Imam established a war college (*al-maktab al-harbi*) in which potential commanders of the new army were educated in modern warfare by Ottoman instructors. This educational effort ran parallel to other efforts to open (or in some cases reopen) a number of other schools, including a school for orphans, a school for state hostages, and later the *madrasa 'ilmiyya*, a state administered school, in Sanaa.[55]

The creation of the regular army figures in all of the Western narratives of the foundation of Imam Yahya's state. Most of these, however, fixate on the inadequacies of the military.[56] The impression of most European travellers who observed the new army in action gives little sense of the novelty of this new form of military organization. The Dutch traveller D. Van der Meulen visited Yemen on behalf of his government in 1931 and remained in Yemen as a guest of the Imam. Among his observations is a description of the weekly military review which was held on *al-'urdi* every Friday after the noon prayer:

First came infantry in bare feet with bayonets fixed on their rifles—soldiers and officers alike were dressed according to their own taste and means. The result was that as individuals they appeared to be most shabby but as a mass most colorful. The officers wore an assortment of former Western uniforms in which the Turkish antecedents of the army could be clearly traced. Some relied on civilian dress to help them out and above a military pair of trousers a black evening or morning coat with the tails cut off would be worn. Some officers were mounted on horseback, some on mules or on poor little donkeys. The onlookers gave all this not even the suggestion of a smile—they seemed really to be impressed by the army.[57]

Indeed, in European terms, the new army offered little to recommend it. It was extremely under-funded, ill-trained, and poorly equipped in terms of uniforms, weapons, ammunition, and general provisions. The combination of antiquated weaponry, lack of uniforms, and the sight of Yemeni soldiers goose-stepping to Ottoman military marches did little to convince Europeans of the Imam's claim to a modern state. Even at the height of the undeclared war between the British in Aden and the Imam's forces in the 1920s (see Chapter 6) a British report stated with some hyperbole that the "so-called regulars are but pure and simple wild tribesmen who are thoughtful of nothing but of resorting to their hobby of hostile activities and who find intoxicating pleasure in cleaving the skulls or severing the necks of their enemies."[58]

In the Yemeni context, however, the creation of a regular standing army based on modern drill signaled a fundamental change in the organization of the state and its armed forces. While the new army seemed little more than a rag-tag assemblage of semi-armed and impoverished tribesmen, the impact of this new form of military organization, with its formalized hierarchy and machine-like organization, was not lost on al-Mutahhar, who devoted several lines to its description:

He divided the army into several columns (*tabur*), the first of which was called the first column, the second, the second column, and so on. Three columns were called an *Ay* and five *Ays* were called a *firqa*; the whole was called the "victorious army" (*al-jaysh al-muzaffari*). Every column was composed of four blocks (*buluk*), one of which was equivalent to one hundred men, each of which was called the first, second and so on. In each block there was a corporal (*'arifa*), a sergeant (*shawush*), a commander referred to as the first or second lieutenant (*mulazim*), and a *yuzbashi* which in Arabic means "the commander of one hundred men." Each column has a commander called the "commander of the column" (*amir al-tabur*) or a *bikbashi* which means the commander of one thousand.[59]

The novelty of this new military organization, as Timothy Mitchell observed earlier in a powerful analysis of Mehmed Ali's Egypt, was in its recognition of order as a goal in its own right.[60] The new "Ottoman" military organization divided the army into discrete compartments, theoretically interchangeable, under a recognizable hierarchy. The movement of the soldiers within the army was now codified and reproduced in official drills, also adopted from the Ottoman military. Al-Mutahhar indicates that the new troops conducted daily drills in ordered movements (*intizam al-harakat*), the principles of military mobilization, advancing and falling back, and attacking elevated positions. While this new style of training and drilling was meant to discipline the movements of the new army, the commanders were mastering the use of the military bugle to control the large-scale movement of soldiers. The value of this method of organization through communication was not lost on al-Mutahhar, who remarked that "its utility is evident, for in a single moment whatever is desired reaches the hearing of thousands of soldiers and they execute it immediately. If this were tried without this instrument, it would take hours."[61]

DISORDER AND THE DOMAIN OF OBEDIENCE

Figure 8: Imam Yahya's royal procession, escorted by troops of the regular army.

Implicit in this new ability to control the bodies of soldiers as parts of a larger military machine was the development of a new technology of space that saw the mastery of geography as integral to the constitution of state power and the extension of political control.[62] To that end, the Imam expanded the Ottoman telegraph network that had been built prior to the First World War, bridging the vast distances of the country.[63] According to al-Mutahhar, he opened offices in Sanaa, Haraz and Arhab. Taʿizz in the south was connected to the capital and to smaller towns such as Maʿbar. Under the administration of another Ottoman technician, the line was extended to Dhamar, Yarim, Ibb and Taʿizz. While al-Mutahhar spends some time discussing the scientific principles behind the telegraph and wireless telegraph, he devotes greater attention to the application of this technology. While explaining its invention in the West and its movement to the rest of the countries of the world, al-Mutahhar noted that "nations soon saw it as an indispensable necessity."[64] He then makes explicit this relation between modern political organization and communication. Explaining the value of the telegraph, he gives the example of a local gover-

125

nor in need of the Imam's attention to some matter. Instead of contacting him by post, which would take at least twelve days, the governor could send a telegraph in the morning and receive a response in as little as an hour. The new technology, he asserted, would be to the benefit of the Imam's subjects and to the government itself.[65] The benefit to "government" was made more explicit in Haddad's comments on the new forms of communication. He notes that in addition to the telegraph, the Imam connected the citadel in Sanaa to the major forts in the outlying regions of Kawkaban, Kuhlan, Suda, Hajja, Shihara, Sharaf, and Qaflat al-'Adhr via heliograph, creating a communications network linking the military and the local administrations. Even more important, he notes, was the wireless radio (*tar al-hawa*) which was used to connect the Imam's palace, Dar al-Sa'ada, with those of his sons in Ta'izz, Hajja and Hudayda.[66] In this way the social and political hierarchy was replicated in a hierarchy of communicative ability: the knowledge of the Imam, and therefore his authority, would always be more complete than his subjects.'

This new technology of space located in the new military and network of communications did not displace the moral order of obedience, but was effectively mapped onto it. Military hierarchy was now linked explicitly to the moral hierarchy of knowledge and was seen as essential to the restoration of the normative moral and political order. In 1922, for example, Imam Yahya issued an order that *naqib* 'Aziz b. Yahya, the commander of a company of regular troops in Sanaa, be promoted to Second Lieutenant in view of his service to the new army. The order begins with the text of the Qur'anic injunction: "Obey God, his messenger and those in authority among you," emphasizing both a military and divine order of authority. It continues by extolling the role of the army in the protection of Muslims and their wealth, but issues the warning that the proper performance of the army depended upon "obedience and submission to whosoever is made commander over them."

We have ordered their affairs in the most complete way so that each individual knows that he has a *shawush* and an *'arifa* over him, and the *shawush* and the *'arifa* know that they have an officer over them, and the officer knows that he has a commander (*amir*) over him, and that they know they have an *amir* over them. The individual defers to the *'arifa*, the *'arifa* to the *shawush*, the *shawush* to the officer, the officer to the commanders (*umara*), and the commanders to the *amir*. This will achieve your goal and the army, God willing, will be at its best.[67]

As the verse from the Qur'an indicated, this official order from the hand of the Imam was not only the confirmation of promotion in the ranks of

DISORDER AND THE DOMAIN OF OBEDIENCE

the military, but also the reaffirmation of the importance of obedience. That is, a more modern form of military hierarchy was not justified by utility or practicality alone, but by the obligatory nature of obedience within a religious hierarchy, at the top of which stood Imam Yahya.

It is useful to return to Van der Meulen's description of the Friday military review, which he found so amusing in its tired grandeur, and compare it with a description of the military left by Qadi Yahya al-Haddad, a member of the learned elite. Describing the sight of the military as it escorted the Imam to the great mosque to perform the Friday congregational prayer, al-Haddad's account suggests a much different order (cf. fig. 8):

> You see the army preceding the Imam with its regiments (*tawabir*) ordered into lines. Preceding them are the military drummers and the buglers whose music was to instill fear in the enemy and which had a great effect on the children, as it did in the Ottoman garrisons. The whole was ordered according to military mobilization. After them came the artillery, then the cavalry, and then our lord the Imam's bodyguards (*al-'ukfa*) and the palace guards walking behind. Behind this whole procession was our lord the Imam and those *sayyids* and *'ulama'* and notables (*al-khassa*) both riding and walking. The Imam, God support him, was in his royal carriage.[68]

What Van der Meulen did not understand, but was clear to al-Haddad, was that it was not a display of the military but of the state itself. The new regular army, with "its regiments ordered into lines," was merely the material force on which the state was based. The world view, the moral force of this new state, was that of the Imam Yahya, rounding out the procession, surrounded by the learned elite and the descendants of the Prophet. In this short account, we see a fantasy of the state in which the regimented, disciplined space of the new military is effortlessly juxtaposed with a social and religious hierarchy, based on religious knowledge and noble birth. It was the naturalized space of this hierarchy that the Imam then attempted to restore throughout geographical Yemen.

Mapping the boundaries of obedience

With the technical and conceptual capacity to order space in new ways, the Imam launched a series of campaigns throughout the country in an attempt to unify an increasingly coherent "Yemeni land" or *al-qutr al-yamani*. A series of small-scale wars pitted the Imam and his growing state apparatus against local notables and tribal leaders who either had gained a semblance of autonomy during the Ottoman period or now saw the opportunity to achieve it. In the writings of the learned elite, these campaigns were not acts of aggression but of moral necessity. The collapse of Ottoman authority meant a collapse of established hierarchies beyond the Zaydi highlands and thus the spread of dissension and chaos at the margins of the Imamate. The narratives of the elite elicit a moral panic at these events, even more so with the growing awareness of the region's place in a much larger world. In particular, the specter of European colonialism became a grim reality in the inter-war period and was invoked with greater frequency by the elite to justify the obedience of the Imam's subjects internally.

After the Ottoman defeat in the First World War and the announcement of the evacuation of its military and administration in 1918, Imam Yahya directed his forces to proceed south. The area controlled by the Ottoman administration in the post-Da"an period was largely contiguous with Ta'izz province.[69] The Ottomans had claimed sovereignty over the south in part because the majority of its population is Sunni-Shafi'i, but also because the region's greater fertility ensured the state a continued tax base. The southern highlands catch enough of the monsoon rains to permit rainfed agriculture, which historically has been organized in large landholdings farmed by peasants. Historically, the south has provided the tax base for all major states in the region, and was thus integral to the formation of the new Imamate.

As the Ottoman administration began to dismantle itself and its army was slowly evacuated, authority in the south devolved to local Shaykhs and notables. Geographical place and elite lineage were nearly inseparable. 'Udayn was divided among Shaykhs of the Al al-Basha, Al 'Abd al-Rabb Sinan, and by Shaykh Mansur b. Nasr. The district of the Hujariyya was under the authority of the Shaykhs of the Al Nu'man and Mawiya in the Qama'ira district was controlled by Shaykh Muhammad Nasir Muqbil, who had control of an Ottoman weapons depot. The city of Ta'izz and the mountain which overlooked it, Jabal Sabr, were under the authority of Shaykhs Ahmad Ali Basha and 'Abdullah b. Yahya al-Sabri. Moreover, Shaykhs from the tribes of Bakil who had been granted land in the southern highlands in return for their support of the Imam were a power unto themselves. Shaykhs of Al Shayif of Dhu Husayn, Al Salahi of Dhu Muhammad, Bayt Abu Hilayqa of Khawlan, and Bayt Abu Luhum of Nihm all owned land in the vicinity of the southern town of Ibb; Shaykhs of Al Abu Ras in Dhi Sufal were particularly entrenched in the south.[70]

Much on these early campaigns was narrated by Hamud b. Muhammad al-Dawla in his biography of 'Ali b. 'Abdullah al-Wazir (d. 1948), a noted

DISORDER AND THE DOMAIN OF OBEDIENCE

sayyid close to Bayt Hamid al-Din and the principal military leader of the southern campaigns. Dawla's text as spatial story narrates the incorporation of the south and its local elites into the domain of obedience, beginning in the town of Hubaysh. Muhammad b. 'Ayid al-'Uqab, one of the Shaykhs of the town, attacked the Imam's troops stationed in the region and besieged them in the local capital of al-Zalma. At Imam Yahya's command, 'Ali b. 'Abdullah al-Wazir was dispatched to "reform" (*islah*) Lower Yemen (*al-yaman al-asfal*). As his army descended south, he sent warnings to Shaykh Muhammad to submit. When he did not, the Imam's army attacked the Shaykh's followers and continued on to al-Zalma where the siege was lifted, houses burned to the ground, and the slain decapitated as a warning to others. The next day, the army pursued the Shaykh to Jabal 'Uqab where his houses were looted and burned.[71]

As al-Dawla tells it, with the occupation of al-Zalma all the surrounding tribes submitted and offered hostages as surety for their good behavior. Moreover, as the news of the Imam's victory spread in the region, major Shaykhs, *sayyid*s and notables from Ta'izz, 'Udayn, Dhi al-Sufal, Shar'ab, the Hujariyya, and even Mawiya—representing most of the province—came and "turned to obedience" (*ila al-ta'a mubinin*).[72] Wazir's biographer wrote that the purpose of the attack was the regeneration of religious learning, enforcement of religious duties, extending the rule of the *shari'a*, and protection of the "blessed homeland." Yet his call to reform was also tinged with menace, as he was said to have declared that if people did not enter into obedience by desire (*raghibin*), they would do so from fear (*rahibin*). Mutahhar was far more aware of the precedent this battle posed in the conquest of the south, as he noted when he declared ominously that at the defeat of al-'Uqab, "lower Yemen shook in all regions."[73]

Indeed, following the military victory at Hubaysh and the return of its people to "obedience," a number of towns in the province, including the city of Ta'izz, submitted to the Imam's forces. In the town of 'Udayn, for example, the majority of its inhabitants in the surrounding villages submitted without incident. 'Ali b. 'Abdullah was said to have collected hostages from every Shaykh and tribe in the region, and the place was said to have entered a "new age." In the time of the Ottomans, al-Mutahhar argued, knowledge was replaced with hostility, the strong lorded it over the weak, and every Shaykh "did whatever he wanted with the peasantry." When the people accepted the rule of the "righteous state" (*dawlat al-haqq*), however, the law was enforced and the peasantry were protected in body and wealth.[74] In the city of Taʿizz, the Shaykhs and notables handed over hostages to ʿAli b. ʿAbdullah with little resistance. The level of security that resulted from the establishment of law and order by the new administration, al-Dawla writes, was such that thereafter the people became "one body" and that "the peasant and the soldier came to be like brothers."[75] From Taʿizz, the call to obedience was extended to the surrounding region down to the border with the Aden Protectorate: the notables of the Hujarriyya, al-Mukha and al-Qamaʿira all submitted with little or no resistance.[76]

The rapid conquest of lower Yemen had resulted in the submission of the independent local notables and ended what al-Mutahhar called the "reign of the strong over the weak."[77] If the independence of these local Shaykhs was intolerable, the Yemeni tribes who existed at the margins of state authority and the moral influence of the Imam were simply beyond the pale. This was not a new position for them. As Paul Dresch has noted on several occasions, the tribes never fared well in the writings of Zaydi scholars. I have argued elsewhere, however, that to reduce Zaydi historiography to a conflict between the learned class and the tribes is to misrepresent the narrative thrust of this literature.[78] Indeed, the tribes were merely one element in a hierarchy of religious knowledge, although their position in this hierarchy was not a favorable one. This was because they were in large part beyond state rule, and the boundaries of political authority and religious knowledge were synonymous.

The opening line of Qadi Hasan b. Ahmad al-Iryani's history of the campaigns against Hashid and the Zaraniq in the decade following the conquest of lower Yemen suggested the new state's approach to tribal resistance to its expansion: "Praise be to God who has made jihad and the foundation of religion by the sword obligatory, and who has appointed someone in every age to put the affairs of mankind in order."[79] The combination of religious learning and military prowess deemed necessary to both subdue and educate the unruly tribes is best exemplified by Iryani's own account of an extemporaneous speech delivered by Sayf al-Islam Ahmad, Imam Yahya's son, in the town of Qaflat al-ʿUdhr in the early part of the campaign against Hashid. In a booming voice, he delivered a lengthy sermon suffused with references to the Qurʾan and *hadith* that was, in the words of the author, both "rousing and terrifying" (*targhiban wa-tarhiban*). In one hand he held a copy of the Qurʾan and in the other, his sword.[80]

In 1921, Ahmad led the campaign against the Hashid tribe of ʿUsaymat in the Yemeni highlands. The tribe's previous Shaykh, Nasir b. Mabkhut al-Ahmar, had supported the Imam's *da'wa* in 1904, but had later opposed him after the Treaty of Da"an. With the ability to muster upwards of 10,000 armed men, the current Shaykh Nasir b. Nasir had the potential to stall any effort to create a centralized state. The campaign against Bayt al-Ahmar began ostensibly with the construction of several forts by Sayf al-Islam Ahmad in the village of al-Najra which was within Hashid territory in Hajja, as a means to project the power of the Imam into this otherwise largely independent region. Ahmad assembled some 300 *nizami* troops and 700 irregulars from Hayma and descended on Hajja. Similar forces were sent to Kawkaban and 'Iyyal Yazid in order to encircle 'Usaymat. In the meantime, Nasir b. Nasir had taken the fort in the town of Nisa, killing the Imam's appointed Governor and his family while under tribal guarantee.[81] Ahmar's forces thereafter became disorganized and the Imam's army was able to force them out of Hajja. With this victory, Ahmad returned to Sanaa at his father's order, leaving 'Abdullah b. Ahmad al-Wazir (the cousin of 'Ali b. 'Abullah al-Wazir) to follow up Ahmad's successes.[82]

When Shaykhs from 'Usaymat refused to submit to the state and hand over hostages to secure their future behavior, Ahmad ordered a force into the town of Huth and the outlying village of Dhu 'Inash, where homes belonging to Bayt al-Ahmar were destroyed and their wealth confiscated, a course also taken in 'Affar shortly afterwards.[83] Likewise, their forts in Hajja and Habur were ordered razed. The fort in Habur was spared only with the appeal of the Shaykhs of Khamir, who attempted to mediate between the two sides, and their presentation of slaughter beasts (*'aqa'ir*) from 'Usaymat. Only in 1927, with the arrival of the regular army at the borders of 'Usaymat territory, did the various sections of the tribe (such as Dhu Qutaysh and Dhu 'Aliyi) finally submit and offer hostages. Shaykh Nasir b. Nasir, however, fled to the region of Najran in the north and made his way to the city of Mecca where he was welcomed as a guest by King 'Abd al-'Aziz b. Sa'ud.

While the rebelling Shaykhs of Bayt al-Ahmar sent hostages on to Sanaa, several members of the *sayyid* community of Huth were accused of aiding the rebels and were called upon to submit. Members of the learned families of Bayt Zayd, Bani 'Ushaysh, Bani Shar'i, Bani Sari and Bani Rassas were called upon to send hostages whom Ahmad enrolled at the Madrasa 'Ilmiyya for their education, or one could say "re-education," in the "noble science" (*al-'ilm al-sharif*).[84] In 'Usaymat, Muhammad Jahhaf al-Jawri was appointed as both Governor and judge.[85] As he and the body of *nizami* and *barrani* troops made their way to the Ba'ira pass, Ahmad again took the pulpit in the local mosque to deliver an extemporaneous *khutba* or sermon. He welcomed the troops, praised his father, the Imam, and praised God for preventing the fragmentation of the Muslims and securing Yemen's unity (*ittihad al-yaman*).[86]

The litany of crimes for which 'Usaymat was attacked and forced to submit was familiar. The tribe was accused of violating the Islamic law governing the inheritance rights of women, of ruling according to the *taghut* or tribal custom, and finally of neither submitting to the Imam's authority nor handing over hostages to secure peace.[87] But as the later speech by Ahmad indicated, the moral transgressions of the tribe had direct implications for the unity of Yemen, increasingly represented in the chronicles of the educated elite as a bounded moral, political, and social space. If the tribal threat to unity had been only suggested in the campaign against the Ahmars, it became far more explicit when the state turned its attention to the Zaraniq tribe.

The Zaraniq were a branch of the Ma'aziba tribe of the Tihama, which had as its capital the town of Bayt al-Faqih. The tribe was divided into northern and southern branches: the Zaraniq al-Shimal and the Zaraniq al-Yaman. Living along the coast, a great number of the tribe made a living through either fishing or engaging in the lucrative business of weapons smuggling (it is in this context that the tribe was mentioned in Chapter 2). Numbering around 10,000 fighting men, the tribe had been able to mount effective resistance against previous efforts of state centralization under the Ottomans.[88] Recounting their history of resistance to the Ottomans, the Idrisi, and now the Imam's government, Iryani notes that they are a tribe known for their "savagery" and inability "to distinguish between right and wrong," a sentiment echoed by one of Sayf al-Islam Ahmad's biographers, who wrote that they "had not known total submission to any government for a lengthy period."[89]

While they had maintained a semblance of autonomy under the Ottoman administration, there was at least some apprehension before the end of the First World War that this would not continue if the Ottomans withdrew. In 1922 a number of Zaraniq headmen sent a letter to the Aden Residency seeking British protection along the lines of the "nine tribes."[90] Shortly afterwards, a group of sections from the Zaraniq al-Yamani allied themselves with the Idrisi in opposition to Imam Yahya. 'Abdullah b. Ahmad al-Wazir was sent to convince the other sections to remain loyal to the Imam while he simultaneously dealt with the uprising. With the occupation of Hudayda by Zaydi forces in 1924 and the realization that direct rule was to follow, Zaraniq resistance developed into full-blown opposition to the centralizing state of Imam Yahya, culminating in the wholesale slaughter of a Zaydi garrison in 1925.

In 1928, the Imam delegated his son Ahmad to lead the regular army with tribal irregulars from the north to the Tihama to end the tribe's resistance.[91] As his army marched south, the Crown Prince composed a lengthy proclamation to be read to the local population in the Tihama. As in other proclamations, Ahmad stressed the necessity of obedience to the Imam's orders and the preservation of traditional social and political hierarchies. His statement goes further than this, however, calling not only for the restoration of a social and religious order, but also for the protection of a unified homeland from its external enemies:

> You are aware of the struggle with our enemies over these parts and of their deeds, their methods, and their intentions to divide us against one another (*tafriq al-kalima*) and gain authority over our land. They do not seek this out of love for the believers or for the regeneration of this land—No! Their purpose is to conquer and enslave God's servants, the Muslims; to take their weapons, wipe out their religion, and take their country, just as they have done in many other great civilizations such as Sind, India, Egypt, Iraq and so on.[92]

Like the campaign against Hashid, Iryani narrates the war against the Zaraniq as a battle against the religious ignorance of the tribes which itself was embodied in their refusal to accede to religiously sanctioned hierarchies. It is important, however, to note in the above quotation that the tribe's cooperation with foreign powers set on the occupation of the country was seen as equally reprehensible. These accusations, which hitherto had been reserved for the Idrisi, were directed at the tribe precisely because of their history of resistance to centralized state power. Their position in the vast Red Sea smuggling trade, which they secured by means of a sizeable fleet of dhows, was made possible precisely because of their interstitial relationship to the Imamate and the colonial order. It was this relationship to the rest of the world and the possibility that the tribe was conspiring with European empire that distinguished them from Hashid. For Iryani, failing to defeat the Zaraniq would risk Yemen's eventual colonization by the West.

Ahmad began the campaign by occupying the port towns of Ta'if and Ghulayfiqa and destroying the tribe's small fleet of dhows that had been employed so effectively in Red Sea commerce.[93] As his forces moved south in the following weeks, he accepted the submission of the Shaykhs of several sections, slowly isolating the rest of the tribe. Those who were accused of inciting discord (*fitna*) had their lands confiscated and their date trees cut down. In intense fighting, regular forces and sections of Hashid took town after town, at one point even taking hostages from their own troops to keep the army fighting through the hot season.[94]

Although the tribe was brought back to the fold of obedience, the victory was not without consequences. Bayt al-Faqih was garrisoned by Ahmad's troops, hundreds were jailed and many of their Shaykhs sent to the infamous prison in Hajja. Moreover, the population was forced to hand over all weapons and the more important families were ordered to deliver hostages to the army. Most significantly, to mark the Imam's claim to sovereignty and the incorporation of the Zaraniq into the domain of obedience, Ahmad ordered the destruction of the tomb of Ahmad b. Musa 'Ujayl, the patron saint of Bayt al-Faqih. The tomb had historically been a popular site of veneration for the surrounding population, but in the moral language of the state it was a center of deviant beliefs (*'aqa'id zayigha*). According to Iryani, a local Sufi had also stored weapons in the tomb and encouraged the population to rise against the Imam's armies in the name of their patron saint. The representation of the tomb as both a site of heterodox Sufi practices and of resistance to the Imamate allowed the elision of two different social and political fields into a common framework of opposition.[95]

The erasure of the spiritual centre of Bayt al-Faqih allowed the tribes reentry into the domain of obedience through the rebuilding of the city. Ahmad first assigned a garrison to the town (*takhtit*) and rebuilt a fort overlooking the eastern part. He then opened a school which was open to all. Most indicative of the campaign's representation as a dual battle against foreign influence and religious ignorance, Ahmad was said to have ordered the restoration and binding of the city's books and hired a number of scholars to teach them to willing students in newly built libraries. All were said to be welcome to come and memorize the works on the condition that they "take care of them and not neglect that which they took from them."[96]

The end of the Zaraniq *fitna* was not the end of the campaign to secure the boundaries of obedience. Rebellions in the Jawf and Ma'rib in 1929–30 and in Khawlan and Ma'rib in 1931–32 were put down by forces under the command of 'Abdullah b. Ahmad al-Wazir and the head of the regular army, 'Abdullah al-Dumayn. In 1932, Ahmad was sent east to subdue parts of the Jawf and to take on the major Bakil tribes of Dhu Muhammad and Dhu Husayn in Jabal Barat, which itself became the subject of a panegyric chronicle by Muhammad Sharaf al-Din.⁹⁷ After Ma'rib was brought under the sway of the state, the Murad tribe of Harib was still looked at suspiciously by the state's agents. Nowhere is this more evident than in the 1934 tax index of the region in which the majority of Murad were categorized as *khawarij*, in reference to the early Islamic secessionist faction—a telling comment on their position at the margins of belief, practice, and state authority.⁹⁸

Conclusion

If Nazih Mu'ayyad found no evidence of the art of cartography in the Imam's kingdom, Ameen Rihani was thoroughly convinced of his obsession with geography and his desire to master it. Despite Rihani's conviction of Imam Yahya's fanatical adherence to an uncompromising Zaydi faith, he believed the ruler was also a man of great forethought and patience. It would only be a matter of time, he opined, before the Imam would act on his ambition to conquer all of geographical Yemen: "He, therefore, abides his time, keeping the maps of Al-Yaman, of Arabia, before him. And there is Aden, the pearl in the crown of his ancestors. It is not only on the map, but also in his dream."⁹⁹

Rihani's comments suggest a blurred boundary between the modern perspective of the map and the perspective of the world of dreams, between the modern art of government, with its emphasis on territory and security, and the pastoral power of an Imamate concerned with guarding the boundaries of a moral geography. One could contrast Imam Yahya's Imamate with Henri Lefebvre's understanding of the production of modern abstract space as part of the formation of a capitalist modernity. Modern space for him meant the destruction of previous symbolic orders, not only spatial practices but entire ways of being in the world. "In some cases," he wrote, "entire countries—certain Islamic countries, for example—are seeking to slow down industrialization so as to preserve their traditional homes, customs and representational spaces from the buffeting of industrial space and industrial representations of space."¹⁰⁰ That is, a singular modernity is formed only through the erasure of an ill-defined "traditional" that is inevitably associated with religion, and one's only choice is acquiescence or resistance.

As I have argued in this chapter, to understand the particular way in which power operated during the Hamid al-Din Imamate, one must look not only at Imam Yahya's resistance to the Ottoman state and the modernizing project of the Tanzimat but also at his selective adoption of the modern instruments of coercive power in the post-war period from the empire he had so recently opposed, and their mobilization in defense of an older notion of Islamic sovereignty. The very power of the Hamid al-Din Imamate, I have suggested, rested on its ability to combine modern techniques of producing and controlling geography through the modern military with a notion of moral authority rooted in the eighteenth-century transformation of the Zaydi Imamate by a group of Sunna-oriented scholars allied with the Qasimi state. The resulting political formation located piety in obedience to the Imam and the state he was constructing. Beyond the domain of obedience was a landscape of chaos, dissension and corruption that was all the more dangerous because it was linked in the 1920s with the dangers of European empire and foreign domination. Imam Yahya justified the sweeping military campaigns that followed the formation of the modern military in the name of the *shari'a* and the defense of the community of Muslims, the *umma*, but just as important was the idea of geographical "Yemen," whose boundaries were understood to coincide with those of the moral terrain of obedience.

If by the 1930s much of what was understood as Yemen was now within the moral space of obedience, there was also a concrete awareness that both were under threat from a resurgent empire that had occupied much of the Islamic Middle East after the collapse of the Ottoman Empire. In the next chapter, I will look more closely at Imam Yahya's careful mobilization of the dual discourses of anti-imperialism and Salafi reformism that were current in the inter-war Islamic world, as a way of remaking Yemen's global image and local politics in a way that emphasized his credentials both as a just Islamic ruler, and as one of the principal actors in a global war of resistance against European empire, the British in particular. In this view, it was clear that the defense of Yemen, as the last independent Islamic kingdom presided over by a descendant of the Prophet who was both scholar and warrior, was integral to the preservation of the entire Islamic community. Yemen, for Imam Yahya, would indeed become, if only for a brief moment, the last and greatest hope for a revived Islam and a triumphant anti-imperialism.

5

THE CENTRE OF RENEWAL AND REFORM

With all this, however, a particular Central Power is clearly visible in every age, and the eye of an historian can see it conspicuously standing out of all division and dispersion.

Abul Kalam Azad, 1920[1]

Introduction

"As for the Zaraniq in general," an anonymous writer in the state newspaper *al-Iman* wrote, "they are an important part of Yemen, among the hardiest of its people and most God-fearing. They are well known for their patriotic zeal (*hamiya wataniyya*), bravery, and fortitude."[2] However, the author continued, there were those among them whose faith had weakened and whose character could not withstand the temptation of "the enemy's gold." It was they who had necessitated a forceful response from Sayf al-Islam Ahmad, acting in the name of his father. The article appeared at the end of the Imam's war against the Zaraniq tribe in 1928 and was intended as an explanation and justification of what had been one of the most vicious of the military campaigns of the 1920s. Although the paper had only printed its first issue in 1926, it was the first time that the front page had been devoted to the state's defense of one of its military campaigns.

The war was quite necessary, the author wrote, for it was conducted in defense of a singular and indivisible Yemeni homeland, whose "expansive natural borders have been delimited and well-known from east to west and north to south forever." Yemen's unity was not merely a matter of geographical cohesion, but also of its special status in the history of divine revelation. Yemen had been mentioned in revelation and the traditions of the Prophet, its people as a whole had accepted Islam, and the country was a place of refuge for the Prophet's descendants. It was a blessed land, the author asserted, and those who would attempt to turn the Yemeni people against one another would be met with "God's anger and punishment." The following year, an unnamed writer for the paper, responding to criticisms from what he called "Islamic newspapers," declared that the war against the Zaraniq was a matter of defending not only Yemeni unity, but the entire Islamic community. "Oh Muslims," he declared, "you've seen with your own eyes what has happened in the Islamic lands and kingdoms these days and the foreign subjugation and despotism that has befallen Muslims. Indeed, among the people of Islam there is not a single kingdom or individual safe from their hostility!"[3]

The point of the author, and one could assume Imam Yahya as well, was that the battle against the Zaraniq tribe had repercussions far beyond Yemen's borders and affected the entire community of Muslims. It was simultaneously a war against irreligion and European empire, both issues of near universal importance, as the anonymous author's response to the collective "Islamic" press suggests. Moreover, the state paper did so in the language of anti-imperialism and Islamic unity, both of which had great political and social currency not only in Yemen but in the greater Islamic world in the inter-war period. When Imam Yahya famously asserted in an interview in the 1920s that he would rather his people ate sorghum stalks than allow a single foreigner in his land, he was emphasizing Yemen's singular status as an independent Arab and Muslim country in a world dominated by European empire.[4] In the context of the establishment of the British and French mandates in Syria, Palestine and Iraq after the collapse of the Ottoman Empire, and with continued colonial presence in countries with sizeable Muslim populations, such as India and Indonesia, Yemen stood out both in its independence and in its maintenance of an Islamic Imamate, headed by a descendant of the Prophet and scholar of the law, in a world of nation states and empires. In fact, it was recognized among some Muslim scholars and activists that Imam Yahya was one of the few potential contenders, along with 'Abd al-'Aziz b. al-Sa'ud, for a renewed Caliphate in the period after its abolition by the Turkish Republic in 1924, despite the fact that he was from the minority Zaydi community.

The reason for Imam Yahya's high profile in the larger Islamic world had less to do with the desperation of reformers such as Rashid Rida to find the

THE CENTRE OF RENEWAL AND REFORM

next leader of the global *umma* than with the fact that the Imam effectively entered a shared discursive field dominated by the reformist ideology and anti-colonialism of the Sunni Salafi movement. He did so by actively engaging the trans-local Islamic public sphere, which was rooted in modern print culture and the unifying terrain of an Islamic discursive tradition that mobilized activists and scholars around the notion of a "public good" (*maslaha 'amma*).[5] The importance of the public sphere stemmed from its relative independence from the political community of the Ottoman Empire. With its collapse after the First World War and the abolition of the Caliphate between 1922 and 1924, a thriving debate over the future of the Islamic community continued, often using the very tools of European empire in a counter-hegemonic fashion. The Syrian scholar, activist and Editor of the Islamist paper *al-Manar*, Rashid Rida, noted as much in 1922 when he asserted that, even in the absence of the Ottoman state, the structural conditions for an Islamic public sphere were already in place:

> Distant lands have united by land and sea with the steamship, the railroad, by airships (airplanes and balloons) that have begun to transport the post and people distances of hundreds and thousands of miles in an hour or hours. That is not to mention the dissemination of news electrically from one side of the world to the other in seconds. If these instruments had existed in the age of our predecessors they would have ruled the entire world.[6]

By establishing the state newspaper *al-Iman* in 1926 under the editorship of 'Abd al-Karim al-Mutahhar and by contributing to papers such as *al-Mu'ayyad* and Rida's *al-Manar*, Imam Yahya actively presented his conquest of Yemen as the first step toward the fulfillment of the Salafi movement's goal of reasserting Islamic orthodoxy and communal unity in the face of empire. This goal was supported by efforts to publicize the Zaydi community's closeness to Sunni Islam and the Imam's opposition to sectarian conflict, through editorials targeting the difference between Sunnis and Shi'is locally and by publishing the works of Sunna-oriented scholars with Cairo publishers for the greater Muslim reading audience. Delegates were similarly sent to the major Pan-Islamist congresses of the inter-war period, in particular the Mecca conference of 1926. That is, in contrast to the accounts of contemporary commentators and more recent historians pointing to the late Imamate's isolation from global intellectual trends, forms of economy, and modes of political organization, Imam Yahya placed himself and Yemen at the heart of a resurgent Islamic world.

In this chapter I will trace Yemen's integration into inter-war movements of Islamic activism, emphasizing its local specificity and trans-local resonance. It begins by revisiting the conquest of Yemen in the inter-war period, looking not at the technology of space and state power, but at the ways in which new state discourses and governing practices were directed towards the cultivation of a new Muslim subject who was morally upright, oblivious to sectarian difference, and obedient to the Imam. I then situate this moral discourse in the larger framework of the inter-war Salafi movement, looking in particular at Imam Yahya's intervention in the debate over Islamic unity, especially in the context of the Caliphate's abolition, and the formation of a broad movement of resistance to empire. This discourse of Islamic unity and anti-colonialism, however, was mobilized simultaneously with his effort to engage the Western world as a state like any other. Domestically, the Imam adopted the title of King, marking the transformation of the Hamid al-Din Imamate to the Mutawakkilite Kingdom of Yemen, a move that increasingly alienated his Zaydi supporters. Internationally, he signaled his entrance into the world state system by signing treaties with European nations as an independent sovereign. It was ultimately the short Saʿudi-Yemeni war of 1934 that laid bare the ambivalent relationship between the Imam's state-building project and his effort to assume leadership of a global Islamic community.

The reordering of Islamic Yemen

At the end of the war against the Zaraniq, *al-Iman* published a front page article extolling the role of Sayf al-Islam Ahmad in restoring the town of Bayt al-Faqih to its historical place of pride after it had been "destroyed by chaos and ignorance."[7] The article noted many of the accomplishments lauded by Iryani in his chronicle of the war: he had revived religious knowledge by organizing study circles in the mosque, restored libraries and collected books, appointed teachers to local mosques, restored buildings, and aided the peasantry in cultivating the land. Obedience had its rewards, the article suggested, which were no less than the complete restoration of true religious knowledge and general prosperity.

In part, the expansion of state power or the "domain of obedience," as the histories of Imam Yahya's chroniclers attested, was meant to end the period of moral, social and political dissension that had prevailed in the period of Ottoman rule and directly after the First World War. If the military campaigns discussed in the previous chapter had ended outright opposition to the Imam's order, the cultivation of morally upright and obedient subjects

THE CENTRE OF RENEWAL AND REFORM

had yet to be accomplished. And this project, as much as the initial military campaigns that preceded it, required the intervention of the state to reshape the conditions in which people lived. The chronical literature, the official proclamations of the Imam, and the state newspaper couched the state project of moral uplift in the idiom of "reform" or *islah*. As Samira Haj has recently argued, reform (*islah*), and revival and renewal (*ihya'* and *tajdid*), are concepts deeply embedded in an Islamic discursive tradition that assumes the continued need to safeguard against the deterioration of the moral community. Reform itself is a normative act of periodic reassessment that checks current belief and practice against the Qur'an and the traditions of the Prophet, and as such is not concerned with liberal notions of progress but with continued conformity with an already perfect revelation.[8]

In inter-war Yemen, reform, especially as it was articulated in the state press, was less concerned with confronting ideas such as secularism than with confronting the problems of Islamic unity and the ongoing struggle against empire. Under Mutahhar's editorship, *al-Iman* drew approvingly on the Lebanese reformer Shakib Arslan's argument that the Islamic community was in a state of decline (*inhitat*), leaving it vulnerable to European hegemony, and that the cause of this decay was internal to the community itself.[9] In particular, the newspaper argued, the Islamic world had witnessed a general decline in the ethical capacities of the faithful, which required a renewed effort to cultivate morals (*tahdhib al-akhlaq*) among the Yemeni population, both collectively and individually. The current age was characterized by a deviation from the Qur'an and the Sunna and an emphasis on the mere formalities of worship. This state of affairs had led both to the spread of reprehensible innovations in belief and practice (*bid'a*) and to the more pernicious rise of the "worship of self" (*'ibadat al-dhat*) among all classes. The result was an acute unwillingness on the part of Muslims to view their well-being in relation to that of their community, a problem that could have been prevented had not the *ulama* in the current age neglected to actively command good and forbid evil.[10] The notion that a civilization's renaissance was dependent on the active cultivation and practice of personal virtue on the path to spiritual perfection was typical of the Salafi trend, especially as it was influenced by the work of Jamal al-Din al-Afghani and Muhammad 'Abduh. However, contrary to 'Abduh's understanding that the goal of moral development was to cultivate an "interiorized conviction in God," the cultivation of morality as it was discussed in the state press, as I will clarify below, was intimately related to obedience to the Imam.[11]

UNMAKING NORTH AND SOUTH

This meant that the reform of the self as an interiorized corrective act was not sufficient, but could only be accomplished in conjunction with willfully acting for the general good (*naf' 'amm*) of the community on the basis of the Qur'anic injunction to "help one another in goodness and piety" (5:2).[12] This was an imperative that applied not only to matters of the faith, the editors of *al-Iman* argued, but to matters of the world as well. It was all too clear, the paper argued, that animated by a spirit of cooperation, the countries of the West had been able to achieve great feats in industry and, as Muslims were very much aware, military conquest. Achieving the general good meant overcoming internal differences within the community of Muslims and realizing unity on the basis of the normative model of the pious ancestors (*al-salaf al-salih*). If the mode of communal reform suggested in the paper appeared rooted in a Sunni tradition of renewal and revival, it also alluded to parallels with growing anti-imperial movements in the colonized world. Gandhi's *swaraj* movement for self-rule in India and his tactics of non-cooperation were looked on approvingly as a model of cultural authenticity and independence that had to be adopted in Yemen.[13] The protection of local "customs and habits" in the face of the foreign was integral to the preservation of the moral community, but it also was directed towards the goal of asserting the single truth that all of Yemen's inhabitants were Muslims, regardless of rank and status (for the state was not opposed to social hierarchy). What was becoming clear was the assertion that unity in the Yemeni homeland (*al-watan al-yamani*) was synonymous with securing the unity of the community at large, an understanding that was especially evident in the paper's discussion of sectarian identity.

The specter of sectarian difference and its relationship to the promotion of patriotic and religious unity arose in the context of the expansion of Imam Yahya's state and the wars of conquest that supported it. The military occupation of lower Yemen brought the largely Shafi'i south under the authority of an ostensibly Zaydi Imamate, even if Imam Yahya in his concept of state power and authority was closer to the Sunna-oriented scholars of the eighteenth century. In the pages of the state newspaper, however, the state's position, and presumably the Imam's, was that the difference between Sunnis and Shi'a was largely irrelevant except to the imperial powers which exploited it in order to turn Muslims against one another, an assertion consistent with other thinkers of the Salafi trend in the late nineteenth and early twentieth centuries.[14] The paper forcefully argued that the British had justified the occupation of Iraq on the assumption that the Sunni and Shi'i

THE CENTRE OF RENEWAL AND REFORM

populations could not be reconciled, and would do so again in Yemen. It was imperative, then, that Muslims understand that there was no basis for sectarian difference in Islam—only the Qur'an and the Prophet's Sunna were sources of the faith. There was no basis, therefore, for sectarian strife in Yemen: "Just as Yemen is for the Yemenis, so is Islam, in the sense that they are brought together by it. And Yemenis are part of Islam whether they are Shafi'i, Zaydi, Hanafi, or Shi'i, for they are all Muslims. There are only Muslims in Yemen and they are all Yemenis as well."[15]

Yemenis were not defined by *madhhab* in this formulation, but by *tawhid* or the doctrine of God's absolute oneness. Division within the community was tantamount to the rejection of *tawhid* and therefore contrary to Islam itself. The argument against sectarian division was not a new one in Yemen's history. As Haykel has argued, it was integral to Shawkani's defense of the necessity of *ijtihad* in the face of received precedent (*taqlid*).[16] In the inter-war period, the power of this discourse of unity was not only that it addressed the specifically Yemeni context in which Imam Yahya had to ameliorate a large Shafi'i population wary of Zaydi rule, but also that it intersected with the general Salafi critique of sectarian factionalism within the universal community of Muslims, or what the activist Rashid Rida would refer to as the "partisanship of legal schools" (*ta'assub madhhabi*).[17] This critique of sectarianism was not unique to the Yemeni context, but arose as the subject of similar debates among Syrian activists and even among the trans-local group of 'Umani and North African scholars that Amal Ghazal associates with what she calls the "Ibadi *Nahda*."[18] Without a doubt, the critique of the *madhhab*s had been part of the rise of Sunna-oriented scholars in the eighteenth century, but the inter-war invocation of Muslim unity on the basis of the Qur'an and Sunna placed Yemen within the mainstream of Sunni Pan-Islamism and anti-imperialism. By the late 1920s, the assumption of Yemen's place within orthodox Sunni Islam was promoted to state policy as the works of tradition-oriented Yemeni scholars were published in Cairo for a global audience of readers under the auspices of the Imam.[19]

In practice *islah* as a means of enacting moral reform with Islamic and Yemeni unity as its goal was guided by the state and was thus inseparable from expansion of the state space of obedience discussed in the previous chapter. The state newspaper noted as much in an article praising the goal of unity, in which it was asserted that the whole country was united in its love of God and its "obedience and observance of the commands of our lord the Commander of the Faithful."[20] Piety before God and obedience to the Imam and his state were thus coequal. The idiom of state power was that of the Imam's ever-present "piercing gaze" (*nazr thaqib*) which could discern hidden truths from outward appearances and therefore guarantee justice and uproot sin. Underlying the metaphorical gaze was a continuous public performance of the dispensation of justice in which Imam Yahya would sit in the courtyard of his palace, the Dar al-Sa'ada, receiving the petitions of his subjects, as Ameen Rihani put it, "of every rank and class."[21] It was a public performance of state in which the Imam was shown to uphold God's law while enforcing a social order of hierarchy rooted in descent and religious knowledge. Accounts of the Imam's personal attention to the most mundane of administrative matters supported the contention that he was acutely aware of and deeply engaged in the affairs of his subjects.[22] In all it was a vision of sovereignty that saw the Imam himself as the guarantor and guardian of moral life and constituted a form of "ocular domination," to quote T. Fujitani's discussion of a similar idiom of state power in Meiji Japan.[23]

One constitutive element of the "piercing gaze" was the evermore intrusive form of government that followed the military conquest of much of historical Yemen, although in practice the Imam's rule was always contested in some fashion. If, as the chroniclers of this period suggest, the aim of the Imam was to enforce the *shari'a* and ensure that Yemen's Muslims performed their religious obligations (*ada' al-wajibat*), it was accomplished as part of a complex of state practices that were enforced by the regular army. The provincial administration was generally the purview of men from the *sayyid* and *qadi* class, often bound to the Imam through marriage, descent or learning, who took responsibilities as governors (singular *'amil*) and judicial experts (singular *hakim*). Their responsibilities were, as generally conceived, to maintain security, enforce the law, and to ensure the collection of the myriad taxes that were necessary to support the state's expansion. That being said, both government and the judiciary were micro-managed by the Imam, even though in doing so he was often at odds with other powerful contenders for the Imamate. Such was the case with the powerful Wazir family of *sayyid*s, in particular 'Ali b. 'Abdullah and 'Abdullah b. Ahmad al-Wazir. 'Ali had led the regular army in its conquest of the south after the withdrawal of the Ottoman administration and was later appointed the commander of Ta'izz province. 'Abdullah had worked as a judge in Dhamar and later led the army against the northern tribes and against Sa'udi forces

THE CENTRE OF RENEWAL AND REFORM

Figure 9: Imam Yahya's "piercing gaze".

in 1934. The Wazir family, with its noble genealogy, boasting several Imams, and its history of scholarship, was a point of opposition to the Imam that he both accommodated, through access to political power and strategic marriage alliances, and ultimately opposed by slowly removing them from their positions.[24]

Obedience to the Imam, and the process of reform that accompanied it, was itself a highly contingent process, often embedded in other political languages and processes. While the state targeted in the most visible ways what it considered to be heretical beliefs by the destruction of sites of veneration—such as the tomb of Ahmad b. Musa 'Ujayl in Bayt al-Faqih and, some years later, that of the Sufi Shaykh Ahmad b. 'Alwan near Ta'izz—Imam Yahya could make the claim to reforming the moral terrain of the country and uniting it in correct belief and practice through the administration of the law, a field of language and practice that was highly contested. A letter of the Imam appointing Qadi Muhammad 'Ali al-'Ulfi to the posi-

145

tion of *hakim* of the Zaydiyya province in 1925 is instructive. The Imam entrusted al-'Ulfi with enforcing the *shari'a* according to the Zaydi *madhhab* and the Imam's personal legal decisions, but also instructed him to see to the general education of local Muslims in their religious obligations, including the paying of the canonical taxes and "the conditions of prayer and ritual purity."[25] The underlying assumption of the order was that he was to enforce both the legislative and the pedagogical parts of the *shari'a* as a means of actively cultivating the moral capacities of the Imam's subjects. Yet, the administration of the law in all of its forms was contextually specific, varying according to region and social grouping.

The state's approach to the northern tribes is illustrative of the encounter with local practice in the application of Islamic law. Tribal customary law (*'urf*), so often criticized by the Zaydi *'ulama'* as a form of *taghut* (a Qur'anic term invoking a general evil), was as often as not accommodated by the state so long as the tribes accepted the Imam's sovereignty. In 1919, Sayyid Ahmad al-Kibsi signed a document of submission with a number of Shaykhs of Dhu Muhammad in Dammaj in the north, in which they agreed to "uphold the *shari'a*, and to settle rulings … and every matter according to God's law, to forbid *taghut* [which was] cursed in the Qur'an, and to eradicate all abominable innovation (*bid'a shani'a*)."[26] Much hinged on the ambiguities of the term *taghut* which, contrary to the *ulama*'s understanding, was not seen as synonymous with customary law among the northern tribes.[27]

In fact, as Paul Dresch has argued, the Imamate's claim to uphold *shari'a* was in many ways a claim to sovereignty which did not attempt to eradicate locally specific forms of customary law so much as to bring them under the observation of the state.[28] Thus, customary practices such as the slaughtering of bulls as an act of appeasement (singular *'aqira*) could be, in effect, made licit if directed towards the state, as Mutahhar records on countless occasions by noting the sacrifice of "bulls of obedience" (*'aqa'ir al-ta'a*), a practice otherwise criticized by the *ulama*, and presumably the Imam, as a form of idolatry or *shirk*.[29]

Similarly, the collection of the canonical taxes—described as either zakat or *wajibat*—covered a wide array of fees in cash and kind from the Imam's subjects, especially the peasant sharecroppers of the southern-Shafi'i uplands. In addition to the *'ushr*, the ten per cent tax on grain crops, and a capitation tax, special imposts were levied on cash crops, on imports and exports, and in support of the Imam's military efforts.[30] Teams of state-appointed surveyors (*mukhkhamin* or *tawwaf*) assessed crops prior to autumn and summer harvests and were followed by the Imam's tax collectors, many of whom were recruited from the regions for which they were responsible. As Isaac Hollander has shown in his study of the Jewish community in Lower Yemen, at the provincial and sub-provincial levels of government the collection of taxes could often cross lines of communal difference, such that Shaykh Muhammad ʿAbd al-Qawi, Governor of the sub-province of Nahiyat al-Sabra, could make Hayyim Misha, a local Jewish notable, responsible for collecting taxes on Muslims and Jews alike.[31] Tax collection as a state practice was often supported by soldiers who could occupy the homes of delinquent taxpayers at their expense in the despised practice of *khitat*, one of the many aspects of the Imam's regime that would draw the ire of the opposition in the 1930s and 1940s.

Even so, the collection of taxes as religious obligation and ethical imperative was a site at which the Imam's inherent justice was regularly performed and sometimes questioned. While the assessment of unpaid taxes could result in the imposition of *khitat*, the Imam's surveyors and collectors were monitored by an appointed investigator or *kashshaf* who was to carefully monitor conditions in the countryside, guarding against potential abuse of the peasantry by the tax assessors and collectors. Thus Muhammad b. Muhammad Zabara could record in verse his inspection tour through lower Yemen, noting that:

> With zeal I transformed mal-administration
> in many of these lands to good
> I removed despotic soldiers and reported
> the measurements of the harvest as it lay on the threshing floor.[32]

Any subject, if he received no satisfaction at the provincial level, could appeal directly to the Imam either in person or in written form through the presentation of petitions (singular *shakwa*). "We have consulted the *ʿamil* according to lawful directives," wrote one farmer in a petition to the Imam in 1933 after he had been taxed in excess of the *mukhkhamin*'s estimates and consequently was forced to suffer the burden of *khitat*, "and we have achieved nothing; indeed, the soldiers are still upon us."[33] Petitioning the Imam was sufficiently established in practice for Imam Yahya to ban all appeals to his justice that had not first been reviewed by provincial governors, in an attempt to delegate authority.[34] The practice of petitioning both questioned the Imam's piercing gaze, which if truly omnipresent would not permit the practice of injustice (*zulm*) against pious subjects, and also reinforced a vision of the state that placed the Imam at the heart of a moral order in which he was responsible, as custodian of the law, for cultivating the moral capacities of his subjects through the enforcement of religious duties.

The implication of Islamic reform as it was imagined in the period of Imam Yahya was that the moral renewal of the community was possible only insofar as it was embodied in everyday forms of obedience to the Imam. In practice this meant submitting to the greater power of the state and its ability to intervene in the lives of its subjects in the fields of taxation and the application of the law—behind which stood the ubiquitous presence of the military. But one of the results of the expansion of government in this period was the production of a moral geography in which everyday state practices created the effect of a single Yemen, united under the attentive gaze of the Imam.[35] In part, many of the innumerable practices of governance were represented in the pages of the state newspaper *al-Iman*, which made the idea of a single moral, geographical and political community of Yemen increasingly coherent to a reading audience. The paper regularly reported administrative appointments and military promotions, but most importantly the regular execution of the *hudud* and *qisas* punishments. As Messick has noted, the administration of the *hudud* was "shari'a shorthand for the existence of legitimate government," and the geographical coverage of the cases was a statement of the extent of state authority: in addition to the capital of Sanaa, punishments were meted out in Ta'izz in the south, Luhayya in the Tihama, Mahwit in the highlands, and even Qa'taba on the border of the Aden Protectorate.[36] That is, despite the contextually specific form state practices took, the overall effect was the constitution of a single territory united by a moral order encompassing all of its inhabitants and overseen by Imam Yahya. This was not a national political community, despite the invocation of the language of patriotism (*wataniyya*), as much as a local iteration of the greater Islamic community comprising numerous pious subjects.

Yemen and the movement for Islamic unity

While Imam Yahya's project of reform was bound intimately to the effort to expand state power within what became the moral space of geographical Yemen, it was also understood to be an element in the greater trans-regional project of Islamic unity and anti-imperial activism that was characteristic of the inter-war period. Despite the local resonance of the state's call to arms

THE CENTRE OF RENEWAL AND REFORM

in the name of a Yemeni homeland, it was understood that Yemen did not exist as an autonomous political/national community but was part of the larger community of Muslims. State discourse in fact supported Rashid Rida's earlier critique of nationalism as he saw it in Europe, noting that "the correct national life is part of the life of the Islamic community."[37] In the absence of a state that acted as the political embodiment of the Islamic community, as the Ottoman Empire had for centuries, the uncertainty regarding the future of the *umma* created a space of possibility in which rival forms of political belonging and association could compete. The Wilsonian idea of national self-determination was at this time one of many conceptions of association that sat uncomfortably alongside trends such as Pan-Asianism, socialist internationalism, and, indeed, the movement for Islamic unity or Pan-Islamism. Rather than accept the inevitability of the idea of the autonomous nation state embodied in the Wilsonian model, the Salafi project of Islamic unity was rooted in a critique of the divisiveness inherent in both European empire and the contemporary politics of nationalism. Just as religious reform necessitated the abandonment of legal partisanship, the inter-war movement for unity required a rejection of the "ethnic partisanship" (*ta'assub jinsi*) that was endemic to the nation form.[38] In this view, the universal brotherhood of Islam would mediate among differences of language, ethnicity and geography, reaffirming a global ethical community that could withstand the onslaught of the West.

'Abd al-Karim al-Mutahhar's chronicle typifies the mood of anxiety that permeated the period after the First World War. In his otherwise triumphant account of the formation and expansion of Imam Yahya's state, he expressed palpable apprehension at the dangers facing the Islamic world after the defeat of the Ottoman Empire and the rise of the politics of national liberation. In an extended account of the Allied occupation of Istanbul, he notes with dismay the 1922 decision by the Turkish National Assembly in Ankara to separate the temporal power of the Ottoman Sultan from the spiritual authority of the Caliph, suggesting that by doing so they had "entered the ranks of apostasy."[39] The next year, he wrote, Imam Yahya received a visit from Harold Jacob, no longer in the service of the Indian government, on behalf of his recently established trading company Zayd International. As al-Mutahhar reminded his readers, the British colonization of India began as a commercial endeavor, and Jacob could very well represent the initial stage of the British occupation of the Yemeni North. This was not mere hyperbole. The Aden Protectorate was south of the

149

Imam's domains and the Idrisi family, first Sayyid Muhammad and then his son Sayyid 'Ali, occupied parts of the Red Sea coast with British financial support. For al-Mutahhar, then, the formation of the post-war Yemeni state was taking place in a global landscape under European hegemony and divided starkly among the imperial powers—the British, French, Italians, Russians, and their local proxies. What distinguished Yemen from the rest of the Islamic world was the presence of Imam Yahya, who had maintained the country's moral purity and political independence, which al-Mutahhar explained as a sign of the Imam's piety and righteousness: "if God on high had not blessed this land with Imam Yahya then its fate would be that of other lands."[40]

But al-Mutahhar was not alone in locating a special providence in Yemen's independence after the collapse of the Ottoman state. Many activists, indeed, saw Yemen and its Imam as playing an important role in the reformulation of an Islamic caliphate and what was increasingly seen as an Arab public sphere. In the years prior to the war, Rashid Rida attempted to secure the agreement of Imam Yahya, 'Abd al-'Aziz b. al-Sa'ud, and Sharif Husayn to form a political union in the Arabian Peninsula that would actively oppose the Ottoman government and form the core of a later Arab caliphate.[41] After the collapse of the empire and the abolition of the Caliphate, Rida argued for the creation of an Arab caliphate that would guard the moral life of the community and act as a unifying element against the threat of empire in the period after the war. Ideally, the future Caliph would conform to the legal conditions established by the consensus of the community and would be charged with guaranteeing the application of the *shari'a* and therefore securing the moral community of Muslims for the future.[42]

He located his future caliphate, as the Syrian 'Abd al-Rahman al-Kawakibi had several years before, in the Arabian Peninsula and the holy city of Mecca, a geographical imagination that he shared with the activists of the Indian Khilafat movement. United by the annual Hajj and the Prophet's testamentary command that two faiths should not be left in the Hijaz, Rida and South Asian activists such as Abul Kalam Azad saw Arabia as the eternal center of the Muslim world.[43] Although sometimes drawing on conflicting trends from within the Islamic tradition, activists in India and the Middle East invoked a shared vision of Arabia and Mecca as the antithesis of European empire and the Western state system: where the West was divided by race, class and nation, Arabia was united by the common brotherhood of submission to God, which erased all distinctions save those of

THE CENTRE OF RENEWAL AND REFORM

piety. But for Rida, Arabia was also a site of cultural authenticity, which had preserved a specifically Arab character in language and habit. It had avoided the slavish adoption of Western ideas and habits, in particular discourses of race and nationalism that had been adopted in places such as republican Turkey. As he understood it, the future caliphate would be uniquely Arab, locating in the Prophet's tribe of the Quraysh an innate virtue, religious knowledge and political savvy.

Rida also read the Prophet's injunction as a form of colonial critique, writing that "He wanted the cradle of Islam to be a fortress in which it could take refuge, to avoid giving those nations who wished to do it harm a path to intervene in its affairs as the great imperial powers are doing now."[44] It had already served this function, he suggested, when Mecca and Medina opposed the accession of Yazid b. Muʻawiya to the Umayyad Caliphate in the eight century. In his formulation, then, the Hijaz and the holy cities were the last bastions of religious, ethnic and linguistic purity which would serve as the center of the universal community and the site of a future Islamic and Arab resurgence—a place of both past and future resistance. The irony, of course, was that the Hijaz was under the control of Sharif Husayn who had allied with the British against the Ottoman state and, at least to Rida, claimed to be the King of the Arabs with Western support. Yemen, however, was quite different for "Yemen alone has preserved its independence and the Imamate for over one thousand years."[45] Moreover, he noted that Imam Yahya fulfilled all of the conditions of the Imamate as stipulated by the four Sunni schools (and the Zaydi school rarely contradicted the four schools), but he also pointed out that the Imam was well-known for his "knowledge, justice, and capability."[46] Contrary to Western observers, then, Yemen's political and, some would say, intellectual isolation was for Rida a virtue in a world dominated by European empire.

Yet, even sympathetic observers such as Rida seemed to ignore the extent to which Yemen's isolation was as much affect directed at a global Muslim and Arab public as it was real policy. Imam Yahya had, in fact, carefully engaged the Islamic public sphere through the medium of the trans-regional press since his assumption of the Imamate in 1904, a strategy that only accelerated in the inter-war period with the establishment of the state press. As he took command of the uprising against the Ottoman state, he vigorously defended his opposition in the pages of Shaykh ʻAli Yusuf's popular Egyptian newspaper *al-Muʼayyad*. His choice of this paper, popular for its anti-British tone and Pan-Islamist sympathies, suggests the Imam's astute observance of the Arabic press. Ameen Rihani noted as much in 1923 when he visited the Imam in his *diwan*, writing that "he keeps himself informed of the principal events of the world, without having to read all the newspapers of Cairo and Damascus and Baghdad, even of New York and Rio Janeiro (Arabic, of course), which are sent to him. His secretaries read them and give him a summary of the news."[47] In the inter-war period, however, the Imam turned to the journal *al-Manar* in light of Rashid Rida's sympathies with his project of reform and his political independence but also of the journal's commitment to the issues of Islamic unity and anti-imperial activism. In particular, it would be a forum to address his confrontation with the British in the Aden Protectorate, which he initiated in 1918, to a reading audience far beyond Yemen's boundaries.

In June 1923 Imam Yahya's state press (Matba'at al-Maqam al-Sharif) produced a lengthy proclamation (*bayyan*) that was sent simultaneously to the chiefs of the Aden Protectorate and to the editors of *al-Manar*, who published it that month.[48] The immediate context of its dissemination and publication was the Imam's rapid military invasion and occupation of the Protectorate and annexation of the Emirate of Dali' after 1918 (see Chapter 6). While the Imamate had long appealed to the native chiefs of the "nine tribes" to submit to his authority as the legitimate head of the community of Muslims in Yemen, the elite and the state press approached the question of the British presence in the Yemeni South as part of the larger anti-imperial moment that characterized the interwar period. In the Salafi discourse of Islamic unity, the Aden Protectorate and the construct of the "nine tribes" (*al-nawahi al-tis'a*) stood as a vivid reminder of the divisive power of colonial rule and the embodiment of Britain's goal "to leave not a single independent Islamic kingdom standing on the face of the earth."[49] The document for our purposes is important for its attempt to integrate the themes of Yemeni unity, Islamic unity and anti-imperialism in a single statement that was produced for local and trans-local consumption.

The proclamation was divided topically into two sections. The first was a non-sectarian call for unity amongst the Muslims in Yemen, and the second and lengthier section was a political call to action against the myriad forces aligned against the country. "This is a sufficient communiqué and clear statement by which we intended to give counsel to our brothers of faith and to wake the Muslims," the Imam wrote. In what followed, the Imam called for Islamic unity under a party "commanding good and forbidding wrong," arguing that a return to the straight path according to the normative model of the pious ancestors was necessary to resist successfully the encroachment of the imperial powers. Up to this point, the discourse of the proclamation was little different from similar appeals by Rashid Rida, and even earlier appeals by Jamal al-Din al-Afghani, for Muslim unity in the face of the divisive effects of European imperialism. What distinguished it from the discourse of the Salafi movement was his appeal for God's blessings on the descendants of the Prophet Muhammad who were "like the ship of Noah: those who boarded it were saved, while those who did not drowned." The message was a none too subtle celebration of his own noble genealogy and his role in uniting the community of Muslims, whether real or perceived, under his own leadership.

From there the document moved to address the issue of the Aden Protectorate. The Islamic community in the current age, the Imam argued, was in a state of fragmentation (*tafarruq*) that had as its origins conflict and dissension among believers. This ran counter to the past, in which the community enjoyed unparalleled unity (*tawhid*) in all fields of life, including religion, politics, and the pursuit of knowledge. Rather, the current time saw foreign powers dividing Muslims against one another and robbing the region of past glories and accomplishments. It was now time, he wrote, for Muslims to look inside themselves with "reflection" (*'ayn al-istibsar*) and work to restore Islam's victory and honor. As he and his supporters had stated in various announcements during the late Ottoman period, the key to unity and a resurgence of Islamic power was for all to submit to the *shari'a* and to follow the straight path set forth in God's book. In a note of triumphal self-reference, he stated that this goal had been achieved in much of his country, and the affairs of the land had been organized "according to that which pleases the all-knowing God." Yemen, he asserted, was now unified under God's law. His non-sectarian call to Islamic unity was mirrored in his understanding of Yemen as a singular historical, social, and religious formation:

Yemen is a single piece of land, its people united in race and religion, in conformance in language, close in descent with no difference between the *ashraf* and the tribes, their God is one, their Prophet is one, their Book is one, and their religion is one, with no disagreement to resolve except for those with no knowledge of the *shari'a* or its vast and clear methods. As for the people of religion and knowledge and those of minds with which they know the paths of goodness, they know that the people of this blessed Yemeni land are as the people of a single city and that it is incumbent upon them to unify word and opinion, to unify the way and ensure true allegiance until we become as one body, or like fingers (on a hand), or like a building just as God's messenger—peace and prayers of God be upon him, his companions, and his family—described the people of faith [i.e. the Yemenis].

Imam Yahya's imaginative mapping of modern Yemen suggested a unified moral and social space, a space of inclusion on the basis of the universal summons to Islam as opposed to the Aden Protectorate's space of tribal division. The call to this new space of unity was not like earlier appeals, because it was directly aimed at the rule of difference created by the British through the institutionalization of the "nine tribes" as part of the durbar model of colonial rule described in the previous chapters. This would be accomplished through universal submission to the Imam, the *shari'a*, and the normalizing practices of Islamic ritual life. In this reading, directed as it was to both a Yemeni and a global Muslim audience, the specifically Yemeni encounter with British imperialism stood metonymically for the entire community's war with empire and made Yemen's struggle the responsibility of the entire *umma*.

Yet, in its specific attention to the ongoing conflict with the British, the Imam betrayed a politics that was not necessarily governed by the interests of the community as much as it was related to his state interests. Noting that he was not interested in acquiring wealth or establishing his authority in the South, the Imam reiterated his desire for Muslim unity in geographical Yemen. He also stated, quite contrary to state practice elsewhere in the country, that "we will keep all lands in the hand of their chiefs and turn over to them their districts and ports." His only condition, of course, was that they must rule according to the Qur'an and Sunna, end bloodshed, and avoid all oppressive acts. The conciliatory tone of the message was a far cry from later dismissal of the protectorate chiefs as nothing but lowly tribal Shaykhs, wearing nothing but "sarongs to cover their genitals," who had been given the lofty title of "sultans."[50] The message then shifted to a gentle admonition to the collective *ulama* to fulfill their obligation to provide moral guidance to the faithful (presumably the "nine tribes" of the Protectorate), to command good and forbid wrong, and to revive the way of the pious ancestors (*al-salaf al-salih*). If there was any doubt that he was addressing the Yemeni South, he pointed specifically to Imams Shafi'i and Abu Hanifa as models of normative behavior. Imam Yahya ended on a note of flattery directed at the British, noting that what he was calling for was universally accepted, especially in the modern nations (*al-duwal al-mutamaddina*). This was especially so with the British, who took pride "in their love for the Arabs" and their commitment to protecting the rights of all of humanity. Yet, his invocation of a shared vision of universal rights revealed less a capitulation to imperial liberalism than a conviction of the universality of the revelation and the Sunna of the Prophet. It is difficult to say whether the Imam's reference to British affection for the Arabs was written ironically or not, in view of his occupation of much of the Protectorate by the time the document was promulgated, but his appeal to the British elicited the criticism of Syrian activists who accused him of actively seeking imperial protection, an accusation that Rashid Rida himself sought to dispel.[51]

In fact, Imam Yahya's intimation of a possible reconciliation with the British in the Yemeni South suggested the tensions that were becoming visible in his call to Yemeni and Islamic unity. Indeed, the universal aspirations of the global community of believers sat uncomfortably with the more specific goals of a thoroughly local political project. In the aftermath of the Caliphate's abolition, a series of conferences were convened that were meant to formalize the type of Islamic unity that had been the focus of so many intellectuals and activists in the previous decades. In 1926, the Rector of the al-Azhar mosque and seminary in Egypt convened a conference on the future of the Caliphate. It was only sparsely attended, marred by Egypt's limited sovereignty under British occupation and rumors that King Fuad coveted the title himself. Many notable activists on the issue declined to show up, such as Mohamed and Shaukat Ali of the Indian Khilafat movement. The conference itself moved away from its initial goal of naming a new Caliph and instead merely issued a statement that declared "the renewal of the legitimate Islamic Caliphate is possible, and it is therefore incumbent upon all Muslims in the East and West to prepare the way for it and make ready that which is necessary."[52] This otherwise positive assessment came after several delegates, including the Tunisian reformer 'Abd al-'Aziz al-Tha'alibi, argued the impossibility of reviving the Caliphate when so much of the Islamic world was under occupation or exercised limited sovereignty.

The conferences that followed did not take the revival of the Caliphate as their goal, but instead attempted to create an institutional framework in which Islamic unity could be achieved through the cooperation of states and individuals on issues of concern to the community. A few months after the Cairo conference, 'Abd al-'Aziz b. al-Sa'ud convened an Islamic conference in Mecca, only a year after his military conquest of the holy cities. Representatives from much of the Arab world attended, as did delegates from Russia, Afghanistan and Java, and Indian associations such as the Khilafat committee, the Jam'iyyat-i Ulama-yi Hind, and the Ahl-i Hadith movement. The meeting was contentious, and the issues dealt largely with the management of the Hajj and the status of the holy cities. Far from fostering Muslim unity, the conference was the scene of bitter debates over Ibn al-Sa'ud's adoption of the title King of the Hijaz, the destruction of the tombs of the Prophet's companions in the Mu'alla and Baqi' cemeteries in Mecca and Medina by his followers, and the policing of public prayer and private devotional practices by the Sa'udi committees of public virtue.[53] The Jerusalem Muslim Congress of 1931 fared little better. Organized by Amin al-Husayni and, to a lesser extent, by Shaukat Ali, the meeting avoided the caliphate issue altogether, instead looking to establish a Muslim university in Jerusalem. Again, delegates from much of the Islamic world attended, including the noted intellectuals and activists al-Tha'alibi, Rashid Rida, Shakib Arslan and India's Muhammad Iqbal.

Yemen sent delegates to all three of these conferences. Shaykh 'Abd al-Rahman b. 'Ali attended the Cairo conference, the Governor of Hudayda Husayn b. 'Ali 'Abd al-Qadir attended the Mecca conference, and Qadi Muhammad b. Muhammad Zabara represented Imam Yahya in Jerusalem. What is surprising is that in spite of the Imam's appeal—through his official announcements or the pages of *al-Iman*—to Islamic unity in the war against empire, the participation of his delegates in the Islamic conferences by all accounts was minimal. Despite the British assumption that Imam Yahya had sent Qadi 'Abd al-Wasi' al-Wasi'i to Egypt at the end of the 1926 conference to "promote the Imam's claims to the Caliphate," there is little evidence to suggest this was the case.[54] Even Qadi Muhammad Zabara, an otherwise prolific writer, mentioned only that he attended the conference in Jerusalem, saying little else of the proceedings beyond his summary of its resolutions.[55]

A number of delegations to the Imam's court seeking to enlist his aid in either Pan-Islamist or Arabist causes were similarly rebuffed. Late in 1923, the same year that Harold Jacob had visited the Imam, the Syrian Salafi activist Kamil al-Qassab made his way to the Yemeni capital as part of a project to "unite the word" of the Arabs and to quell what was becoming a growing antagonism between the Imam and Ibn al-Sa'ud. While expressing sympathy with the political project of uniting the community of Muslims against "the hostility of the Frankish nations," al-Mutahhar tells us, the Imam assured him that no reconciliation would take place between him and Ibn al-Sa'ud until the latter's continued aggression against Yemeni pilgrims had ceased.[56] In 1925, members of a Khilafat delegation led by Sayyid Sulaiman Nadvi, who had travelled to the Hijaz to assess the effects of Ibn al-Saʿud's occupation of the holy cities, went thereafter to Sanaa where they met Imam Yahya. After returning to India, they supposedly sent the Imam a number of articles critical of the Saʿudi occupation, which were "full of rancor for the Najdi."[57] The Egyptian Arabist Ahmad Zaki Pasha was similarly received a year later, and after the Jerusalem conference Zabara returned with the Indian Khilafat leader Shaukat Ali, who was given an audience with the Imam. Although all of these missions were received cordially, at least according to local accounts, they shared the singular distinction of leaving with little more than Imam Yahya's expression of general support.

Underlying Imam Yahya's hesitant participation in these conferences, it seems, was a general ambivalence toward engaging trans-local movements of Islamic reform in their institutional forms, even though he showed little reticence in claiming sovereignty over the Yemeni diaspora in neighboring Arab and Islamic countries.[58] It was becoming clear to many that by the end of the 1920s the creation of an institutional framework for the universal brotherhood of Muslims was an increasingly distant possibility. After the failed conference at Mecca, Rida published an open letter to Mohamed and Shaukat Ali of the Khilafat delegation, criticizing their opposition to Ibn al-Saʿud for having adopted the title of King of the Hijaz at a time when they were working to revive the Caliphate. On the subject of the Caliphate, Rida noted with some despair that "the Islamic world is not prepared at the moment to examine the issue or to do what is necessary for it."[59] In this age, he wrote, Muslims understand that the Caliphate meant "true Islamic governance" according to the normative model of the rightly-guided Caliphs. Only Ibn al-Saʿud fitted this model, he argued, departing from his earlier enthusiasm for Imam Yahya. In fact, he noted that although the Imam met the conditions of the Caliphate, his own people, both Zaydi and Shafiʿi, did not support his rule except when they were paid or their relatives were taken hostage. It was now Ibn al-Saʿud rather than the Imam who most completely fulfilled the project of Islamic reform and anti-imperialism that Rida had championed since the end of the war.[60] What Rida had failed to understand, at least at this time, was that Imam Yahya's commitment to the project of Islamic unity and anti-imperialism sat in ever greater tension with what became a tentative engagement with the Western state system.

A state like any other

In 1926 Imam Yahya signed a treaty with Italy, represented by the governor of Eritrea, Jacopo Gasparini. The text of the agreement was published on the front page of the first issue of *al-Iman*. In addition to establishing friendly relations between the two countries, it also called for the encouragement of bilateral trade and guaranteed Italian material and technical assistance in the development of various technical fields in Yemen, the most important of which was the military. This translated into direct assistance in the form of expertise and materials for the building of a new munitions workshop, the purchase of weapons, and even the training of a few pilots to fly two aircraft recently purchased by the Imam. Italian doctors were brought in to tend to the royal family and to open a clinic in Hudayda. By 1927, Sayf al-Islam Muhammad and Qadi Muhammad Raghib Bey were on their way to Italy to meet Mussolini personally.[61]

The entry of Yemen and the new Imamate into the community of nations was greeted with a mixture of celebration and caution in Yemen and beyond. The occasion was even thought important enough to be covered by Rida's periodical, *al-Manar*, which commended the Imam's decision to end Yemen's "political isolation" (*'uzla siyasiyya*). The article also suggested that the Imam Yahya should practice a great degree of caution concerning the country's entry into the international arena. Among other things, its author noted that history had taught that military and political influence generally follow economic influence. Indeed, from the examples of the British in India and the Dutch in Java he concluded that "the flag follows trade" (*inna al-tijara tatba'uha al-raya*).[62] The reception of the treaty within the Zaydi elite close to the Imam was no less cautious. With the announcement of the treaty, Qadi Hasan b. Ahmad al-Iryani composed a lengthy ode to the Imam on the subject of foreign relations, entitled "Candid Advice" (*nasiha sidq*), in which he warned of the danger posed by interaction with the West.[63] Any agreement with Europe, he suggested, would lead eventually to Yemen's occupation and subjugation:

> *He who takes refuge with his enemies will soon be forsaken by them*
> *And be blinded to truth and right guidance*
> *They express friendship publicly, however*
> *They are setting him up to be tricked*
> *At times giving gifts, at others growing closer to him*
> *The cunning enemy [does this] so that he might later forsake him*
> *So have the unbelievers of every age*
> *Interfered with Islam and the Muslims*

Iryani's apprehension was not shared by all. 'Abd al-'Aziz al-Tha'alibi, the Tunisian reformer whose presence at the Cairo caliphate conference was so prominent, wrote after meeting with the Imam in 1924 that his sole purpose in engaging with the European nations was ensuring their "recognition of Yemen's independence and that it is but one of the states in Asia."[64] Thereafter, the internationally recognized bilateral treaty became the framework for conducting relations with other countries. In 1928, diplomatic and economic relations were established with the Soviet Union, which was followed by treaties with Iraq (1930) and the Netherlands (1933).

Yet the treaty with Italy not only placed Yemen within the complex of global treaties that indicated its place as a state among others, it also made explicit the political direction in which the Imamate was heading. While the treaty recognized the independence of Yemen, it also recognized the Imam as "His Majesty, the King of Yemen" (*jalalat malik al-yaman*). The use of this title was revolutionary. As I suggested in the previous chapter, the concept of obedience had become a principal concept around which the modern Imamate was formulated, but the formal recognition of Imam Yahya as monarch indicated that he had broken irrevocably from the Zaydi past and had resituated the Imamate squarely within Sunni understandings of kingship.

Although the move was not met with strong opposition, it was, at least, privately criticized by members of the Zaydi elite. 'Ali b. 'Abdullah al-Wazir, the commander who had conquered the south and was sometimes critical of the Imam, was said to have stated in his *maqyal*, his regular afternoon *qat* chewing session, that the designation set a dangerous precedent, and that he and his colleagues had not "fought the Turks for the sake of a kingdom ... but for the sake of the Islamic Caliphate." Similarly, 'Ali b. Husayn al-Shami, who had served as a *qadi* in several different places at the Imam's command, was said to have argued with the Imam himself that the word "majesty" (*jalala*) was reserved for God alone. Moreover, he stated that even God only referred to himself in the singular first person as "I" and never as "we" as the Imam was doing by referring to himself as "our Majesty" (*nahnu sahib al-jalala*).[65] Nonetheless, the Imamate was now the Mutawakkilite Kingdom of Yemen.

To these criticisms, the Imam was said to have responded that the title itself did not indicate a change in the Imamate; rather it conformed to "the exigencies of the international situation and nothing more."[66] But the transformation of the Imamate into a kingdom had actually been preceded by the adoption of primogeniture as a basis for political succession. In the year 1343 (1924) a group of prominent *ulama* were approached to address the legal basis of the title of Crown Prince (*wali al-'ahd*), by which Sayf al-Islam Ahmad was addressed in practice.⁶⁷ By the end of the year they had written a lengthy document in which they presented their opinion, copies of which were delivered to Imam Yahya and Ahmad.⁶⁸ The opinion began with the statement that all major scholars of all legal schools had agreed by consensus that the Imamate was necessary in defending Islam and the borders of the Islamic community. Moreover, it was necessary to have an Imam to oversee *jihad*, to maintain the application of the *shari'a*, and to rule by commanding right and forbidding wrong. Up to this point the statement was uncontroversial, but what followed indicated another radical shift in the legal basis of the Zaydi Imamate. The authors of the document no longer stressed the traditional summons (*da'wa*) or rising (*khuruj*) against illegitimate rule as the obligatory path to the Imamate, instead asserting the importance of maintaining an Islamic social order and the necessity of obedience to the Imam. Drawing on the Prophetic Hadith, they asserted that the Imam should be obeyed, but also that any other claimants to the title should be actively resisted according to the Prophet's Sunna, writing, for example, that "if another [Imam] comes, fight him and cut off his head with a sword."⁶⁹

In their written legal opinion, they argued that Yemen was blessed by God with the presence of an Imam who had protected the country from foreign powers which were now "stretching their necks" (*tatawwul a'naqihim*) towards them. It was only due to the efforts of Imam Yahya, they suggested, that these countries had been kept from sowing discord among the Muslims, and for that reason they decreed that the Imamate should be bequeathed to the heirs of the Imam, beginning with his son Ahmad.

And he entrusts this position after him to his son, God on high grant him long life, Sayf al-Islam, the most learned and generous, Ahmad, son of our lord the commander of the faithful, may God increase his praises. He will be the Crown Prince executing that which God and his messenger desired from those they appointed successors in this *umma*. It is in accordance with His law (*shari'atahu*) that this is one of the established paths to the Imamate, as Abu Hashim defined it, and the majority of Imams transmitted it on [his authority], and on which the four schools [are in agreement]. Indeed, their unambiguous statements that the previous Imam specifies whom he entrusts as qualified for the Imamate [was arrived at] by consensus.⁷⁰

The legal opinion, Haykel notes, was "purely Sunni."⁷¹ Both in its emphasis on obedience to rulers and in its reference to the four Sunni legal schools rather than specifically Zaydi law, the decision represented a major departure in the configuration of the Imamate. The decision was considered

THE CENTRE OF RENEWAL AND REFORM

momentous enough for the Jamiʿiyyat-i ʿUlama of Calcutta to issue a general appeal to the Yemeni people (*al-shaʿb al-yamani*) which decried the adoption of hereditary rule, especially in light of Ahmad's unsavory character, when the Imamate had traditionally been decided according to religious qualifications.[72]

The foundation of the Mutawakkilite Kingdom sat in tension with the inter-war project of Islamic unity insofar as it signaled a rejection of a particular kind of Yemeni exceptionalism: it was no longer an isolated bastion of just Islamic rule, but a Sunni monarchy like those of Egypt, Iraq, Jordan, Afghanistan, and what would soon become Saʿudi Arabia—increasingly bound to the Western state system through international agreements. As part of the effort to promote the Mutawakkilite Kingdom's status as a state like any other in the region, we see government in the 1920s and 1930s restructured to conform to the representation of the modern, rationally organized state. Imam Yahya divided government functions among newly established ministries to which he appointed a number of his sons. There were now ministries of War, the Treasury (*maliyya*), Transport and Education (*maʿarif*). The Interior Minister was Qadi ʿAbdullah b. Husayn al-ʿAmri, who had helped negotiate the Treaty of Daʿʿan for the Imam. The face of Yemen to the rest of the world was the so-called Foreign Minister, the French-speaking former Ottoman diplomat Qadi Muhammad Raghib Bey.[73] The importance of the institution of government ministries was not so much in the bureaucratization of rule, for as the Italian traveller Salvator Aponte remarked, "it is useless to attempt to detect their ministries, by which I mean their offices or the [different] grades of the bureaucracy."[74] Rather, the creation of ministries placed the kingdom within the linguistic framework of the state, even if the Imam and his sons still monopolized power.

The Saʿudi-Yemeni War

Recalling his 1929 pilgrimage, the Salafi activist Shakib Arslan wrote hopefully of the Arabian Peninsula and its role in the future prosperity of the community of Muslims and Arabs: "All Arabs in the world take interest in strengthening, preserving, and reforming the Arabian Peninsula just as they do their own countries and birthplaces, if not more, because it is the abode of Arabism, the homeland of those who speak Arabic, and the center from which they were scattered to distant lands, and the refuge to which they will journey when repelled by fate."[75] His invocation of the holy cities as centers of undiluted Arabism and Islam was central to the inter-war project of Islamic unity, at least at it was envisioned by a number of Arab activists. By the late 1920s, however, it became clear to many that Arabia's special status could only be protected by either union of or reconciliation between the two kingdoms of Saʻudi Arabia and Yemen. If the political union of Arabia seemed unlikely in the late Ottoman period when Rashid Rida actively canvassed local rulers for their support, it seemed just as unlikely in the inter-war period, despite the declarations in favor of Islamic unity by both Ibn al-Saʻud and Imam Yahya. By the end of the decade both states were set resolutely on the path to war, one which shook the faith of Salafi activists in the moral and political project of Islamic and Arab unity.

The conflict between Ibn al-Saʻud and Imam Yahya stemmed from the collapse of the Idrisi Emirate in the mountainous ʻAsir region north of Yemen. Under the leadership of Sayyid Muhammad b. ʻAli al-Idrisi, the Emirate challenged the rule of Imam Yahya and the Ottoman state after the peace of Daʻʻan. In 1915 he signed a treaty with Britain that recognized his authority over ʻAsir and guaranteed him the political, financial, and military support of the British. After the First World War, his alliance with the British was rewarded by the continuation of his financial support and the tacit approval of his occupation of the Yemeni Tihama, including the port city of Hudayda. A conflict with another ʻAsiri tribe, however, forced Sayyid Muhammad to accept the protection of Ibn al-Saʻud, formalized in a 1920 treaty, which allied the Idrisi with the Saʻudi king and gave him a status similar to the protectorate signatories in the Aden hinterland.[76] Sayyid Muhammad was succeeded by his son ʻAli in 1923, and during his tenure his forces were expelled from Hudayda and most of the Tihama during Imam Yahya's conquest of the Yemeni South. Sayyid ʻAli was then overthrown by his uncle Hasan who, in his capacity as the new Imam, accepted full Saʻudi suzerainty in the 1926 Treaty of Mecca. ʻAli fled to Aden and later sought refuge with Imam Yahya. By 1930, the remainder of the Idrisi Emirate was annexed by the Saʻudis.

In the years following the treaty, the Yemeni military clashed with local tribes in the northern Idrisi territories, taking hostages and forcing the submission of local populations. After heated exchanges between Ibn al-Saʻud and Imam Yahya, a treaty was negotiated in 1931 that agreed to the general principle of non-interference in each other's territories. The treaty, Ibn al-Saʻud noted in a telegraph to the Imam, was not like "modern international treaties" (*muʻahhadat duwaliyya ʻasriyya*), but was built on a foundation of "Islamic and Arab fraternity."[77] This Islamic comity was broken with the outbreak of an Idrisi uprising in concert with a group of disaffected Hijazis against Saʻudi rule that ended when Hasan al-Idrisi took refuge in Yemen in the face of the Saʻudi occupation of ʻAsir.[78] Although Ibn al-Saʻud and Imam Yahya continued to exchange hostile telegrams, each accusing the other of fostering moral and social chaos and tempered only by their emphasis on preserving the unity of Muslims and Arabs, war did not break out until 1933, when Sayf al-Islam Ahmad and a military force of regular troops and tribal auxiliaries entered the oasis of Najran under the pretext of subduing the northern Yam tribe which he accused of instigating social and moral upheaval (*fitna*).

A chronicle written shortly after the war by a *sayyid* close to the Hamid al-Din family describes the conflict much as the occupation of the Yemeni South had been described just a few years earlier. We are told that Sayf al-Islam Ahmad delivered the Friday sermon in the northern town of Saʻda, in which he called on Muslims to strive for "unity of word and sincerity of intentions" in their war against the largely Ismaʻili population of Najran to whom he referred as the "party of Satan."[79] In the fighting that followed, it was said not only that the population had returned to "obedience" but that the Imam's soldiers destroyed the Ismaʻili mosques and domed tombs which "they venerated in their ignorance."[80] After a joint Saʻudi-Yemeni delegation failed to defuse the situation, which hinged in Saʻudi eyes on the Imam's refusal to agree upon a shared border and to expel Hasan al-Idrisi, Ibn al-Saʻud initiated an invasion of the Red Sea Coast and the northern mountains to expel the Yemeni forces. "We have shown patience which no person could bear," Ibn al-Saʻud announced in the state newspaper *Umm al-Qura*, and he vowed to publish the contents of the telegrams exchanged with the Imam to prove his intransigence.[81] In the brief war that followed, Saʻudi forces marched southward, ultimately capturing the port city of Hudayda. Imam Yahya's forces were expelled from Najran, but otherwise neither side reached a clear victory in the mountainous terrain of ʻAsir. Nonetheless, Imam Yahya finally contacted Ibn al-Saʻud via telegraph in early 1934, stating "what has taken place is enough" and indicating his desire to negotiate a peace treaty.

Even though the war was fought over issues that could be considered of purely local import, both Ibn al-Saʻud and Imam Yahya framed their discussion of the conflict, conducted through rapid telegraphic exchanges and editorials published in the Saʻudi and Yemeni state newspapers, by issues of

Islamic and Arab solidarity. Indeed, the means of modern communication that Rida had earlier extolled as the structural precondition for modern Islamic unity now facilitated a war between two states that had been seen as integral to the future of the Arab world and possibly even the entire *umma*. As the conflict intensified in the late 1920s and early 1930s, it was covered in ever greater detail by Rida's *al-Manar*, in which he reiterated his desire to effect a general political alliance, if not union, between the Sa'udi and Yemeni kingdoms. His principal concern, several years after abandoning the cause of the post-Ottoman caliphate, was protecting the Arabian Peninsula from the ever present danger of empire and "foreign intervention" (*tadakhkhul ajnabi*). This intervention emanated from both east and west. Rida argued at one point that Muslims hostile to Ibn al-Sa'ud's occupation of the Hijaz were secretly encouraging hostilities between the two kings, pointing specifically to the Raja of Mahmudabad and a group of Hadrami 'Alawis resident in Java who had vehemently opposed the Sa'udi conquest of the holy cities.[82] But it was the British who continued to pose the greater threat, and as the conflict intensified after 1930 Rida's appeals to both monarchs to resolve their dispute quickly and amicably betrayed an ever greater frustration. With the news that Imam Yahya's army had moved on Najran, he reiterated that, in all the Arab world, the Arabian Peninsula was the "one place in which the Western imperialists have neither sovereignty nor rule," but the Sa'udi-Yemeni conflict increased the possibility of Western intervention.[83] It was for this reason that in 1933 he could only recount the Prophetic Hadith, "woe to the Arabs from the evil that has approached."

Ending the conflict in Arabia, Rida would argue, was in the general interest (*maslaha 'amma*) of the entire Muslim and Arab community. His journal published widely on the deteriorating relations between the two kings, reproducing articles from both the Yemeni *al-Iman* and the Sa'udi state paper *Umm al-Qura*. Yet, in its coverage of the events leading up to the war and during the war itself, *al-Manar* criticized Imam Yahya with greater and greater frequency, accusing him of instigating the conflict with a Sa'udi king who had otherwise desired peace and subjecting the region to colonial intrigue. When the war finally began, the quick victory of the Sa'udi army over the Yemeni forces took Rida by surprise, especially since, as he argued, the Imam had claimed that his military was unassailable. With the cessation of hostilities, a delegation of Muslim activists representing the Islamic Conference of Jerusalem, comprising Shakib Arslan, the Palestinian Hajj Amin al-Husayni, the Egyptian Muhammad 'Ali al-'Aluba and the Syrian Hashim

THE CENTRE OF RENEWAL AND REFORM

Bey al-Atasi, set out for the Hijaz and Hudayda to negotiate a treaty between the two powers.[84] The result was the 1934 Treaty of Ta'if, which ended the state of hostility between the two kingdoms, demarcated the boundary between them, and recognized Sa'udi sovereignty over 'Asir, Najran, and the Yam tribe which had been at the heart of the conflict. The treaty was published simultaneously in *al-Iman, Umm al-Qura,* and *al-Manar,* indicating the extent to which the conflict was understood simultaneously as a local, trans-local, and Islamic conflict.[85]

For many activists in the cause of Islamic and Arab unity, the war had threatened to engulf Arabia in a divisive politics dominated by territorial and dynastic nationalisms, incited and encouraged by the European powers. After the treaty was signed, *al-Manar* pointed to its use of the phrases "Islamic brotherhood" and "Arab friendship" as indicators of a new politics of cooperation and the embodiment of earlier Salafi appeals to unity in the face of empire. There was no greater emblem of its realization than the fact that the treaty was concluded between two Imams representing the Sunni and Shi'i communities, a potent sign of hope for the ultimate union of the Islamic *umma* and its renewal.[86] In Yemen, the outcome of the war was not received in such a sanguine manner, despite the state's representation of the conflict as a momentary interruption in an otherwise amicable relationship between monarchs. Soldiers' accounts of the poor preparation of the regular army, in which many had inadequate clothing, outdated weapons from the Ottoman period, and limited ammunition, indicated the failure of Imam Yahya's military reforms, even though his soldiers had proved so effective in the earlier conquest of Yemen.[87] Italian support in the end meant less than Ibn al-Sa'ud's 1933 agreement with the Standard Oil Company, which provided the hard currency used to equip his army. But the military loss also suggested that Imam Yahya's reputation as a *mujahid,* a warrior in the name of Islam, was in question as well. For Muhammad al-Zubayri, the war was "a massive shock in the life of Yemen which exposed the failings of Mutawakkilite rule" that generated of a multi-sited opposition movement, a movement all the more important because it arose not only from the class of *sayyid*s who challenged Imam Yahya from within the Zaydi Islamic tradition of just rule, but also from an increasingly politicized group of "young" activists, inspired by nationalist discourse and a narrative of liberal progress in the face of Imam Yahya's tyranny.[88]

UNMAKING NORTH AND SOUTH

Conclusion: the limits of the gaze

Foucault wrote that "power is tolerable only on condition that it mask a substantial part of itself. Its success is proportional to its ability to hide its own mechanisms."[89] The Saʿudi-Yemeni war and the Treaty of Taʾif had the effect of unmasking the contradictions inherent in Imam Yahya's state building project and the project of Islamic reform that it claimed to encompass. The state that had been constructed since the Ottoman evacuation, with its claims to restoring Islamic rule through the power of the new regular army, appeared fragile and decrepit. Instead of the righteous Imamate Imam Yahya had created a monarchy and designated his son Crown Prince to rule what was increasingly thought of as an autonomous Yemeni homeland. Instead of Islamic unity, he had offered fratricidal conflict and division with the Guardian of the Holy Cities. Instead of resisting the West, he would secretly negotiate with the British, signing a treaty with them the very same year as the Saʿudi war. By the late 1930s Imam Yahya's "piercing gaze" which saw all and guaranteed a just Islamic order was increasingly seen by many of his subjects as woefully myopic.

In this chapter I have argued against the claim made by Western and Arab nationalist historians that Imam Yahya had committed to a firm policy of political, economic and intellectual isolation, which resulted in the preservation of his kingdom as an outpost of oriental despotism, ill-suited to the modern world. On the contrary, from the Ottoman evacuation on, Imam Yahya deftly invoked the twin discourses of Islamic reformism and anti-imperialism that had been so integral to the trans-local Salafi movement through an active engagement with the reformist Islamic public sphere that represented a trans-local "general good" (*maslaha 'amma*). The local conflicts associated with the expansion of the domain of obedience were represented as a singular instance of the larger project of moral reform (*islah*) in which the entire community of Muslims was engaged after the collapse of the Ottoman Empire and the abolition of its Caliphate. In this view, the war against the Zaraniq and later the British in the South were assaults on irreligion and European empire, just as the efforts to erase distinctions between Zaydi and Shafiʿi were essential to achieving Islamic unity. In practice, however, the project of inter-war Islamic solidarity was difficult to reconcile with Imam Yahya's state building project, which was ultimately dynastic in character and limited in its political aspirations. Thus, Yemen's participation in the inter-war Islamic conferences, the debate over the future of the Caliphate, and the general wave of anti-imperial

THE CENTRE OF RENEWAL AND REFORM

resistance were contradicted by the establishment of the Mutawakkilite Kingdom, the war with Sa'udi Arabia, and ultimately Imam Yahya's negotiations with the British in Aden—all of which were occurring as the Yemeni state claimed itself at the forefront of the interwar Islamic resurgence.

If the war with Sa'udi Arabia, despite Rida's assurances to the contrary, had revealed that Imam Yahya's concerns were local and primarily political, the discourse of reformism that he had so regularly evoked did not fall on deaf ears. In fact, while the political and discursive order of the Imamate, which had assumed the concurrence of state power and moral reform (the "piercing gaze" of elite chronicles), had come under question from members of the religious class and a politicized group of young activists, it had not abandoned the cause of reform. Indeed, the rise of opposition groups such as the Youth for Commanding Good and Forbidding Evil (Shabab al-Amr bi-l-Ma'ruf wa-Nahi 'an al-Munkar) and the Reform Association (Jam'iyyat al-Islah) did not indicate a rupture insomuch as a re-articulation of reform from within the Islamic tradition, seeking to curb the sovereign powers of the Imam and reinvigorate the faith along the lines of earlier Salafi figures and, later, the Egyptian Muslim Brotherhood.

In the final chapter of this study, I will at last look at how the two political and discursive orders under study, the Mutawakkilite Kingdom and the Aden Protectorate, converged in the inter-war period. These two geographies of rule, one rooted in the post-1857 elaboration of imperial rule based on the durbar model of consultative government and the other located in the inter-war movement of Islamic unity and anti-imperialism, entered into a period of warfare that lasted over a decade and challenged the coherency of these already unstable discursive and practical orders—these imperial spaces, to enlist Paul Carter's terminology. It is the purpose of the next chapter to investigate the way this early conflict between North and South both opened and eventually closed new horizons for politics and action in the spaces in between.

6

THE RETURN OF INDETERMINACY

Space that has been seized upon by the imagination cannot remain indifferent space subject to the measures and estimates of the surveyor. It has been lived in, not in its positivity, but with all the partiality of the imagination.

Gaston Bachelard[1]

Introduction

Harold Jacob submitted a lengthy report in 1907 which dealt with social and political conditions in the Aden hinterland. One of the few officers with lengthy experience outside Aden, he brought disturbing news from afar. In recent years, he reported, a local Sufi Shaykh had taken up residence on Jabal Harir in territory which the British had claimed in the name of the Amirs of Daliʿ. He was said to be an unofficial emissary of Imam Yahya Hamid al-Din, and although he was supposed to have been expelled from Jabal Harir by the local population, Amir Nasr b. Shayif reinstated him there. He was popularly known as "*al-majnun*" or the "mad one." His name and origins were unknown, but he was said to have miraculous powers. Soon after he settled there, he began to preach about a coming struggle or *jihad* against the British occupiers and to intrigue among some of Amir Nasr's subjects. Around the same time, a rather ominous incident occurred at the home of a tribal Shaykh to the east. This Shaykh had an enchanted brass bowl that for some time had rung of its own accord every two years. At this time in 1907, it began to ring incessantly—as if, many thought, a harbinger of things to come.[2]

UNMAKING NORTH AND SOUTH

What many felt locally was the possibility of a political realignment in the Yemeni South, for the expulsion of the British and the return of the rule of Islam. Although the sentiment was never stated explicitly, Jacob frequently heard the following verse in Daliʻ, which indicated its presence in popular culture:

> *From Haf to Jahhaf*
> *From al-Raqqa to al-Daqqa*
> *From ʻAqraqa to Hardaba*
> *From the gate of Aden to ʻAqraqa*

Each line suggested movement through the northernmost reaches of the Protectorate, through the territory of the Shaʻiri tribe, Jabal Jahhaf, the town of Qaʻtaba, and Hardaba to the gates of the British colony in Aden— poetic fulfillment of the desire for their expulsion. At roughly the same time, one of Jacob's local informants, a man of the Ismaʻili branch of Shiism who was resident in Aden, suggested that someone might come to power in Yemen after the withdrawal of the Ottoman government, a man to whom he cryptically referred in the sentence "The Imam of truth will arise" (*imam al-haqq yazhar*). When Jacob later asked him to clarify his remarks, the man explained that in Arabic numerology the value of the letters when added together indicated the year of this Imam's appearance: the Islamic year 1336 (1917/18).[3] Jacob was writing then after the end of the First World War, and he added that the man's savior had still not arrived. Perceptive on many other issues, he perhaps can be forgiven for not immediately seeing the significance of the date.

The historian Qadi ʻAbd al-Wasiʻ al-Wasiʻi recorded two major events that occurred in the year 1336. The first was the order given by Sultan Mehmed V for the beginning of the Ottoman withdrawal from Yemen. The second was Imam Yahya's arrival from Hashid territory in the garden town of al-Rawda, outside Sanaa, where he received emissaries from the tribes and *ulama*. Describing the events surrounding the event, al-Wasiʻi wrote, "there was great joy among the people at the Imam's return, the likes of which had never been seen, whereupon the senior sayyids, ulama, merchants, and notables came from Sanaa to al-Rawda to visit the Imam."[4] As I have argued in the previous two chapters, the great appeal of Imam Yahya's state lay in its ability to frame a largely local struggle within the global discourse of moral reform, Islamic unity, and anti-imperialism. His return to Sanaa at the end of the First World War fulfilled not only the vague prophecy of Jacob's informant but also, to a certain extent, Jacob's own claim that the

THE RETURN OF INDETERMINACY

Imam would "bring order out of chaos." The universalist vision of the Imamate with its message of moral and political revival, made possible by the dissolution of the Ottoman Empire and the abolition of the Caliphate, brought it into inevitable conflict with Britain's vision of empire as an association of native princes. Shortly after his arrival in Sanaa, the Imam's regular army launched an invasion of the Yemeni South and began an occupation that would last for a decade.

This chapter looks at the clash between the Mutawakkilite Kingdom and the British Aden Protectorate in the southern borderlands as part of what was an undeclared war between 1918 and 1934. Although historians have mentioned this period as essential to the constitution of the Yemeni state, the conflict was emblematic of the larger crisis of empire in the inter-war period that saw, in the Middle East alone, the 1919 revolution in Egypt, the 1920 uprising in Iraq, and the Syrian Revolt of 1925–27.[5] While Erez Manela is no doubt correct to suggest the importance of Wilsonian internationalism embodied in the Fourteen Points in inspiring a wave of inter-war anti-imperialist activism, the Imam's call for Yemeni unity in the face of British aggression was simultaneously a claim for his own role in crafting a globalized vision of Islamic internationalism in opposition to empire. Alternately referred to as a new Kaiser Wilhelm, an Arab Bolshevik, or at best an Arab Mussolini, the Imam was a specter for British imperial power on the wane.[6]

The purpose of this chapter is to explore the erasure, both ideological and practical, of the protectorate border by the Imamate in this period, and to map out the types of tactics it made possible on the part of the local population along the southern borderlands. This conflict is fascinating because it created an interstitial political space between the North and South that was not fully part either of the Imam's "domain of obedience" or of the British Aden Protectorate. Rather, both were present and absent in the borderlands. No historians, however, have drawn attention to the intense struggle over the conceptual geography of the hinterland and the practices deployed to make "real" the Imamate as it decisively erased the borders of the already fragile colonial order. Moreover, they have yet to investigate the complex interaction between the colonial, Imamic and local political and social orders, and even less so the kinds of tactics deployed by the border populations in order to maneuver through these multiple and often overlapping fields of power.

These spaces, subject as they were to both the Mutawakkilite Kingdom and the agreements of the British Protectorate, were heterotopic in nature—juxtaposing in a single space multiple and competing forms of institutional

UNMAKING NORTH AND SOUTH

and discursive power. This period of warfare in the borderlands was a direct challenge to the British concept of the "nine tribes" and the long process by which they, as a cultural and political construct, came into being. If language and colonial knowledge were integral to the production of a class of native princes, founded in history and made relevant through their incorporation into the rituals of empire, the border war brought this language into question. As Foucault argued, "*heterotopias* are disturbing, probably because they secretly undermine language, because they make it impossible to name this *and* that, because they shatter or tangle common names."[7] The profound ambivalence this conflict produced was narrated in various ways. For the British, this was a momentary setback which would be settled with the reassertion of the agreement concluded with the Ottomans delimiting the frontier between North and South. For the Zaydi chroniclers it was *fitna*, a state of moral and political dissension, which could only be resolved by the implementation of Islamic law under the authority of the Imam. For the population of the Protectorate, overrun by soldiers from the north and left by the British to fend for themselves, this was *rabsha*, a term that in the Yemeni dialect invoked disorder, chaos and fear.

This chapter takes as its point of departure Imam Yahya's general call or *da'wa* to the population of the Protectorate to return to obedience and a unified Islamic community in Yemen, free from tribal and sectarian discord. The appeals of the Imam and their quick reception among many parts of the protectorate population revealed the tensions inherent in the form of indirect rule practiced by the British. I then move to the military occupation of the Emirate of Dali' and the governmental practices that were imposed by the Imam's administrators as the Amir's domain was incorporated into the metaphorical and practical space of obedience. I argue, drawing on the example of the Qutaybi tribe, that the heterotopic space of the borderlands enabled a particular kind of tactics in which the local population was able to move deftly between the conceptual and practical orders of obedience and protection. The war was ultimately concluded by force with the British introduction of aerial bombardment to the Yemeni South and the reinstatement of the Anglo-Ottoman status quo. That is, the border between North and South remained the same.

The call to obedience

The military invasion and occupation of the Aden Protectorate did not come unannounced. Prior to the end of Ottoman rule and the evacuation of its

THE RETURN OF INDETERMINACY

soldiers, Imam Yahya had begun an organized campaign to call the tribes under British protection to rejoin the "domain of obedience." As mentioned in Chapter 4, a tendency by historians to take the Treaty of Da'an at face value in terms of its creation of a sectarian form of rule has meant that the Imam's decidedly non-sectarian claims to rule have been ignored. Although he was recognized as the legitimate head of the Zaydi community in the northern highlands, as has been noted he was already addressing himself to "the people of Yemen, both Zaydi and Shafi'i." This appeal to the people of what could be called "greater" Yemen, in fact, preceded his treaty with the Ottomans and went beyond the borders of Ottoman authority. As early as 1909, Imam Yahya was in communication with several of the protectorate signatories in the South; most of the messages came to the British in Aden through rumor and messages filtered through local informants. The message was consistent with that heard elsewhere from the Imam: submit, enforce the *shari'a*, and institute correct ritual practice.

The Imam's appeals were first directed along the borders of British authority, especially in Wadi Bayhan and Jabal Yafi'. The inhabitants of Wadi Bayhan in the north-east of the Protectorate only came into contact with the British during the Anglo-Ottoman Boundary Commission. The population of the valley, like that of many of the areas in treaty relations with the British, was mixed and did not conform to the British concept of the "tribe." The British, in fact signed the protectorate treaty of 1903 with a *sharif* or descendant of the Prophet, Ahmad am-Muhsin, rather than with the powerful Bal Harith or Mas'abayn tribes in and around Bayhan al-Qisab.[8] As the British later admitted, the hereditary *sharifs* of Bayhan had influence only with the Bal Harith and none with the much larger Mas'abayn tribe who lived in the largest settlements in the valley.[9] By the terms of the treaty, they had only agreed to protect those peoples and areas under the control of the *sharifs* rather than the entirety of the valley, a seemingly minor point which would later haunt the British in Aden. Like in other regions, especially along the margins of British authority, the fragmentary nature of local authority made Bayhan fruitful ground for the Imam's appeals.

In 1909, notables from Wadi Bayhan began writing to the Aden Residency warning the British government of Zaydi preparations against them. They had received letters from the Imam and his supporters and, worried that his soldiers in the nearby region of Ma'rib could easily move against them, they forwarded these messages to Aden. Some of the tribes of Khawlan had submitted to the Imam, as had those of Ma'rib, and their region could be next. It was reported that an influential *sayyid* of the Al Bu Bakr b. Salim, the hereditary administrators of the *hawta* or shrine of 'Inat in the Hadramawt, had allied himself with Imam Yahya and joined his forces in Ma'rib.[10] More important, this *sayyid* had begun contacting the tribes and *sharifs* of Bayhan, commanding them to return to the fold of the Imamate. In a letter to the principal Shaykhs of the Mas'abayn tribe, the *sayyid* called upon them to submit to the Imam, noting that "obedience to our lord the Imam is obligatory (*fard lazim*) on all Muslims as stated in the Holy Quran: 'Obey God, His Messenger and those in authority among you.'"[11] That the summons was cast in terms of obedience should not be surprising, nor should the fact that it was being made by a non-Zaydi descendant of the Prophet. The call to submission from this Shafi'i *sayyid* was couched in a characteristically Sunni claim to political authority: the obligatory nature of obedience to the Imam. While it could be argued that this letter, and others like it which the *sayyid* sent to several notables in the region, was tailored to appeal to the Sunni population of the South, it was in keeping with the doctrinal and political shift in the Imamate that was discussed in the context of the creation of the Mutawakkilite Kingdom after the Ottoman withdrawal in 1918. That is, even prior to the institutionalization of Imam Yahya's position as Head of the Zaydi community in the Treaty of Da"an, he was making claims to the leadership of the entire Muslim population of Yemen by appealing across sectarian lines.

Imam Yahya's claims to authority in Bayhan were little different from the ones given by those who chronicled his campaigns in the tribal northern and eastern parts of the country. In a communication with the 'Abdali Sultan of Lahj, the Imam wrote that his interest in the valley and its inhabitants was merely related to his desire to implement the *shari'a* and enforce the worship of God.[12] His interference was necessary to bring order, security and correct religious practice to the region. In spite of the large community of descendants of the Prophet, the country had lapsed into a chaos whose source was the absence of religious knowledge. "We hear," he wrote in another letter, "that people living in the east do not discriminate between what is lawful and what is not." They had fallen into a condition in which they engaged in innovations in belief and practice (*bid'a*) and relied, not on God's law, but on custom or *taghut*.[13] The South, however, differed significantly from the rest of the country by its relationship with the British colony in Aden and the protectorate system put in place to manage the tribes.

THE RETURN OF INDETERMINACY

The same *sayyid* from the Bu Bakr b. Salim clan wrote letters criticizing the *sharifs* and the tribes for their contact with the British, or the "Nazarenes" (*nasara*) as they were called. It was a particularly grievous offence for the *ulama* of Bayhan to send people to see British officials or present grievances before British courts.[14]

In Jabal Yafi', in which political authority was fragmented between the ruling houses of the Upper and Lower Yafi'i Sultanates as well as among numerous tribal sections, Imam Yahya's appeals found a receptive audience. The British had signed a protectorate treaty with the Bani Qasid Sultan of Lower Yafi' in 1895, but the treaties signed at the time of the Boundary Commission were evidence of the growing realization that the "native chiefs" of the region did not command full authority. As I mentioned in previous chapters, the relationship between ruling houses and surrounding tribes often entailed complex and overlapping rights and obligations that bore little resemblance to the type of full authority the British had hoped they could command. The treaties signed in Upper Yafi' were an admission of this complexity. In 1903 the British signed protectorate agreements with the Al Harhara Sultan of Upper Yafi', but they also signed separate treaties with the Shaykhs of the major tribal sections (as they had not done in the case of the agreements with the Bani Qasid Sultans in Lower Yafi'); these were the Dubi, Mawsatti, Muflahi, Hadrami, and related Shu'aybi sections.[15]

As in Bayhan, by 1909 the Shaykhs of the Yafi'i tribes began receiving letters from Imam Yahya and his supporters calling them to enter into "obedience." In Aden, letters were sent from local informants and some of the treaty signatories reporting that numerous Shaykhs had been contacted by the Imam and called to visit him. Stipends, honorific robes, and payments of other kinds were said to have been promised.[16] Sayyid Muhammad 'Ali al-Sharif, referred to in British reports as the Imam's "emissary," was in intermittent correspondence with the 'Abdali Sultan at this time and actually sent him a list of the men with whom the Imam was corresponding. In all, the Imam had contacted the Sultans of the Upper and Lower Yafi'i Sultanates and thirty-eight Shaykhs of the various sections under them.[17] The principle was one of divide and rule as the later critics of Britain's Protectorate would say, and many Shaykhs who were otherwise unimportant found themselves courted by the Imam.

The conditions of submission were always the same: obedience to the Imam was obligatory, as was the payment of *zakat*. One letter written by Imam Yahya himself in 1911 was forwarded by one of the Mawsatti *naqib*s to the Aden Residency. In content, it was similar to other letters sent by the Imam to various regions after the peace of Da"an, extolling the conclusion of the treaty and the danger presented by both the British and the Idrisi in 'Asir. The Imam presented the treaty as a great victory for Islam, especially in the face of potential foreign aggression from the British in the South and against the Ottoman Empire in the world at large. The main body of the message, however, was an affirmation of the religious obligations of all Muslims and the role of the Imamate in enforcing them. He reiterated the duty of Muslims to perform the ritual acts of worship, the fast, the pilgrimage, and to engage in "commanding good and forbidding wrong." As in much of the *sira* literature, however, the payment of *zakat* was emphasized above all. It was necessary, he stated, to support the poor, the beggars, and one's neighbor: "such *zakat* will purify the giver" (*tuhra tutahhiru sahibaha*).[18]

In the British records one can follow the movement of the Imam's appeals to the protectorate tribes across the hinterland as reports of contact increasingly arrived from areas in greater proximity to Aden. By 1912 the Amir Nasr b. Shayif of Dali' (the son of Amir Shayif b. Sayf from Chapter 3) was in contact with Imam Yahya, as were the Shaykhs of the Hawshabi and 'Alawi tribes. Sayyid Muhammad Taha, a local informant on Jabal Jahhaf, reported that representatives of the Zindani Shaykhs had travelled to Sanaa to meet the Imam, and later reported that he had himself received a letter from Shaykh Muhammad Salih al-Akhram al-Qutaybi concerning Qutaybi correspondence with the Imam.[19] A Shaykh of the Azraqi tribe, one of the tribes considered subject to the Amir of Dali', wrote that Sayyid Muhammad 'Ali al-Sharif had come to Dali' to reconcile the Amir with the Sha'iri tribe and the people of Jabal Jahhaf with whom he was in conflict (see Chapter 3).[20] Again, the presumed motive behind these attempts to contact individual Shaykhs and to claim the right to resolve disputes between them and the protectorate signatories was to undermine the fragile appearance of order on which the British had based their presence in South Arabia. This was already apparent to Amir Nasr b. Shayif who wrote to the Political Resident that the Imam was "now writing secretly and openly in all directions and is arranging and collecting all his forces and their requirements for the time when it shall arrive."[21]

This could not have been welcome news. As was mentioned in Chapter 3, the British had only just managed to negotiate an end to the conflicts between the Amir of Dali' and the 'Alawi and Hawshabi Sultans over the control of the road leading from Lahj to the northern border along the

THE RETURN OF INDETERMINACY

Amir's territory. It was only in 1912 that an agreement was signed with the Qutaybi tribe, theoretically subject to the Amir, to take responsibility for securing parts of the road in return for some of the privileges of a protectorate signatory. Similarly, new treaties regularizing customs dues were only signed with the 'Alawis, Hawshabis and Qutaybis between 1914 and 1915. For the British, the period following the removal of the Dali' Agency in 1907 and the conclusion of these treaties was a time of major realignment of the space of the "nine tribes" on which the British Protectorate was based. The multiple forms of sovereignty exercised by the Amir had become quite clear through his inability to bring a modicum of security to the trade routes and to command the type of loyalty the British assumed he should. Harold Jacob's earlier assertion that the Indian model of the "native chiefs" had failed was only too true.

Erasing the Protectorate

Although an internationally recognized boundary between the British Aden Protectorate and the Ottoman province of Yemen had been delimited, the line itself remained little more than an administrative fiction. It was a political boundary indicating spheres of influence that had limited effect on the everyday lives of the population. To turn again to Harold Jacob, he was one of the few British officers to suggest that most people living on either side of the boundary were little affected by it. To a certain extent this was true. In legal matters, those living in Dali' could bring their cases before the *qadi*s of the Amir or they could just as easily appeal to those in the Ottoman town of Qa'taba. Nor were relationships and alliances necessarily mirrored in the border either. The *naqib*s of Mawsatta, themselves part of the Upper Yafi'i Sultanate and protectorate signatories, counted as their clients the inhabitants of Juban, Na'wa, and Muris on the Ottoman side of the border.[22] Yet, Jacob's assumption of the boundary's relative unimportance as part of everyday life in the Protectorate is deceptive insofar as it failed to consider the extent to which the boundary and the idea of protection or *himaya* might have repercussions in extraordinary circumstances or in moments of crisis. With the withdrawal of the Ottoman administration at the end of the First World War, Imam Yahya's expansionist form of state formation was extended into the area of the British Protectorate. As Jacob himself noted, in the view of many inhabitants in the Aden hinterland "the Imam was "*barrah*," or like the cyclone which drives all before it."[23]

The borderlands of the Daliʿ Emirate once again became the epicenter of the conflict with Imam Yahya as they had during the Anglo-Ottoman confrontation at the turn of the century. Not unlike the period of confrontation surrounding the Boundary Commission's work, there were again questions regarding the Amir's authority. In this case, Amir Nasr b. Shayif had fallen out of grace with the British during the First World War. With the Protectorate occupied by Ottoman soldiers and the absence of British assistance, the Amir had allied himself with the Ottoman government. After their withdrawal, the Amir was left without British recognition and without the financial and military assistance on which his power and authority were based. It was largely on account of the possibility of conflict along the borders that Amir Nasr was rehabilitated in British eyes, and primarily through the insistence of the ʿAbdali Sultan who argued that he had lost his influence among his tribesmen as a result this policy. By the autumn of 1919, the British could no longer afford to neglect the Amir.[24]

What prompted the British to renew Amir Nasr's status as protectorate chief were the increasingly urgent reports of what were routinely described as "suspicious" movements by the Imam's military along the borders. Reports arrived of the Imam's soldiers in the border areas of Juban and Naʿwa of the Rubiʿatayn tribe, and later in the area of Muris.[25] These were not merely reconnaissance operations but part of what would become the incorporation of the protectorate polities into the complex of state practices that constituted the "domain of obedience" to the north of the boundary. If we are to believe the letters sent to the Aden Residency by its informants, the soldiers of the Imam were not only making a show of military strength but also setting the stage for the fiscal and possibly the bureaucratic incorporation of the Aden hinterland into the Imam's state. Prior to the outright occupation, soldiers were sent to assess the borderland villages for the purpose of future taxation.[26] At roughly the same time, both the Imam and his representatives in the town of Qaʿtaba were contacting Amir Nasr, the tribes theoretically subject to him, and the ʿAlawi Shaykh. The letters called the men and their followers to return to obedience, to pay the *zakat*, and to maintain security on the roads.[27] More specifically, the territories of the Shaʿiri tribe, the people of Jabal Jahhaf, and the region of Daliʿ itself were claimed as part of the district (*qada*) of Qaʿtaba, a claim made real when the Imam's soldiers constructed a customs post in the village of Sana in Shaʿiri territory. The claims made by the Imam, over both the conduct of the local Shaykhs and the economic life of the region proved, in the words of the

THE RETURN OF INDETERMINACY

'Abdali Sultan, "the ambitions of the Zeidis to occupy the whole country, extending as far as Hadramout."[28]

What followed this first attempt to create a physical claim on those residing within the boundaries of the Aden Protectorate was an occupation by the armies of Imam Yahya which lasted over a decade and challenged the appearance of order meticulously constructed over nearly one hundred years. By the end of 1919, several thousand soldiers under the command of Sayyid Yahya b. Muhammad b. 'Abbas (d. 1962) entered Dali', claimed the region as part of the Imam's domains, and forced Amir Nasr to hand them a hostage from his own family to ensure his obedience. Sayyid Muhammad b. Muhammad al-Shami was appointed Governor. The new government even tried to bolster the Amir's brother, 'Abd al-Hamid b. Shayif, as a local figurehead. Amir Nasr fled the town, making his way to Aden where he took refuge in the Aden Residency.

For 'Abd al-Karim al-Mutahhar, the occupation of Dali' was part of the extension of the domain of obedience as an absolute space of moral rectitude, within which there was no room for compromise. As in his accounts of the Imam's campaigns elsewhere in Yemen, his narrative pointed to the general disobedience of local Shaykhs and headmen who had upset traditional hierarchies based in historical custom and practice; only the specifics of time and place differentiated the campaigns. From the perspective of the learned elite, the people of Dali' had realized that their country was in a state of "chaos and dissension" (*fawda wa-fasad*) and immediately wrote to the Imam offering their obedience. The principal point of contention, in this view, was that Amir Nasr had previously submitted to Imam Yahya during the First World War and had turned over a hostage from his family, but that he had now broken his covenant with the Imam by turning to the British. For Mutahhar, this betrayal was not of contemporary significance only, for it overturned a longstanding hierarchy by which the Amirs of Dali' had recognized the suzerainty of the Zaydi Imams, at least since the early eighteenth century. This much was made clear in a letter of advice supposedly written by Sayyid Yahya after his initial victory, in which he urged Amir Nasr to remember "the blessings of previous Imams on his forefathers, for their authority over Dali' had benefited from the Imams' beneficence and was extracted from their ocean, even though his great grandfather was a slave (*mamluk*) to those who gave him command over this land."[29] Mutahhar's reference to the less than noble origins of the ruling house of Dali' was likely meant not only as an insult but also as a reassertion of the primacy of the Prophet's house or *ahl al-bayt* in the formation of a polity united under God's law.

The Imam's armies subsequently moved against Jabal Yafi', defeating the Lower Yafi'i tribes at the Shu'aybi village of Quz'a.[30] By 1921, the Imam's soldiers were moving out from the Dali' plateau against the Ahl Aj'ud confederation of the Radfan mountains while in the west, 'Ali b. 'Abdullah al-Wazir's soldiers moved into the Wadi Sha'b and Wadi Ma'adin in Subayhi country. By 1925 there were ongoing skirmishes and occasionally full-blown battles along most of the protectorate frontier, from the westernmost part of Subayhi country to the eastern reaches of the 'Awlaqi and 'Awdhali territories. This was accomplished with mostly small numbers of *nizami* troops and tribal irregulars, generally in the hundreds, armed with rifles and often accompanied by tribesmen from local communities who had submitted to the Imam. By the spring of 1921, it was estimated that Imam Yahya had fielded some 3,000 men in the area of the Protectorate who were then reinforced with local recruits from the Sha'iri, Shu'aybi, Rubi'atayn, and Halimayn tribes.[31]

"But the main point," Imam Yahya wrote to Sultan 'Abd al-Karim in Lahj in explanation of the occupation of Dali' by his soldiers, "is the desire of our lad Sayid Yehia bin Mohamed to put on a proper footing the rules for the security of the roads and to maintain order wherever he is."[32] What constituted order became increasingly clear as a pattern of colonizing practices emerged that was intended to rewrite the political geography of the Protectorate hinterland. Imam Yahya's claim to the *zakat* of the region was enforced by groups of soldiers who visited the major tribes and villages to collect taxes. Reports came in that Sayyid Muhammad was sending soldiers to collect taxes amongst the Azariq, the communities on Jabal Jahhaf (*ahl Jahhaf*) and the Radfan tribes, and into Hawshabi, 'Alawi, and Subayhi territory.[33] Perhaps less obvious was the practice of demolishing the small forts (referred to as *dar*s or *buyut*) that dotted the hinterland and were used for defense and garrisoning. Rather, as had happened in the protracted conflict over the trade routes in the early part of the century, the Imam's army would lay claim to particular areas by erecting small forts and placing small numbers of soldiers in them as permanent garrisons. The Imam's troops were also simply destructive, confiscating household belongings and crops to sustain their own military campaign and to force local communities to submit, a tactic that was extremely effective after successive years of drought. The Imam's position on these activities was quite clear. In a letter

THE RETURN OF INDETERMINACY

to the Aden Resident, responding to British complaints, the Imam simply wrote that they were part of the internal procedures related to "royal Yemeni administration" (*al-idara al-malakiyya al-yamaniyya*).[34]

The Imam's military incursion across the border put the British in the awkward position of having to fulfill the terms of their protectorate treaties. The treaties of protection both outside Aden and in the wider Persian Gulf had been concluded on the basis of the perceived threat from other European colonizing powers, not local states. While the government in Aden demanded that Imam Yahya recognize its relationship with the "nine tribes," there was still a question as to what the British obligation to the tribes actually was. The minority opinion, which was quickly dismissed, was that the Imam was not a "foreign" power at all and therefore did not fall within the parameters of the treaties.[35] Yet, there was no talk of sending British troops (or Indian, since the garrison in Aden was drawn from the Subcontinent) to Dali' to protect their Arab protégés, which would have run counter to the general policy of non-intervention that had held since the end of the Dali' Agency in 1907. Rather, an intermediate policy was accepted by which protectorate signatories in the areas under threat would be supplied with modest numbers of rifles and ammunition. The policy was one of minimal confrontation and was meant to forestall full British military engagement outside Aden.

The perhaps over-legalistic reading of the protectorate treaties did little to make sense of the local context of British aid and its role in the creation and maintenance of alliances. By early 1920, the Amir had returned to his family's ancestral homeland of al-Kharafa to organize resistance against the Imam. In addition to ammunition, rice, flour and dates, he requested blood money payments for the families of future casualties and cloth for burial shrouds. In a series of letters to the major Shaykhs of the Radfan tribes, the Halimayn and Ahl Aj'ud confederation, Amir Nasr made a general call to resistance. The tribes responded according to the very general terms of their allegiance with the Amir, stating that "everyone will do such acts as is becoming of his reputation."[36] The relationship was one of "*sum'a wa-tub'a*" or "hearing and following" in which the tribes were under an obligation to answer the Amir's summons to war. Nonetheless, as was argued in Chapter 3, this relationship was largely contextual and in no way implied a permanent alliance. As the Amir himself understood, the coalition was cemented, not by a shared sense of allegiance to his leadership and cause, but by his role as patron and source of largesse. This was made clear to the Aden Residency in a letter prior to the Amir's counteroffensive, in which he made requests for food, money, weapons and ammunition for those tribes who had offered to fight: "We have told you of the customs and usages (*qawaʿidna wa-siyarna*) between us and our tribesmen and their customary rights which we have to bear at the time of necessity and demand (*waqt al-lazm wa-l-talab*). The time has now come when they ask for them."[37] The united front the Amir presented to oppose the Imam was created through the deliberate and careful distribution of largesse and the conclusion of short-term arrangements with local Shaykhs and headmen. While in purely material terms the Amir's financial support was needed in a time of ongoing drought and near famine conditions, the distribution of wealth was also part of the expected magnanimity of someone with claims to leadership and authority. By no means could the loyalty of his supposed subjects be taken for granted, and his requests for ammunition and financial support were constant lest his fragile coalition disintegrate.

The Amir's attempt to retake the town of Daliʿ was unsuccessful. Although the coalition held together, they found the buildings of the town garrisoned by the Imam's soldiers. The initial assault against the lightly garrisoned town seemed successful; surrounding villages were captured and a fort built by the occupying force was retaken. Shortly thereafter, however, the garrison was reinforced by troops from Qaʿtaba and the surrounding region, and they were in turn joined by men from the Ahl Muris, Ahl Shuʿayb and Ahl Jahhaf, and the Shaʿiri tribe. Why exactly so many of the Amir's supposed subjects joined the Imam's forces will be discussed below. Sayyid Yahya had managed to field around two thousand men with rumors circulating of five thousand more arriving as reinforcements, while the Amir's men were in the hundreds. In light of the asymmetry of the two sides, the Imam's troops easily retook Daliʿ and destroyed one of the Amir's forts.[38] The army then began to move against the tribes of Jabal Radfan who provided the bulk of the Amir's fighting force.

The conflict then shifted to the Wadi Taym, the valley at the bottom of the northern slopes of Jabal Radfan, whose course could be followed into Yafiʿi country. Following the pattern established in the campaigns in and around Daliʿ, the offensive began with the Imam's representatives appealing to the Shaykhs of tribal sections in an attempt to fragment local opposition. Individual Shaykhs and headmen of the Ahl Ajʿud confederation were ordered to submit to the Imam's authority and forestall military defeat. The Hujayli tribe which sat at the northernmost part of the valley

THE RETURN OF INDETERMINACY

was the first to receive such an offer. The principal Hujayli Shaykh resisted, but a lesser Shaykh named Haytham Hasan gave his own brother as a hostage and led the Imam's soldiers in early 1921 to the homes of the principal Shaykhs. In the fighting that ensued, the Hujayli Shaykh's own sister was reported to have been beheaded by the invading force.[39] The Shaykh and his followers then fled to the territory of the Ahl 'Abdullah tribe where they were reinforced by a number of the other Ja'di (plural Aj'ud) sections, including the Qutaybi. In spite of the previous years of famine which had caused many of the local men to emigrate and sell their weapons and the incessant shortage of rifles and ammunition, an estimated three to four thousand of the Imam's soldiers were stopped.[40] They were similarly repulsed after the Bakri tribe's Shaykh, whose son was taken as a hostage to Qa'taba, led the Imam's soldiers to his territory. While they managed to loot and burn a number of villages, including the house of the Qutaybi Shaykh Muhammad Salih al-Akhram, they were again repulsed and withdrew from the Radfan area by April.

Imam Yahya's effort to defeat and conquer the Radfan tribes had failed, but the greater part of the Amir of Dali''s domains remained under his control. Nor did the Imam's offensive end in the Taym valley. As a local *sayyid* wrote to the various Yafi'i tribes, "Taim is the door and Yafa is the store room." This was not an exaggerated claim meant to bolster the resolve of those who would resist the Imam. Indeed, fighting continued in the ensuing years along the Yafi'i frontier into the area of Bayda' and the 'Awlaqi and 'Awdhali territories on the eastern edges of the Protectorate. Perhaps more alarming, both for the British and for their protégés, was that the early fighting revealed the limits of the protectorate treaties. On the one hand, the British had been taken by surprise by the rapidity with which many of the Amir's subjects had sided with Imam Yahya and had even joined his army to move against Amir Nasr. The tribal order that early on had been reduced to an "Amiri" tribe was no more stable than in the period of the Dali' Agency in the first decade of the twentieth century. The defection of Jabal Jahhaf and the Sha'iri, Hujayli and Bakri tribes suggest what a heterotopic place South Arabia could be; that is, it was a space whose organizing principles were not visible, certainly not to the British. As we shall see, for the protectorate signatories this descent into indeterminacy meant that the order of the protectorate agreements was even more important, even while the inactivity of the British brought their worth into question. "It is a well known fact to all Powers and tribesmen," wrote a local Shaykh, quick to remind the British of their agreements, "that you are the protector of the nine directions (*al-tis'a al-nawahi*) from the aggression of every enemy. These parts bear your name and they are your borders and the tribesmen are yours and under your protection."[41]

Rabsha and the tactics of the everyday

A letter was sent to the Kathiri Sultan in Hadramawt by the 'Awlaqi Shaykh's son Farid b. Muhsin in 1929.[42] He reported the efforts of the Imam to force the population of Wadi Bayhan to submit and hand over hostages to the state. His fear was that the 'Awaliq would be next and that they were poor in both fighting men and treasure. The letter suggested overwhelming alarm as he noted, "the people of Bayhan and those near them are in *rabsha*." The word *rabsha* in Yemeni dialect means a general condition of fear, chaos, or disorder. In many of the letters to the Aden Residency prior to Imam Yahya's invasion of the South, the term was invoked repeatedly to suggest a general confusion or an apprehension of things to come.[43] The vague premonitions of near apocalyptic change that were repeated to Harold Jacob ten years prior to the Ottoman evacuation were at least partially fulfilled with the beginning of the Imam's military occupation in the South. In everyday terms, the violence and destruction caused by the Imam's army created a general climate of fear and anxiety, at least so far as can be told from the colonial archives. The attempt to incorporate the region into the conceptual geography of the "domain of obedience" also created a situation in which the political hierarchy based on the British concept of the "nine tribes" was almost immediately undone.

Without a doubt, much of the anxiety expressed by the protectorate signatories stemmed from the very real conditions brought on by war, but there was also a general *rabsha* brought on by the very indeterminacy of the protectorate agreements and, by association, the meaning of British support. Invocation of the treaties of protection was nearly universal in the letters penned by Britain's protégés in the Aden hinterland. Expressing vexation at Britain's hesitance in fulfilling what they considered to be the Aden's obligation to defend them, writers couched requests for ammunition and weapons in the language of "treaties" (*mu'ahadat*) and "protection" (*himaya*). The notion of protection as *himaya* here is especially important as it paralleled local concepts of refuge and protection. The obligation to come to the defense of the protectorate signatories was not merely a legal require-

THE RETURN OF INDETERMINACY

ment, but a moral duty as well. In a political language that called on British military support on the basis of the "sanctity of the state, its treaties, and its protection" the Aden government was honor-bound to support its agreements, just as the Amir of Daliʿ expected the Ahl Ajʿud to come to his aid in a time of need.[44]

The initial British hesitation to enforce the text of their protectorate agreements beyond shipping small amounts of rifles and ammunition left large parts of the population to fend for themselves. At the intersection of obedience and the remnants of the protectorate order, people engaged in what can best be described as de Certeau's "tactics," which he also described as ways of "making do." That is, rather than engaging in forms of outward resistance (although there was armed resistance too) people engaged the various modes of ordering and the ruling practices that were being imposed on the countryside by the British and Imam Yahya, subverted them, and used them for their own purposes. In the process of doing so they produced a new spatial history, in Paul Carter's terms, through the various tactics used to ameliorate their disadvantageous position in a complex of asymmetric power relations. Again, the situation in the Emirate of Daliʿ is instructive.[45]

After the initial occupation of Shaʿiri country, Jabal Jahhaf, and the town of Daliʿ, it will be recalled, Amir Nasr b. Shayif was able to put together a loose coalition of the Radfan tribes, the Ahl Ajʿud confederation in particular, for defense against the Imam's army. The diffuse nature of the Amir's authority, as I suggested in Chapter 3, was really a form of multiple sovereignty by which his rule was maintained through the conclusion of multiple agreements with different populations in time and space. These entailed very different rights and obligations, meaning that any alliance would require great expenditure of social and material capital and could only exist in very particular contexts. This alliance, as the Amir informed the British on countless occasions, would only last so long as the threat was immediate and he could supply cash, supplies, and most importantly, weapons. Nearly two decades after the British first began to remark on the limited nature of the Amir's authority, they still did not seem to understand that his power to persuade and unite was dependent on the generous distribution of gifts. "Do not think that our departure without assistance, maintenance nor sufficient supply of ammunition is an honor to you," the Amir wrote after a disappointing visit to Aden in 1921, "it is on the contrary a reflection on both you and ourselves."[46] By offering only intermittent assistance, the British had both reduced their own honor in the eyes of the local population and, by restricting the Amir's ability to show his generosity to his people, put his honor into question as well. In the vernacular, they had "blackened" the Amir's face as well as theirs.[47] The failure of British authority, and by association of the Amir's authority, pushed his subjects to seek other political relationships.

The limits of the Amir's authority over the surrounding population were indicated by the rapidity with which the Shaʻiri tribe and the residents of Jabal Jahhaf submitted to the Imam's forces and actually participated in the campaigns against the town of Daliʻ and the Ahl Ajʻud. Similarly, Shaykhs from the Hujayli and Bakri tribes of the Ahl Ajʻud were quick to cooperate with the invading armies after submitting relatives as hostages. In the case of the Bakri and Hujayli Shaykhs there was a basis for the general British understanding that they allied themselves with the Imam unwillingly as a result of, as one officer put it, *"force majeure."* With the people of Jabal Jahhaf and the Shaʻiri tribe, however, their cooperation was due less to compulsion than to the possibilities presented by the political upheaval resulting from the Imam's invasion. Imam Yahya himself targeted the polities and populations theoretically under the Amir's authority, offering official recognition, stipends, and bestowing gifts liberally. In fact, as the Imamate expanded into the Protectorate, we see the empowerment of hitherto unimportant Shaykhs who had, in British terms, been considered subjects of Amir Nasr.

Through the mid-1920s we see the slow extension of the politics of the Imamate into the Protectorate and their entanglement in the local political landscape. Again the Qutaybi example is useful insofar as it sheds light on the types of tactics that were available to the local population at the intersection of Imamic, British, and local power. The Qutabyi Shaykh, Muhammad Salih al-Akhram, who had given the British so much trouble in the period of the Daliʻ Agency had joined Amir Nasr in his opposition to the Imam's army. During the Amir's failed attempt to retake the town of Daliʻ the support of the Qutaybi tribe was absolutely essential, fulfilling its role as the "spearhead" or *sinan* of the Ahl Ajʻud confederation. By the beginning of 1920, however, the Imam had already been in contact with Muhammad Salih's nephew, Muqbil ʻAbdullah, along with a number of the protectorate signatories in an effort to convince him to submit to his rule and enter into "obedience."[48] Just as the Imam had earlier formed a relationship with Amir Nasr's own brother, ʻAbd al-Hamid, in an attempt to create a rival figurehead in Daliʻ, he was now trying to do the same within the tribe that was arguably the strongest military force in the area.

THE RETURN OF INDETERMINACY

When the Imam's armies attempted to take Jabal Radfan through the Taym valley, the extent of Muqbil 'Abdullah's role in the conflict became apparent. 'Ali Ibrahim, who was in the field with the Amir's forces as an agent of the British, wrote to Aden describing what amounted to a geographical and political convergence in the territory of the Qutaybi tribe.[49] He noted some fifteen villages along the Wadi Taym that had submitted to the Imam under the threat of military force. All of these, he wrote, were situated along the bed of the valley rather than in the hills like other Qutaybi sections and were therefore vulnerable. These villages, however, were also theoretically under the leadership of Muqbil 'Abdullah, rather than Shaykh Muhammad Salih. Ibrahim suggested that impetus for Muqbil 'Abdullah's submission and active alliance with Imam Yahya had to do with a dispute over money. Shaykh Muhammad Salih was said to have refused to pay his nephew a portion of his British stipend, and his submission to the Imam had been rewarded with both a stipend and an allotment of the taxes gathered locally. This supposed agreement does bear some resemblance to those al-Wasi'i argued were concluded between the Imam and the protectorate tribal leadership.[50] Whether the dispute with his uncle actually took place—it was typical of the British to attribute all forms of what they considered treachery to pecuniary interests—is unclear. Just as likely an explanation was that Muqbil 'Abdullah, sensing the imminence of an invasion and the vulnerability of the low-lying villages of the Taym valley, willingly made terms with the Imam. That the Imam also offered a stipend and a portion of taxes was merely an additional incentive.

Both Muqbil 'Abdullah and 'Abd al-Hamid had travelled to the town of al-Nadira of which Sayyid Yahya was the Governor, where they submitted hostages and, one presumes, consulted with the Governor on their role in Radfan.[51] Thereafter both men began to correspond with the Shaykhs and headmen of the various Radfan tribes in an effort to convince them to submit to the rule of Imam Yahya while collecting taxes in the Imam's name.[52] In effect, Muqbil 'Abdullah became an intermediary for the Imam, forwarding letters written by those in his employ. In one such letter Shaykh Muhammad Salih urged him to submit without resistance while taking care to note the Imam's interest that there should be no bloodshed. "We would like to come to a peaceful arrangement," one Qayid b. Rajih wrote, "in order to avoid bloodshed among the Moslems."[53] Yet the letter also contained the explicit warning to cease his disobedience and resistance, adding, "if you are doing so in order to assist the Infidels and displease the Lord of the Universe, there is no remedy but to turn you out (of your country) in order to please God." This pattern of discreet warnings and overt threats was used by Muqbil 'Abdullah himself in his correspondence with his uncle and other notables of the Qutaybi tribe:

> You have wisdom like mountains but God has deprived you of them. You do not accept advice from him who offers it to you. You have neither revolved your minds nor taken into consideration the position of those who are more powerful than you such as Bin Mohsin [the 'Abdali Sultan] and others. They are corresponding with the Imam and are friendly to him. You desire to become Khalifs and copy the Somali Mulla who was a Somali. The Imam is powerful. It is no good for you to try to emulate him. Wait till God determines. Your exilement in the hills and that of your families is worst [sic] than death. It is wonderful (strange—*'ajib*) when sections desire to fight and make such of himself while it cannot furnish a hostage. When I left Dala they were building houses. If they built houses in your country you run away and later you would sue for peace, and at that stage you will not get it. Please dissuade our father Mahomed Saleh to excuse himself and not to cause the devastation of the country and people. The Akhram family are not angels. They are of the ordinary creatures of God. Let him come to pay a visit and we shall undertake that the hostages are kept for certain months. My son is already in Dthala. The other clans should also leave their hostages for certain appointed months. It is better to save yourselves than to spread yourselves on the hills of the World.[54]

Muqbil 'Abdullah's letter castigated his uncle by comparing his desire for independence to the infamous "Mad Mullah" who had so challenged the British in Somalia earlier in the century. To become like a caliph or "khalif," as it was translated by the British, meant to ignore the legitimate authority of the Imam and the inherent right of those descended from the Prophet Muhammad to rule the Islamic community. Muhammad Salih was not of noble descent, but an "ordinary creature of God," and therefore should rightfully submit. Eventually Muqbil 'Abdullah's efforts paid off.

In the summer of 1923 news began to reach Aden that Shaykh Muhammad Salih al-Akhram had submitted to the Governor of Dali' Muhammad al-Shami. Word was received from the Aden hinterland that he had received several loads of grain from the government in Dali', and shortly thereafter the Shaykh himself contacted Aden to inform the Resident that he would be making terms with the Imam. This was not a surprise; one official went as far as admitting that the British could not counter the Imam's message nor his threat of force, making it "most difficult to persuade the tribes of our Protectorate from yielding eventually to Zeidi pressure."[55] The Qutaybi Shaykh, who had been on the frontlines of the fighting, apparently felt he

THE RETURN OF INDETERMINACY

could no longer sustain an active resistance and wrote that he would be "left like a bird without wings" if he did not at some point give in to the Imam's entreaties. Yet, this was not submission in the sense of surrender, but the engagement in a shared ritual of alliance and political incorporation. As narrated by 'Abd al-Karim al-Mutahhar, the righting of the Qutaybi hierarchy becomes synonymous with the righting of the religious hierarchy on which the domain of obedience was based:

> When the Amir [Sayyid Yahya] learned of the anxiety with which they had arrived and of which they had swallowed in this matter, and that they had repented and desired to enter the door of peace, he began to correspond with them and welcomed Muhammad Salih al-Qutaybi to enter into obedience. They found in this the fresh breeze of virtue and sincerity under whose influence they tired of their anguish, so they came running to obedience and rushing to their homelands. They gave that which was demanded of hostages and documents of obedience and submitted. Their grief then ended and they were protected from the vicissitudes of resistance. Shaykh Muhammad Salih al-Qutaybi arrived at the Amir's residence and he was accepted with honor and respect. The Amir then garrisoned Jabal Radfan, improved its state, pulled up the roots of deviance, and returned to Dali' enveloped in the joy of God, the Designer.[56]

The return of the Qutaybi Shaykh to obedience and his placement in a hierarchy at the top of which sat the Imam was also effected through a series of rituals performed when the Shaykh visited Dali' to submit. Muhammad Salih al-Akhram arrived in Dali' with two hundred and fifty supporters and was greeted with the firing of four cannon shots. Whether this bit of state pageantry was intended to mimic the British symbols of rank used in the Protectorate is unclear, but it does suggest an explicit message from the Imam that the Shaykh's status would not change. While there, he was given what the British called "robes of honor" for both himself and his grandson along with a monetary gift. The gift is itself important as it suggests parallels with Mughal and Ottoman ritual acts of incorporation through the bestowal of robes or *khil'a*, by which the recipient symbolically became part of the ruler and shared in his authority.[57] The fact that this was a political language shared both by the Imam and the tribal Shaykh indicates the extent to which the "domain of obedience" easily accommodated local practices. Shaykh Muhammad was appointed Governor or *'amil* of Jabal Radfan and assigned thirty soldiers and an army officer. More importantly, the rank he was assigned and the benefits it brought reasserted his position in the local social and political hierarchy. He was given the right to one tenth of all taxes collected and the right to twelve annas per camel from any caravan.[58] His nephew, Muqbil 'Abdullah, was only allowed four. The order had been righted.

Especially intriguing in this episode is the ease with which people moved between the various forms of social and political ordering, the myriad ways in which boundaries material and conceptual were crossed. Disrupting the carefully constructed boundaries of obedience and protection, the Qutaybi Shaykh moved deftly between his positions as tribal Shaykh, protectorate chief, and *mujahid* in the name of the Imam. For Paul Carter, it was the "wandering state" of the indigenous Australian population that disrupted European imperial histories, rooted as they were in the supposed universalism of the map and the geography it represented. In the case of the Qutaybi Shaykhs, as well as other inhabitants of the Aden hinterland, it is more useful to think in terms of de Certeau's concept of "tactics" by which cultural consumers navigate the spaces created by hegemonic power. Tactics are not forms of resistance but ways of using these spaces at cross purposes as a form of reappropriation: "a tactic insinuates itself into the other's place, fragmentarily, without taking it over in its entirety, without being able to keep it at a distance."[59] On this basis, it is possible to understand the ease with which people maneuvered between the British protectorate order and the moral order of Imam Yahya without fully committing to the terms of either. Protection was cast as the moral obligation of *himaya* which the British had failed, at least early on, to fulfill. Submission to the Imam was acceptable only insofar as it reasserted the local hierarchy of the Qutaybi Shaykh over his rivals and was cemented through rituals not especially different from the British version of the durbar as practiced in the South. It was this ease of movement between different regimes of power that the British then tried to stop.

Defending the map

The situation that had developed in the protectorate borderlands since the Qutaybi Shaykh's submission to the Imam was slowly becoming intolerable for the British. There had been no more incursions outside Dali' after the ill-fated campaign in Jabal Radfan; only a garrison of one hundred soldiers remained in the town of Dali' itself.[60] By the late 1920s, military activity had moved further to the east, into the mountainous areas of the 'Awlaqi and 'Awdhilli tribes and the Bayda area. Nonetheless, the Amir of Dali' was still in exile as a guest of the Sultan of Lahj and there was little indication

THE RETURN OF INDETERMINACY

that the Imam's soldiers would withdraw from the area. In 1926, the British sent General Gerald Clayton to Sanaa for negotiations with Imam Yahya to discuss a potential treaty and the ongoing conflict along the border.[61] The negotiations failed when neither the Imam nor Clayton could agree over the status of the protectorate territory under occupation. The failure of the negotiations and the growing relationship between the Imam and the Italian and Soviet governments made it clear to the British that the issue of the occupation should be settled before the Imam received much-needed military aid from abroad.

Perhaps more alarming than the Imam's growing willingness to deal with outside powers was the fact that his government was providing a measure of security and stability in the areas recently brought under its control, the like of which the British had never been able to provide in their Protectorate. Both Imam Yahya and 'Ali b. 'Abdullah al-Wazir in Ta'izz, for example, had complained to the British on several occasions, deploring the lack of security along the trade routes, especially in Subayhi country. In a particularly ironic letter, Imam Yahya complained of the Sabayha's "interference with the route, their terrorizing the travellers thereon, and their depredatory and homicidal acts while the whole of Yemen, by the grace of God, is in a state of entire quietude and rest."[62] His solution to the matter of securing the trade routes was little different from that so often proposed by the British: disciplining the Sabayha was the duty of the 'Abdali Sultan of Lahj.

Nor had the Imam's occupation of Dali' and his control of the trade routes into Aden affected the trade between North and South. While the Imam had early on redirected inland trade to the Red Sea port of Mukha, its subsequent silting caused merchants to move back to the overland routes. Despite the continuous skirmishes along the borders of the Protectorate, trade continued to move through Subayhi, Hawshabi and Amiri territory, so much so that it could be written in 1926 that, "the occupation of Dala and other British Protectorate districts has consequently not interfered with the trade by land between Aden and the interior."[63] Figures on inland imports and exports suggest that this was indeed the case; with only minor fluctuations, trade remained relatively stable through 1926.[64] It was only because of the Imam's occupation of the port of Hudayda in 1925 that some exports were redirected to that port rather than to Aden.

Despite British protests, the Imam's incorporation of parts of the protectorate, especially Dali', into the administrative structures of his kingdom, no matter how rudimentary, had not created chaos but a certain level of order. Moreover, the relative calm that followed the early clashes on the Daliʿ plateau and Jabal Radfan once again put the utility of the Protectorate agreements into question. In the negotiations between Imam Yahya and Gilbert Clayton in 1926, the Imam refused to relinquish territories within the British Protectorate in which he had established "regular administration."[65] Although initial drafts of a treaty deferred the delimitation of the boundary between the Imam's lands and the British to a later period, the British position was that a full withdrawal should occur before full negotiations. No agreement was reached before Clayton's departure and the status quo remained. The general climate of calm and security that prevailed in at least some parts of the Protectorate convinced Harold Jacob, always an admirer of Imam Yahya, that all of Britain's tribal protégés excluding Lahj should be abandoned to the Imam. He was perhaps the first British official to remark publicly on the utter lack of security in the British Protectorate compared to the Imam's domain. Leaving the Aden hinterland to the Imam, in his mind, would return South Arabia to its "natural" leader and earn for the British the general gratitude of the Arab population.[66]

British reticence ended in February 1928 when the Imam's soldiers abducted the ʿAlawi Shaykh and Shaykh Muqbil ʿAbdullah al-Qutaybi. The Political Resident in Aden wrote in a letter to the Colonial Office, "The outrage now reported is the culminating act."[67] It just so happened that this "culminating act" had occurred only one year after the responsibility for Aden's defense was transferred from the British Army to the recently formed Air Ministry.[68] The use of the aeroplane as a means to project state power and to punish and discipline subject populations had already been tested in Iraq in the early 1920s. Both cheaper and more effective than ground troops, air power was soon portrayed as the military panacea for defeating and even preventing rural uprisings and potential revolts. From then on, Aden was to be defended primarily through preemptive and punitive bombing, supported secondarily by small groups of infantry.

After warnings to release the Shaykhs went unheeded, permission was granted to commence bombing.[69] Prior to the aerial assault on the Northern army's positions, reconnaissance flights took extensive photos, not only of the towns of Daliʿ and Qaʿtaba, but also of the city of Taʿizz, the major southern city of the Imamate. The precision photographs taken by reconnaissance flights suggested that the British had now attained the perspectiveless gaze that allowed them to see beyond the indeterminacy of tribe and landscape. Their "piercing gaze" was now more complete than that of the

THE RETURN OF INDETERMINACY

Imam himself. Bombing began in March 1928, targeting Daliʿ, Qaʿtaba, and the village of Mawiya. The British also threatened to support the Zaraniq tribe in the Tihama who had just begun their revolt against the Imam's government. Efforts to negotiate ended when the Imam refused to withdraw from the Protectorate and bombing recommenced, extending to the town of Taʿizz.

The introduction of the aeroplane into South Arabian military culture was almost immediately evident as tribesmen began writing letters calling for support from the *tayyara* against the Imam's soldiers. After nearly ten years of hesitation, the military calculus had shifted in favor of the British and their protégés, who were quickly provisioned and organized to attack the Imam's garrisons in Daliʿ. Qadi Yahya b. Muhammad al-Iryani (d. 1943) reflected on this new balance of power in great dismay after witnessing the effects of aerial bombardment:

> *Don't think the destruction of cities will sap*
> *our strength or soften hard fortitude*
>
> *This is savagery; you've come*
> *with that which we don't have*
>
> *Battle is only battle if you are among those*
> *who in war fear not enemy soldiers*
>
> *You'll see who among you and who among us stays*
> *firmly bound to his adversary*
>
> *Indeed, if you took to the field you'd see*
> *each man of strength melt steel!*
>
> *You'd see us inflict on you devastation*
> *of such greatness that a child would go gray!*[70]

Despite the arrival in Qaʿtaba of reinforcements from Taʿizz, the Amir of Daliʿ was able to return to his palace with an army of allied tribesmen and the support of the aeroplane. The Aden Protectorate was evacuated and the Imam's troops fled north. The Air Ministry pilots were instructed to target those fleeing, whether by pack animal or car, with machine guns.[71] For those who fled their positions after the British bombardment, the reaction of the Imam was far harsher. Iryani notes that a group of tribesmen from ʿIyal Yazid fled Daliʿ after the attacks and returned to their homes in Arhab. As punishment for their desertion, Sayf al-Islam Ahmad sent troops to destroy their Shaykhs' houses and confiscate their property.[72] Even so, for at least some of the Imam's supporters, their defeat by the British and their allies did

193

not diminish the discursive power of the Imamate's imagined moral geography, in which piety and righteousness could defeat technology. As one young *sayyid* encountered by Ameen Rihani put it, "yes, the *taiyara* [aeroplane] came and threw two bombs at us. But we read the Fatihah [opening chapter of the Koran] against it, and she straightway disappeared."[73]

Conclusion: geography triumphant

Kevin Hetherington has argued that heterotopias are by nature points of passage in the larger process of ordering.[74] That is, heterotopias are located outside but relative to normative spaces, but by providing an alternative to hegemonic spaces they also create a space of possibilities that is ultimately generative of new forms of potentially hegemonic power. The indeterminate spaces that were constructed on the borderlands of the Imamate and the Protectorate, perhaps inadvertently, provided the context for greater ordering, for the reinforcement of boundaries rather than their erasure. Imam Yahya's defeat in Dali' and subsequent retreat north of the border encouraged the commencement of full-scale negotiations with the British that resulted in the 1934 Anglo-Yemeni treaty, signed on 11 February of that year.

The treaty in its final form differed little from that negotiated with and rejected by Imam Yahya in 1926. While the occupation of Britain's Protectorate was no longer at issue, it reserved the settlement of Yemen's southern frontier to a later, unspecified date. Moreover it specified that both parties would "maintain the situation existing in regard to the frontier on the date of the signature of this treaty."[75] This article, in particular, would become a point of contention in later years under Imam Yahya's successor, his son Imam Ahmad, precisely because no one could define what specifically "the situation" at the time of the treaty's signing was. The argument was not merely about semantics. The period of heterotopia on the borderlands had resulted in a drastic shift in British colonial policy in the Protectorate in the three years preceding the treaty.

With the arrival of Bernard Reilly, who was Political Resident of Aden and then Governor from 1930 to 1940, the British government officially adopted what was called the "forward policy" in the Protectorate.[76] The Imam's occupation of Dali' had revealed the fallacy of non-intervention and it was decided that direct British influence was needed, financially, militarily and culturally. A 1930 conference of the major "native chiefs"

THE RETURN OF INDETERMINACY

convened in Lahj provided a space in which the importance of tribal authority and its link to the British in Aden was reinforced. Aden and the hinterland were now to be inextricably intertwined, a point brought home in the conference when the Political Resident at the time, G.S. Symes, noted the increasing numbers of surveillance flights that had taken place over the Protectorate and the increasing need for new landing grounds upcountry "to facilitate communications with the Chiefs in the Interior."[77] British policy in the hinterland thereafter was conducted with various forms of small-scale institution building, supported by aerial bombardment. In 1928 the Aden Protectorate Levies were formed, following the pattern of Jacob's earlier Yemen Light Infantry, to support the RAF's activities in the hinterland. British personnel were later sent upcountry to organize tribal guards on modern lines for their protectorate signatories. In 1937 a medical dispensary was established in Dali', the first of its kind since Harold Jacob's Dali' Agency was withdrawn from the region in 1907. That same year a school for the sons of the native Chiefs was opened to educate the hinterland aristocracy in the methods of benevolent authoritarianism. Also in that same year, the administration of Aden was relinquished by the Indian government and placed under the Colonial Office. The Protectorate, with the inclusion of the Hadramawt region, was divided into Western and Eastern regions.

For Imam Yahya as well the conclusion of the treaty presented the opportunity to concentrate on the ordering of the Mutawakkilite Kingdom, both internally and externally. The Yemeni-Saudi war broke out in April of that year and the tribesmen and regular soldiers who had been stationed in the south were now needed in 'Asir and the Tihama to defend the Kingdom's northern borders. Internally, it was in the period after the treaty that the Hamid al-Din dynasty was institutionalized through the appointment of the Imam's sons to official positions as governors and ministers in the newly-formed ministries. In particular, it was in this period that Sayf al-Islam Ahmad and Hasan took over the Ta'izz and Ibb provinces and helped to break permanently the power of Bayt al-Wazir in Lower Yemen. It was also the end of conflict in both North and South that allowed the Imam to institute ever more intrusive forms of fiscal and military power, as I argued in the previous chapter, which resulted in the collapse of the Imam's "piercing gaze" as people began to question the benevolence of his rule.

For the moment, however, both the Mutawakkilite Kingdom and the Aden Protectorate as imperial spaces had been reinforced through the experience of, and ultimately opposition to, the indeterminate space of the borderland. The period after 1934 was, for the moment, one of "geography triumphant" as Joseph Conrad wrote just ten years earlier for *National Geographic* magazine.[78] He was referring to the end of what he called the period of "geography militant," the period of the great explorers scrambling to fill in the blank spaces on the map in the name of scientific progress, commerce, and empire. Felix Driver is right to describe the essay as a "nostalgic lament for the spirit of heroic exploration."[79] While no one, as far as I know, lamented the 1934 treaty on either side of the border, it marked the end of imperial expansion in South Arabia, just as it marked the end of the triumphalist vision of Islamic rule in all of geographical Yemen.

CONCLUSION

UNMAKING NORTH AND SOUTH

In the Western desert there are scattered Ruins of the Map, inhabited by Animals and Beggars. No other relics of the Geographic Discipline can be found anywhere else in the Land.

Jorge Luis Borges[1]

In the early 1950s, Wendell Phillips and his recently organized American Foundation for the Study of Man began several years of exploration and archaeological fieldwork in the easternmost areas of the Aden Protectorate. The team was most eager to explore the ancient site of Timna, which was located in the territory of the Sharifs of Bayhan. Although Bayhan was technically within the British Protectorate, Imam Yahya had never ceded his claim to the area. After Yahya's assassination in 1948, his son and successor Imam Ahmad came to power and was just as reluctant to recognize British claims over the Yemeni South. Beyond Bayhan, Phillips also wanted to extend his work to the desert town of Ma'rib, far in the eastern desert and only under nominal state control. He and his team, after much effort, were given an audience with Imam Ahmad. After polite introductions and the presentation of a number of gifts from the American team, Phillips and the Imam discussed the object of their journey and the possibility of new archaeological discoveries. One subject of discussion was a map of the disputed areas made by the expedition's cartographer, Friso Heybroek. What aroused the Imam's interest in particular was the fact that Heybroek had drawn the border between the Aden Protectorate and the Mutawakkilite

UNMAKING NORTH AND SOUTH

Kingdom with a series of dashes and question marks. A situation that Phillips assumed would provoke an angry response from Imam Ahmad was met instead with gentle though slightly wry humor: "Next time, please remove the dashes and leave only question marks."[2]

Geography is never static. Imam Ahmad's implicit recognition (and whether it was intentional or not is irrelevant) that boundaries and spaces are contingent and ultimately contextually specific has been at the heart of this study. If the national historical narrative of modern, unified Yemen has assumed the presence of a singular Yemeni space and identity waiting to be discovered, I have attempted to show that all such spaces are effects of particular constellations of knowledge, power, and practice. Spatial practice as I have used it here is an attempt to narrate the processes by which "imperial histories," representations of space as eternal and unchanging, are produced. The historiography of the Yemeni nation and its Northern and Southern precedents has been far too wedded to a narrative of state-formation and nation building that has, in effect, attempted to erase the question marks from Yemen's modern map. That is, most histories have taken for granted a universalist assumption that takes the state and nation as historical subjects. I have tried instead to look at the highly contested nature of spatial history by writing the histories of the Yemeni North and South into those of Britain's Indian empire, the post-Tanzimat Ottoman state, and the inter-war movement for Islamic unity.

Of particular importance to this project has been the explicit recognition of the contingency of space as an effect of complexes of knowledge and power on both sides of the North-South border. Each chapter has been illustrative of the process of making and unmaking of particular spaces, and, in fact, each chapter has ended with the collapse of a particular mode of ordering or disciplining spaces and those who inhabited them. The meticulous process of constructing an edifice of order based on the histories and genealogies of "ruling Chiefs" in the Aden Protectorate had the unintended consequence of undermining the very Chiefs it was meant to strengthen. The incorporation of the Protectorate tribes into the symbolic and administrative framework of the Indian Residencies was part of the careful elaboration of an idea of sovereignty rooted in an idealist conception of the Indian and Yemeni past that posited a political landscape of what Dirks in the Indian context called "little kingdoms." Yet, the protectorate system, by making the tribal hinterland legible through the complex of state ritual, treaties, stipends and ethnographic knowledge, tended to produce its

CONCLUSION: UNMAKING NORTH AND SOUTH

own negative—a landscape that was just as chaotic and illegible as the way in which the Protectorate was ordered.

Both the Sabayha and Qutaybi tribes, in a manner of speaking, were products of the very processes of ordering that marked off the "nine tribes" as objects of colonial knowledge and administration. In Chapter 1, for example, I argued that the Sabayha tribe was criminalized by the Aden government precisely because it did not correspond to the typology of the tribe that had been established earlier, based on the example of the 'Abdali Sultanate. Moreover, the Sabayha were problematic because they were enmeshed in larger networks of trade and migration in the Red Sea, which put into question the very notion of geographically bounded tribes. The Qutaybi on the other hand were the product of the British inability to reconcile the boundary determined by the Anglo-Ottoman Boundary Commission with the forms of multiple sovereignty exercised by the Amirs of Dali'. If British delimitation of the boundary was as much an effort to make legible a hostile tribal landscape as it was a political arrangement with the Ottoman administration to the north, the period of the Dali' Agency (1902–07), as I argued in Chapter 3, revealed the impossibility of absolute order. The Qutaybi tribe arose as a problem of the colonial order when it became apparent that the tribe was not a subject of the Amir, but a potential challenger. The failure of colonial knowledge in this instance was enough to cause the seasoned colonial officer Harold Jacob to declare the end of the Indian model of indirect rule and call for a new form of colonial administration that took into account what he called the "vast democracy" of the tribal hinterland.

These histories illustrate Zygmunt Bauman's contention that the defining characteristic of modernity has been the ceaseless quest to order as a means to exterminate ambivalence. "Modern practice," he wrote, "is not aimed at the conquest of foreign lands, but at the filling of the blank spots in the *compleat mappa mundi*."[3] Although he was writing metaphorically, the equation of geographical knowledge and European colonialism has been one of the principal concerns of this book. As I suggested in the second half of the book, however, the war to eradicate indeterminacy was not unique to the colonial state but was also integral to the constitution of the Mutawakkilite Kingdom as the domain of obedience. The representation of Imam Yahya's Yemen as an absolute moral space was dependent on a geographical imagination which distinguished between the areas under just Islamic rule and those in a state of moral and political dissension (*fitna*), disorder (*fawda*) or opposition (*khilaf*). But if the narrative thrust of much of the rhetoric of Imam Yahya's state allowed no room for spaces in between, the everyday practices of governance allowed careful accommodation of local practices otherwise considered at odds with the form of just rule supposedly exercised by the Imam. Imam Yahya's "piercing gaze" (*nazr thaqib*) was to ensure the continuous application of reform (*islah*) in his domains in an effort to cultivate the moral capacities of his subjects, primarily through the administration of the law and the collection of *zakat*. Yet, the state's unprecedented ability to intervene in the everyday lives of its subjects, and its use of violence in doing so, was increasingly seen as incommensurate with Imam Yahya's assertion that he ruled according to God's law. This was also the case in the greater Islamic community, in which the formation of the Mutawakkilite Kingdom, the war with Saʿudi Arabia, and the Imam's negotiations with the British in Aden sat in contradiction to his claims to leadership in the trans-local movement for Islamic unity and the anti-imperial struggle.

As I suggested in Chapter 6, however, heterotopic spaces, spaces of radical indeterminacy, were integral to the formation of new "imperial histories" in both North and South. The border war between the Mutawakkilite Kingdom and the British Aden Protectorate in the period between 1918 and 1934 created a social and political space in which the colonial and Imamic orders came into conflict, but also overlapped in a way that was unprecedented since the delimitation of the boundary between North and South in 1905. The radical juxtaposition of these competing social, political, and moral orders generated a palpable sense of anxiety in the local population, often expressed in letters as *rabsha*, a word which indicated both fear and a general sense of chaos. Nonetheless, the space between the Imam's domain of obedience and the Aden Protectorate made possible a particular set of tactics that allowed someone like Muhammad Salih al-Akhram al-Qutaybi to exist simultaneously as a tribal Shaykh, a protectorate "chief" subordinate to the Amir of Daliʿ, and a *mujahid* or holy warrior in the name of the Imam and Islam. At the same time, however, both the Imamate and the colonial state saw this type of ambivalence as a danger, and both initiated renewed efforts to reassert the previous orders. In fact, after the conclusion of the treaty of 1934, both the British and Imam Yahya embarked upon unprecedented projects of state centralization in their respective domains. That is not to say that these spatial orders post-1934 were any more stable, any less productive of the ambivalence they attempted to police and regu-

CONCLUSION: UNMAKING NORTH AND SOUTH

late, if not eradicate. In both cases, by the 1940s and 1950s the twin ideologies of secular nationalism and modernist Islam had brought both the colonial and the Imamic order into question.

The British did not abandon the edifice of colonial rule that they had constructed so meticulously, based on the notion of the "nine tribes." They came instead to the conclusion that more intervention, not less, was needed in the Protectorate. The 1930s marked the beginning of the "forward policy" first started by Bernard Reilly, which entailed the projection of British military power into the furthest reaches of the hinterland by means of the aeroplane and the concurrent projection of British power through the assignment of "Resident Advisers" to the native Chiefs. The discourse of colonial rule in the hinterland shifted from its emphasis on protection to the post-war concern with economic development and good administration, both of which were to be accomplished with British assistance. If the native aristocracy in India was outmaneuvered by the middle class nationalism of the Indian National Congress, it was the intention of the British government in Aden to ensure its continued survival in the Protectorate. The Indian model of a federation of formerly colonized areas and native states, embodied in the Government of India Act of 1935, was reintroduced in 1959 as the Federation of South Arabia, which included all of the former protectorate chiefs except for those of the Hadramawt and Upper Yafi'. The Aden Protectorate Levies, formerly an instrument of colonial policing in the Aden hinterland, was recast as the Federal Army. A capital city was founded just outside Aden, called the City of the Federation (Madinat al-Ittihad), even if it was so only in name.[4]

By the early 1950s a particular form of bourgeois nationalism arose among the commercial classes of Aden, both Arab and Indian, linked by their slogan "Aden for the Adenese," and their fear of becoming absorbed by the immigrant working class of East Africa, the Aden Protectorate, and the Yemeni North. In the same decade, the appeal of bourgeois nationalism declined in the face of the influence of Nasser's pan-Arabism and the call from a group called the South Arabian League for the unification of Aden and the Protectorate as an independent state. As the best indication of the demise of the hegemonic framework of the Indian native states, the 'Abdali Sultan himself, 'Ali b. 'Abd al-Karim, was deposed by the British in 1958 for his opposition to the federation plan and his active support of Nasserism. That the "native chief" most invested in the structure and culture of the Protectorate was both able and willing to conceive other political possibilities was perhaps ultimately more relevant to the end of colonial rule in the Yemeni South than the outbreak of an organized resistance movement on 14 October 1963 under the banner of the National Liberation Front (NLF).

In the North, the assassination of Imam Yahya in 1948 led to the formation of a short-lived constitutional Imamate under Sayyid 'Abdullah b. Ahmad al-Wazir. Sayf al-Islam Ahmad's mobilization of the northern tribes against the coup and the burning of Sanaa that followed ensured the survival of the Hamid al-Din Imamate, until 1962, but the "domain of obedience" as a political space was no longer possible once Ahmad had become Imam. As I suggested at the end of Chapter 5, the growing contradictions between the state's ability to intervene more directly in the everyday lives of its subjects and the discourse of just rule, coupled with the defeat in the 1934 war, slowly undermined the domain of obedience. In the interstices of state power, themselves an effect of these contradictions, new spaces of political possibility allowed the mobilization of a diverse group of reformers in the name of an often ill-defined republicanism. When Imam al-Badr Muhammad, Ahmad's son and successor, was deposed by a group of junior offices led by 'Abdullah al-Sallal (who were themselves products of Imam Yahya's programme of military reform in the 1930s) on 26 September 1962, the Imamate as it existed under Yahya had already fallen apart.

But what is left of these geographies, these spatial histories that were supposed to be effaced by the creation of the Yemeni nation? Contemporary Yemen is littered with the "Ruins of the Map" as Borges wrote, or, one could say, the question marks that Imam Ahmad was so desperate to erase. In spite of the efforts of 'Ali 'Abdullah Salih's government to inculcate an authentically Yemeni national identity in the country's citizens, the traces of its pasts are ubiquitous. In Aden, for example, the victory of the Northern army over that of the South in the civil war of 1994 left in its wake a resurgent nostalgia for the "civilized" government of the British. The subsequent marginalization of the Southern political class and hegemony of Sanaa led some to frame unified Yemen as a form of Northern colonization. It is no surprise, then, as Lucine Taminian has pointed out, that opponents of the government in the South revived the old slogan of the pre-independence nationalists, "Aden for the Adenese."[5] Indeed, the collapse of the Yemeni economy, felt acutely in Aden after the attack on the USS *Cole*, pushed shipping companies to find safer ports, has led some to question the idea of unification as a remedy to the ills of the political system and the economy. "*Khalas*," I was told by a young journalist in 2001 who had been praising

CONCLUSION: UNMAKING NORTH AND SOUTH

unification only a year earlier, "we've had it with unification; we've grown weary of it." He, like others I knew in Aden, looked wistfully back to the final years of colonial rule as a period of prosperity, order and hope. It is perhaps for this reason that the town has recently seen growing interest in a past otherwise condemned as an aberration in Yemen's national history. By 2002, the British government had already agreed to renovate two classic landmarks of the city's colonial past: the passenger terminal of what was formerly the Prince of Wales pier, and the clock tower, a replica of London's Big Ben or "Little Big Ben" as it is called—both in the former administrative and shopping district of Tawahi. Even the "Park of the Revolution" (Hadiqat al-Thawra) is once again graced with the statue of Queen Victoria that had up until 1967 been its centerpiece, a vivid reminder of the port's history as the first colonial acquisition of the Victorian period, until 1967 locked safely away in the British Consulate in the Khur Maksar neighborhood. In 2007, Southern frustration coalesced into a broad movement of old guard activists, members of the Yemeni Socialist Party, and the newly mobilized youth, who in largely popular demonstrations pressed the government on issues of political representation, economic policy in time of harsh structural adjustment, and the rule of law.[6] Having so far eschewed unified organization and structures of leadership, the movement has rejected unified Yemen in its current form and has called for revision of the North-South relationship, some even calling once again for Southern secession.

Nor have the vestiges of the Imamate been erased from unified Yemen. If the memories of the cemetery groundskeeper mentioned in the Introduction were fixated on the image of Imam Yahya as a pious and just ruler, the Imamate has also found ways to intervene more forcefully in the dream of unity propagated by the government. While the Zaydism of the Imams was thoroughly discredited after the revolution and the *sayyid*s politically marginalized in an anti-hierarchical culture of republican "brotherhood," the promise of just rule embodied in Zaydism has found a way of reiterating its importance in unified Yemen.[7] In its least threatening manifestation, a self-identified Zaydi political party, "The Party of Truth" (Hizb al-Haqq), was formed to participate in parliamentary elections, though with only limited success. Its participation in public life, however, has been dependent on its rejection of the concept of the Imamate and the principle of *khuruj* or armed opposition against unjust rule. In the summer of 2004, however, Sayyid Husayn Badr al-Din al-Huthi rose against the state, in opposition to Salih's alliance with America in its "Global War on Terror" and his silent support for the US invasion and occupation of Iraq. The rise of an opposition movement led by a Zaydi scholar and *sayyid* had unleashed the specter of the Imamate for the republican government and its supporters in the Islah party, a political coalition of Northern tribes, the Yemeni Muslim Brotherhood, and factions of the Salafi movement.[8] Backed by a ragtag militia called the "Believing Youth" (al-Shabab al-Mu'minin), al-Huthi resisted attempts by the government to arrest him, which led to a devastating military assault on his supporters and their villages. Huthi was killed, but his father continued the struggle, even attempting to enlist the aid of the global Shi'i community. His efforts to globalize the conflict as part of a greater Sunni-Shi'i confrontation were matched by the government's own rhetoric which placed Huthi's movement in the framework of the US-led "Global War on Terror." The conflict itself has resulted in hundreds dead, many more wounded, and the arrest and prosecution of those who have supported al-Huthi's movement, and it continues, punctuated by periods of truce, to the present day.

The dates 14 October 1963 and 26 September 1962 have now been subsumed by 22 May, the date of Yemeni unification in 1990. They all, however, have in common the assumption that they constitute both a break with the past and the resumption of a history deferred. Although this book has, as a whole, avoided an analysis of nationalism and the nation, I have framed it in part as a critique of the very notion of a national space, both timeless and uniform in character. The nation, in its geographical aspect, is a product of imperial history according to Paul Carter's formulation precisely because of its negation of history and contingency. At least in part, the nation's power as a cultural construct derives from its claim to exist beyond history—its history is not one of becoming, but of awakening. Spatial history is meant to deny the nation its ability to silence the voices that speak against it and its power to erase the presence of other, potentially alternative formulations of community. Yemen's fragile post-colonial present has been defined, at least in part, by the current state's attempt to censure and police expressions of social, religious, political, and geographical belonging that deviate from the current formulation of Yemeni unity. The recent series of economic and political crises suggest that necessity of reimagining the space of the Yemeni nation, based on a culture of inclusiveness and possibility, one that could accommodate the polyvalence of spatial history, rather than its effacement. In part, it would call for what Bauman has described as the transfer of "contingency from the vocabulary of dashed

CONCLUSION: UNMAKING NORTH AND SOUTH

hopes into that of the opportunity, from the language of domination into that of emancipation."⁹ Indeed, to return to the quote with which I began, we should celebrate the "Ruins of the Map" and the end of the "Geographic Discipline," not mourn them.

At the time of this writing, popular mobilization and concerted political action have unseated both Tunisia's Zine El Abidine Ben Ali and Egypt's Husni Mubarak. Opposition movements have arisen in Bahrayn, Oman, Syria, and Saʻudi Arabia. The Libyan government has initiated a brutally violent civil war against its own movement of opposition that has been met by US and NATO military intervention. Yemen has also seen the formation of a vigorous protest movement against the government of ʻAli ʻAbdullah Salih, which has called for his removal. The regime's violent response to protesters has resulted in an attempt by the Gulf Cooperation Council, under the guidance of Saʻudi Arabia, to negotiate Salih's resignation in the name of preserving the state. Many of these movements are calling for similar things: an end to authoritarian rule, the establishment of representative institutions guarded by the law, an end to American and Israeli hegemony in the region, and a revision of programs of neo-liberal economic reform. What these movements also have in common is their truly popular character, their inclusiveness, and their unwillingness to subordinate their movements to the parochial interests of institutionalized opposition parties. They have, thus far, refused to exchange one sovereign for another, to replace the sovereign of authoritarian rule with the sovereign of an established opposition leader or party. While revolutions, if one can indeed refer to these movements as revolutions at this time, are themselves contingent events, we can say at the moment of this writing that they carry the possibility of representing what Hardt and Negri have called the power of the "multitude."[10] That is, these movements represent the internal opposition of new global forms of dispersed sovereignty: they are inclusive, represent many classes and diverse political interests, lack a political center, but nonetheless are mobilized around particular shared social, political, and economic goals. At least for now, this is cause enough for hope.

NOTES

INTRODUCTION

1. Michel Foucault, "The Eye of Power," in Colin Gordon (ed.), *Power/Knowledge: Selected Interviews and Other Writings* (New York: Pantheon Press, 1980), 149.
2. Yahya 'Abd al-Raqib al-Jubayhi, "No More North and South," *Yemen Times*, 5–7 June 2006.
3. Lisa Wedeen, *Peripheral Visions: Publics, Power, and Performance in Yemen* (University of Chicago Press), 81–8.
4. Prasenjit Duara, *Rescuing History from the Nation* (University of Chicago Press, 1995), 4. The critique of the nation as the universal subject of history has been one of the principal concerns of Dipesh Chakrabarty, especially in his *Provincializing Europe: Postcolonial Thought and Historical Difference* (Princeton University Press, 2000). See also Ranajit Guha, *History at the Limit of World-History* (New York: Columbia University Press, 2002) and Partha Chatterjee, *The Nation and its Fragments* (Princeton University Press, 1993), esp. ch. 5.
5. Barbara D. Metcalf and Thomas R. Metcalf, *A Concise History of India* (Cambridge University Press, 2002), 133.
6. For the North, see Manfred Wenner, *Modern Yemen, 1918–1966* (Baltimore: Johns Hopkins University Press, 1967), Robert Stookey, *Yemen: The Politics of the Yemen Arab Republic* (Boulder, Colorado: Westview Press, 1978), and J.E. Peterson, *Yemen: The Search for a Modern State* (Baltimore: Johns Hopkins University Press, 1982). On the South, see Robert Stookey, *South Yemen: A Marxist Republic in Arabia* (Boulder: Westview Press, 1982) and Helen Lackner, *PDRY Yemen: Outpost of Socialist Development in Arabia* (London: Ithaca Press, 1985).
7. See, for example, Paul Dresch, *A History of Modern Yemen* and Muhammad Ahmad al-'Ashmali, *al-Tarikh al-Siyasi li-l-Dawla al-Haditha* (Cairo: Maktabat al-Madbuli, 2002). Robin Bidwell's *The Two Yemens* (Boulder: Westview Press, 1983) is the one book that tried in a single volume to write outside the param-

eters of national history, though his histories of North and South were relegated to separate chapters.

8. Although much of the work in Arabic is either implicitly or explicitly engaging in a Marxian critique of either the colonial policy of "divide and rule" of the British or the reactionary agenda of the Zaydi Imamate, it shares the same historical assumptions of liberalism: the slow and determined development of the modern state as the embodiment of human freedom. On the South see R.J. Gavin's otherwise magisterial *Aden Under British Rule, 1839–1967* (London: C. Hurst & Company, 1975) and Sultan b. Muhammad al-Qasimi, *al-Ihtilal al-Britani li-'Adan* (Dubai: Dar al-Ghurayr li-l-Taba'a wa-l-Nashr, 1992), Faruq 'Uthman Abaza, *'Adan wa-l-Siyasa al-Britaniyya fi al-Bahr al-Ahmar, 1839–1918* (Cairo: al-Hay'a al-Misriyya al-'Amma li-l-Kuttab, 1987), and Jad Taha, *Siyasat Britaniya fi Janub al-Yaman* (Cairo: Dar al-Fikr al-'Arabi, 1969). On the North see see 'Abd al-'Aziz Qa'id al-Mas'udi, *al-Yaman al-Mu'asir* (Sanaa: Maktabat al-Sanhani, 1992), 'Abdullah al-'Amri, *Tarikh al-Yaman al-Hadith wa-l-Mu'asir* (Damascus: Dar al-Fikr, 2001), and 'Abdullah b. 'Abd al-Wahhab al-Shamahi, *al-Yaman: al-Insan wa-l-Hadara* (Cairo: al-Dar al-Haditha, 1972). The Egyptian historian Sayyid Mustafa Salim is one of the few historians to expressly associate Imam Yahya with the foundation of the modern Yemeni state. That he does so only serves to illuminate the power of modern historicism. See his *Takwin al-Yaman al-Hadith, 1904–1948*, 4th ed. (Cairo: Dar al-Amin, 1993).

9. Paul Carter, *The Road to Botany Bay: An Exploration of Landscape and History* (New York: Alfred A. Knopf, 1988), xvi-xxi. His view is sympathetic with Timothy Mithcell's *Colonising Egypt* (Berkeley: University of California Press, 1991).

10. Michel de Certeau, *The Practice of Everyday Life*, trans. Steven Rendall (Berkeley: University of California Press, 1984), 91.

11. Fred Halliday, "The Formation of Yemeni Nationalism: Initial Reflections," in James Jankowski and Israel Gershoni (eds), *Rethinking Nationalism in the Arab Middle East*, (New York: Columbia University Press, 1997), 37. See also Wedeen's account of the historical development of the idea of "unified" Yemen, *Peripheral Visions*, 22–66.

12. Doreen Massey, *For Space* (London: Sage, 2005), 63.

13. de Certeau, *The Practice of Everyday Life*, 92–3. On the concept of tactics, see pp. xvii-xx. His concept of tactics is similar to Lefebvre's concept of "representational spaces," which he describes in part as "space as directly *lived* through its associated images and symbols, and hence the space of 'inhabitants' and 'users.'" Henri Lefebvre, *The Production of Space*, trans. Donald Nicholson-Smith (Oxford: Blackwell, 1991), 39.

14. Benedict Anderson, *Imagined Communities*, revised ed. (London: Verso, 1991), 170–78, Thongchai Winichakul, *Siam Mapped: A History of the Geo-Body of a*

Nation (Honolulu: University of Hawa'i Press, 1994), Firoozeh Kashani-Sabet, *Frontier Fictions: Shaping the Iranian Nation, 1804–1946* (Princeton University Press, 1999), and Manu Goswami, *Producing India: From Colonial Economy to National Space* (University of Chicago Press, 2004).

15. e.g. Felix Driver, *Geography Militant: Cultures of Exploration and Empire* (London: Blackwell, 2001), D. Graham Burnett, *Masters of All they Surveyed: Exploration, Geography, and a British El Dorado* (University of Chicago Press, 2000), Matthew H. Edney, *Mapping an Empire: The Geographical Construction of British India, 1765–1843* (University of Chicago Press, 1997), and Simon Ryan, *The Cartographic Eye: How Explorers Saw Australia* (Cambridge University Press, 1996). In addition to Carter's work, a number of these writers have been influenced by the work of J.B. Harley on mapping. See J.B. Harley, "Deconstructing the Map," in Trevor J. Barnes and James S. Duncan (eds), *Writing Worlds: Discourse, Text and Metaphor in the Representation of Landscape* (London: Routledge, 1992) and "Maps, Knowledge, and Power," in Denis Cosgrove and Stephen Daniels (eds) *The Iconography of Landscape: Essays on the Symbolic Representation, Design and Use of Past Environments* (Cambridge University Press, 1988).

16. Gyanendra Pandey, "In Defense of the Fragment: Writing About Hindu-Muslim Riots in India Today," *Representations*, no. 37 (Winter 1992), 28–9.

17. The inspiration here is Thomas R. Metcalf's argument that India played a sub-imperial role within the British Empire, providing personnel and modes of government to the colonial acquisitions in the Indian Ocean. See his *Imperial Connections: India in the Indian Ocean Arena, 1860–1920* (Berkeley: University of California Press, 2007). Also useful for conceptualizing empire beyond its administrative or military capacities is Tony Ballantyne, "Rereading the Archive and Opening up the Nation-State: Colonial Knowledge in South Asia (and Beyond)," in Antoinette Burton (ed.), *After the Imperial Turn: Thinking with and through the Nation* (Durham, NC: Duke University Press, 2003), 113.

18. Robert J. Blyth, *The Empire of the Raj: India, Eastern Africa, and the Middle East, 1858–1947* (London: Palgrave Macmillan, 2003).

19. James Onley, *The Arabian Frontier of the British Raj: Merchants, Rulers, and the British in the Nineteenth-Century Gulf* (Oxford University Press, 2007), 20–29 and 216–17. We could also point to Roger Owen's *Lord Cromer: Victorian Imperialist, Edwardian Proconsul* (Oxford University Press, 2005) and Toby Dodge's *Inventing Iraq: The Failure of Nation Building and a History Denied* (New York: Columbia University Press, 2003) for their discussion of the influence of the Indian empire in formulating policies in the Middle East in Egypt and Iraq.

20. *Laws of the Aden Protectorate* (Aden: Government of the Colony of Aden, 1939), 26. It should be noted that historians of the eastern Hadramawt region have convincingly argued the importance of modes of mobility, the elaboration of

genealogies, and the place of diaspora in the constitution of Hadrami identity and history. See in particular Engseng Ho, *The Graves of Tarim: Genealogy and Mobility across the Indian Ocean* (Berkeley: University of California Press, 2006), Ulrike Freitag, *Indian Ocean Migrants and State Formation in Hadhramaut: Reforming the Homeland* (Leiden: Brill, 2003), and Linda Boxberger, *On the Edge of Empire: Hadhramawt, Emigration, and the Indian Ocean, 1880s-1930s* (Albany: SUNY Press, 2002).

21. Sugata Bose, *A Hundred Horizons: The Indian Ocean in the Age of Global Empire* (Cambridge, MA: Harvard University Press, 2006), 43.

22. Thomas R. Metcalf, *Ideologies of the Raj* (Cambridge University Press, 1995), 72–4. See also Ian Copland, *The British Raj and the Indian Princes: Paramountcy in Western India, 1857–1930* (Bombay: Orient Longman, 1982), 88–123 and Barbara N. Ramusack, *The Indian Princes and Their States* (Cambridge University Press, 2004), 88–131.

23. On the role of the press in facilitating the formation of an Islamic public sphere in the late nineteenth and early twentieth centuries, see Juan Cole, "Printing and Urban Islam in the Mediterranean World, 1890–1920," in Leila Tarazi Fawaz and C.A. Bayly (eds), *Modernity and Culture: From the Mediterranean to the Indian Ocean* (New York: Columbia University Press, 2001) and Francis Robinson, "Technology and Religious Change: Islam and the Impact of Print," *Modern Asian Studies* 27 no. 1 (Feb. 1993), 229–51. For an account of the Arabic language print revolution that emphasizes its role in the dissemination of leftist thought, rather than Islamic, see Ilham Khuri-Makdisi, *The Eastern Mediterranean and the Making of Global Radicalism, 1860–1914* (Berkeley: University of California Press, 2010), 35–59.

24. I am using the term "Salafi" here not to indicate an institutionalized intellectual or political movement, but as a heuristic term to indicate a diverse group of intellectuals and activists who, whether belonging to legalist or mystical traditions, invoked the necessity of reforming Islam by conforming to the normative model of the Prophet and the "pious ancestors" (*al-salaf al-salih*) however realized in thought and practice. For a critique of the use of "Salafi" to describe the reform movements of the nineteenth and twentieth centuries, see Henri Lauzière, "The Construction of Salafiyya: Reconsidering Salafism from the Perspective of Conceptual History," *IJMES* 42 no. 3 (2010), 369–89. For a discussion of what "Salafi" Islam might entail, see Bernard Haykel, "On the Nature of Salafi Thought and Action" in Roel Meijer (ed.) *Global Salafism: Islam's New Religious Movement*, (New York: Columbia University Press, 2009), 33–57. For a discussion of reformist thought rooted in the mystical orders and the intellectual tradition of Ibn 'Arabi (d. 1240), see Itzchak Weismann, *Taste of Modernity: Sufism, Salafiyya, and Arabism in Late Ottoman Damascus* (Leiden: Brill, 2001).

25. I am obviously indebted to the work of Talal Asad and Samira Haj for the understanding of Islam as a discursive tradition. See Talal Asad, "The Idea of an Anthropology of Islam," Occasional Papers Series (Washington DC: Georgetown University, Center for Contemporary Arab Studies, 1986) and Samira Haj, *Reconfiguring Islamic Tradition: Reform, Rationality, and Modernity* (Stanford University Press, 2009).
26. Charles R. Crane, "Visit to the Red Sea Littoral and the Yaman," *Journal of the Central Asian Society* 17 (1928), 57.
27. David Harvey, *The Condition of Postmodernity* (London: Blackwell, 1990), 252.
28. Johannes Fabian, *Time and the Other: How Anthropology Makes its Object* (New York: Columbia University Press, 1983), 25–36.
29. On reform movements in Southeast Asia, Central Asia, and India, see Michael Francis Laffan, *Islamic Nationhood and Colonial Indonesia: The Umma Below the Winds* (London: Routledge, 2003), Natlie Mobini-Keshek, *The Hadrami Awakening: Community and Identity in the Netherlands East Indies, 1900–1942* (Ithaca, NY: Cornell Southeast Asia Program, 1999), Adeeb Khalid, *The Politics of Muslim Cultural Reform: Jadidism in Central Asia* (Berkeley: University of California Press, 1999), Gail Minault, *The Khilafat Movement: Religious Symbolism and Political Mobilization in India* (New York: Columbia University Press, 1982).
30. See Erez Manela, *The Wilsonian Moment: Self-Determination and the International Origins of Anticolonial Nationalism* (Oxford University Press, 2009). It is worth comparing Manela's emphasis on Wilsonian internationalism to formulations of Pan-Islamism and Pan-Asianism as frameworks for counter-imperial thought and action. See Cemil Aydin, *The Politics of Anti-Westernism in Asia: Visions of World Order in Pan-Islamic and Pan-Asian Thought* (New York: Columbia University Press, 2007).

1. DEFINING AUTHORITY ON THE INDIAN FRONTIER

1. Curzon's speech during for the ceremonial installation of the Nawab of Bahawalpur, 12 November 1903. Quoted in *Lord Curzon in India, Being a Selection From His Speeches as Viceroy and Governor General* (London: Macmillan and Co., Ltd., 1906), 226.
2. IOR R/20/A/434, Haines to the Superintendent of the Indian Navy, 20 January 1838. The conversation took place on 13 January 1838.
3. Surat was annexed by the British in 1842 under the doctrine of lapse by which independent "states" without recognized heirs were inherited by the East India Company. On the longstanding commercial ties between the port of al-Mukha and Surat, see Ashin Das Gupta, *Indian Merchants and the Decline of Surat, c. 1700–1750* (Wiesbaden: Franz Steiner Verlag, 1979), 20–93, *passim* and Nancy

Um, *The Merchant Houses of Mocha: Trade and Architecture in an Indian Ocean Port* (Seattle, WA: University of Washington Press, 2009), 28–32.
4. Michael H. Fisher, *Indirect Rule in India: Residents and the Residency System, 1764–1858* (Delhi: Oxford University Press, 1991), 56–8.
5. Metcalf and Metcalf, *A Concise History of India*, 133.
6. For useful overviews of the Indian princely states and the development of the British residency system, see Ramusack, *The Indian Princes and their States*, and Fiona Groenhout, "The History of the Indian Princely States: Bringing the Puppets Back onto Centre Stage," *History Compass*, 4 no. 4 (June 2006), 629–44.
7. On the early development of the port and settlement of Aden, see Gavin, *Aden Under British Rule*, 48–61 and 102–108, Z.H. Kour, *The History of Aden, 1839–1872* (London: Frank Cass, 1981), 13–62 and 77–104, and the entirety of F.M. Hunter's *An Account of the British Settlement of Aden in Arabia* (1877; reprint, London: Frank Cass, 1968).
8. Haines to government of Bombay, 13 April 1854, ROY, 2: 711–12.
9. For Satia, the emphasis on personal intuition as a mode of intelligence gathering (as opposed to empiricism) was typical of the British encounter with Arabia between the two World Wars. See Priya Satia, *Spies in Arabia: The Great War and the Cultural Foundations of Britain's Covert Empire in the Middle East* (Oxford University Press, 2008), esp. ch. 3.
10. See IOR R/20/A/434, "Estimates of Tribute annually paid by Sultan Mo'haussain to the undermentioned Chieftains," in Haines to Willoughby, Secret Dept., 5 Feb. 1839. The tribes mentioned are the Fadli, Yafi'i, Hawshabi, Amiri, 'Alawi and Subayhi. The 'Abdali Sultan's stipend of 6,500 dollars was somewhat paltry compared to past income from the port, calculated at anywhere from 7,000 to 50,000 dollars annually, depending on the source. See Kour, *History of Aden*, 64 and 116–17. The dollars referred to are the Maria Theresa dollars that were in circulation in Yemen into the twentieth century.
11. Gordon Waterfield, *Sultans of Aden* (London: John Murray, 1968), 225. Waterfield treats the trial in great detail, 205–241.
12. For background on the Indian Political Service in Aden, see Copland, *The British Raj and the Indian Native Princes*, 74–5. On the backgrounds of the Aden residents, see Robin Bidwell, "The Political Residents of Aden: Biographical Notes," *Arabian Studies*, 5 (1979), 149–59.
13. See Bidwell, "The Political Residents of Aden," 149–50. On Outram's policies toward the Bhils and his time at the Baroda Residency, see Lionel J. Trotter, *The Bayard of India: A Life of General Sir Charles Outram* (London: J. M. Den & Co., 1909), 16–26 and 106–108.
14. Nicholas B. Dirks, *Castes of Mind: Colonialism and the Making of Modern India* (Princeton University Press, 2001), 43–60.
15. In this case, the Aden experience was quite different from that of India, in so

NOTES pp. [22–24]

far as the pre-revolt residencies there adopted Mughal bureaucratic practices and Persian as an administrative language. In most residences, therefore, it was typical to employ a *munshi* as a specialist in administrative practices, the Persian language, and court etiquette rather than a native informant using local vernaculars. See Fisher, *Indirect Rule in India*, 324–30.

16. Gavin, *Aden under British Rule*, 127.
17. Gavin, *Aden under British Rule*, 127–9 and Copland, *The British Raj and the Indian Princes*, 62–3. In Copland's view the independent power of translators through their monopoly on information was typical of the entire residency system, a point supported by Fisher. See Fisher, *Indirect Rule in India*, 328–31.
18. Nonetheless, the Arabic Department, as it had come to be known, was the primary point of entry and distribution for all correspondence from the tribes. The correspondence collected in the department can be found in IOR R/20A/4520–4847.
19. See Schneider to Gonne, 10 February 1873, in Doreen Ingrams and Leila Ingrams (eds), *Records of Yemen, 1798–1960* (London: Archive Editions, 1993), 4:45–46. Gavin is the only historian to point out the fact that the "nine tribes" represented a political, not an economic unit. Even then, the politics represented were not British colonial but the lines drawn by the resistance to Qasimi rule in the late eighteenth century. Gavin, *Aden under British Rule*, 140–42.
20. The results of which were organized and reproduced in Hunter and Sealey's handbook. See F.M. Hunter and C.W.H. Sealy, *The Arab Tribes in the Vicinity of Aden* (1909; reprint, London: Darf Publishers, 1986), 235–321.
21. F.M. Hunter and C.W.H. Sealy, *An Account of the Arab Tribes in the Vicinity of Aden* (Bombay: Government Central Press, 1886) and *Arab Tribes in the Vicinity of Aden* (1909).
22. These memoranda are in IOR R/20/A/4873 (Subayhi), R/20/A/4874 (Subayhi), R/20/A/4868 (Upper Yafi'i), R/20/A/4869 (on Wadi Bayhan and the 'Awalqi), R/20/A/4871 ('Abdali), R/20/A/4875 (Fadli), R/20/A/4876 (Subayhi), R/20/A/4877 ('Alawi), R/20/A/4878 (Hawshabi), R/20A/4879 (Lower Yafi'i), R/20/A/5002 and 5003 (Amiri/Dali').
23. General Staff, India, *Military Report on the Aden Protectorate* (Simla: Government Press, 1915) in *Military Handbooks of Arabia, 1913–1917* (London: Archive Editions, 1988), 1:13 and G.A. Joy, "A Summary of the Raising and Training of the Yemen Light Infantry," *Journal of the Royal Central Asian Society*, 11 pt. 2 (1924), 148. For J. Wyman Bury, the "hill tribes" by virtue of their military abilities and status as small landholders were little different from the romanticized vision of the English yeoman farmer. See G. Wyman Bury, *The Land of Uz* (London: Macmillan and Co., 1911), 300.
24. The first treaties were signed with the 'Aqrabi (1888), the Fadli (1888), the Lower 'Awlaqi (1888), the Barhimi and 'Atifi sections of the Sabayha (1889),

213

the Lower Yafi'i (1895), the Hawshabi (1895) and the 'Alawi (1895). During the Anglo-Ottoman Boundary Commission, treaties were signed with the Upper 'Awlaqi Shaykh (1903), the Upper 'Awlaqi Sultan (1903), the Upper Yafi'i Sultan and several sections and notables ostensibly under the authority of the Lower Yafi'i Sultan (1903), the Amir of Dali' (1904) and the Sharifs of Bayhan (1904).
25. IOR R/20/A/54, fol. 14.
26. IOR R/20/E/89, "Report by Captain Prideaux on the Various Tribes which the Government of India have Treaty Relations," 5. Its importance to Lahj should not be underestimated; the text of the treaty signed with Haines in 1843 stipulates that "certain revenue and territorial books styled Deiras" should be returned to the Sultan. They had formally been in the possession of the British agent to Lahj, Hasan 'Abdullah al-Khatib. See C.U. Aitchison, *A Collection of Treaties, Engagements and Sanads Relating to India and Neighbouring Countries*, 4th ed. (Calcutta: Superintendent Government Printing, India, 1909), 13:81.
27. Cf. with the identification of the *zayl* as the basis of tribal social and economic life in the Punjab. See David Gilmartin, *Empire and Islam: Punjab and the Making of Pakistan* (Berkeley: University of California Press, 1988), esp. Ch. 1. Also, Frederick J.D. Lugard, *The Dual Mandate in British Tropical Africa* (reprint New York: Routledge, 1965), 193–213. In contrast to the Aden Protectorate, in both the Punjab and in Lugard's work the village was the basic unit of administration. Since the Protectorate was not directly administered, the Aden government took the "Chief" as the basic unit.
28. Robert Playfair, *A History of Arabia Felix or Yemen* (Bombay, 1859), 159–63.
29. See Hunter and Sealey, *Arab Tribes*, 6–17 for the historical narrative of the 'Abadil. The local genealogical discourse, of course, has little to do with the foundation of "states" but of descent. Al-'Abdali traces the ruling family, the Al Salam, to the Yafi'i tribe of Kalad from the village of Barakat. See Ahmad Fadl b. 'Ali Muhsin al-'Abdali, *Hadiyat al-Zaman fi Akhbar Muluk Lahj wa-'Adan* (Beirut: Dar al-'Awda, 1932), 39–40. From a northern perspective, al-'Arshi claims they can be traced to 'Ayyal 'Abdullah of Arhab (Hashid). See Husayn b. Ahmad al-'Arshi, *Kitab Bulugh al-Maram fi Sharh Misk al-Khitam*, ed. Anastase-Marie de St-Elie (Beirut: Dar Ihya' al-Turath al-'Arabi, 1939), 81. More recently, Shihab has claimed that both texts are incorrect. 'Arshi, he claims, asserted that the Al Salam were from Arhab merely to reflect a contemporary political closeness between Imam Yahya and the 'Abdali Sultan, while al-'Abdali was simply wrong. Instead, he suggests that the 'Abadil are named for the Al 'Abdullah in the eastern Radfan mountains. See Hassan Salih al-Shihab, *al-'Abadil: Salatin Lahj wa-'Adan, 1832–1959* (Sanaa: Markaz al-Shar'abi lil-Taba'a, wa-l-Nashr wa-l-Tawzi', 1999), 6–7.
30. See, for example, the refutation of Imam Yahya's claim that the area of the Protectorate had historically been subject to the Zaydi Imamate, BNA CO 725/17/12.

31. The date itself has provoked very little debate, especially since the revolution of 1967 and the purge of the former ruling families in the Protectorate removed their pasts from the realm of possible historical inquiry. Kour's *History of Aden* accepts 1728 as the date of 'Abdali independence without question (page 3), as does al-Qasimi's *al-Ihtilal al-Britani* (page 20). Gavin's *Aden under British Rule* is more circumspect and suggests the more realistic date of c. 1730, noting as well that Lahji independence was, by necessity, backed by Yafi' military power (page 20). Shihab's *al-'Abadil* makes more of a point of the question and argues expressly for the date 1145 AH (i.e. 1732) based on his reading of *al-Sira al-Mansuriyya* (page 11). In his earlier text, al-'Abdali more properly considers the longer period of 1682–1732 as a series of wars which eventually led to the independence of the 'Abadil. He, like Shihab, bases his account largely on al-Rusi's text (much of which is simply reproduced with little comment) and upholds 1732 as the date of independence. See *Hadiyat al-Zaman*, 109 and 123.
32. Michel-Rolph Trouillot, *Silencing the Past: Power and the Production of History* (Boston: Beacon Press, 1995), 46.
33. Husayn b. Husayn al-Rusi, *al-Barahin al-Mudi'a fi al-Sira al-Mansuriyya*. pt. 2, EL (Tarikh: 2198) (hereafter referred to as *al-Sira al-Mansuriyya*). As far as I have been able to ascertain, the first and third parts are not extant. 'Abdali's *Hadiyat al-Zaman*, however, does contain a number of extracts from the third part in his chapter on the independence of Lahj. For the period after 1142 AH, I rely on this work.
34. On the decline of Qasimi state power and the loss of territory in the eighteenth century, see Bernard Haykel, *Revival and Reform in Islam: The Legacy of Muhammad al-Shawkani* (Cambridge University Press, 2003), 43–6 and 62–3.
35. al-Rusi, *al-Sira al-Mansuriyya*, fols. 3–4.
36. Upper Yafi' comprised the Hadrami, Bu'si, Dubi, Mawsatti and Muflihi tribes. Lower Yafi' comprised the Kaladi, Nakhibi, Yazidi, Yahari, and Sa'di. It should be noted that these lines of authority also represented administrative divisions indicating the limits of taxation, agreed upon by both Sultanates in the seventeenth century. See Nasir Salih Husayn Haytham Sab'a al-Yahari al-Yafi'i, *Min Yanabi' Tarikhina al-Yamani wa-Ash'ar Rajih Haytham Sab'a al-Yafi'i* (Damascus: Matba'at al-Katib al-'Arabi, 1994), 60–62 and 143–4. The type of authority wielded by both the Bani Qasid Sultans and the Al Harhara, and the multiple forms of allegiance expressed by the tribes, are treated by R.B. Serjeant in his "Yafi', Zaydis, Āl Bū Bakr b. Sālim and Others: Tribes and Sayyids," in *On Both Sides of al-Mandab* (Swedish Research Institute in Istanbul, 1988), 85–7.
37. See al-Yahari al-Yafi'i, *Min Yanabi' Tarikhina*, 145. Five documents from Imam Mahdi Muhammad recognizing Yafi'i rights in Aden (two dated 1687/88 and 1698, the other three undated) are included in the appendices (pp. 185–8). It should also be noted that it was during the reign of Mahdi Muhammad as well

that the rights of the Amir of Dali' over certain territories were reconfirmed. See the letter from the Imam to Amir Ahmad b. Qasim al-Sha'fal, dated 1687, in IOR R/20/A/1198 and two letters from the Imam to Amir Mutahhar b. Muqbil b. Sha'fal, dated 1702 and 1711 in IOR R/20/A/1200. The case of Dali' will be considered more closely in Chapter 3.

38. In its most obvious form, the very real threat of Yafi'i opposition to the Qasimi state is represented by al-Rusi's careful attention to their constant attacks on Zaydi garrisons in Qa'taba and elsewhere in the South. But he also makes a point of criticizing Yafi'i claims to authority, or at least those proffered by the Al Harhara. When the Bani Qasid Sultan, Sayf b. Qahtan b. al-'Afif, momentarily sided with the Imam, al-Rusi explained this turn of events by noting that the Al 'Afif represented the original Yafi'is who had held the leadership of the tribe from time immemorial (*wa-lahum al-riyasa min qadim*). As for the Harhara, they were merely appointed (*manasib*) by the Al Bu Bakr b. Salim in violation of the customary legal bases of leadership (*'ala ghayr qawanin al-riyasa*). Al-Rusi, *al-Sira al-Mansuriyya*, fols. 31–2.

39. The offering of slaughter-beasts in Yemeni (especially tribal) society is a ritual act of appeasement or recognition of error. See Paul Dresch, *Tribes, Government and History in Yemen* (Oxford: Clarendon Press, 1993), 50–53.

40. According to al-Rusi as quoted in al-'Abdali, *Hadiyat al-Zaman*, 118–22.

41. IOR R/20/A/54, fol. 26. Playfair repeated this assertion in his history: *History of Arabia Felix*, 43. See also M. Niebuhr, *Travels through Arabia and other Countries of the East*, trans. Robert Heron (Edinburgh: R. Morison and Son, 1792), 2:68–9. Even in the period of the Anglo-Ottoman Boundary Commission this was commonly held to be true, as the Political Resident, James Maitland, expressed: Maitland to Gov. of Bombay, 2 Aug. 1903. ROY, 5:148.

42. Serjeant, "Yafi', Zaydis, Āl Bū Bakr b. Sālim," 83 and al-Yahari al-Yafi'i, *Min Yanabi' Tarikhina*, 55.

43. See IOR R/20/E/89, Prideaux, "Report," 3, Playfair, *A History of Arabia Felix*, 33–4, Hunter and Sealey, *Arab Tribes* (1909), 4–5, and Bury, *The Land of Uz*, 9.

44. IOR R/20/A/120, Outram, "Report on Arab Tribes," fol. 50.

45. Haines estimated the number of "fighting men" as 4,000 in 1851, IOR R/20/A/54, "The Principal Tribes in the neighbourhood of Aden," fol. 25; Outram estimated their number at around 2,000 in 1854, IOR R/20/A/120, "Report on Arab Tribes," fol. 51; Prideaux estimated a total population of 5,000, IOR R/20/E/89, "Report," 3; and Playfair estimated the population at 10,000, 4,000 of which were "fighting men," *History of Arabia Felix*, 32.

46. As Outram was quick to note in his report on the tribes, when he wrote "There can be no doubt, indeed, that however galling the recollection of that transaction may be to some of the more patriotic and fanatical Arabs, the sale of Aden has proved an increased advantage to the Abdali tribe." See IOR R/20/A/120, "Report on Arab Tribes," fol. 50.

47. Aitchison, *A Collection of Treaties*, 4th ed., 13:84–87. See also Hunter, *Account of the British Settlement*, 67–69 for the cultivation of European vegetables in Lahj.
48. Gavin, *Aden under British Rule*, 80.
49. IOR R/20/E/89, Prideaux, "Report," 6–7.
50. Gavin, *Aden under British Rule*, 120–21. It is important to note as well that South Yemen suffered from successive periods of drought and rinderpest in the 1860s, which decimated local agriculture. Sultan Fadl was compelled by economic necessity to pursue avenues of income that promised greater regularity and security, although one assumes that this only accelerated a course of action that would have been taken eventually anyway. This was especially so since Sultan Fadl had been forced to cement his tenuous accession to the throne with liberal gifts in land revenues to his opponents, 'Abdullah b. Muhsin and Fadl b. 'Ali. See Gavin, *Aden under British Rule*, 117–18.
51. Gavin, *Aden under British Rule*, 85.
52. In fact, many of the villages devastated by the British in this assault were still either in ruins or entirely deserted when the Aden Troop passed through Fadli territory in 1872. See G.J. Stevens, "Report on the Country around Aden," *Journal of the Royal Geographical Society of London*, 43 (1873), 298.
53. The Hawshabi Sultan had allowed the Ottoman government to build a customs post in the village of al-'Anad, near the Lahj route to the highlands, to check the flow of tobacco and safeguard the local monopoly of the Ottoman Tobacco Co. See Gavin, *Aden under British Rule*, 209–210 and Aitchison, *A Collection of Treaties*, 4th ed., 13:89–90 for the 1881 agreement on Zayida. According to al-'Abdali, the dispute involved the Hawshabi Sultan's mistreatment of merchants in Musaymir and the exactions on caravans within Hawshabi territory. *Hadiyat al-Zaman*, 176–82.
54. See Aitchison, *A Collection of Treaties*, 4th ed., 13:156–7.
55. Harold Jacob, *Kings of Arabia: The Rise and Set of the Turkish Sovranty in the Arabian Peninsula* (London: Mills & Boon Limited, 1923), 44.
56. *Rudyard Kipling: The Complete Verse* (London: Kyle Cathie Ltd., 2002), 6.
57. "Proclamation by the Queen in Council, to the Princes, Chiefs and People of India," in *Calcutta Gazette*, Extraordinary, 1 November 1858, in John Marriot and Bhaskar Mukhopadhyay (eds), *Britain in India, 1765–1905*, (London: Pickering and Chatto, 2006), 5:298–300.
58. Metcalf, *Ideologies of the Raj*, 193–4. See also Bernard Cohn, "Cloth, Clothes, and Colonialism," in *Colonialism and Its Forms of Knowledge*, 119 and "Representing Authority in Victorian India," in *An Anthropologist Among the Historians and Other Essays* (Delhi: Oxford University Press, 1987), 649–50.
59. For a standard definition of "durbar" in the British imperial context, see the entry in Henry Yule and A. C. Burnell, *Hobson-Jobson: The Anglo-Indian Dictionary* (1886; repr., Ware: Wordsworth Editions, 1996), 331.

60. Metcalf and Metcalf, *Concise History of India*, 133.
61. Chatterjee, *The Nation and Its Fragments*, 16–17.
62. For an elaboration of the privileges associated with each class, see the unsigned memo from 24 April 1907 in IOR R/20/A/1859. The tribes and their classification, as listed in the same file, were as follows: Class I: Qu'ayti, Qishn and Suqutra, 'Abdali, Fadli. Class II: Amiri, Lower Yafi'i, Hawshabi, Upper Yafi'i sultan, Upper 'Awlaqi Sultan, Upper 'Awlaqi Shaykh, Lower 'Awlaqi Sultan. Class III: 'Aqrabi Shaykh, 'Alawi Shaykh, Sharif of Bayhan, Upper Yafi'i stipendiaries (Mawsatta, Dubi), Wahidi Sultans (Balhaf, Bir 'Ali), Hawra Shaykh and 'Irqa Shaykh. Class IV: Upper Yafi'i stipendiaries (Muflahi, Hadrami), Subayhi stipendiaries (Mansuri, Makhdumi, Rija'i, Barhimi, 'Atifi).
63. For the protocol governing visits by native chiefs to the Aden Residency, see "Draft Memo, Aden Residency, 1906," IOR R/20/A/1859. For the importance of personal visits to the Residency, see "Notes on System of Presents and Entertainment," 6 May 1906, IOR R/20/A/1419.
64. On the frequency of visits see the letter from Political Resident O'Moore Creagh to the Governor of Bombay, 15 February 1900 in Ingrams and Ingrams, *Records of Yemen*, 5:27.
65. Cohn, "Representing Authority," 636–40. On the symbolic function of the *darbar* as an act of incorporation, see F.M. Buckler, "The Oriental Despot," in M.N. Pearson (ed.), *Legitimacy and Symbols: The South Asian Writings of F.W. Buckler*, Michigan Papers on South and Southeast Asia, No. 26 (1985), 176–87.
66. See, for example, "Notes on System of Presents and Entertainments," as well as the related files in IOR R/20/A/1419. For some basic figures on funds granted to specific tribes for the year 1905–06, see IOR R/20/A/1420.
67. Harold Jacob, *Perfumes of Araby: Silhouettes of Al Yemen* (London: Martin Secker, 1915), 234.
68. *Lord Curzon in India*, 290.
69. IOR R/20/A/955, Maitland to Wahab, 29 October 1902.
70. IOR R/20/A/956, Foreign Office, Simla, 4 November 1902.
71. The protectorate chiefs were ranked higher than others with salutes of nine guns primarily because they were believed to exercise greater independence from British rule. See notes by the Bombay Political Department from 1916 in IOR R/20/A/1391. The chiefs from the Bombay Presidency who attended the Durbar in order of precedence were the following (followed by salute): Maharaja of Kolhapur (17), Rao of Cutch (17), Mir of Khairpur (15), Maharaja of Idar (15—personal), Sultan of Shihr and Mukalla (12—personal), Nawab of Junagarh (11), Thakur sahib of Bhavnagar (11), Rana of Porbandar (11), Nawab of Cambay (11), Thakur Sahib of Morvi (11), Thakur Sahib of Gondal (11), Sultan of Lahj (9), Raja of Bansda (9), Raja of Baria (9), Thakur Sahib of Palitana (9), Thakur Sahib of Limri (9), Nawab of Janjira (9), and the Amir of

Dali', the Pant Sachiv of Bor and the Chief of Miraj, none of whom had salutes. See Stephen Wheeler, *History of the Delhi Coronation Durbar* (London: John Murray, 1904), 303 and the list of precedence within the Bombay Presidency included in IOR R/20/A/956. For a slightly later period, see the lists of salutes forwarded to the Aden Residency in 1910 for the purposes of the 1911 Durbar in IOR R/20/A/2650.

72. Wheeler, *History of the Delhi Coronation Durbar*, 60.
73. Ibid., 79.
74. Ibid., 123.
75. Ibid., 128–30.
76. Al-'Abdali narrates the whole affair, at which he was present, quite succinctly: "In 1319 His Majesty the King of the English blessed him [Sultan Fadl] with the medal of the Star of India, second class (K.C.S.I.) with the title of "Sir." In the month of Ramadan 1320, he travelled to India and attended the coronation of His Majesty the King, Edward VII, in Delhi, and the author was in the group which accompanied him." *Hadiyat al-Zaman*, 198.
77. Quoted in Michael Edwardes, *High Noon of Empire: India Under Curzon* (London: Eyre & Spottiswoode, 1965), 169.
78. Metcalf, *Ideologies of the Raj*, 197–9. Manu Bhagavan looks more closely at these contradictions in the context of educational reform in the princely states of Baroda and Mysore. See his *Sovereign Spheres: Princes, Education and Empire in Colonial India* (New Delhi: Oxford University Press, 2003).
79. Nicholas B. Dirks, *The Hollow Crown: Ethnohistory of an Indian Kingdom* (Ann Arbor, MI: University of Michigan Press, 1993).

2. MASTERLESS MEN

1. Zygmunt Bauman, Modernity and Ambivalence (Cambridge: Polity Press, 1991), 8.
2. Carlo Landberg, *Etudes sur les dialectes de L'Arabie méridionale* (Leiden: E.J. Brill, 1905), 1:163, 268. For a facsimile of the letter which contains the text and annotations see Muhammad 'Abd al-Qadir Ba Faqih, a*l-Mustashriqun wa-Athar al-Yaman* (Sanaa: Markaz al-Dirasat wa-l-Buhuth al-Yamani, 1988), 2:869–85. The informant was Hasan b. Ahmad 'Ali al-Hitari. The incident was also one of the reasons given justifying the construction of a new guest house away from downtown Crater. Although a new building was never built, the guest house was moved by 1909 into the former residency building on the edge of town, in what would become the neighborhood of Khusaf. See the collected correspondence on the subject in IOR R/20/A/2046.
3. A.L. Beier, *Masterless Men: The Vagrancy Problem in England, 1560–1640* (London: Methuen, 1985).

4. Heather Streets, *Martial Races: The Military, Race, and Masculinity in British Imperial Culture, 1857–1914* (Manchester University Press, 2004), 2–33 and Dirks, *Castes of Mind*, 177.
5. Dirks, *Castes of Mind*, 179.
6. Metcalf, *Ideologies of the Raj*, 126.
7. See Streets, *Martial Races*, 93–5 and Richard G. Fox, *Lions of the Punjab* (Berkeley: University of California Press, 1985), esp. Ch. 8 and Bernard Cohn, "Cloth, Clothes, and Colonialism," 107–111 for the creation of a uniform and inherently "martial" Sikh culture.
8. Sanjay Nigam, "Disciplining and Policing the 'Criminals by Birth,' Part 1: The Making of a Colonial Stereotype—The Criminal Tribes and Castes of North India," *The Indian Economic and Social History Review*, 27 no. 2 (April-June 1990), 155–8 and Metcalf, *Ideologies of the Raj*, 124–5.
9. On the Criminal Tribes Act, see David Arnold, *Police Power and Colonial Rule: Madras 1859–1947*, (Delhi: Oxford University Press, 1986), 143–7 and Sanjay Nigam, "Disciplining and Policing the 'Criminals by Birth,' Part 1," 131–64 and "Disciplining and Policing the 'Criminals by Birth,' Part 2: The Development of a Disciplinary System, 1871–1900," *The Indian Economic and Social History Review*, 27 no. 3 (July-September 1990), 257–88.
10. Metcalf, *Ideologies of the Raj*, 123–4.
11. General Staff, India, *Military Report on the Aden Protectorate* (Simla: Government Press, 1915) in *Military Handbooks of Arabia, 1913–1917* (London: Archive Editions, 1988), 1:194. Hereafter referred to as MRAP.
12. MRAP, 1:197. The comparison was based on general conditions of life, the similar style of small, fortified towers, and the constant feuds in which both the Arabs and the Pathans engaged. A review of the performance of the Yemen Light Infantry in 1924 compared the hill Arabs to the Gurkhas of Nepal. G.A. Joy, "A Summary of the Raising and Training of the 1st Yemen Infantry," *Journal of the Royal Central Asian Society*, 11 pt. 2 (1924), 148.
13. See Haines, "The Principal Tribes in the neighbourhood of Aden," fol. 26, IOR R/20/A/54, Prideaux, *Report*, 17–18, IOR R/20/E/89, and Hunter and Sealey, *Arab Tribes* (1909), 54.
14. Dirks, *Castes of Mind*, 177.
15. Prideaux, *Report*, 4, IOR R/20/E/89, Hunter and Sealey, *Arab Tribes* (1909), 3, and Playfair, *History of Arabia Felix*, 33. See also Jacob's description of their investment in the "Pax Britannica." *Perfumes of Araby*, 229–30.
16. Dresch, *A History of Modern Yemen*, 38. For the relationship between land ownership and notions of honor in the Yemeni highlands, see Dresch, *Tribes, Government, and History in Yemen*, 54–5 and 81–2.
17. Bury, *The Land of Uz*, 300.
18. There were various estimates of the Subayhi population. In 1845, Haines esti-

NOTES   pp. [51–56]

mated a population of 10,000 fighting men, IOR R/20/A/54, fol. 25; in 1854, Outram estimated a total population of 12,000, IOR R/20/A/120, fol. 54; Hunter and Sealey estimated a total of 3,450 fighting men, *Account of the Arab Tribes* (1886), 13; and according to the statistics collected by Maitland on a village by village basis in the period of the Anglo-Ottoman Boundary Commission, the total population of the interior (excluding the 'Atifi and the Barhimi) was around 5,071, although the entries for three villages were missing owing to slight damage to the document, IOR R/20/A/4874.

19. S.B. Haines, "Memoir, to Accompany a chart of the South Coast of Arabia from the entrance of the Red Sea to Misenát, in 50° 43′′ 25′," *Journal of the Royal Geographical Society of London*, vol. 9 (1839), 130.
20. Aitchison, *A Collection of Treaties*, 4th ed., 13:97–101. While Haines' uneven command of Arabic makes it difficult to discern with any certainty which sections signed treaties, it is clear that they represented very little of the population of what was later considered the Sabayha. Treaty signatories, for example, represented communities in Hujariyya, in what would later be Ottoman Yemen, and a village in 'Abdali territory inhabited by *sayyid*s, not tribes.
21. IOR R/20/A/120, fols. 54–55.
22. Even then, the Sabayha were deemed relatively unimportant from the vantage point of Aden. Hunter's *Account of the British Settlement* notes that relations exist between the British and the Sabayha, but writes of them (as well as of the Hawshabi, Amiri, 'Alawi and Yafi'i) "as they do not reside in the immediate vicinity of Aden it is unnecessary to refer more particularly to them." Hunter, *Account of the British Settlement*, 157.
23. Aitchison, *A Collection of Treaties*, 4th ed., 13:91.
24. See IOR R/20/A/4874 and al-'Abdali, *Hadiyat al-Zaman*, 198–9.
25. Hunter and Sealey, *Account of the Arab Tribes*, (1886), 13.
26. Hunter and Sealey, *Account of the Arab Tribes* (1886), 10. The authors were quoting an earlier report by Capt. Prideaux from 1872. See IOR R/20/A/89.
27. Hunter and Sealey, *Account of the Arab Tribes* (1886), 12.
28. See the texts of the treaties in Aitchison, *A Collection of Treaties*, 4th ed., 13:106–9.
29. IOR R/20/A/4874.
30. Bauman, *Modernity and Ambivalence*, 3.
31. Verse recorded by Harold Jacob. Jacob, *Perfumes of Araby*, 173.
32. Gavin, *Aden Under British Rule*, 203–06.
33. Bury, *The Land of Uz*, 296.
34. Dresch, *History of Modern Yemen*, 22 and 226, note 46. Gavin equally seems to forget that the matchlock itself was an innovation in its time and was hardly the cause of "social disintegration." One can point to texts such as Husayn b. Muhammad al-Ibriqi's nineteenth-century manual on the use of the matchlock

221

as an indication of the rapidity and ease with which innovations in weaponry were adopted. See his *al-Adab al-Muhaqqaqa fi Mu'tabarat al-Bandaqa*, ed. 'Abdullah Ahmad Muhayraz (Aden: PDRY Ministry of Culture and Information, 1988).

35. R.W. Beachey, "The Arms Trade in East Africa in the Late Nineteenth Century," *Journal of African History*, 3 no. 3 (1962), 452. Unless otherwise indicated, the information on the East Africa arms trade comes from this article. For a more detailed account of the innovations in small arms development and the role of new weapons in modern African history see Gavin White, "Firearms in Africa: An Introduction," *Journal of African History*, 12 no. 2 (1971), 173–84. Unfortunately, his focus is on the trade musket rather than the decommissioned military breech-loaders, which supplied the bulk of the market in Arabia.

36. IOR R/20/A/1289, DeBrath to Political Dept., Bombay, 31 March 1907.

37. IOR R/20/A/1289. See also the similar chart in IOR R/20/A/1288, letter from B.H. Adler to Hancock, 29 Nov. 1907.

38. Farah deals with smuggling and piracy (with a few words on the arms trade) in Ottoman Yemen in brief and very much from the perspective of the state. See Ceasar Farah, *The Sultan's Yemen: Nineteenth-Century Challenges to Ottoman Rule* (London: I.B. Tauris, 2002), 192–211.

39. IOR R/20/A/1289, Warneford to?, 1 April 1903. Warneford notes that the price of Martini-Henry ammunition at Dali' was ten rounds to the dollar while Le Gras ammunition sold at twelve to the dollar.

40. IOR R/20/A/1290, 'Abdali Sultan to Resident, 15 Aug. 1910.

41. IOR R/20/A/1214, Extract from notes of an interview with 'Abdali Sultan, 5 Oct. 1904. See also the description of the port of Ras 'Imran and the inaction of the 'Abdali post in curbing the trade in HMS *Prosperine* to Mason, 26 Jan. 1905, IOR R/20/A/1221.

42. IOR R/20/E/280, Gen. Mason to HM Sec. of State for India, 17 Jan. 1906, enclosing "Report on the Illicit Traffic in Arms from the French Possessions in the Red Sea and their Subsequent Importation into the Districts Lying in the Aden Protectorate and British Somaliland."

43. IOR R/20/A/1290, M.M. O'Byrne, chief of customs in Berbera to Commissioner of the Somaliland Protectorate, 9 June 1910.

44. IOR R/20/E/280, Political Resident to Political Dept., Bombay, 29 Oct. 1905.

45. IOR R/20/A/1221, see particularly Notes from an interview between the 1st Assistant Resident and the Julaydi Shaykh, 'Imad b. Ahmad Salih, 27 April 1905, Notes of an Interview between Col. R.J. Scallon and the 'Abdali Sultan, 9 Aug. 1905 and Shaykh 'Imad b. Salih al-Julaydi to Political Resident, n.d.

46. Jacob, *Perfumes of Araby*, 70. It should be mentioned that up to the present day, the Suq al-Milh in Sanaa is still filled with le Gras rifles which can be bought for around US$20–25. Equally abundant is the German Mauser of Ottoman manufacture used by the Ottoman military.

47. IOR R/20/A/1287, 14 May 1906.
48. IOR R/20/A/1287, Shaykh Saʻid Ba ʻAli al-ʻAtifi to DeBrath, n.d.
49. IOR/20/A/1287, Notes of an interview between the ʻAtifi Shaykh and the Political Resident, 18 Dec. 1906.
50. This was attempted by Lugard in Uganda as well, with little success. See Beachey, "The Arms Trade in East Africa," 459.
51. See IOR R/20/E/280, "Proposals for Checking the Importation of Arms and Ammunition into the Aden protectorate," Political Resident to Political Department, Bombay, 29 Oct. 1905; and IOR R/20/A/1294, Notes of an interview between the Governor of Djibouti, the Political Resident, the Commissioner of the Somaliland Protectorate, the Senior Naval Officer, Aden and the 1st Assistant Resident, 5 Jan. 1906.
52. IOR R/20/E/280, ʻAbdali Sultan to Political Resident, 4 Sep. 1905.
53. These are Confidential Files, R/20/A/1350, 1351, and 1352, entitled "Outrages committed by the Subehi on the roads."
54. IOR R/20/A/1200. This description of the trade routes notes that the route from Mawiya through al-Madraja in Makhdumi country, mentioned by Hunter, was no longer in use. See Hunter, *An Account of the British Settlement*, 87.
55. Hunter and Sealey, *Account of the Arab Tribes* (1909), 352.
56. IOR R/20/A/1400, memo, 22 Aug. 1907.
57. Gavin, *Aden under British Rule*, 119.
58. The duty at the time Hunter wrote his description of Aden was Rs. 1 for every 25 lbs. of Maqtari *qat* and 30 lbs. of Sabri *qat*, which came from Jabal Sabr outside of Taʻizz and was more likely to be carried along the routes in Hawshabi country. Hunter, *Account of the British Settlement*, 138. For duties collected in the period 1900–5 in the markets of Shaykh ʻUthman, see IOR R/20/A/1338, marginal note, 20 Feb. 1908.
59. Hunter and Sealey, *Account of the Arab Tribes* (1909), 352. The list of *muqaddim*s is in a memo by Mosse, 17 July 1907. IOR R/20/A/1400.
60. IOR R/20/A/1350, Lysaght to Political Dept., Bombay, 22 June 1908.
61. IOR R/20/A/1350, Sayyid Ahmad Saʻid to DeBrath, 31 March 1908.
62. IOR R/20/A/1350, Saʻid al-Jurabi and Muhammad ʻAli Muqbil to ʻAbdali Sultan, n.d.
63. The *qat* merchants were Thabit Hasan al-Hindi, Ahmad b. Ahmad Hasan al-Hindi, Nuʻman Hasan, ʻAli b. Salih and ʻAbdulla Sumayl. See their letters to the Political Resident, dated 5, 11, 15 May 1908, IOR R/20/A/1350. Also, for the comment on the arms trade, Thabit Hasan al-Hindi to 1st Assistant Resident, 15 June 1908, IOR R/20/A/1351.
64. IOR R/20/A/1350, Muqbil ʻAli al-Kabir al-Humaydi and sons to ʻAbdali Sultan, May 1908.
65. IOR R/20/A/1350, Shaykh Salih b. Ahmad al-Mansuri to Political Resident, n.d. and Shaykh Saʻid Jaʻfar al-Maʻmai to Political Resident, May 1908.

66. IOR R/20/A/1350, 'Abdali Sultan to Shaykh Nasir Ba Sa'id al-Sulami, 28 May 1908.
67. MRAP, 142.
68. IOR R/20/A/1350, Sa'id al-Jurabi and Muhammad 'Ali Muqbil to 'Abdali Sultan, n.d.
69. IOR R/20/A/1350, Letters from the Political Resident, dated 18 May 1908, to Shaykhs 'Imad b. Ahmad al-Julaydi, Sa'id Muhammad Ya'qub al-Masfari, 'Ali al-Bughayli, Haza' Qasim Muqbil al-Mashaqi, and Hasan 'Imad al-Juraywi.
70. IOR R/20/A/1350, Letter to the Political Resident and 1st Assistant Resident, n.d.
71. IOR R/20/A/1350, Notes on meeting with the Shaykhs at Dar al-Amir. Compensation was distributed as follows: Shaykh 'Imad Rs 80, 'Ali al-'Bughayli Rs 30, Darwish Battash Rs 30, Haza' Qasim Muqbil Rs 30, Qasim 'Abd al-Rab al-Makmahi Rs 15, Sa'id Muhammad al-Masfari Rs 30, Qadri Yasin Rs 20, Ahmad Abdallah al-Ruzayhi Rs 8, Muhammad 'Abd al-Rabb Rs 8, Ahmad b. Muhammad Rs 8, Hasan Thabit al-'Awbali Rs 10.
72. The *hijra* is a form of tribal protection applied to particular spaces and people, whether socially "weak" (*da'if*) or prestigious (such as *sayyid*s and *qadi*s). See Dresch, *Tribes, Government, and History in Yemen*, 145–50 and G.R. Puin, "The Yemenite *hijrah* Concept of Tribal Protection," in Tarif Khalidi (ed.), *Land Reform and Social Transformation in the Middle East* (Beirut: American University, 1984), 483–94.
73. While the record IOR R/20/A/1351 is seemingly concluded with the signing of the truce, the remaining files in the series pick up again with another series of conflicts between different sections of the interior along the same roads in the Wadis Ma'baq and Ma'adin.
74. IOR R/20/A/1338, Sultan Ahmad b. Fadl to Political Resident, 5 March 1909.
75. C.U. Aitchison, *A Collection of Treaties, Engagements and Sanads Relating to India and Neighbouring Countries*, 5th ed. (Delhi: Manager of Publications, 1933), 11:76. For negotiations leading up to the new agreement, see IOR R/20/A/1357.
76. Carter, *The Road to Botany Bay*, 336.
77. Bauman, *Modernity and Ambivalence*, 7.
78. Nigam, "Disciplining and Policing, Pt. 1," 152 and 163. On the reformative effects of military discipline on the Bhils, see Trotter, *Bayard of India*, 20–22 and Anand A. Yang, "Bhils and the Idea of a Criminal Tribe in Nineteenth-Century India," in Anand A. Yang (ed.), *Crime and Criminality in British India* (Tucson, AZ: The University of Arizona Press, 1985), 137–8.
79. Such as the attempted settlement of the Magahiya Doms in agricultural colonies in the 1880s. See Edith S. Brandstadter, "Dangerous Castes and Tribes: The Criminal Tribes Act and the Magahiya Doms of Northeast India," in Yang (ed.), *Crime and Criminality*, 122–6.

80. Bury, *The Land of Uz*, 14. See also MRAP, 197.
81. Joy, "A Summary of the Raising and Training of the 1st Yemen Infantry," 148 and Gavin, *Aden Under British Rule*, 286.
82. BNA CO 725/11/3, Stewart to Sec. of State for the Colonies, 6 Jan. 1927. The same sentiment was expressed by Stewart in a letter to the same when discussing the resistance of the Yafi'i and 'Awlaqi tribes to the Imam's offensives. 19 Jan. 1927. This opinion was echoed earlier in the MRAP, 194.
83. BNA CO 725/17/10, Sir Steward Symes to HM Secretary of State for the Colonies, 8 Sep. 1928, enclosing report on operations against the Zaydis by Maj. Fowle.
84. See the series of letters exchanged between 'Ali b. 'Abdullah al-Wazir and the 'Abdali Sultan on Subayhi raids in 1920–21 which form the bulk of IOR R/20/A/4764.

3. A LANDSCAPE OF UNCERTAINTY

1. Carter, *Road to Botany Bay*, xxiv [emphasis in original].
2. Freya Stark, *East is West* (London: John Murray, 1945), 19–20. This chapter, entitled "Christmas at Dhala," was first published in *The Times*, 28 March 1940.
3. Donald Foster, *Landscape with Arabs: Travels in Aden and South Arabia* (Brighton: Clifton Books, 1969). Foster served for fifteen years in various positions in the Aden Government and later the government of the Federation of South Arabia. These included the Cabinet and the Ministries of the Interior, Information and Agriculture.
4. Ibid., 49–50.
5. This literature is quite extensive, but among the more important works are Ann Bermingham, *Landscape and Ideology: The English Rustic Tradition, 1740–1860* (Berkeley: University of California Press, 1986), Denis E. Cosgrove, *Social Formation and Symbolic Landscape* (London: Croom Helm, 1984), John Barrel, *The Dark Side of the Landscape* (Cambridge University Press, 1980), and Raymond Williams, *The Country and the City* (Oxford University Press, 1973). On the relationship between European empire and landscape, see Burnett, *Masters of All They Surveyed*, 131–165, Ryan, *The Cartographic Eye*, 60–100, and Edney, *Mapping an Empire*, 57–63.
6. W.J.T. Mitchell, "Imperial Landscape," in W.J.T. Mitchell (ed.), *Landscape and Power*, (University of Chicago Press, 1994), 10.
7. Harold Ingrams, "The Exploration of the Aden Protectorate," *Geographical Review* vol. 28, no. 4 (Oct. 1938), 638. For a summary of the exploration of South Arabia in the nineteenth century, see David George Hogarth, *The Penetration of Arabia* (Westport, CT: Hyperion Press, Inc., 1981; repr., New York: F.A. Stokes Co., 1904), 191–205.

8. e.g. Carter, *Road to Botany Bay*, Ryan, *The Cartographic Eye*, Burnett, *Masters of All They Surveyed*.
9. Hunter, *Account of the British Settlement*, 86–8.
10. Aitchison, *A Collection of Treaties*, 4th ed., 13:161.
11. Hunter and Sealey, *An Account of the Arab Tribes* (1909), 230–34.
12. Ibid., 37.
13. Hunter and Sealey, *Account of the Arab Tribes* (1886), 38.
14. Baron von Maltzen, "Geography of Southern Arabia," *Proceedings of the Royal Geographical Society of London*, 16 no. 2 (1871–72), 119. The British explorer Hugh Scott echoed this sentiment in 1937 on his visit to Amir Nasr b. Shayif. See Hugh Scott, *In the High Yemen* (London: John Murray, 1942), 34.
15. Walter B. Harris, *A Journey Through the Yemen* (1893; reprint, London: Darf Publishers, 1985), 176.
16. Ibid., 182.
17. Ibid., 188.
18. Despite his inability to find written records of the *wali* Hasan, he was well known locally according to Harold Jacob. See Jacob, *Perfumes of Araby*, 174–5 and MRAP, 1:120.
19. Cf. John Noyes, *Colonial Space: Spatiality in the Discourse of German South West Africa, 1884–1915* (Philadelphia: Harwood Academic Publishers, 1992), 123.
20. Harris, *A Journey Through the Yemen*, 192. The material from the following paragraph is drawn from the same page.
21. Cater, *Road to Botany Bay*, 247. Dane Kennedy has similarly shown how Indian landscapes were appropriated linguistically and materially in the context of the establishment of the nineteenth century hill stations. See Dane Kennedy, *The Magic Mountains: Hill Stations and the British Raj* (Berkeley: University of California Press, 1996), especially Ch. 3.
22. IOR R/20/E/274, "Proceedings of a Committee assembled at D'thala," 27 Nov. 1905. IOR R/20/E/266 also presents some of the debate on the merits of the Daliʿ plateau and Jabal Jahhaf as sites for possible sanatoria for British troops.
23. Williams, *The Country and the City*, 120. This theme, of course, was elaborated much more fully in the context of landscape art in John Barrell's *The Dark Side of the Landscape*. Mary Louise Pratt has argued that the effacement of a human presence in colonial travel writing was a common trope. See Mary Louise Pratt, "Scratches on the Face of the Country; or, What Mr. Barrows Saw in the Land of the Bushmen," *Critical Inquiry*, 12 no. 1 (1985), 119–43.
24. Harris, *A Journey Through the Yemen*, 190–91.
25. Ryan, *Cartographic Eye*, 120.
26. Gavin, *Aden Under British Rule*, especially Ch. 8.
27. For a summary of the Ottoman documentary evidence presented to the Commission and the British point by point response see IOR R/20/E/234, Wahab

to Sec. to Govt. of India, enclosing "Memorandum on the Amiri Frontier," Appendix II, 2 Dec. 1902.
28. IOR R/20/E/233, Political Resident to Political Dept., Bombay, 13 May 1902. The fort at Laqmat al-Salah was destroyed on 8 May 1902, Political Resident to Political Dept., Bombay, 14 May 1902.
29. See IOR R/20/A/1472 for coverage of the Zindani-Ottoman alliance. See also IOR R/20/E/233, Political Resident to Political Dept., Bombay, 9 May 1902 and Political Resident to Political Dept., Bombay, 14 May 1902 for Wahab's account of a clash between two *sayyids*, one supportive of the Amir and the other of the Ottoman-appointed Shaykh, in the village of Lakmat al-Salah.
30. See IOR R/20/E/233, Political Resident to Political Dept., Bombay 24 April 1902 for Wahab's account of tax collection in Humada territory, Wahab to Sec. to Govt. of India, 23 April 1902 for collection in Habil al-Suq in the Wadi Safiya, and IOR R/20/E/234, Political Resident to Political Dept., Bombay, 21 May 1902 for collection in Sha'iri villages, Political Resident to Political Dept., Bombay, 11 Oct. 1902 on collection among the 'Ammara on the Yafi'i border.
31. IOR R/20/E/233, Wahab to Sec. to Govt. of India, 4 March 1902.
32. G.H. Fitzmaurice to Foreign Office, 12 Dec. 1902. ROY 5:108. Fitzmaurice had been Dragoman at the British embassy in Istanbul until he was seconded to the Boundary Commission in October 1902, specifically for his diplomatic experience in the Ottoman capital. See Gavin, *Aden under British Rule*, 223 and Wahab to Sec. to Gov. of India, Foreign Dept., 10 June 1904. ROY, 5:190.
33. IOR R/20/E/233, memo by H.M. Abud, Dali', 12 Feb. 1902.
34. IOR R/20/E/233, memo by H.M. Abud, forwarded to Maitland, 25 April 1902.
35. Gavin, *Aden under British Rule*, 220.
36. Curzon to Sec. of State for India, 26 Nov. 1901. ROY, 5:55.
37. IOR R/20/E/233, Wahab to Gov. of India, Foreign Dept., 7 April 1902. See also IOR R/20/E/234, Maitland to Political Dept., Bombay, 6 Dec. 1902.
38. IOR R/20/E/233, Sec. of State for India to Political Resident Aden, 13 May 1902, enclosed in Political Resident to Political Dept., Bombay, 13 May 1902.
39. IOR R/20/E/234, Curzon to Sec. of State for India, 13 June 1902.
40. IOR R/20/E/233, Wahab to Sec. to Gov. of India, Foreign Dept., 16 May 1902.
41. IOR R/20/E/234, Wahab to Sec. to Gov. of India, Foreign Dept., 13 June 1902. For the Amir's accounts, see IOR R/20/A/1198 for the full text of the account for the year 1902. See also, IOR R/20/A/5002 for a summary of the accounts.
42. On the absence of a trained surveyor in the Ottoman commission, see Wahab to Gov. of India, 25 May 1903. ROY, 5:134.
43. For incidents in which the British surveyors were turned back or fired upon see IOR R/20/E/233, Political Resident to Political Dept., Bombay, 31 March 1902, and IOR R/20/E/234, Wahab's diary entry for 21–28 May 1902 in Polit-

ical Resident to Political Dept., Bombay, 31 May 1902 and his entry for 16 Oct. 1902 in Wahab to Maitland, 23 Oct. 1902, and Wahab to Foreign Dept., India, 20 Nov. 1902.
44. IOR R/20/E/233, Political Resident to Political Dep., Bombay, 14 May 1902, diary entry for 7–12 May inclusive.
45. Wahab's diary entries can be found in IOR R/20/E/233 and IOR R/20/E/234.
46. The abstracts of the documents can be found in IOR R/20/E/234, Wahab to Foreign Dept., India, 2 December 1902, "Memorandum on the Amiri Frontier," Appendix 1. At least some of the full documents in translation are collected in IOR R/20/A/1198, although they are badly damaged.
47. As stated by Warneford in his notes, IOR R/20/A/5003.
48. For the Azraqi, see Warneford's notes and the MRAP, 100. For the Ahmadi, see Warneford's notes. For the Sha'iri see Warneford's notes and MRAP, 92. For the Halimayn tribes, see Warneford. For agreements on the pattern of *sum'a wa-tub'a*, see Serjeant, "Yāfi'ī Zaydīs, Āl Bū Bakr Sālim," 85.
49. See Warneford's notes and Hunter and Sealey, *Arab Tribes* (1909), 80–81.
50. IOR R/20/A/1198, letters collected and translated by Boundary Commission, 1902.
51. Winichakul, *Siam Mapped*, 97–109, *passim*.
52. IOR R/20/E/289, Jacob, *Monograph on the Aden Hinterland*, 2.
53. Jacob, *Kings of Arabia*, 83–4.
54. IOR R/20/A/1339, 5 Jan. 1907.
55. IOR R/20/A/1339, Jacob to DeBrath, 4 Dec. 1906.
56. IOR R/20/A/5003, Warneford, "Notes on the Territory of the Amir of Dhala," 1903.
57. IOR R/20/A/4853, "Precis of the Kotaibis Transit Dues on the Kafila Routes." See also Hunter and Sealey, *Account of the Arab Tribes*, (1909), 84–7.
58. IOR R/20/A/4853, Merewether to Davies, 21 Oct. 1904.
59. Which was later echoed by Hamilton in the period of the "forward policy." See, R.A.B. Hamilton, "The Social Organization of the Tribes of the Aden Protectorate," *Journal of the Royal Central Asian Society* vol. 30 (1943), 144.
60. IOR R/20/E/289, *Monograph on the Aden Hinterland*, 7.
61. A sentiment he expressed several times to the Aden Residency. See IOR R/20/A/1338, Jacob to 1st Ass. Resident, 31 Jan. 1905, Political Resident to Political Dept., Bombay, 30 April 1905, and Jacob, "Memorandum on the Radfan Tribes," 7 Sep. 1905.
62. The urgency of maintaining this appearance of order had already arisen in 1894 when the Hawshabis elected the 'Abdali Sultan as their own Sultan, thus eliminating the Hawshabi Sultanate and one of the "nine cantons" recognized by the British. See Gavin, *Aden under British Rule*, 210. As for the Qutaybi, Hamilton would later say that placing them under the authority of the Amir of Dali'

was a "political mistake." Hamilton, "The Social Organization of the Tribes of the Aden Protectorate," 155.
63. IOR R/20/A/1338, Harold Jacob, "Memorandum on the Proposed Change of Trade-Route," (1905) and Harold Jacob, "Memorandum on the Kotaibi Radfan Tribe," 8 April 1906.
64. For the general events surrounding this conference and drafts of the agreements see Hunter and Sealey, *Account of the Arab Tribes* (1909), 94–5 and 229. Also, GAT, 1:344–5.
65. Jacob, *Perfumes of Araby*, 78.
66. IOR R/20/A/1340, note by 'Ali Ja'far, 17 Jan. 1908 and Muhammad Taha to DeBrath, 21 Jan. 1908.
67. IOR R/20/A/1340, extracts from notes of an interview granted to the 'Abdali Sultan, 9 Feb. 1908.
68. IOR R/20/A/1340, see the text of the agreement; notes on a meeting between the Political Resident, the 'Abdali Sultan, the Hawshabi Sultan, the Amir of Dali', and Muqbil 'Abdullah al-Qutaybi, the nephew of Shaykh Muhammad Salih al-Akhram, 9 March 1908; and 'Abdali Sultan to Political Resident on the disputed clause, 24 March 1908.
69. IOR R/20/A/1340, Extract from weekly letter, 3 Oct. 1908 and IOR R/20/E/289, Jacob, *Monograph on the Aden Hinterland*, 19. See also Hunter and Sealey, *Account of the Arab Tribes* (1909), 347.
70. IOR R/20/A/1340, Shaykh 'Ali Nashir to Political Resident, Aug. 1908.
71. IOR R/20/A/1340, Ag. Secretary to the Gov. of Bombay to Secretary to Gov. of India, Foreign Dept., 31 March 1908.
72. The text of the agreement can be found in IOR R/20/A/1341.
73. IOR R/20/A/1341, Secretary of State for India to Gov. of India in Council, 14 Nov. 1913, approving the terms of the agreements. The texts of these agreements are found in Aitchison, *Collection of Treaties, Engagements and Sanads*, 5th ed., 11:144–8.
74. IOR R/20/A/1339, memo by Harold Jacob, 7 July 1907.
75. For detailed records on the planning of the initial bombing campaigns against the Imam's positions in Dali' as well as the towns of Qa'taba and Ta'izz see IOR R/20/A/1266 and 1267. See the correspondence in IOR R/20/A/3303 and 3646 for the punitive use of air power against the Qutaybi tribe in 1929 and in 1934.
76. See Priya Satia, "The Defense of Inhumanity: Air Control and the British Idea of Arabia," *American Historical Review*, 3 no. 1 (February 2006), 16–51. Satia also argues that the British use of punitive bombing was an effect of a moral imagination that viewed Arabia as inherently and irredeemably different.

4. DISORDER AND THE DOMAIN OF OBEDIENCE

1. Nazih al-Mu'ayyad al-'Azm, *Rihla fi Bilad al-'Arabiyya al-Sa'ida* (London: Fadi Press, 1985), 173–4.
2. Ameen Rihani, *Arabian Peak and Desert: Travels in Al-Yaman* (London: Constable & Co, Ltd, 1930), 98.
3. Hugh Scott, *In the High Yemen* (London: John Murray, 1942), 171.
4. Michel Foucault, *Security, Territory, Population*, trans. Graham Burchell (New York: Palgrave, 2007), 87–114 and 135–61.
5. Muhammad b. Muhammad Zabara, *A'immat al-Yaman bi-l-Qarn al-Rabi''Ashr* (Sanaa: al-Dar al-Yamaniyya li-l-Nashr wa-l-Tawzi', 1984), 156.
6. On the ethical imperative of "commanding good" in the Zaydi tradition, see Michael Cook, *Commanding Right and Forbidding Wrong in Islam* (Cambridge University Press, 2000), 227–51.
7. Muhsin b. Ahmad al-Harazi, *Fatrat al-Fawda wa-'Awdat al-Atrak ila Sanaa: al-Safr al-Thani min Tarikh al-Harazi (Riyad al-Rayahin), 1859–1872*, ed. Husayn b. 'Abdullah al-'Amri (Sanaa: Dar al-Hikma al-Yamaniyya, 1986), 178.
8. On events in 'Asir in the 1830s and 1840s, see Anne K. Bang, *The Idrīsī State in 'Asīr, 1906–1934* (Bergen: Centre for Middle Eastern and Islamic Studies, 1996), 11–25. For the Egyptian occupation, see 'Abd al-Hamid El-Batrik, "Egyptian-Yemeni Relations (1819–1840) and Their Implications for British Policy in the Red Sea," in P.M. Holt (ed.), *Political and Social Change in Modern Egypt: Historical Studies from the Ottoman Conquest to the United Arab Republic* (London: Oxford University Press, 1968), 281–90. Faqih Sa'id's uprising is covered in Kour, *The History of Aden*, 128–30, and the appearance of the "Jewish sorcerer" in al-Harazi, *Fatrat al-Fawda*, 145.
9. For an overview of the contested meaning and practice of citizenship in the late Ottoman Empire, see Ariel Salzmann, "Citizens in Search of a State: The Limits of Political Participation in the late Ottoman Empire," in Michael Hanagan and Charles Tilly (eds), *Extending Citizenship, Reconfiguring States* (Lanham, MD: Rowman & Littlefield Publishers, 1999), 37–66.
10. Ussama Makdisi, "Ottoman Orientalism," *American Historical Review* 107 no. 3 (June 2002), 768–96.
11. Ibid., 772.
12. On Abdül Hamid's mobilization of Islam as a form of state politics see Kemal H. Karpat, *The Politicization of Islam: Reconstructing Identity, State, Faith, and Community in the Late Ottoman State* (Oxford University Press, 2001) and Selim Deringil, *The Well-Protected Domains: Ideology and the Legitimation of Power in the Ottoman Empire, 1876–1909* (London: I.B. Tauris, 1998), 44–92.
13. Farah, *The Sultan's Yemen*, 143.
14. On the early administrative development, see Farah, *The Sultan's Yemen*, 97–100.

On the use of architecture and urban design as a mode of enacting state power, see Thomas Kühn, "Ordering Urban Space in Ottoman Yemen, 1872–1914" in Jens Hanssen *et al.* (eds), *The Empire in the City: Arab Provincial Capitals in the Late Ottoman Empire* (Würzburg: Ergon in Kommission, 2002), 329–47 and Messick, *The Calligraphic State*, 247.

15. See Thomas Kühn, "Clothing the 'uncivilized:' Military Recruitment in Ottoman Yemen and the Quest for 'Native' Uniforms, 1880–1914," in Suraiya Faroqhi and Christoph K. Neumann (eds), *Ottoman Costumes: From Textile to Identity* (Istanbul: Eren Publishers, 2004), 143–56.
16. Brinkley Messick, *The Calligraphic State: Textual Domination and History in a Muslim Society* (Berkeley: University of California Press, 1993), 101–05.
17. Ibid., 84–8.
18. See Thomas Kühn, "Ordering the Past of Ottoman Yemen, 1872–1914," *Turcica* 34 (2002), 189–220 and "An Imperial Borderland as Colony: Knowledge Production and the Elaboration of Difference in Ottoman Yemen, 1872–1914," *The MIT Electronic Journal of Middle East Studies* 3 (Spring 2003), 5–17.
19. See Jon Mandaville, "Memduh Pasha and Aziz Bey: Ottoman Experience in Yemen," in B.R. Pridham (ed.) *Contemporary Yemen* (London: Croom Helm, 1985), 20–33.
20. See Ussama Makdisi, *The Culture of Sectarianism: Community, History, and Violence in Nineteenth-Century Lebanon* (Berkeley: University of California Press, 2000), 105–08.
21. 'Ali b. 'Abdullah al-Iryani, *Sirat al-Imam Muhammad bin Yahya Hamid al-Din*, ed. Muhammad 'Isa al-Salihiyya ('Amman: Dar al-Bashir, 1996), 1:219. On the concept of *tajdid* in Zaydi thought, see Ella Landau-Tasseron, "Zaydī Imams as Restorers of Religion: *Ihyā'* and *Tajdīd* in Zaydī Literature," *Journal of Near Eastern Studies* 49, no. 3 (July 1990), 247–63.
22. al-Iryani, *Sirat al-Imam Muhammad*, 1:218.
23. Sayyid Muhammad al-Hariri al-Hamawi to Imam al-Mansur, 2 Nov. 1891, as quoted in ibid., 1:373.
24. Ibid., 1:377.
25. Ibid., 1:380.
26. 'Abdullah b. 'Abd al-Karim al-Jirafi, *al-Muqtataf min Tarikh al-Yaman* (Beirut: Manshurat al-'Asr al-Hadith, [1951] 1987), 285.
27. 'Abd al-Wasi' al-Wasi'i, *Tarikh al-Yaman* (Cairo: al-Matba'a al-Salafiyya, 1927/8), 198.
28. Yahya b. 'Ali al-Haddad, *Silsilat al-Darari*, WL (Tarikh: 104), fol. 2. On Yahya's *da'wa*, see Ahmad b. 'Abdullah al-Jindari's, *al-Jami' al-Wajiz bi-Wafiyat Dhui al-Tabriz*, WL (Tarikh: 37), fol. 218 and his *al-Durar al-Muntaqa fi Sirat al-Imam al-Mutawakkil 'ala Allah wa-Khasaluhu al-Murtada*, WL (Tarikh: 2521), fol. 4.

29. al-Jindari himself was said to have moved from Zaydism toward the Sunni traditionalists after he dreamed of the Prophet. See Ismaʿil b. ʿAli al-Akwaʿ, *Hijar al-ʿIlm wa-Maʿaqiluhu fi al-Yaman* (Damascus: Dar al-Fikr, 1995), 3:1476–8. In his history, al-Haddad refers to Jindari as the Imam of "*kalam* and *hadith*." See Yahya b. ʿAli b. Naji al-Haddad, *ʿUmdat al-Qari' fi Sirat Imam Zamanina Sayf al-Bari'*, WL (Tarikh: 2594), 13.
30. Ahmad b. Yahya al-Murtada, *Kitab al-Azhar* (Sanaa: Dar al-Hikma al-Yamaniyya, 1993), 314.
31. Muhammad b. Muhammad Zabara, *A'immat al-Yaman bi-l-Qarn al-Rabiʿ ʿAshr: Sirat al-Fatih al-Shahid* (Cairo: al-Matbaʿa al-Salafiyya, 1956), 1:105–06 and *Nuzhat al-Nazar fi Rijal al-Qarn al-Rabiʿ ʿAshr* (Sanaa: Markaz al-Dirasat wa-l-Abhath al-Yamaniyya, 1979), 241–4. See also al-Akwaʿ, *Hijar al-ʿIlm*, 1:131–2.
32. al-Wasiʿi, *Tarikh al-Yaman*, 305–07. See also the 1909 letter by the Imam published in the Egyptian newspaper *al-Mu'ayyad*, in which he defended his war against the Ottoman administration in similar terms. Zabara, *Sirat al-Fatih al-Shahid*, 1:147.
33. al-Wasiʿi, *Tarikh al-Yaman*, 219 and Wenner, *Modern Yemen*, 46.
34. See the text of the agreement in al-Wasiʿi, *Tarikh al-Yaman*, 236–9.
35. Thomas Kühn, "Shaping and Reshaping Colonial Ottomanism: Contesting Boundaries of Difference and Integration in Ottoman Yemen, 1872–1919," *Comparative Studies of South Asia, Africa and the Middle East* 27, no. 2 (2007), 27–9.
36. See the letter from Muhammad al-Idrisi to Imam Yahya dated 5 March 1912 in Zabara, *Sirat al-Fatih al-Shahid*, 1:244 and the letter he wrote to the Imam published in the Egyptian newspaper, *al-Ahram*, around the same time in Muhammad b. Ahmad al-ʿAqili, *Tarikh al-Mikhlaf al-Sulaymani* (Riyadh?: Matabiʿ Walid, 1989), 2:704. On the war with Italy as well as details on Italian support of the Idrisi, see John Baldry, "The Turkish-Italian War in the Yemen, 1911–1912," *Arabian Studies III* (1976), 51–65. For a coastal view of the war, see Ismaʿil al-Washali, *Dhayl Nashr al-Thana' al-Hasan*, ed. Muhammad al-Shuʿaybi (Sanaa: Matabiʿ al-Yaman al-ʿAsriyya, 1982), 109–110 and 115–16.
37. For a summary of events after the conclusion of the treaty of Daʿan, see John Baldry, "Al-Yaman and the Turkish Occupation," *Arabica* 23 no. 2 (1976), 190–95.
38. ʿAbd al-Karim b. Ahmad al-Mutahhar, *Sirat al-Imam Yahya bin Muhammad Hamid al-Din*, ed. Muhammad ʿIsa al-Salihiyya (ʿAmman: Dar al-Bashir, 1998), 2:100,119, 124, and Jacob, *Kings of Arabia*, 125.
39. Mutahhar collection, undated draft announcement (most likely from 1913 or 1914) to the *ashraf*, ulama, Shaykhs, and notables of Yemen. The mufti was Khayri b. ʿAwni al-Arkubi.

40. Paul Dresch, "A Letter from Imam Yahya concerning the Idrisi," *New Arabian Studies* 3 (1996), 66. See also the Imam's letter to the *sayyids* and *'ulama'* of Huth from 5 July 1912 in Zabara, *Sirat al-Fatih al-Shahid*, 1:254–7.
41. Haykel, *Revival and Reform in Islam*, 84–5.
42. Ibid., 127.
43. al-Mutahhar, *Sirat al-Imam*, 2:22–3.
44. De Certeau, *The Practice of Everyday Life*, 120. For Messick this type of spatial narration was part of the greater politico-discursive formation he called "the calligraphic state." Messick, *The Calligraphic State*, 248. For the Moroccan example of royal sovereignty constituted through the mobility of the court as it travelled through the king's domains, see Clifford Geertz, "Centers, Kings, and Charisma: Reflections on the Symbolics of Power," in *Local Knowledge* (New York: Basic Books, 1983), 134–42.
45. Makdisi, *The Culture of Sectarianism*, 42.
46. al-Mutahhar, *Sirat al-Imam*, 2:93. He uses this language specifically in description of the situation in the southern town of 'Udayn during the period of Ottoman rule.
47. Haykel, *Revival and Reform*, 202 and Rihani, *Arabian Peak and Desert*, 90–91.
48. For example, the appointment of the traditionist scholar Husayn b. 'Ali al-'Amri to the Head of the Court of Appeals. See Zabara, *Sirat al-Fatih al-Shahid*, 1:242 and Haykel, *Revival and Reform*, 198–9 and 204–05.
49. On education, see Messick, *The Calligraphic State*, 108–09.
50. al-Mutahhar, *Sirat al-Imam*, 2:21.
51. Ibid., 2:37–38. Mutahhar's account is summarized by Zabara, *Sirat al-Fatih al-Shahid*, 2:3–4.
52. al-Mutahhar, *Sirat al-Imam*, 2:50.
53. There are no hard and fast statistics available on the military and military service in this period; for estimates of total enlistments, see Raymond Davis to Sec. of State, 20 Dec. 1923 in Reginald W. Sinclair (ed.), *Documents on the History of Southwest Arabia* (Salisbury, NC: Documentary Publications, 1976), 1:110–11; IOR R/20/A/3207, "Report on Zaidi Garrison"; Wenner, *Modern Yemen*, 57–9; Peterson, *Yemen: The Search for a Modern State*, 53; and Sultan Naji, *al-Tarikh al-'Askari li-l-Yaman* (Beirut: Dar al-'Awda, 1985), 111.
54. al-Mutahhar, *Sirat al-Imam*, 2:57. See also al-Haddad, *'Umdat al-Qari'*, 38.
55. al-Haddad, *'Umdat al-Qari'*, 33–5. On the modern system of education, the introduction of new subjects, and the spatial relocation of education from the mosque to a separate structure, see Messick, *The Calligraphic State*, 107–09.
56. Peterson, *Yemen: The Search for a Modern State*, 53, Bidwell, *The Two Yemens*, 108, and Wenner, *Modern Yemen*, 57–8.
57. D. Van Der Meulen, *Faces in Shem* (London: John Murray, 1961), 136–7. For eye-witness accounts of the military and the Friday procession, see Ameen

Rihani, *Muluk al-'Arab*, 8th ed. (Beirut: Dar al-Jil, n.d.), 1:152–3, Edgar O'Balance, *The War in the Yemen* (Hamden, CT: Archon Books, 1971), 38–40, and Salvator Aponte, *Hadhihi Hiya al-Yaman al-Sa'ida*, trans. Taha Fawzi (Beirut: Manshurat Dar al-Adab, n.d.), 94–7.

58. IOR R/20/A/3207, "Report on Zaidi Garrison."
59. al-Mutahhar, *Sirat al-Imam*, 2:52–3. For similar descriptions see al-Haddad, *'Umdat al-Qari'*, 36–7, and Zabara, *Sirat al-Fatih al-Shahid*, 2:13–14. Both of these authors relied largely on al-Mutahhar for their descriptions.
60. Mitchell, *Colonising Egypt*, 35–9.
61. al-Mutahhar, *Sirat al-Imam*, 2:53.
62. Michel Foucault, "Space, Knowledge, and Power," in Paul Rabinow (ed.), *The Foucault Reader* (New York: Pantheon, 1984), 242–3.
63. The following towns were connected to the main lines: Dhamar, Yarim, Qa'taba, al-Mukha, Bayt al-Faqih, Zabid, Hays, Luhayya, and Midi. See Arab Bureau, *Handbook of Yemen* (Cairo: Government Press, 1917), 17–31.
64. al-Mutahhar, *Sirat al-Imam*, 2:61.
65. Ibid., 2:61.
66. al-Haddad, *'Umdat al-Qari'*, 31–2.
67. As quoted in Naji, *al-Tarikh al-'Askari*, 131.
68. al-Haddad, *'Umdat al-Qari'*, 48. See also al-Mutahhar, *Sirat al-Imam*, 2:63–4 and al-Haddad's description of the Imam's 'Id procession, 49–51.
69. The *liwa'* of Ta'izz consisted of the districts of Ta'izz, al-Qama'ira, Hujarriyya, al-Mukha, Yarim, Nadira, Ibb, and 'Udayn. The boundaries of the *liwa'* were largely those of the Ottoman *sanjak* of Ta'izz after the administrative reorganization of 1872. See Farah, *The Sultan's Yemen*, 276. The latter four districts would later be attached to the *liwa'* of Dhamar and by 1944 incorporated into a new *liwa'* of Ibb.
70. Ahmad b. Muhammad al-Wazir, *Hayat al-Amir 'Ali bin 'Abdullah al-Wazir* (n.p.: Manshurat al-'Asr al-Hadith, 1987), 89–90. More than any other scholar, Paul Dresch has consistently argued the importance of state largesse and the rise of the large shaykhly houses in the highlands. See Dresch, *Tribes, Government, and History*, 207–212. On patterns of landholding in the southern uplands, see Sheila Carapico and Richard Tutwiler, *Yemeni Agriculture and Economic Change* (Sanaa: American Institute for Yemeni Studies, 1981), 23–5 and 98–9.
71. Hamud b. Muhammad al-Dawla, *al-Zawraq al-Halwa fi Sirat Qa'id al-Jaysh wa-Amir al-Liwa'*, ed. Zayd b. 'Ali al-Wazir (Beirut: Manshurat al-'Asr al-Hadith, 1988), 184–6 and al-Mutahhar, *Sirat al-Imam*, 2:80–2. See also and al-Wazir, *Hayat al-Amir*, 94–9.
72. al-Dawla, *al-Zawraq al-Halwa*, 188–9 and Yahya Mansur b. Nasr, *Shi'r wa Dhikriyyat* (Beirut: Manshurat al-'Asr al-Hadith, 1987), 37–8.
73. al-Dawla, *al-Zawraq al-Halwa*, 188–189 and al-Mutahhar, *Sirat al-Imam*, 2:82.

74. al-Mutahhar, *Sirat al-Imam*, 2:92–93 and al-Dawla, *al-Zawraq al-Halwa*, 197–8.
75. al-Dawla, *al-Zawraq al-Halwa*, 222.
76. For details on the campaigns in these regions see al-Mutahhar, *Sirat al-Imam*, 2:96–7 and al-Dawla, *al-Zawraq al-Halwa*, 267–2. Shaykh Muhammad Nasir Muqbil of Mawiya (Qama'ira) was said to have even left one third of his wealth to Imam Yahya. Al-Wazir, *Hayat al-Amir*, 117.
77. al-Mutahhar, *Sirat al-Imam*, 2:180.
78. John M. Willis, "Leaving Only Question-Marks: Geographies of Rule in Modern Yemen," in Madawi Al-Rasheed and Robert Vitalis (eds), *Counter-Narratives: History, Contemporary Society, and Politics in Saudi Arabia and Yemen* (New York: Palgrave Macmillan, 2004), 119–50.
79. Hasan b. Ahmad al-Iryani, *Sadiq al-Tahaqiq bi-ma Hadatha fi Qabilatay Hashid wa-l-Zaraniq*, WL (Majmu' 781), fol. 2.
80. Ibid., fol. 5.
81. Zabara, *Sirat al-Fatih al-Shahid*, 2:89–91, Shamahi, *al-Yaman*, 191–4, and anon., *al-Rawd al-Bassam fi Sirat al-Mawlay Sayf al-Islam Ahmad bin Amir al-Mu'minin Yahya al-Imam*, WL (Majmu' 148), fols. 170–75.
82. 'Abdullah al-Wazir to Ba Salama, 11 Feb. 1925. In the final paragraph of an otherwise everyday letter, Imam Yahya informed Ba Salama that the whole of Hashid had been "thoroughly subdued" and that nearly 200 hostages were taken. Both letters are reproduced in Muhammad b. 'Ali al-Akwa' Hawali, *Hayat 'Alim wa-Amir* (Sanaa: Maktabat al-Jil al-Jadid, 1987), 1:454–7.
83. al-Iryani, *Sadiq al-Tahaqiq*, fol. 16–18.
84. Ibid., fol. 21.
85. Ibid., fol. 25.
86. Ibid., fol. 22.
87. Zabara, *Sirat al-Fatih al-Shahid*, 2:197–8. Muhammad b. 'Ali al-Akwa', writing after the revolution, suggests that the accusations were deliberate cover for a carefully planned and executed campaign against Bayt al-Ahmar devised by Imam Yahya and Ahmad. al-Akwa' al-Hawali, *Hayat 'Alim wa-Amir*, 2:118–19.
88. For population estimates see Wenner, *Modern Yemen*, 73; and even Iryani, *Sadiq al-Tahaqiq*, fol. 33. The Arab Bureau estimated their numbers at 20,000. *Handbook of Yemen*, 1917, 52–3. For their ability to resist Ottoman forces, see G. Wyman Bury, *Arabia Infelix or the Turks in Yaman* (London: Macmillan, 1915), 23–4.
89. al-Iryani, *Sadiq al-Tahaqiq*, fol. 33, and Ahmad b. Muhammad al-Shami, *Imam al-Yaman Ahmad Hamid al-Din* (Beirut: Dar al-Kitab al-Jadid, 1965), 71.
90. IOR R/20/A/ 3038, letter to Political Resident, 10 July 1922.
91. At different moments in the campaign, the regular army was joined by mem-

bers of Hada (Madhhij), Anis, Hajur (Hashid), Arhab (Bakil), Hayma, Waʿizat ('Akk), and Sharaf.
92. al-Iryani, *Sadiq al-Tahaqiq*, fol. 34.
93. Ibid., fols. 37 and 44 and Shami, *Ahmad Hamid al-Din*, 72.
94. al-Iryani, *Sadiq al-Tahaqiq*, fol. 63.
95. Ibid., fol. 83 and al-Akwaʿ, *Hijar al-ʿIlm*, 1:222–5. Ahmad would later order the destruction of the tomb of the Sufi, Ahmad b. ʿAlwan, in Yafrus, Jabal Habashi south-west of Taʿizz. The poet and member of the Free Yemenis, Muhammad Mahmud al-Zubayri, wrote a scathing critique of the move. See al-Akwaʿ, *Hijar al-ʿIlm*, 2:750–51. For a more positive appraisal of Ahmad's actions, see al-Shami, *Ahmad Hamid al-Din*, 90–2.
96. al-Iryani, *Sadiq al-Tahaqiq*, fol. 85.
97. Muhammad b. ʿAbd al-Rahman Sharaf al-Din, *al-Barq al-Mutaʿallaq fi Rihlat Mawlana Sayf al-Islam ila al-Mashraq*, WL (Jughrafiya: 1). See also al-Jirafi, *al-Muqtataf min Tarikh al-Yaman*, 312–14.
98. Abdualaziz K. Msaodi ['Abd al-'Aziz al-Mas'udi], "The Yemeni Opposition Movement, 1918–1948." Unpublished PhD Dissertation, Georgetown University (1987), 137.
99. Rihani, *Arabian Peaks and Desert*, 142.
100. Lefebvre, *The Production of Space*, 122.

5. THE CENTRE OF RENEWAL AND REFORM

1. Abul Kalam Azad, *Khilafat and Jaziratul-Arab*, trans. Mirza Abdul Qadir Beg (Bombay: Central Khilafat Committee, 1920), 190.
2. "al-Zaraniq," *al-Iman*, Nov.-Dec. 1928, 1–2.
3. "al-Zaraniq wa-l-Wahda al-Yamaniyya," *al-Iman*, Nov. 1929, 2.
4. al-'Azm, *Rihla fi Bilad al-'Arabiyya al-Sa'ida*, 308.
5. For the role of print capitalism in the formation of national and largely secular publics, see the now classic account of Anderson, *Imagined Communities*, 37–46. Laffan is critical of the secular underpinnings of Anderson's approach, looking instead at the formation of an Islamic public sphere, embedded in an Islamic print culture and ecumenical notions of religion. See Laffan, *Islamic Nationhood*, 9–10. On the formation of a Muslim public sphere, see Dale F. Eickelman and Armando Salvatore, "Muslim Publics," in Dale F. Eickelman and Armando Salvatore (eds), *Public Islam and the Common Good* (Leiden: Brill, 2004), 3–27.
6. Muhammad Rashid Rida, *al-Khilafa* (Cairo: al-Zahra' li-l-'Ilam al-'Arabi, 1988), 59.
7. "A'mal al-Islah fi Bayt al-Faqih," *al-Iman*, Dec. 1929, 1.
8. Haj, *Reconfiguring Islamic Tradition*, 7–8. See also John O. Voll, "Renewal and Reform in Islamic History: *Tajdid* and *Islah*," in John L. Esposito (ed.), *Voices of Resurgent Islam*(Oxford University Press, 1983), 34.

9. "Asbab Ta'akhkhur al-Muslimin," *al-Iman*, Oct. 1932, 1–2. Cf. Shakib Arslan, *Limadha Ta'khkhara al-Muslimun wa-Limadha Taqaddama Ghayruhum* (Beirut: Dar al-Anwar, n.d.), 61–2.
10. "Marad al-Akhlaq," *al-Iman*, July 1934, 1–2.
11. Haj, *Reconfiguring Islamic Tradition*, 114. See also Charles C. Adams, *Islam and Modernism in Egypt* (New York: Russel & Russel, 1968), 169.
12. See "Fi Sabil al-Ta'awun," *al-Iman*, Aug. 1929, 1–2 and "Fi Sabil al-Ta'awun al-Nafi'," *al-Iman*, Nov. 1931, 1.
13. "al-Yaman Maqarr al-Iman wa-l-Hikma," *al-Iman*, Oct. 1932, 1–2 and "al-Bilad al-Hindiyya," *al-Iman*, Sep./Oct. 1931, 4.
14. See Hourani, *Arabic Thought*, 115–17 and Jamal al-Din al-Afghani and Muhammad 'Abduh, "al-Ta'assub," in *al-'Urwa al-Wuthqa* (Beirut: Dar al-Kitab al-'Arabi, n.d.), 85.
15. "al-Shafi'i wa-l-Zaydi," *al-Iman*, April 1929, 2. See also, "Madhahib Ahl al-Islam, *al-Iman*, Dec. 1928, 1–2.
16. See for example Bernard Haykel, "Reforming Islam by Dissolving the *Madhhabs*: Shawkanī and his Zaydī Detractors," in Bernard G. Weiss (ed.), *Studies in Islamic Legal Theory* (Leiden: Brill, 2002), 337–64.
17. e.g. Rida, *al-Khilafa*, 60.
18. See David Dean Commins, *Islamic Reform: Politics and Social Change in Late Ottoman Syria* (Oxford University Press, 1990), 69 and Amal Ghazal, *Islamic Reform and Arab Nationalism: Expanding the Crescent from the Mediterranean to the Indian Ocean (1880s-1930s)* (London: Routledge, 2010), 32–4.
19. Haykel, *Revival and Reform*, 206–09 and al-'Akwa', *Hijar al-'Ilm*, 2:591.
20. "Ijtima' al-Kalima wa-Ijma' al-Umma fi al-Yaman," *al-Iman*, April/June 1928, 1.
21. Rihani, *Arabian Peak and Desert*, 104.
22. See for example Ameen Rihani's account of Imam Yahya's daily *majlis* in which he attended to the minutiae of governance, *Arabian Peak and Desert*, 221–6.
23. T. Fujitani, *Splendid Monarchy: Power and Pageantry in Modern Japan* (Berkeley: University of California Press, 1996), 25.
24. On the genealogy of Bayt al-Wazir and the contested relationship between 'Ali b. 'Abdullah, 'Abdullah b. Ahmad and Imam Yahya, see Gabriele vom Bruck, *Islam, Memory, and Morality in Yemen: Ruling Families in Transition* (London: Palgrave, 2005), 76–80 and Dresch, *History of Modern Yemen*, 44–5.
25. Rashad Muhammad al-'Alimi, *al-Taqlidiyya wa-l-Hadatha fi al-Nizam al-Qanuni al-Yamani* (Cairo: Matabi' al-Shuruq, n.d.), 274–5. Cf. Muhammad b. Husayn al-Kibsi's letter of appointment from the same year, in Haykel, *Revival and Reform*, 203.
26. Mutahhar collection. On the Zaydi attitude towards tribal customary law, see Dresch, *Tribes, Government, and History*, 183–8.

27. Shelagh Weir, *A Tribal Order: Politics and Law in the Mountains of Yemen* (Austin: University of Texas Press, 2007), 148.
28. See Paul Dresch, "Guaranty of the Market at Ḥūth," *Arabian Studies* 8 (1990), 63–91 and "Keeping the Imam's Peace: A Response to Tribal Disorder in the 1950's," *Peuples Méditerranéens* 46 (Jan.-March, 1989), 77–95. It would seem, then, that Serjeant's anecdotal account of Imam Yahya's hostility to tribal customary law had as much to do with a state performance of Islamic piety as with actual policy. See R.B. Serjeant, "The Interplay between Tribal Affinities and Religious (Zaydī) Authority in the Yemen, *al-Abhath* 30 (1982), 43–4.
29. Dresch, *Tribes, Government, and History*, 184.
30. For two critical, often polemical, overviews of the taxation policies of Imam Yahya's state, see Hasan Muhammad al-Kuhlani, "al-Nizam al-Dara'ibi wa-'Alaqatuhu bi-l-Jawanib al-Iqtisadiyya wa-l-Siyasa fi 'Ahd ma qabla al-Thawra," *Dirasat Yamaniyya*, 30 (Oct., Nov., Dec. 1987), 131–59 and Muhammad Sa'id al-'Attar, *al-Takhalluf al-Iqtisadi wa-l-Ijtima'i fi al-Yaman* (Algiers: al-Matbu'at al-Wataniyya al-Jaza'iriyya, 1965), 240–41. A more sober account of taxation in Sanaa during this period is given in R. B. Serjeant and Husayn al-'Amri, "Administrative Organization," in R. B. Serjeant and Ronald Lewcock (eds), *Ṣanʿāʾ—An Arabian Islamic City* (London: World of Islam Festival Trust, 1983), 154–60.
31. See Isaac Hollander, *Jews and Muslims in Lower Yemen: A Study in Protection and Restraint, 1918–1949* (Leiden: Brill, 2005), 119.
32. Muhammad b. Muhammad Zabara, *al-Anba' 'an Dawlat Bilqis wa-Saba'* (Sanaa: Dar al-Yamaniyya li-l-Nashr wa-l-Tawzi', 1984), 71.
33. Mutahhar collection, petition from 'Abduh 'Ali al-Jabiri of Mafhaq.
34. *al-Iman*, Nov./Dec. 1933, 2.
35. Cf. Timothy Mitchell's discussion of the state as "an effect of mundane practices of spatial organization, temporal arrangement, functional specification, supervision and surveillance, and representation that create the appearance of a world fundamentally divided into state and society or state and economy." "Society, Economy, and the State Effect," in George Steinmetz (ed.), *State/Culture: State-Formation after the Cultural Turn* (Ithaca, NY: Cornell University Press, 1999), 95.
36. Messick, *The Calligraphic State*, 51. For the coverage of the application of the *hudud* punishments in the *al-Iman*, see Gerald J. Obermeyer, "*Al-Iman* and Al-Imam: Ideology and State in the Yemen, 1900–1948," in Marwan R. Buheiry (ed.), *Intellectual Life in the Arab East, 1840–1939* (Beirut: American University of Beirut, 1981), 181–2.
37. Rashid Rida, "Rawabit al-Jinsiyya wa-l-Hayat al-Milliyya," *al-Manar*, 13 Dec. 1905/vol. 8, 789.
38. The critique of ethnic nationalism as an inherently divisive ideology in com-

parison with Islam's unity was widespread in reformist circles in the Arab world and beyond. See, for example, Muhammad 'Abduh's *fatwa* "Fi al-Jinsiyya wa-l-Qawmiyya," in Muhammad 'Amara (ed.), *al-A'mal al-Kamila li-l-Imam Muhammad 'Abduh* (Cairo: Dar al-Shuruq, 2006), 2:497–500, Rida, "Rawabit al-Jinsiyya," 784–91, and Muhammad Iqbal, *The Reconstruction of Religious Thought in Islam* (Dubai: Kitab al-Islamiyyah, n.d.), 158–9.

39. al-Mutahhar, *Sirat al-Imam*, 2:355–6.
40. Ibid., 2:194.
41. See Eliezer Tauber, "Rashīd Riḍā as Pan-Arabist before World War I," *The Muslim World* 79 no. 1–2 (1989), 108–111.
42. For an extended discussion of Rida's work on the Caliphate, see Malcolm H. Kerr, *Islamic Reform: The Political and Legal Theories of Muḥammad 'Abduh and Rashīd Riḍā* (Berkeley: University of California Press, 1966), 153–86 and Hamid Enayat, *Modern Islamic Political Thought* (Austin: University of Texas Press, 1982), 70–83.
43. Azad, *Khilafat*, 257 and Mohamed Ali's 10 July 1920 letter to Lloyd George on the postwar status of Mecca in Mushirul Hasan (ed.), *Mohamed Ali in Indian Politics* (New Delhi: Atlantic Publishers, 1986), 3:123–38.
44. Rashid Rida, *al-Wahhabiyyun wa-l-Hijaz* (Madinat Nasr: Dar al-Nada, 2000), 49.
45. Rida, *al-Khilafa*, 79.
46. Ibid., 78.
47. Rihani, *Arabian Peak and Desert*, 99.
48. IOR R/20/A/3075 and *al-Manar*, 14 July, 1923/vol. 24, 551–5.
49. "al-Yaman wa-Inkiltira wa-l-'Alam al-Islami," *al-Iman*, June/July, 1928, 4.
50. al-Wasi'i, *Tarikh al-Yaman*, 358.
51. *al-Manar*, 13 Aug. 1923/vol. 24, 638.
52. "Qarar al-Mut'tamar al-Islami al-'Amm li-l-Khilafa bi Misr," *al-Manar*, 7 Sept. 1926/vol. 27, 458. See also Martin Kramer, *Islam Assembled: The Advent of the Muslim Congresses* (New York: Columbia University Press, 1986), 100–102. On the Egyptian context and King Fuad's interest in being named Caliph, see Israel Gershoni and James P. Jankowski, *Egypt, Islam, and the Arabs: The Search for Egyptian Nationhood, 1900–1930* (Oxford University Press, 1986), 63–6.
53. See Kramer, *Islam Assembled*, 106–122 and Achille Sékaly, *Le congrès du Khalifat et ce congrès du monde musulman* (Paris: Éditions Ernest Leroux, 1926), 211–12. Hafiz Wahba, one of Ibn Sa'ud's advisers, argued that the conference failed primarily because of the differing opinions between Ibn Sa'ud and many of the foreign delegates concerning the proper path of reform (*islah*), see his *Jazirat al-'Arab fi al-Qarn al-'Ishrin* (Cairo: Lajnat al-Ta'lif wa-l-Tarjama wa-l-Nashr, 1935), 297.
54. IOR R/20/A/2922, Major B.R. Reilly, Acting Political Resident, Aden to High Commissioner of Egypt, 28 July 1926.

55. Zabara, *Sirat al-Fatih al-Shahid*, 2:282–3 and *al-Anba'*, 76.
56. al-Mutahhar, *Sirat al-Imam*, 2:445–6. See also Zabara, *Sirat al-Fatih al-Shahid*, 2:96.
57. Zabara, *Sirat al-Fatih al-Shahid*, 2:131. For an account of the Khilafat delegation to the Kingdom of the Hijaz, see BNA FO 686/139, Wizarat al-Kharijiyya li-l-Hukuma al-Hijaziyya, "Muhimmat al-Wafd al-Hindi fi al-Hijaz," 1925.
58. See for example his letter to Qadi al-Wasi'i ordering him to "enquire into the welfare of our brethren the Moslems" and to collect *zakat* in Egypt and elsewhere in 1928–29. IOR R/20/A/2922, J.C. Penney, Controller of Public Security Intelligence, Khartoum to Sudan Agent, Cairo, 23 Jan. 1929. See also the account of 'Abd al-Rahman al-Saqqaf's attempts to collect money on behalf of the Imam in Batavia in 1930. IOR R/20/A/3374, Consul General, Batavia to Aden Residency, and DCI, Singapore, 3 Feb. 1931.
59. "al-Radd 'ala al-Za'im Muhammad 'Ali al-Hindi," *al-Manar*, 18 June 1928/vol. 29, 180.
60. See, for example, his collected journalistic writings in defence of Ibn Sa'ud's state and his policy of rigorously enforcing his vision of correct belief and practice in the Hijaz, published in 1927, *al-Wahhabiyyun wa-l-Hijaz*.
61. For descriptions of the visit by Gasparini and the signing of the treaty, see Zabara, *Sirat al-Fatih al-Shahid*, 2:144–8 and al-Jirafi, *al-Muqtataf min Tarikh al-Yaman*, 308. For the international political context of the agreement, see John Baldry, "Anglo-Italian Rivalry in Yemen and 'Asir, 1900–1934," *Die Welt des Islams*, vol. 17 no. 1 (1976–1977), 171–5; Peterson, *Yemen: The Search for a Modern State*, 60–61; Wenner, *Modern Yemen*, 152–4; and Salim, *Takwin al-Yaman al-Hadith*, 304–08.
62. "Mu'ahada Italiyya-Yamaniyya," *al-Manar*, 5 Dec. 1926/vol. 27, 715.
63. Zabara, *Nuzhat al-Nazar*, 208.
64. 'Abd al-'Aziz al-Tha'alibi, *al-Rihla al-Yamaniyya* (Beirut: Dar al-Gharb al-Islami, 1997), 100.
65. al-Wazir, *Hayat al-Amir*, 212. While al-Wazir's criticism of the transformation of the Imamate into a hereditary monarchy can partly be explained by his own desire to defend the legitimacy of 'Ali b. 'Abdullah's claim to the title and his participation in the assassination of Imam Yahya, it would be inaccurate to ignore the very real doctrinal issues at stake here. Even 'Abdullah al-Shamahi, who was at moments sympathetic to Imam Yahya, points out that his adoption of the hereditary monarchy was directly counter to the "revolutionary spirit" (*al-ruh al-thawriyya*) of Zaydism. Shamahi *al-Yaman*, 190. Some contemporary Zaydi thinkers attribute the marginalization of Zaydism in Yemen to Imam Yahya's transformation of the Imamate into a hereditary monarchy in this period. See Muhammad Hakim, *Qira'at fi al-Fikr al-Zaydi: Hiwar ma' al-Ustadh Ibrahim al-Wazir* (Beirut: Dar al-Manhal, 1993), 50–53.

66. al-Wazir, *Hayat al-Amir*, 212.
67. Haykel, *Revival and Reform*, 210.
68. Among others, the group of scholars included al-Husayn b. 'Ali al-'Amri, Zayd b. 'Ali al-Daylami, 'Abdullah b. Ibrahim b. Ahmad b. al-Imam, Ahmad b. 'Ali al-Kuhlani, 'Abdullah b. 'Ali 'Abd al-Qadir, Muhammad b. Sayf al-Islam Ahmad Hamid al-Din, al-Qasm b. Husayn al-'Izzi Abu Talib, Muhammad b. Hasan al-Dallal, 'Abdullah b. 'Ali al-Yamani, Lutf b. Muhammad al-Zubayri and Ahmad b. Ahmad al-Jirafi.
69. Zabara, *Sirat al-Fatih al-Shahid*, 2:108. Again, this is an argument made much more forcefully by Bernard Haykel in his intellectual history of Shawkani's thought. See Haykel, *Revival and Reform in Islam*, 210–12.
70. Zabara, *Sirat al-Fatih al-Shahid*, 2:109–110.
71. Haykel, *Revival and Reform in Islam*, 211.
72. al-Akwa', *Hijar al-'Ilm*, 2:822–4.
73. Most travellers, both Western and Arab, responded positively to Muhammad Raghib, leaving glowing accounts of the Minister. See al-'Azm, *Rihla*, 172–4, Van Der Meulen, *Faces in Shem*, 120, and Aponte, *Hadhihi hiyya al-Yaman al-Sa'ida*, 158–61.
74. Aponte, *Hadhihi hiyya al-Yaman al-Sa'ida*, 154–5.
75. Shakib Arslan, *al-Irtisamat al-Litaf fi Khatir al-Hajj ila Aqdas Mataf* (Beirut: al-Mu'assasa al-'Arabiyya li-l-Dirasat wa-l-Nashr, 2004), 256.
76. For the text of the treaty, see al-'Aqili, *al-Mikhlaf al-Sulaymani*, 2:261–2. On the British view of the Idrisi's legal status, see BNA FO 905/1, Eastern (Arabia) Confidential, 15 Jan. 1934, Sir John Simon to Sir E. Drummond.
77. *The Saudi Green Book, 1934* (London: Archive Editions, 1994), 31.
78. See al-'Aqili, *al-Mikhlaf al-Sulaymani*, 2:944–7 and Alexei Vassiliev, *The History of Saudi Arabia* (London: Saqi Books, 2000), 282–4.
79. Sharaf al-Din, *al-Barq al-Muta'alliq*, fol. 62.
80. Ibid., fol. 72.
81. "al-Mawqif baynana wa-bayn al-Imam Yahya," *Umm al-Qura*, 22 Feb. 1934, 4.
82. "Du'at al-Shiqaq li-l-Harb bayn al-Imamayn Yahya wa-'Abd al-'Aziz," *al-Manar*, 2 April 1927/vol. 28, 159. On the Raja of Mahmudabad's call for the cancellation of the Hajj after the Sa'udi occupation of Mecca, see BNA FO 967/3, extract from the *Indian Daily Telegraph*, 15 June 1926.
83. "Wayl li-l-'Arab min Sharr qad Iqtaraba," *al-Manar*, Sep. 1933/vol. 33, 383.
84. On the Islamic delegation, see "Wafd al-Sulh wa-l-Salam," *al-Manar*, July 1934/vol. 34, 232–5, Sharaf al-Din, *al-Barq al-Muta'allaq*, fol.85, Cleveland, *Islam against the West*, 81–2.
85. Published in *al-Iman*, June/July 1934, *Umm al-Qura*, 7 July 1934, and *al-Manar*, July 1934.
86. "al-Islah wa-l-Tajdid al-Islami," *al-Manar*, July 1934/vol. 34, 207–08.

87. See 'Abdullah Juzaylan, *Lamahat min Dhikriyyat al-Tufula* (Cairo: Maktabat Madbuli, 1984), 15–16.
88. Muhammad Mahmud al-Zubayri, *al-Muntalaqat al-Nazariyya fi Fikr al-Thawra al-Yamaniyya* (Beirut: Dar al-'Awda, 1983), 9. On the opposition of 'Abdullah al-Wazir, see al-Wazir, *Hayat al-Amir*, 285–8. See also J. Leigh Douglas, *The Free Yemeni Movement, 1935–1962* (Beirut: The American University of Beirut, 1987), esp. ch. 2, which details the first wave of opposition after the Sa'udi-Yemeni war.
89. Michel Foucault, *The History of Sexuality*, trans. Robert Hurley (New York: Pantheon Books, 1978), 86.

6. THE RETURN OF INDETERMINACY

1. Gaston Bachelard, *The Poetics of Space*, trans. Maria Jolas (Boston: Beacon Press, 1994), xxxvi.
2. IOR R/20/E/289, Jacob, *Monograph on the Aden Hinterland*, 29–30 and Jacob, *Kings of Arabia*, 113.
3. Jacob, *Kings of Arabia*, 245.
4. al-Wasi'i, *Tarikh al-Yaman*, 261.
5. For discussion of this period of intermittent warfare, see Wenner, *Modern Yemen*, 150–51, Bidwell, *The Two Yemens*, 68–71, and Dresch, *A History of Modern Yemen*, 30–35.
6. IOR R/20/A/1259, 'Ali Ibrahim manages to refer to Zaydi "bolshevism" while simultaneously referring to Imam Yahya as "Kaiser William." Report by 'Ali Ibrahim, 13 Jan. 1920. For Harold Jacob, the Imam was "an Irredentist, like Mussolini of modern Italy," although he always evinced a great deal of admiration for him. *Kings of Arabia*, 113.
7. Michel Foucault, *The Order of Things* (New York: Vintage Books, 1994), xviii. See also his "Of Other Spaces," *Diacritics*, 16 no. 1 (Spring 1986), 22–7.
8. On the population of Bayhan, see HA, 59–60 and MRAP, 125–126. The text of the treaty is in Aitchison, *A Collection of Treaties*, 4th ed., 13:132–3.
9. See the memo of 6 Feb. 1931 which discusses the problematic definition of "Bayhan" in light of the need to fulfill British obligations to defend the area according to the 1903 treaty. The fragmentary nature of local authority is made all the more revealing by an enclosed map based on aerial surveillance of the region that maps out lines of authority. IOR R/20/A/3368.
10. See IOR R/20/A/1257, Qadi 'Atiq b. Ahmad al-Bakri to DeBrath, 9 March 1909. The sections of Khawlan mentioned were the Bani Jabr and Bani Dubyan.
11. IOR R/20/A/1257, Sayyid Ahmad b. Bu Bakr b. Ahmad b. al-Shaykh Bu Bakr b. Salim to various Mas'abi Shaykhs, 13 Feb. 1909.
12. IOR R/20/A/1257, Imam Yahya to Sultan Ahmad b. Fadl, 6 June 1909.

NOTES pp. [174–178]

13. IOR R/20/A/1257, Imam Yahya to Qadi 'Atiq b. Ahmad al-Bakri, 29 April 1909.
14. IOR R/20/A/1257, Sayyid Ahmad b. Bu Bakr b. Ahmad b. al-Shaykh Bu Bakr b. Salim to various Mas'abi shaykhs, 14 March 1909 and same to Qadi 'Atiq b. Ahmad al-Bakri, 14 Feb. 1909.
15. See Aitchison, *A Collection of Treaties*, 4th ed., 13:142–53.
16. See for example IOR R/20/A/1257, letter from Shaykh Zayd b. Salih al-Huraybi of Mawsatta, 17 Nov. 1911.
17. IOR R/20/A/1257, Sayyid Muhammad 'Ali al-Sharif to 'Abdali Sultan, 22 Rabi' al-Awwal, no year listed.
18. IOR R/20/A/1257, Imam Yahya to Shaykh Muhsin 'Askar, 19 Nov. 1911.
19. IOR R/20/A/1257, Sayyid Muhammad Taha, 6 Feb. 1912 and IOR R/20/A/1258, Muhammad Salih al-Akhram to Sayyid Muhammad Taha, 5 Sep. 1912.
20. IOR R/20/E/301, Shaykh Husayn b. Salih al-Azraqi to 1st Acting. Resident, 7 May 1912.
21. IOR R/20/E/301, Amir Nasr b. Shayif to Political Resident, 7 May 1912. Of course, others solicited the Imam's aid in local disputes. Shaykh 'Ali Nashir al-'Alawi, for example, contacted Imam Yahya to intervene on his behalf in his dispute with the Qutaybis, requesting that he "assist us by men and resources and spend from the Treasury of the State." IOR R/20/A/1257, Shaykh 'Ali Nashir to Imam Yahya, 17 June 1912 (?).
22. Jacob, *Kings of Arabia*, 83–4 and IOR R/20/A/1474, notes by Harold Jacob, 8 Feb. 1906 and note by Col. F. Churchill, 20 Feb. 1906. The view from Bombay, of course, was that the line was definitive: all land north of the boundary was by definition "Turkish," a designation that superseded all other claims.
23. Jacob, *Kings of Arabia*, 113.
24. IOR R/20/A/4064, Sultan 'Abd al-Karim b. Fadl to Bernard Reilly, 5 June 1919 and IOR R/20/A/1259, Sultan 'Abd al-Karim b. Fadl to Barret, 18 Oct. 1919. By November of that year, the Amir's stipend and nine gun salute had been restored. On his alliance with the Ottomans in 1915, see *Arabian Personalities of the Twentieth Century* (1917; reprint, New York: Oleander Press, 1986), 250.
25. In 1917 Imam Yahya even sent a letter of appointment to the Upper Yafi'i Sultan, Salih b. 'Umar al-Harhara, recognizing his sovereignty over the Rubi'atayn tribe of Juban and his responsibility for executing the Imam's orders. See a reproduction of the document in al-Yahari al-Yafi'i, *Min Yanabi' Tarikhina*, 200. See also the collected files in IOR R/20/A/4809 and 4814.
26. For reports of tax assessment in Muris, see IOR R/20/A/4064, Amir Nasr b. Shayif to Lees, 14 Oct. 1919 and IOR R/20/A/1259, Amir Nasr b. Shayif to Lees, 18 Oct. 1919. On tax collection in the lands of the Rubi'atayn, see IOR R/20/A/1259, L.H. Beatty to High Commissioner, Cairo, June 1919.

27. In addition to the Shaʻiri, Ahl Jahhaf and ʻAlawis, there is evidence that the Imam or the governor of Qaʻtaba contacted the Dakkam and Humada, as well as the Qutaybis and Busaylis from Radfan, see IOR R/20/A/1259, Sultan ʻAbd al-Karim b. Fadl to 1st Asst. Resident, 16 July 1919, Imam Yahya to Shaykh ʻAli Nashir al-'Alawi, 20 July 1919, Ahmad b. Muhammad al-ʻAnsi to Muhsin ʻAbdullah ʻAbd al-Dayyam, 21 Oct. 1919 and IOR R/20/A/4064, Amir Nasr b. Shayif to Political Resident, 14 Oct. 1919.
28. IOR R/20/A/1259, ʻAbd al-Karim b. Fadl to Barret, 2 Oct. 1919.
29. al-Mutahhar, *Sirat al-Imam*, 2:144. See also IOR R/20/A/1259, "Report on Sharif Nasr b. Shukr's Interview with Imam Yahya," 26 Jan. 1920 for an account of the Amir's submission to the Imam during the First World War.
30. After the battle at Quzʻa, Sultan Ghalib b. ʻAwad al-Quʻayti sent his Chief Minister, Sayyid Husayn Hamid al-Mihdar, to arrange a truce between the Yafiʻi and the Imam. It was said that he was paid for his expenses both by the Quʻayti Sultan and by the Aden Residency. The move by Mihdar even fostered a rumor that the Quʻayti Sultan was gathering a massive army against Imam Yahya with the support of British aeroplanes. See, Salah al-Bakri al-Yafiʻi, *Tarikh Hadramawt al-Siyasi* (Cairo: Maktabat Mustafa al-Babi al-Halabi wa-Awladuhu, 1936), 2:35–36 and BNA CO 725/1. 7th Aden News Letter, 6 Aug. 1924.
31. BNA CO 725/1, 4th Aden News Letter, 17 March 1921.
32. IOR R/20/1259, Imam Yahya to Sultan ʻAbd al-Karim b. Fadl, 9 Dec. 1919.
33. IOR R/20/A/1259, Amir Nasr b. Shayif to Barrett, 6 Jan. 1920 on the Radfan tribes, see BNA CO 725/2, Aden News Letter, 22 Dec. 1920, on Hawshabi and ʻAlawi territory, see BNA CO 725/2, 1st Aden News Letter, 12 Jan. 1921, on collection in the Wadi Maʻadin, see BNA CO 725/3, 8th Aden News Letter, 5 Sep. 1922.
34. IOR R/20/A/1259, Imam Yahya to Political Resident, 3 Jan. 1920.
35. See IOR R/20/A/1259, report from ʻAli Ibrahim, 7 Jan. 1920 and Barrett's response on 21 Jan. 1920.
36. IOR R/20/A/1259, Shaykhs Amir Sayf al-ʻAbdali, Salih ʻAbduh, Salman b. Muhsin, Ghalib Husayn, Naji Muhammad, Salih ʻAbd al-Habib Hujja, and all Halimi and Jaʻdi *ʻaqils* to Amir Nasr b. Shayif, n.d.
37. IOR R/20/A/1259, Amir Nasr b. Shayif to Barrett, 11 Jan. 1920.
38. IOR R/20/A/1259, Amir Nasr b. Shayif to Barret, 11 Feb. 1920.
39. For the general details of the offensive in the Wadi Taym, see IOR R/20/A/4895, Report by ʻAli Ibrahim, March 1921 and ROY, 6:560–2. On the incident of the beheading, see IOR R/20/A/4895, Sayyid Yahya b. ʻAbd al-Rahman to Sultan ʻAbd al-Karim b. Fadl, 23 Jan. 1921.
40. In February and March of 1921 the Aden Residency supplied the Radfan tribes with some 300 rifles of mixed make and 87,000 rounds of ammunition. ROY, 6:562. Even so, the general scarcity of rifles and ammunition was routinely a

subject of correspondence between the protectorate signatories and the Aden government. Many men were still fighting with spears, and many of those who owned rifles did not have ammunition. On the general poverty of the area and the sale of rifles for subsistence, see IOR R/20/A/4895, 'Ali Ibrahim, "Notes on the Nature of the Kotebi Country," 2 March 1921 and BNA CO 725/1, 3rd Aden News Letter, 17 Feb. 1921.

41. IOR R/20/A/4895, Yahya al-Makki to Political Resident, 28 Feb. 1921.
42. SM, Farid b. Muhsin al-'Awlaqi to Sultan 'Ali b. al-Mansur al-Kathiri, 1929.
43. e.g. IOR R/20/4809, Shaykh Salih b. Ahmad 'Ali to Political Resident, April 1911, IOR R/20/A/1257, Shaykh Muhammad 'Ali Muhsin to Political Resident, Feb. 1912, Shaykh Muthanna 'Ali Sha'fi to Political Resident, 25 Feb. 1912, and Salih Muhsin al-'Askar to Political Resident, 9 Feb. 1912.
44. IOR R/20/A/4587, Amir Nasr b. Shayif to Barrett, 24 Jan. 1922.
45. These spaces of practice or tactics are akin to Lefebvre's "representational spaces," which are spaces of everyday life, of symbols, and of dreams of alternative spaces. See *The Production of Space*, 39–46.
46. IOR R/20/A/4895, Amir Nasr b. Shayif to Barret, 11 Feb. 1921.
47. On honour and the metaphor of whitening and blackening one's face, see Dresch, *Tribes, Government, and History in Yemen*, 59–61.
48. The first reference I have come across of Muqbil 'Abdullah's contact with the Imam's state is a letter from Amir Nasr b. Shayif to Barret indicating that several other Shaykhs of Radfan followed their example and submitted. IOR R/20/A/1259, Amir Nasr b. Shayif to Barret, 2 March 1920.
49. IOR R/20/A/4895, 'Ali Ibrahim, reports of 14 Feb. 1921 and n.d., probably late March 1921. See also IOR R/20/A/4895, Sayyid Yahya 'Abd al-Rahman al-Makki to Barret, Feb. 1921 in which he describes Muqbil 'Abdullah's attempts to open local roads to the Imam's troops so that they could cut off the Qutaybi supply routes, not unlike the Hujayli and Bakri Shaykhs who had acted as guides more than active military allies.
50. al-Wasi'i, *Tarikh al-Yaman*, 357.
51. BNA CO 725/1, 12th Aden News Letter, 28 Sep. 1921.
52. See, for example, IOR R/20/A/4587, Amir Nasr b. Shayif to Barret, 24 Jan. 1922, BNA CO 725/3, 5th Aden News Letter, 30 May 1922.
53. IOR R/20/A/4587, Qayid b. Rajih to Muhammad Salih al-Akhram, 13 Feb. 1922. Cf. IOR R/20/A/4587, Muqbil 'Abdullah to Shaykhs of the Ahl 'Abdullah, Dambari and Da'iri tribes, 9 Feb. 1922.
54. IOR R/20/A/4587, Muqbil 'Abdullah to Shaykh Muhammad Salih al-Akhram, Jan. 1922.
55. BNA CO 725/5, 6th Aden News Letter, 11 July 1923.
56. al-Mutahhar, *Sirat al-Imam*, 2:310. Cf. al-Haddad, *'Umdat al-Qari'*, 183–4.
57. Cf. Buckler, "The Oriental Despot," 240–3. For the Ottoman case, see Selim

Deringil, "Legitimacy Structures in the Ottoman State: The Reign of Abdülhamid II (1876–1909)," *International Journal of Middle East Studies* 23, no. 3 (1991), 353.
58. For details of Shaykh Muhammad's visit to Dali', see BNA CO 725/5, 7th Aden News Letter, 31 July 1923, 8th Aden News Letter, 30 Aug. 1923, and 9th Aden News Letter, 30 Sep. 1923.
59. de Certeau, *The Practice of Everyday Life*, xix. Cf. Carter, *The Road to Botany Bay*, esp. Ch. 11.
60. IOR R/20/A/3207, notes on districts, commanders, and garrisons, 1926.
61. For Clayton's account of the mission, see Sir Gilbert Falkingham Clayton, *An Arabian Diary* (Berkeley: University of California Press, 1969), 189–270.
62. IOR R/20/A/4764, Imam Yahya to al-'Arshi, 29 Sep. 1921. The letter was forwarded with others to the 'Abdali Sultan, and then sent to the Aden Government. This point was also put forward by Harold Jacob. See, "The Kingdom of the Yemen: Its Place in the Comity of Nations," *Transactions of the Grotius Society*, 18 (1932), 148.
63. IOR R/20/A/2919, Reilly to H.M's Sec. of State for the Colonies, 11 Aug. 1926.
64. IOR R/20/A/2919, Reilly to H.M's Sec. of State for the Colonies, 11 Aug. 1926, enclosed tables showing value of inland trade for the period 1920–26. See also BNA CO 725/4, table showing value of inland trade for the period 1903–21.
65. Clayton, *An Arabian Diary*, 245–6.
66. Jacob, *Kings of Arabia*, 243–4 and "The Kingdom of the Yemen," 152.
67. IOR R/20/A/1266, Resident to Colonial Office, 11 Feb. 1928.
68. Gavin, *Aden Under British Rule*, 280–2. On the development of air power as part of the governmental structure of Iraq, see Dodge, *Inventing Iraq*, ch. 7.
69. For details on the bombing campaigns, see the collected documents in IOR R/20/A/1266 and BNA CO 725/17/10, Symes to HM Sec. of State for Colonies, 8 Sep. 1928, enclosing Maj. Fowle, "Hostilities with the Imam, June 25 to July 15, 1928."
70. al-Akwa' al-Hawali, *Hayat 'Alim wa-Amir*, 2:43.
71. IOR R/20/A/1266, Aden Brigade Operation Instruction, No. 1, to O.C. No. 8 B Squadron, 21 Feb. 1928.
72. al-Iryani, *Sadiq al-Tahaqiq*, fol. 23.
73. Rihani, *Arabian Peak and Desert*, 69. See also the poem by 'Ali b. Muhammad al-Mutawakkil al-Jibli which also describes the downing of planes through otherworldly power. Zabara, *Nuzhat al-Nazar*, 467.
74. Kevin Hetherington, *The Badlands of Modernity: Heterotopia and Social Ordering* (London: Routledge, 1997), 50–51.
75. Wenner, *Modern Yemen*, 159 and Gavin, *Aden Under British Rule*, 296.

76. For Reilly's own account of this period, see his *Aden and the Yemen* (London: HMSO, 1960), 15–24.
77. BNA CO 725/20/7, Symes to Sec. of State for the Colonies, 17 Dec. 1930.
78. Joseph Conrad, "Geography and Some Explorers," in *Last Essays* (Garden City: Doubleday, Page, & Co., 1926), 1–21.
79. Driver, *Geography Militant*, 4.

CONCLUSION: UNMAKING NORTH AND SOUTH

1. In *Selected Poems*, ed. Alexander Coleman (New York: Viking, 1999), 139.
2. Wendell Phillips, *Qataban and Sheba: Exploring the Ancient Kingdoms on the Biblical Spice Routes of Arabia* (New York: Harcourt, Brace and Company, 1955), 204.
3. Bauman, *Modernity and Ambivalence*, 8.
4. This is not to imply that the Indian experience was the only reference for policy makers in the Aden Protectorate in the post-war period. As Simon C. Smith notes, the un-federated Malay states were just as important a model for the advisory system implemented in the Yemeni South in the 1930s and 40s. See Simon C. Smith, "Rulers and Residents: British Relations with the Aden Protectorate, 1937–59," *Middle Eastern Studies* 31 no. 3 (July 1995), 509–523.
5. Lucine Taminian, "Rimbaud's House in Aden, Yemen: Giving Voice(s) to the Silent Poet," *Cultural Anthropology*, 13 no. 4 (1998), 482.
6. See Susanne Dahlgren, "The Snake with a Thousand Heads: The Southern Cause in Yemen," *Middle East Report*, 256 (Fall 2010), 28–33.
7. vom Bruck has discussed the trauma associated with the political and social marginalization of the descendants of the Prophet in post-revolutionary Yemen. See her *Islam, Memory, and Morality*, 216–36.
8. See Ayman Hamidi, "Inscriptions of Violence in Northern Yemen: Haunting Histories, Unstable Moral Spaces," *Middle Eastern Studies*, 45, no. 2 (2009), 165–87. For an overview of the conflict, see Barak A. Salmoni, Bryce Loidolt, and Madeleine Wells, *Regime and Periphery in Northern Yemen: The Huthi Phenonmenon* (Santa Monica, CA: Rand, 2010).
9. Bauman, *Modernity and Ambivalence*, 234.
10. Michael Hardt and Antonio Negri, *Multitude: War and Democracy in the Age of Empire* (New York: Penguin, 2004).

BIBLIOGRAPHY

Archives and other collections

British National Archives, Kew

Colonial Office, Aden correspondence (CO 725)
Foreign Office, Yemen Political Relations (FO 905)
Foreign Office, Legation, Hejaz: Various Papers (FO 967)
Foreign Office, Jedda Agency: Papers (FO 686)

India Office Records, British Library, London

Records of the British Administrations in Aden, 1837–1967 (R/20)

Say'un Museum (al-Markaz al-Watani li-l-Watha'iq), Say'un, Yemen

Various documents

Private Collection of N. Mutahhar, Sanaa, Yemen

Various documents

Western Library (Dar al-Makhtutat), Sanaa, Yemen

Anon. *al-Rawd al-Bassam fi Sirat al-Mawlay Sayf al-Islam Ahmad bin Amir al-Mu'minin Yahya al-Imam.* (Majmu': 148).

al-Haddad, Yahya b. 'Ali b. Naji. *'Umdat al-Qari' fi Sirat Imam Zamanina Sayf al-Bari'.* (Tarikh: 2594).

———. *Silsilat al-Darari.* (Tarikh: 104).

al-Iryani, Hasan b. Ahmad. *Sadiq al-Tahaqiq bi-ma Hadatha fi Qabilatay Hashid wa-l-Zaraniq.* (Majmu': 781).

al-Jindari, Ahmad b. 'Abdullah. *al-Durar al-Muntaqa fi Sirat al-Imam al-Mutawakkil 'ala Allah wa-Khasaluhu al-Murtada.* (Tarikh: 2521).

———. *al-Jami' al-Wajiz bi-Wafiyat Dhui al-Tabriz.* (Tarikh: 37).

BIBLIOGRAPHY

Sharaf al-Din, Muhammad b. 'Abd al-Rahman. *al-Barq al-Muta'alliq fi Rihlat Mawlana Sayf al-Islam ila al-Mashraq.* (Jughrafiya: 1).

Eastern Library (Wizarat al-Awqaf), Sanaa, Yemen

al-Rusi al-Ahnumi, Husayn b. Husayn. *al-Barahin al-Mudi'a fi al-Sira al-Mansuriyya.* pt. 2 (Tarikh: 2198).

Newspapers

al-Iman (Sanaa)
al-Manar (Cairo)
Umm al-Qura (Mecca)

Published works

Abaza, Faruq 'Uthman. *'Adan wa-l-Siyasa al-Britaniyya fi al-Bahr al-Ahmar, 1839–1918* (Cairo: al-Hay'a al-Misriyya al-'Amma li-l-Kuttab, 1987).
al-'Abdali, Ahmad Fadl b. 'Ali Muhsin. *Hadiyat al-Zaman fi Akhbar Muluk Lahj wa-'Adan* (Beirut: Dar al-'Awda, 1932).
Adams, Charles C. *Islam and Modernism in Egypt* (New York: Russel & Russel, 1968).
al-Afghani, Jamal al-Din and Muhammad 'Abduh. "al-Ta'assub," in *al-'Urwa al-Wuthqa* (Beirut: Dar al-Kitab al-'Arabi, n.d.).
Aitchison, C.U. *A Collection of Treaties, Engagements and Sanads Relating to India and Neighbouring Countries.* 4th ed. 13 vols (Calcutta: Superintendent Government Printing, India, 1909).
———. *A Collection of Treaties, Engagements and Sanads Relating to India and Neighbouring Countries.* 5th ed. 14 vols (Delhi: Manager of Publications, 1933).
al-Akwa', Isma'il b. 'Ali. *Hijar al-'Ilm wa-Ma'aqiluhu fi al-Yaman.* 5 vols (Damascus: Dar al-Fikr, 1995).
al-Akwa' al-Hawali, Muhammad b. 'Ali. *Hayat 'Alim wa-Amir.* 2 vols (Sanaa: Maktabat al-Jil al-Jadid, 1987).
al-'Alimi, Rashad Muhammad. *al-Taqlidiyya wa-l-Hadatha fi al-Nizam al-Qanuni al-Yamani* (Cairo: Matabi' al-Shuruq, n.d.).
'Amara, Muhammad, ed. *al-A'mal al-Kamila li-l-Imam Muhammad 'Abduh* (Cairo: Dar al-Shuruq, 2006).
al-'Amri, 'Abdullah. *Tarikh al-Yaman al-Hadith wa-l-Mu'asir* (Damascus: Dar al-Fikr, 2001).
Anderson, Benedict. *Imagined Communities.* Revised edition (London: Verson, 1991).
Aponte, Salvatore. *Hadhihi hiyya al-Yaman al-Sa'ida.* trans. Taha Fawzi (Beirut: Manshurat Dar al-Adab, n.d).
al-'Aqili, Muhammad b. Ahmad. *Tarikh al-Mikhlaf al-Sulaymani.* 2 vols. 3rd ed. (Riyadh[?]: Matabi' al-Walid, 1989).

BIBLIOGRAPHY

Arab Bureau, *Handbook of Yemen* (Cairo: Government Press, 1917).
Arabian Personalities of the Twentieth Century (1917; reprint, New York: Oleander Press, 1986).
Arnold, David. *Police Power and Colonial Rule: Madras 1859–1947* (Delhi: Oxford University Press, 1986).
al-'Arshi, Husayn b. Ahmad. *Kitab Bulugh al-Muram fi Sharh Misk al-Khitam* ed. Anastase-Marie de St-Elie (Beirut: Dar Ihya' al-Turath al-'Arabi, 1939).
al-'Ashmali, Muhammad Ahmad. *al-Tarikh al-Siyasi li-l-Dawla al-Haditha* (Cairo: Maktabat al-Madbuli, 2002).
Arslan, Shakib. *al-Irtisamat al-Litaf fi Khatir al-Hajj ila Aqdas Mataf* (Beirut: al-Mu'assasa al-'Arabiyya li-l-Dirasat wa-l-Nashr, 2004).
———. *Limadha Ta'khkhara al-Muslimun, wa-Limadha Taqaddama Ghayrahum?* 2nd ed. (Beirut: Dar al-Anwar, n.d).
Asad, Talal. "The Idea of an Anthropology of Islam," Occasional Papers Series (Washington DC: Georgetown University, Center for Contemporary Arab Studies, 1986).
al-'Attar, Muhammad Sa'id. *al-Takhalluf al-Iqtisadi wa-l-Ijtima'i fi al-Yaman* (Algiers?: al-Matbu'at al-Wataniyya al-Jaza'iriyya, 1965).
Aydin, Cemil. *The Politics of Anti-Westernism in Asia: Visions of World Order in Pan-Islamic Thought* (New York: Columbia University Press, 2007).
Azad, Abul Kalam. *Khilafat and Jaziratul-Arab*. trans. Mirza Abdul Qadir Beg (Bombay: Central Khilafat Committee, 1920).
al-'Azm, Nazih al-Mu'ayyad. *Rihla fi Bilad al-'Arabiyya al-Sa'ida* (London: Fadi Press, 1985).
Bachelard, Gaston. *The Poetics of Space*. trans. Maria Jolas (Boston: Beacon Press, 1994).
Ba Faqih, Muhammad 'Abd al-Qadir. *al-Mustashriqun wa-Athar al-Yaman*. 2 vols (Sanaa: Markaz al-Dirasat wa-l-Buhuth al-Yamani, 1988).
al-Bakri al-Yafi'i, Salah. *Tarikh Hadramawt al-Siyasi*. 2 vols (Cairo: Maktabat Mustafa al-Babi al-Halabi wa-Awladuhu, 1936).
Baldry, John. "Anglo-Italian Rivalry in Yemen and 'Asir, 1900–1934," *Die Welt des Islams*, vol. 17 no. 1 (1976–1977): 155–93.
———. "Al-Yaman and the Turkish Occupation 1849–1914," *Arabica* vol. 23 no. 2 (1976): 156–96.
———. "The Turkish-Italian War in the Yemen, 1911–1912," *Arabian Studies*, 3 (1976): 51–65.
Ballantyne, Tony. "Rereading the Archive and Opening up the Nation-State: Colonial Knowledge in South Asia (and Beyond)," in Antoinette Burton (ed.), *After the Imperial Turn: Thinking with and through the Nation* (Durham, NC: Duke University Press, 2003).
Bang, Anne K. *The Idrīsī State in 'Asīr, 1906–1934* (Bergen: Centre for Middle Eastern and Islamic Studies, 1996).

BIBLIOGRAPHY

Barrel, John. *The Dark Side of the Landscape: The Rural Poor in English Painting, 1730–1840* (Cambridge University Press, 1980).
Bauman, Zygmunt. *Modernity and Ambivalence* (Cambridge: Polity Press, 1991).
Beachey, R.W. "The Arms Trade in East Africa in the Late Nineteenth Century," *Journal of African History*, 3 no. 3 (1962): 451–67.
Beier, A.L. *Masterless Men: The Vagrancy Problem in England, 1560–1640* (London: Methuen, 1985).
Bermingham, Ann. *Landscape and Ideology: The English Rustic Tradition, 1740–1860* (Berkeley: University of California Press, 1986).
Bhagavan, Manu. *Sovereign Spheres: Princes, Education and Empire in Colonial India* (New Delhi: Oxford University Press, 2003).
Bidwell, Robin. *The Two Yemens* (Harlow and Boulder: Longman Westview Press, 1983).
———. "The Political Residents of Aden: Biographical Notes," *Arabian Studies*, 5 (1979): 149–59.
Borges, Jorge Luis. *Selected Poems*, ed. Alexander Coleman (New York: Viking, 1999).
Bose, Sugata. *A Hundred Horizons: The Indian Ocean in the Age of Global Empire* (Cambridge, MA: Harvard University Press, 2006).
Boxberger, Linda. *On the Edge of Empire: Hadhramawt, Emigration, and the Indian Ocean, 1880s-1930s* (Albany: SUNY Press, 2002).
Brandstadter, Edith S. "Dangerous Castes and Tribes: The Criminal Tribes Act and the Magahiya Doms of Northwest India," in Anand A. Yang (ed.) Crime and Criminality in British India (Tucson, AZ: University of Arizona Press, 1985).
Buckler, F.M., "The Oriental Despot," in M.N. Pearson (ed.), *Legitimacy and Symbols: The South Asian Writings of F. W. Buckler*, Michigan Papers on South and Southeast Asia, No. 26 (1985).
Burnett, D. Graham. *Masters of All they Surveyed: Exploration, Geography, and a British El Dorado* (University of Chicago Press, 2000).
Bury, G. Wyman (Abdullah Mansur). *Pan-Islam* (London: Macmillan and Co. Ltd, 1919).
———. *Arabia Infelix or the Turks in Yamen* (London: Macmillan and Co. Ltd, 1915).
———. *The Land of Uz* (London: Macmillan and Co. Ltd, 1911).
Carapico, Sheila and Richard Tutweiler. *Yemeni Agriculture and Economic Change* (Sanaa: American Institute of Yemeni Studies, 1981).
Carter, Paul. *The Road to Botany Bay: An Exploration of Landscape and History* (London: Faber and Faber, 1988).
de Certeau, Michel. *The Practice of Everyday Life*. trans. Steven Rendall (Berkeley: University of California Press, 1984).

BIBLIOGRAPHY

Chakrabarty, Dipesh. *Provincializing Europe: Postcolonial Thought and Historical Difference* (Princeton University Press, 2000).

Chatterjee, Partha. *The Nation and its Fragments.* (Princeton University Press, 1993).

Clayton, Sir Gilbert Falkingham. *An Arabian Diary.* (Berkeley: University of California Press, 1969)

Cleveland, William L. *Islam against the West: Shakib Arslan and the Campaign for Islamic Nationalism* (Austin: University of Texas Press, 1985).

Cohn, Bernard. "Cloth, Clothes, and Colonialism," in *Colonialism and its Forms of Knowledge: The British in India* (Princeton University Press, 1996).

———. "Representing Authority in Victorian India," in Eric Hobsbawm and Terence Ranger (eds), *The Invention of Tradition* (Cambridge University Press, 1983).

Cole, Juan R.I. "Printing and Urban Islam in the Mediterranean World, 1890–1920," in Leila Tarazi Fawaz and C.A. Bayly (eds), *Modernity and Culture: From the Mediterranean to the Indian Ocean* (New York: Columbia University Press, 2001).

Commins, David Dean. *Islamic Reform: Politics and Social Change in Late Ottoman Syria* (Oxford University Press, 1990).

Conrad, Joseph. "Geography and Some Explorers," in *Last Essays* (Garden City: Doubleday, Page, & Co., 1926).

Cook, Michael. *Commanding Right and Forbidding Wrong in Islam* (Cambridge University Press, 2000).

Copland, Ian. *The British Raj and the Indian Native Princes: Paramountcy in Western India, 1857–1930* (Bombay: Orient Longman, 1982).

Cosgrove, Denis E. *Social Formation and Symbolic Landscape* (London: Croom Helm, 1984).

Crane, Charles R. "Visit to the Red Sea Littoral and the Yaman," *Journal of the Central Asian Society* 17 (1928): 48–67.

Dahlgren, Susanne. "The Snake with a Thousand Heads: The Southern Cause in Yemen," *Middle East Report*, 256 (Fall 2010): 28–33.

al-Dawla, Hamud b. Muhammad. *al-Zawraq al-Halwa fi Sirat Qa'id al-Jaysh wa-Amir al-Liwa'.* ed. Zayd b. 'Ali al-Wazir (Sanaa: Manshurat al-'Asr al-Hadith, 1988).

Deringil, Selim. *The Well-Protected Domains: Ideology and the Legitimation of Power in the Ottoman Empire, 1876–1909* (London: I.B. Tauris, 1998).

———. "Legitimacy Structures in the Ottoman State: The Reign of Abdülhamid II (1876–1909)," *International Journal of Middle East Studies* 23 no. 3 (1991): 345–59.

Dirks, Nicholas B. *Castes of Mind* (Princeton University Press, 2001).

———. *The Hollow Crown: Ethnohistory of an Indian Kingdom* (Cambridge University Press, 1987).

BIBLIOGRAPHY

Dodge, Toby. *Inventing Iraq* (New York: Columbia University Press, 2003).
Douglas, J. Leigh. *The Free Yemeni Movement, 1935–1962* (Beirut: The American University of Beirut, 1987).
Dresch, Paul. *A History of Modern Yemen* (Cambridge University Press, 2000).
———. "A Letter from Imam Yahya concerning the Idrisi," *New Arabian Studies*, 3 (1996): 58–68.
———. *Tribes Government and History in Yemen* (Oxford: Clarendon Press, 1993).
———. "Guaranty of the Market at Ḥūth," *Arabian Studies* 8 (1990), 63–91.
———. "Keeping the Imam's Peace: A Response to Tribal Disorder in the 1950's," *Peuples Méditerranéens* 46 (Jan.-March, 1989), 77–95.
Driver, Felix. *Geography Militant: Cultures of Exploration and Empire* (Oxford: Blackwell, 2001).
Duara, Prasenjit. *Rescuing History from the Nation: Questioning Narratives of Modern China* (University of Chicago Press, 1995).
Edney, Matthew H. *Mapping an Empire: the Geographic Construction of British India, 1765–1843* (University of Chicago Press, 1997).
Edwardes, Michael. *High Noon of Empire: India Under Curzon* (London: Eyre & Spottiswoode, 1965).
Eickelman, Dale F. and Armando Salvatore. "Muslim Publics," in Dale F. Eickelman and Armando Salvatore (eds), *Public Islam and the Common Good* (Leiden: Brill, 2004).
El-Batrik, 'Abd al-Hamid. "Egyptian-Yemeni Relations (1819–1840) and their Implications for British Policy in the Red Sea," in P.M. Holt (ed.), *Political and Social Change in Modern Egypt: Historical Studies from the Ottoman Conquest to the United Arab Republic* (London: Oxford University Press, 1968).
Enayat, Hamid. *Modern Islamic Political Thought* (Austin: University of Texas Press, 1982).
Fabian, Johannes. *Time and the Other: How Anthropology Makes its Object* (New York: Columbia University Press, 1983).
Farah, Ceasar. *The Sultan's Yemen: Nineteenth-Century Challenges to Ottoman Rule* (London: I.B. Tauris, 2002).
Fisher, Michael H. *Indirect Rule in India: Residents and the Residency System, 1764–1858* (Oxford University Press, 1991).
Foster, Donald. *Landscape with Arabs: Travels in Aden and South Arabia* (Brighton: Clifton Books, 1969).
Foucault, Michel. *Security, Territory, Population*, trans. Graham Burchell (New York: Palgrave, 2007).
———. *The Order of Things* (New York: Vintage Books, 1994).
———. "Space, Knowledge, and Power," in Paul Rabinow (ed.), *The Foucault Reader* (New York: Pantheon Books, 1984).

BIBLIOGRAPHY

———. "The Eye of Power," in Colin Gordon (ed.), *Power/Knowledge: Selected Interviews and Other Writings* (New York: Pantheon Press, 1980).

———. *The History of Sexuality.* trans. Robert Hurley (New York: Pantheon Books, 1978).

Fox, Richard G. *Lions of the Punjab* (Berkeley: University of California Press, 1985).

Freitag, Ulrike. *Indian Ocean Migrants and State Formation in Hadhramaut: Reforming the Homeland* (Leiden: Brill, 2003).

Fujitani, T. *Splendid Monarchy: Power and Pageantry in Modern Japan* (Berkeley: University of California Press, 1996).

Gavin, R.J. *Aden Under British Rule, 1839–1967* (London: C. Hurst & Company, 1975).

Geertz, Clifford. "Centers, Kings and Charisma: Reflections on the Symbolics of Power," in *Local Knowledge* (New York: Basic Books, 1983).

General Staff, India. *Military Report on the Aden Protectorate*, vol. 1 (Simla: Government Press, 1915) in *Military Handbooks of Arabia, 1913–1917*. 10 vols (London: Archive Editions, 1988).

Gershoni, Israel and James P. Jankowski. *Egypt, Islam, and the Arabs: The Search for Egyptian Nationhood, 1900–1930* (Oxford University Press, 1986).

Ghazal, Amal N. *Islamic Reform and Arab Nationalism: Expanding the Crescent from the Mediterranean to the Indian Ocean (1880s-1930s)* (London: Routledge, 2010).

Gilmartin, David. *Empire and Islam: Punjab and the Making of Pakistan* (Berkeley: University of California Press, 1988).

Goswami, Manu. *Producing India: From Colonial Economy to National Space* (University of Chicago Press, 2004).

Groenhout, Fiona. "The History of the Indian Princely States: Bringing the Puppets Back onto Centre Stage," *History Compass*, 4 no. 4 (June 2006), 629–44.

Guha, Ranajit. *History at the Limit of World-History* (New York: Columbia University Press, 2002).

Gupta, Ashin Das. *Indian Merchants and the Decline of Surat, c. 1700–1750* (Wiesbaden: Franz Steiner Verlag, 1979).

Haines, S.B. "Memoir, to Accompany a chart of the South Coast of Arabia from the entrance of the Red Sea to Misenát, in 50° 43′′ 25′." *Journal of the Royal Geographical Society of London*, vol. 9 (1839): 125–56.

Haj, Samira, *Reconfiguring Islamic Tradition: Reform, Rationality, and Modernity* (Stanford University Press, 2009).

Hakim, Muhammad. *Qirā'at fī al-Fikr al-Zaydī: Hiwar ma' al-Ustadh Ibrahim al-Wazir* (Beirut: Dar al-Manhal, 1993).

Halliday, Fred. "The Formation of Yemeni Nationalism: Initial Reflections," in James Jankowski and Israel Gershoni (eds), *Rethinking Nationalism in the Arab Middle East* (New York: Columbia University Press, 1997).

BIBLIOGRAPHY

Hamidi, Ayman. "Inscriptions of Violence in Northern Yemen: Haunting Histories, Unstable Moral Spaces," *Middle Eastern Studies*, 45, no. 2 (2009): 165–87.

Hamilton, R.A.B. "The Social Organization of the Tribes of the Aden Protectorate," *Journal of the Royal Central Asian Society* 30 (1943): 142–57.

al-Harazi, Mushin b. Ahmad. *Fatrat al-Fawda wa-'Awdat al-Atrak ila Sanaa: al-Safr al-Thani min Tarikh al-Harazi (Riyad al-Rayahin), 1859–1872*, ed. Husayn b. 'Abdullah al-'Amri (Sanaa: Dar al-Hikma al-Yamaniyya, 1986).

Hardt, Michael and Antonio Negri, *Multitude: War and Democracy in the Age of Empire* (New York: Penguin, 2004).

Harley, J.B. "Deconstructing the Map," in Trevor J. Barnes and James S. Duncan (eds), *Writing Worlds: Discourse, Text and Metaphor in the Representation of Landscape* (London: Routledge, 1992).

———. "Maps, Knowledge, and Power," in Denis Cosgrove and Stephen Daniels (eds), *The Iconography of Landscape: Essays on the Symbolic Representation, Design and Use of Past Environments* (Cambridge University Press, 1988).

Harris, Walter B. *A Journey Through the Yemen* (1893; reprint, London: Darf Publishers, 1985).

Harvey, David. *The Condition of Postmodernity* (London: Blackwell, 1990).

Hasan, Mushirul (ed.). *Mohamed Ali in Indian Politics*. 3 vols (New Delhi: Atlantic Publishers, 1986).

Haykel, Bernard. "On the Nature of Salafi Thought and Action," in Roel Meijer (ed.), *Global Salafism: Islam's New Religious Movement* (New York: Columbia University Press, 2009).

———. *Revival and Reform in Islam: The Legacy of Muhammad al-Shawkani* (Cambridge University Press, 2003).

———. "Reforming Islam by Dissolving the *Madhhabs*: Shawkanī and his Zaydī Detractors," in Bernard G. Weiss (ed.), *Studies in Islamic Legal Theory* (Leiden: Brill, 2002), 337–64.

Hetherington, Kevin. *The Badlands of Modernity: Heterotopia and Social Ordering* (London: Routledge, 1997).

Ho, Engseng. *The Graves of Tarim: Genealogy and Mobility across the Indian Ocean* (Berkeley: University of California Press, 2006).

Hogarth, David George. *The Penetration of Arabia* (Westport, CT: Hyperion Press, Inc., 1981; repr., New York: F. A. Stokes Co., 1904).

Hollander, Isaac. *Jews and Muslims in Lower Yemen: A Study in Protection and Restraint, 1918–1949* (Leiden: Brill, 2005).

Hourani, Albert *Arabic Thought in the Liberal Age, 1798–1939* (Cambridge University Press, 1983).

Hunter, F.M. *An Account of the British Settlement of Aden in Arabia* (1877; reprint, London: Frank Cass and Company Limited, 1968).

BIBLIOGRAPHY

Hunter, F.M. and C.W.H. Sealy. *An Account of the Arab Tribes in the Vicinity of Aden* (Bombay: Government Central Press, 1886).

———. *The Arab Tribes in the Vicinity of Aden* (1909; reprint, London: Darf Publishers, 1986).

al-Ibriqi, Husayn b. Muhammad. *al-Adab al-Muhaqqaqa fi Mu'tabarat al-Bandaqa*. ed. 'Abdallah Ahmad Muhayraz (Aden: PDRY Ministry of Culture and Information, 1988).

Ingrams, Doreen and Leila Ingrams (eds), *Records of Yemen, 1798–1960*. 16 vols (London: Archive Editions, 1993).

Ingrams, Harold. "The Exploration of the Aden Protectorate," *Geographical Review*, 28 no. 4 (Oct. 1938): 638–51.

Iqbal, Muhammad. *The Reconstruction of Religious Thought in Islam* (Dubai: Kitab al-Islamiyyah, n.d.).

al-Iryani, 'Ali b. 'Abdullah. *Sirat al-Imam Muhammad bin Yahya Hamid al-Din*. 2 vols. ed. Muhammad 'Isa al-Salihiyya ('Amman: Dar al-Bashir, 1996).

Jacob, Harold. "The Kingdom of the Yemen: Its Place in the Comity of Nations," *Transactions of the Grotius Society*, 18 (1932): 131–58.

———. *Kings of Arabia: The Rise and Set of the Turkish Sovranty in the Arabian Peninsula*. (London: Mills & Boon Limited, 1923).

———. *Perfumes of Araby: Silhouettes of Al Yemen* (London: Martin Secker, 1915)

al-Jirafi, 'Abdullah b. 'Abd al-Karim. *al-Muqtataf min Tarikh al-Yaman* (Beirut: Manshurat al-'Asr al-Hadith, [1951] 1987).

Joy, G.A. "A Summary of the Raising and Training of the 1st Yemen Infantry," *Journal of the Royal Central Asian Society*, 11 pt. 2 (1924): 147–51.

Juzaylan, 'Abdullah. *Lamahat min Dhikriyat al-Tufula* (Cairo: Maktabat Madbuli, 1984).

Karpat, Kemal H. *The Politicization of Islam: Reconstructing Identity, State, Faith, and Community in the Late Ottoman State* (Oxford University Press, 2001).

Kashani-Sabet, Firoozeh. *Frontier Fictions: Shaping the Iranian Nation, 1804–1946* (Princeton University Press, 1999).

Kennedy, Dane. *The Magic Mountains: Hill Stations and the British Raj* (Berkeley: University of California Press, 1996).

Kerr, Malcolm H. *Islamic Reform: The Political and Legal Theories of Muḥammad 'Abduh and Rashīd Riḍā* (Berkeley: University of California Press, 1966).

Khalid, Adeeb. *The Politics of Muslim Cultural Reform: Jadidism in Central Asia* (Berkeley: University of California Press, 1999).

Khuri-Makdisi, Ilham. *The Eastern Mediterranean and the Making of Global Radicalism, 1860–1914* (Berkeley: University of California Press, 2010).

Kipling, Rudyard. *The Complete Verse* (London: Kyle Cathie Ltd, 2002).

Kour, Z.H. *The History of Aden, 1839–1872* (London: Frank Cass, 1981).

BIBLIOGRAPHY

Kramer, Martin. *Islam Assembled: The Advent of the Muslim Congresses* (New York: Columbia University Press, 1986).

al-Kuhlani, Hasan Muhammad. "al-Nizam al-Dara'ibi wa-'Alaqatuhu bi-l-Jawanib al-Iqtisadiyya wa-l-Siyasa fi 'Ahd ma qabla al-Thawra," *Dirasat Yamaniyya*, 30 (Oct., Nov., Dec., 1987): 131–59.

Kühn, Thomas. "Shaping and Reshaping Colonial Ottomanism: Contesting Boundaries of Difference and Integration in Ottoman Yemen, 1872–1919," *Comparative Studies of South Asia, Africa and the Middle East* 27, no. 2 (2007), 27–9.

———. "Clothing the 'uncivilized:' Military Recruitment in Ottoman Yemen and the Quest for 'Native' Uniforms, 1880–1914," in Suraiya Faroqhi and Christoph K. Neumann (eds), *Ottoman Costumes: From Textile to Identity* (Istanbul: Eren Publishers, 2004), 143–56.

———. "An Imperial Borderland as Colony: Knowledge Production and the Elaboration of Difference in Ottoman Yemen, 1872–1914," *The MIT Electronic Journal of Middle East Studies* (http://web.mit.edu/cis/www/mitejmes, 3 (Spring 2003): 5–17.

———. "Ordering Urban Space in Ottoman Yemen, 1872–1914," in Jens Hanssen, Thomas Philipp and Stefan Weber (eds), *The Empire in the City: Arab Provincial Capitals in the Late Ottoman Empire* (Würzburg: Ergon in Kommission, 2002).

———. "Ordering the Past of Ottoman Yemen, 1872–1914," *Turcica* 34 (2002): 189–219.

Lackner, Helen. *PDRY Yemen: Outpost of Socialist Development in Arabia* (London: Ithaca Press, 1985).

Laffan, Michael Francis. *Islamic Nationhood and Colonial Indonesia: The Umma below the Winds* (London: Routledge, 2003).

Landau-Tasseron, Ella. "Zaydī Imams as Restorers of Religion: *Ihyā'* and *Tajdīd* in Zaydī Literature," *Journal of Near Eastern Studies* 49, no. 3 (July 1990): 247–63.

Landberg, Carlo. *Etudes sur les dialectes de l'Arabie méridionale*. 4 vols (Leiden: E.J. Brill, 1905).

Lauzière, Henri. "The Construction of Salafiyya: Reconsidering Salafism from the Perspective of Conceptual History," *IJMES* 42 no. 3 (2010): 369–89.

Laws of the Aden Protectorate (Aden: Government of the Colony of Aden, 1939).

Lefebvre, Henri. *The Production of Space*. trans. Donald Nicholson-Smith (Cambridge, MA: Blackwell, 1991).

Lord Curzon in India, Being a Selection From His Speeches as Viceroy and Governor General (London: Macmillan and Co. Ltd, 1906).

Lugard, Lord Frederick J.D. *The Dual Mandate in British Tropical Africa* (reprint New York:Routledge, 1965).

Luqman, Hamza 'Ali. *Tarikh al-Qaba'il al-Yamaniyya* (Sanaa: Dar al-Kalima, 1985).

BIBLIOGRAPHY

Makdisi, Ussama. "Ottoman Orientalism," *American Historical Review*, 107 no. 3 (June 2002): 768–96.

———. *The Culture of Sectarianism: Community, History, and Violence in Nineteenth-Century Lebanon* (Berkeley: University of California Press, 2000).

Mandaville, Jon. "Memduh Pasha and Aziz Bey: Ottoman Experience in Yemen," in B.R. Pridham (eds), *Contemporary Yemen: Politics and Historical Background* (London: Croom Helm, 1984), 20–33.

al-Maqhafi, Ibrahim Ahmad. *Mu'jam al-Buldan wa-l-Qaba'il al-Yamaniyya*. 2 vols (Sanaa: Dar al-Kalima, 2002).

Marriot, John and Bhaskar Mukhopadhyay (eds), *Britain in India, 1765–1905*. 6 vols (London: Pickering and Chatto, 2006).

Massey, Doreen. *For Space* (London: Sage, 2005).

al-Mas'udi, 'Abd al-'Aziz Qa'id [Abdualaziz K. al-Msaodi]. *al-Yaman al-Mu'asir* (Sanaa: Maktabat al-Sanhani, 1992)

———. "The Yemeni Opposition Movement, 1918–1948." Unpublished PhD Dissertation, Georgetown University (1987).

Manela, Erez. *The Wilsonian Moment: Self-Determination and the International Origins of Anticolonial Nationalism* (Oxford University Press, 2009).

Messick, Brinkley. *The Calligraphic State: Textual Domination and History in a Muslim Society* (Berkeley University of California Press, 1993).

Metcalf, Barbara D. and Thomas R. Metcalf. *A Concise History of India* (Cambridge University Press, 2002).

Metcalf, Thomas R. *Imperial Connections: India in the Indian Ocean Arena, 1860–1920* (Berkeley: University California Press, 2007).

———. *Ideologies of the Raj* (Cambridge University Press, 1994).

Miles, S.V. "Account of an Excursion into the Interior of Southern Arabia." *Proceedings of the Royal Geographical Society of London*, 15 no. 5 (1870–71): 319–28.

Millingen, Charles. "Notes of a Journey in Yemen," *Journal of the Royal Geographical Society of London*, vol. 44 (1874): 118–26.

———. "Notes of a Journey in Yemen," *Proceedings of the Royal Geographical Society of London*, 8 no. 2 (1873): 194–202.

Minault, Gail. *The Khilafat Movement: Religious Symbolism and Political Mobilization in India* (New York: Columbia University Press, 1982).

Mitchell, Timothy. "Society, Economy, and the State Effect," in George Steinmetz (ed.), *State/Culture: State-Formation after the Cultural Turn* (Ithaca, NY: Cornell University Press, 1999).

———. *Colonising Egypt* (Berkeley: University of California Press, 1988).

Mitchell, W.J.T. "Imperial Landscape," in W.J.T. Mitchell (ed.), *Landscape and Power* (University of Chicago Press, 1994).

Mobini-Kesheh, Natalie. *The Hadrami Awakening: Community and Identity in the Netherlands East Indies, 1900–1942* (Ithaca, NY: Cornell Southeast Asia Program, 1999).

BIBLIOGRAPHY

al-Murtada, Ahmad b. Yahya. *Kitab al-Azhar* (Sanaa: Dar al-Hikma al-Yamaniyya, 1993).
al-Mutahhar, 'Abd al-Karim b. Ahmad. *Sirat al-Imam Yahya bin Muhammad Hamid al-Din*. 2 vols. ed. Muhammad 'Isa al-Salihiyya ('Amman: Dar al-Bashir, 1998).
Naji, Sultan. *al-Tarikh al-'Askari li-l-Yaman* (Beirut: Dar al-'Awda, 1985).
Niebuhr, M. *Travels through Arabia and other Countries of the East*, 2 vols. trans. Robert Heron (Edinburgh: R. Morison and Son, 1792).
Nigam, Sanjay. "Disciplining and Policing the 'Criminals by Birth,' Part 1: The Making of a Colonial Stereotype—The Criminal Tribes and Castes of North India," *The Indian Economic and Social History Review*, 27 no. 2 (April-June 1990): 131–64.
———. "Disciplining and Policing the 'Criminals by Birth,' Part 2: The Development of a Disciplinary System, 1871–1900," *The Indian Economic and Social History Review*, 27 no. 3 (July-September 1990): 257–88.
Noyes, John. *Colonial Space: Spatiality in the Discourse of German South West Africa, 1884–1915* (Philadelphia: Harwood Academic Publishers, 1992).
O'Balance, Edgar. *The War in the Yemen* (Hamden, CT: Archon Books, 1971).
Obermeyer, Gerald J. "Al-Iman and Al-Imam: Ideology and State in the Yemen, 1900–1948," in Marwan R. Buheiry (ed.), *Intellectual Life in the Arab East, 1840–1939* (Beirut: American University of Beirut, 1981).
Owen, Roger. *Lord Cromer: Victorian Imperialist, Edwardian Proconsul* (Oxford University Press, 2005).
Pandey, Gyanendra. "In Defense of the Fragment: Writing About Hindu-Muslim Riots in India Today," *Representations*, no. 37 (Winter 1992): 28–9.
Peterson, J.E. *Yemen: The Search for a Modern State* (Baltimore: Johns Hopkins University Press, 1982).
Phillips, Wendell. *Qataban and Sheba: Exploring the Ancient Kingdoms on the Biblical Spice Routes of Arabia* (New York: Harcourt, Brace and Company, 1955).
Playfair, Robert L. *A History of Arabia Felix or Yemen* (Bombay, 1859).
Pratt, Mary Louise. "Scratches on the Face of the Country; or, What Mr. Barrows Saw in the Land of the Bushmen," *Critical Inquiry*, 12 no. 1 (1985): 119–43.
Puin, G.R. "The Yemenite *hijra* Concept of Tribal Protection," in Tarif Khalidi (ed.), *Land Reform and Social Transformation in the Middle East* (Beirut: American University, 1984).
al-Qasimi, Sultan b. Muhammad. *al-Ihtilal al-Britani li-'Adan* (Dubai: Dar al-Ghurayr li-l-Taba'a wa-l-Nashr, 1992).
Ramusack, Barbara. *The Indian Princes and their States* (Cambridge University Press, 2004).
Reilly, Bernard. *Aden and the Yemen* (London: Her Majesty's Stationery Office, 1960).
Rida, Rashid. *al-Wahhabiyyun wa-l-Hijaz* (Madinat Nasr: Dar al-Nada, 2000).

BIBLIOGRAPHY

———. *al-Khilafa* (Cairo: al-Zahra' li-l-'Ilam al-'Arabi, 1988).
Rihani, Ameen. *Arabian Peak and Desert: Travels in Al-Yaman* (London: Constable & Co, LTD, 1930).
———. *Muluk al-'Arab*. 8th ed. (Beirut: Dar al-Jil, n.d.).
Robinson, Francis. "Technology and Religious Change: Islam and the Impact of Print," *Modern Asian Studies* 27 no. 1 (1993), 229–51.
Ryan, Simon. *The Cartographic Eye: How Explorers Saw Australia* (Cambridge University Press, 1996).
Salim, Sayyid Mustafa. *Takwin al-Yaman al-Hadith*. 4th ed. (Cairo: Dar al-Amin, 1993).
Salmoni, Barak A., Bryce Loidolt and Madeleine Wells, *Regime and Periphery in Northern Yemen: The Huthi Phenomenon* (Santa Monica, CA: Rand, 2010).
Salzmann, Ariel. "Citizens in Search of a State: The Limits of Political Participation in the Late Ottoman Empire," in Michael Hanagan and Charles Tilly (eds), *Extending Citizenship, Reconfiguring States* (Lanham, MD: Rowman & Littlefield Publishers, 1999), 37–66.
Satia, Priva. *Spies in Arabia: The Great War and the Cultural Foundations of Britain's Covert Empire in the Middle East* (Oxford University Press, 2008).
———. "The Defense of Inhumanity: Air Control and the British Idea of Arabia," *American Historical Review* 3 no. 1 (February 2006): 16–51.
The Saudi Green Book, 1934 (Oxford: Archive Editions, 1994).
Scott, Hugh. *In the High Yemen* (London: John Murray, 1942).
Sékaly, Achille. *Le congrès du Khalifat et le congrès du monde musulman* (Paris: Éditions Ernest Leroux, 1926).
Serjeant, R.B. "Yafi', Zaydis, Āl Bū Bakr b. Sālim and Others: Tribes and Sayyids," in *On Both Sides of al-Mandab: Ethiopian, South Arabian and Islamic Studies Presented to Oscar Lofgren on his 90th Birthday* (Istanbul: Swedish Research Institute, 1988): 83–105.
———. "The Interplay between Tribal Affinities and Religious (Zaydi) Authority in the Yemen," *al-Abhath* 30 (1982): 11–50.
Serjeant, R.B. and Husayn al-'Amri, "Administrative Organisation," in R.B. Serjeant and Ronald Lewcock (eds), *San'a'—An Arabian Islamic City* (London: World of Islam Festival Trust, 1983).
al-Shamahi, 'Abdullah b. 'Abd al-Wahhab. *al-Yaman: al-Insan wa-l-Hadara* (Cairo: al-Dar al-Haditha, 1972).
al-Shami, Ahmad b. Muhammad. *Imam al-Yaman Ahmad Hamid al-Din* (Beirut?: Dar al-Kitab al-Jadid, 1965).
Shihab, Hassan Salih. *al-'Abadil: Salatin Lahj wa-'Adan, 1832–1959* (Sanaa: Markaz al-Shar'abi li-l-Taba'a, wa-l-Nashr wa-l-Tawzi', 1999).
Sinclair, Reginald W. (ed.), *Documents on the History of Southwest Arabia*. 2 vols (Salisbury, NC: Documentary Publications, 1976).

BIBLIOGRAPHY

Smith, Simon C. "Rulers and Residents: British Relations with the Aden Protectorate, 1937–59," *Middle Eastern Studies*, 31 no. 3 (July 1995): 509–523.

Stark, Freya. *East is West* (London: John Murray, 1945).

Stevens, G.J. "Report on the Country around Aden," *Journal of the Royal Geographical Society of London*, 43 (1873): 295–309.

Stookey, Robert. *South Yemen: A Marxist Republic in Arabia* (Boulder: Westview Press, 1982).

———. *Yemen: The Politics of the Yemen Arab Republic* (Boulder, Colorado: Westview Press, 1978).

Streets, Heather. *Martial Races: The Military, Race and Masculinity in British Imperial Culture, 1857–1914* (Manchester University Press, 2004).

Taha, Jad. *Siyasat Britaniya fi Janub al-Yaman* (Cairo: Dar al-Fikr al-'Arabi, 1969).

Taminian, Lucine. "Rimbaud's House in Aden, Yemen: Giving Voice(s) to the Silent Poet," *Cultural Anthropology*, 13 no. 4 (1998): 464–490.

Tauber, Eliezer. "Rashīd Riḍā as Pan-Arabist before World War I," *The Muslim World* 79 no. 1–2 (1989), 108–111.

al-Tha'alibi, 'Abd al-'Aziz. *al-Rihla al-Yamaniyya* (Beirut: Dar al-Gharb al-Islami, 1997).

Trotter, Lionel J. *The Bayard of India: A Life of Sir James Outram* (London: J.M. Dent & Co., 1909).

Trouillot, Michel-Rolph. *Silencing the Past: Power and the Production of History* (Boston: Beacon Press, 1995).

Um, Nancy. *The Merchant Houses of Mocha: Trade and Architecture in an Indian Ocean Port*. (Seattle, WA: University of Washington Press, 2009).

Van Der Meulen, D. *Faces in Shem* (London: John Murray, 1961).

Vassiliev, Alexei. *The History of Saudi Arabia* (London: Saqi Books, 2000).

Voll, John O. "Renewal and Reform in Islamic History: *Tajdid* and *Islah*," in John L. Esposito (Ed.), *Voices of Resurgent Islam* (Oxford University Press, 1983).

Volta, Sandro. *La Corte Di Re Yahia* (Milan: Garzanti, 1945).

vom Bruck, Gabriele. *Islam, Memory, and Morality in Yemen: Ruling Families in Transition* (London: Palgrave, 2005).

von Maltzen, Baron. "Geography of Southern Arabia." *Proceedings of the Royal Geographical Society of London* 16 no. 2 (1871–72): 115–23.

Wahba, Hafiz. *Jazirat al-'Arab fi al-Qarn al-'Ishrin* (Cairo: Lajnat al-Ta'lif wa-l-Tarjama wa-l-Nashr, 1935).

al-Wasi'i, 'Abd al-Wasi' b. Yahya. *Tarikh al-Yaman* (Cairo: al-Matba'a al-Salafiyya, 1927/28).

al-Washali, Isma'il. *Dhayl Nashr al-Thana' al-Hasan*, ed. Muhammad al-Shu'aybi (Sanaa: Matabi' al-Yaman al-'Asriyya, 1982).

Waterfield, Gordon. *Sultans of Aden* (London: John Murray, 1968).

al-Wazir, Ahmad b. Muhammad. *Hayat al-Amir 'Ali bin 'Abdullah al-Wazir* (n.p.: Manshurat al-'Asr al-Hadith, 1987).

BIBLIOGRAPHY

Wedeen, Lisa. *Peripheral Visions: Publics, Powers, and Performance in Yemen* (University of Chicago Press, 2008).

Weir, Shelagh. *A Tribal Order: Politics and Law in the Mountains of Yemen* (Austin: University of Texas Press, 2007).

Weismann, Itzchak. *Taste of Modernity: Sufism, Salafiyya, and Arabism in Late Ottoman Damascus* (Leiden: Brill, 2001).

Wenner, Manfred. *Modern Yemen, 1918–1966* (Baltimore: Johns Hopkins University Press, 1967).

Wheeler, Stephen. *History of the Delhi Coronation Durbar* (London: John Murray, 1904).

White, Gavin. "Firearms in Africa: An Introduction," *Journal of African History*, 12 no. 2 (1971): 173–84.

Williams, Raymond. *The Country and the City* (Oxford University Press, 1973).

Willis, John M. "Leaving Only Question-Marks: Geographies of Rule in Modern Yemen," in Robert Vitalis and Madawi al-Rasheed (eds), *Counter-Narratives: History, Contemporary Society, and Politics in Saudi Arabia and Yemen* (New York: Palgrave, 2004).

Winichakul, Thongchai. *Siam Mapped: A History of the Geo-Body of a Nation* (Honolulu: University of Hawa'ii Press, 1994).

al-Yahari al-Yafi'i, Nasir Salih Husayn Haytham Sab'a. *Min Yanabi' Tarikhina al-Yamani wa-Ash'ar Rajih Haytham Sab'a al-Yafi'i* (Damascus: Matba'at al-Katib al-'Arabi, 1994).

Yang, Anand A. "Bhils and the Idea of a Criminal Tribe in Nineteenth-Century India," in Anand A. Yang (ed.) Crime and Criminality in British India (Tucson, AZ: University of Arizona Press, 1985).

Yule, Henry and A.C. Burnell. *Hobson-Jobson: The Anglo-Indian Dictionary* (1886; repr. Ware: Wordsworth Editions, 1996).

Zabara, Muhammad b. Muhammad. *A'immat al-Yaman bi-l-Qarn al-Rabi' 'Ashr* (Sanaa: al-Dar al-Yamaniyya li-l-Nashr wa-l-Tawzi', 1984).

———. *al-Anba' 'an Dawlat Bilqis wa-Saba'* (Sanaa: Dar al-Yamaniyya li-l-Nashr wa-l-Tawzi', 1984).

———. *Nuzhat al-Nazar fi Rijal al-Qarn al-Rabi' 'Ashr* (Sanaa: Markaz al-Dirasat wa-l-Abhath al-Yamaniyya, 1979).

———. *A'immat al-Yaman bi-l-Qarn al-Rabi' 'Ashr: Sirat al-Fatih al-Shahid*. 2 vols (Cairo:al-Matba'a al-Salafiyya, 1956).

al-Zubayri, Muhammad Mahmud. *al-Muntalaqat al-Nazariyya fi Fikr al-Thawra al-Yamaniyya* (Beirut: Dar al-'Awda, 1983).

INDEX

'Abbas, Sayyid Yahya b. Muhammad: 187; military forces commanded by, 179
'Abd al-Qadir, Husayn b. 'Ali: Governor of Hudayda, 156
'Abd al-Qawi, Shaykh Muhammad: Governor of Nahiyat al-Sabra, 147
'Abdali: 23–4, 30, 35, 52, 69, 78, 191; *da'ira*: 25–6, 28, 83; history of, 25-31; relationship with Subayhi, 52–3; territory of, 80
al-'Abdali, Sultan 'Abd al-Karim b. Fadl b. 'Ali: 69, 180
al-'Abdali, Sultan Ahmad b. Fadl: 41, 98; accession of (1898), 33–4; participation in Coronation Durbar (1903), 39-40
al-'Abdali, Sultan Fadl b. 'Ali: 32–3
al-'Abdali, Sultan Mushin b. Fadl: 17, 32
'Abduh, Muhammad: 141
Abdül Hamid II, Sultan: 109, 110, 112, 113
Aberigh-Mackay, G.R.: *The Native States and their Chiefs* (1877), 23
Aden Protectorate: 6, 10–11, 13–15, 18, 21, 34, 36–7, 40, 42–3, 49, 57–61, 75, 77, 85, 149–50, 152–3,
167, 170, 177, 180, 188, 194–5, 197–9; Arabic Guest House and Translation Department, 35, 45; borders of, 130, 148, 179; conflict with Mutawakkilite Kingdom of Yemen (1918–34), 171
Aden Protectorate Levies: 201; formation of (1928), 195
al-Afghani, Jamal al-Din: 141, 153
Afghanistan: 11, 21, 39, 86, 155, 161
al-'Afifi, Mu'awwada b. Muhammad: founder of Bani Qasid Sultanate, 30
al-'Afifi, Sultan Sayf b. Qahtan: 30
Ahl 'Abdullah: territory of, 96
Ahl Aj'ud: 185; population of, 95; territory of, 96; tribes of, 186
Ahl-i Hadith movement: 155–6
Ahmadi: 90, 92
al-Ahmar, Shaykh Nasir Mabkhut: 116, 130
al-Ahmar, Shaykh Nasir b. Nasir: military forces of, 131
'Alawi: 23, 31, 78, 176–7, 192; conflict with Qutaybi, 101; territory of, 100, 180
al-'Alawi, Sa'id Du'gri: 99
'Alwan, Shaykh Ahmad b.: destruction of tomb of, 145

INDEX

Ali, Mohamed: 155, 157
Ali, Shaukat: 155-7
'Ali, Shaykh 'Abd al-Rahman b.: 156
al-'Aluba, Muhammad 'Ali: representative of Islamic Conference of Jerusalem, 164-5
American Foundation for the Study of Man: 197
Amiri: 23, 78; territory of, 84
al-'Amri, Qadi 'Abdullah b. Husayn: Yemeni Interior Minister, 161
Anglo-Ottoman Boundary Commission (1902–5): 23–4, 30, 39, 54, 63, 76, 81, 84–5, 97, 178; conclusion of, 94–5, 199; impact of, 102; mission statement of, 87
Anglo-Yemeni Treaty (1934): provisions of, 15; signing of, 15, 194
'Aqrabi: 23, 52
Arab Spring: Egyptian Revolution (2011–12), 205; Tunisian Revolution (2010–11), 205
Arslan, Shakib: 156, 161; representative of Islamic Conference of Jerusalem, 164
al-Atasi, Hashim Bey: representative of Islamic Conference of Jerusalem, 164–5
Athwari: territory of, 50
al-'Atifi, Shaykh Sa'id Ba 'Ali: 60
'Atifi: 52–4; acquisition of weaponry by, 59; territory of, 51
Australia: 7, 70
Austria: military of, 56
'Awdhilli: 71; territory of, 190
'Awlaqi: 23, 71; territory of, 190
Azad, Abul Kalam: 150
al-'Azm, Nazih Mu'ayyad: visit to Yemen (1927), 105
Azraqi: 92

Bakri: 186; territory of, 96

Bani al-Harith: 122
Bani Hushaysh: 122
Barhimi: 53–4, 60; acquisition of weaponry by, 59; Khalifi section of, 52; territory of, 51
Bauman, Zygmunt: 54, 71, 199, 204
Bey, Jurji: 122
Bey, Kanan: 122
Bey, Qadi Muhammad Raghib: 105–6, 158; background of, 161
Bhil: 21
al-Bid, 'Ali Salim: President of People's Democratic Republic of Yemen, 3
Bilad al-Bustan: 122
Blythe, Robert: 10
Borges, Jorge Luis: 202
Bose, Sugata: 10
Brussels Treaty (1890): 62; aims of, 56–7
Bu Bakr b. Salim: 175
al-Bughayli, Shaykh 'Ali: 63
Burma: 38
Buraymi: Bushbushi, 66
Bury, G. Wyman: 71; Extra Assistant Resident, 46

Caliphate: abolition of (1922-4), 138, 139, 140, 150, 155, 164, 166, 171; Cairo conference on, 155; Khilafat movement, 13, 150, 155, 157; Rashid Rida on, 150-1; Imam Yahya's claim to, 156; Umayyad, 151
Carter, Paul: 9, 76, 83, 167, 185, 190; *The Road to Botany Bay*, 7–8, 70; concept of 'spatial history', 8-9
de Certeau, Michel: 8–9, 119, 185; concept of 'tactics', 190; 'spatial stories', 119
Chatterjee, Partha: 35
Christianity: 106, 113
Clayton, General Gerald: 191

INDEX

Cohn, Bernard: 36
colonialism: British, 4, 6, 10, 25; indirect rule, 19-20, 26, 34, 49, 69, 79, 94, 95, 102, 116, 172, 199
Conrad, Joseph: 196
Crane, Charles R.: 12
Criminal castes: concept of, 40, 48-9
Curzon, Lord George: 40, 85, 88, 90; Viceroy of India, 19; role in Coronation Durbar (1903), 37-8, 40-1

al-Dahyani, Sayyid Hasan b. Yahya: 114
Daʾiri: territory of, 96
Daliʿ: 31, 58, 73–4, 81, 84, 86, 88, 91, 93, 95, 101–2, 152, 170, 177, 179, 182, 189–90, 192, 200; amirs of, 77-8; military occupation of, 172; pastoral population of, 75
Daliʿ Agency: 183, 186; end of (1907), 181; personnel of, 76, 195
Dambari: territory of, 96
al-Dawla, Hamud b. Muhammad: chronicle of ʿAli b. ʿAbdullah al-Wazir's military campaigns, 128-30
DeBrath, Ernest: Political Resident, 57
Dirks, Nicholas: 22, 42, 49, 198
Dresch, Paul: 56, 130, 146
Duara, Prasenjit: 6
Dubayni: 52, 63, 65–6; territory of, 51
al-Dumayn, ʿAbdullah b. Muhammad: 134; military forces commanded by, 122

East India Company: 18, 34
Eden Commission (1879): recommendations of, 47
Edward VII, King: 41; coronation of, 13, 37

Egypt: 124, 156, 161; British occupation of (1882–1952), 155; Cairo, 143, 155, 158; Free Officers movement, 7; military of, 108; Revolution (1919), 171; Revolution (2011–12), 205
Ethiopia: Shoa, 57

Fabian, Johannes: 12-13
Fadli: 23, 35, 52
Federation of South Arabia: 73
First World War (1914–18): 12, 15, 33, 69, 71, 102–3, 105, 107–8, 116, 122, 125, 128, 132, 139–40, 149, 162, 170, 177–9; Ottoman entry into, 117
Foster, Donald: 74-5
Foucault, Michel: 6, 166; concept of 'heterotopia', 172; concepts of 'pastoral' and 'governmental' power, 106
France: 150; colonies of, 55; government of, 61; military of, 56
Fujitani, T.: 144

Gandhi, Mohandas: *swaraj* movement of, 142
Gasparini, Jacopo: Governor of Eritrea, 157
German East African Company: 56
Germany: military of, 56
Gilmartin, David: 26
Gulf Cooperation Council: 205

al-Haddad, Qadi Yahya b. ʿAli: 114, 126, 127
Hadramawt: 13, 16, 76, 106, 179, 184
Haines, Capt. S.B.: 17, 25–6, 28, 31–2, 51; role in occupation of Aden, 20–1

267

INDEX

Haj, Samira: 141
Halimayn: 180
Hamid al-Din, Imam al-Badr Muhammad b. Ahmad: family of, 202; coup against (1962), 202
Hamid al-Din, Imam al-Mansur Muhammad b. Yahya: 30, 107, 113, 121; death of (1904), 113; family of, 11; reign of, 108; revolt of, 112-13
Hamid al-Din, Imam Yahya b. Muhammad: 4, 6, 13–14, 102, 106, 111, 113, 118, 120–1, 123, 127, 135, 138–9, 143, 148, 150, 153, 157, 160, 162, 171, 174, 190–1, 194, 199–200; assassination of (1948), 197, 202; background of, 111–12; daʿwa of, 113–14, 131, 172; family of, 115, 126, 130, 132–3, 166, 197; grave of, 5; military forces of, 70, 122, 179–80, 185; military reforms of, 165, 202
Hamid al-Din, Sayf al-Islam Ahmad b. Yahya: 137, 140, 160, 193, 198; family of, 130, 132–3, 197, 202; military campaigns led by, 130–1, 133; named 'Crown Prince,' 159-61
Hamid al-Din, Sayf al-Islam Muhammad b. Yahya: 158
Harris, Walter: 79, 81, 83; fellow of Royal Geographical Society, 76
Harvey, David: 12
Hashid: 130–1
Hawshabi: 23, 31, 78, 101, 176–7; territory of, 80, 85, 180
Haykel, Bernard: 114, 117, 118, 120, 143, 160
Hetherington, Kevin: 194
Heybroek, Friso: 197
Hizb al-Haqq: formation of, 203
Hujayli: 186; Shaykhs of, 183; territory of, 96, 182–3

Hunter, F.M. and C.W.H. Sealey: *An Account of the Arab Tribes in the Vicinity of Aden* (1886 and 1909), 23, 24, 28, 53, 78, 79, 83, 84, 85, 96
Husayn, Dhu: 134
al-Husayni, Hajj Amin: 156; representative of Islamic Conference of Jerusalem, 164
al-Huthi, Sayyid Husayn Badr al-Din: 203; supporters of, 204

al-Idrisi, Sayyid Muhammad b. ʿAli: 116; leader of Idrisi Emirate, 162
Idrisi Emirate: 162
ijtihad: 12, 143; concept of, 112
al-Iman: 140, 156, 158, 164–5; editorial staff of, 139, 142
imperialism: 164; British, 154
India: 6–7, 34–5, 84, 97, 102, 142, 157, 181, 199: Baroda, 40; Bengal, 26; Bombay, 20, 28, 40; British Raj, 13, 19, 36, 40; Buddhuks, 48; caste system of, 71; Coronation Durbar (1903), 19, 34, 37–43; Delhi, 19; government of, 149; Hyderabad, 19, 40; Imperial Assemblage (1877), 10; Indian Revolt (1857), 10, 21, 37, 42, 47; Interpretation Act (1889), 10; military of, 47–8; Mysore, 40; Penal Code, 20; princely states, 7, 10, 11, 14, 18, 19, 37, 41, 80; Punjab: 11, 21; Simla, 37; Sind: 11, 21; Surat, 18; Thags, 48
Indian National Congress: formation of (1885), 10; ideology of, 37, 201
Indian Ocean: 5, 6, 10, 11, 13, 18, 58, 77
Iqbal, Muhammad: 156
Iraq: 102, 142, 159, 161; Basra, 57; British mandate of, 138; Iraqi Up-

INDEX

rising (1920), 171; Operation Iraqi Freedom (2003–11), 204
al-Iryani, Qadi 'Ali b. 'Abdullah: 112
al-Iryani, Qadi Hasan b. Ahmad: 'Candid Advice', 158; chronicle of Hashid and Zaraniq campaigns, 130
al-Iryani, Qadi Yahya b. Muhammad: 193
islah: 143
Islam: 7, 11, 108, 110, 118, 120, 136, 151, 162, 188, 200; *hadith*, 112, 117, 130, 141, 160; Hajj, 156; Hanafi legal school, 115, 143; modernist, 201; reformism, 8, 13; Qur'an, 94, 112, 126, 130, 141–3, 154, 174, 194; *shari'a*, 107, 111–13, 118, 136, 146, 150, 153–4, 160, 173; Shafi'i legal school, 115, 142–3, 146, 154, 157, 166, 173–4; Shi'a, 13, 23, 116, 142, 165, 204; *sunna*, 143, 155; Sunni, 13, 114, 116, 121, 128, 139, 142, 159–61, 165, 174, 204; *umma*, 136, 139, 149, 154; *zakat*, 146, 176, 180; Zaydi, 143, 157, 166, 173
Islamic Conference of Jerusalem: representatives of, 164
Italy: 150, 158–9; colonies of, 57; government of, 61

Jacob, Harold: 33, 36, 59, 101, 149, 156, 169–71, 177; critique of 'Indian model,' 94-95, 102; head of Dali' Agency, 76, 195
Jam'iyyat-i Ulama-yi Hind: 155
al-Jawri, Muhammad Jahhaf: Governor of 'Usaymat, 131
Java: 13, 155, 158
Jerusalem Muslim Congress (1931): 156

al-Jindari, Ahmad b. 'Abdullah: 114
al-Jirafi, 'Abdullah b. 'Abd al-Karim: 113
al-Jubayhi, Yahya 'Abd al-Raqib: 1
Judaism: 31, 78, 109, 113, 147
Julaydi: territory of, 51
Jurabi: 'Atawi section of, 52; 'Ayyari section of, 65–6; Za'wari section of, 65–6
al-Jurabi Shaykh Sa'id: 65–6, 68
al-Juraywi, Shaykh Hasan: 63

Kaye, John William: *People of India* (1868-75), 23-4
al-Kibsi, Sayyid Ahmad: 146
Kingdom of Jordan: 161
Kühn, Thomas: 111, 115

Landscape: 73-6; and Emirate of Dali', 76-85
Lebanon: 112; Beirut, 82
Lefebvre, Henri: 9, 135
Libya: 116
Lugard, Frederick: 26

Mahla'i: territory of, 96
Makdisi, Ussama: 119; concept of 'Ottoman orientalism', 109-10
Makhdumi: 52; territory of, 51
al-Manar: 139, 152, 164–5
Mansuri: territory of, 51
Maqtari: territory of, 50
Martial races: concept of, 40, 47-8
Mas'abayn: 174
al-Masfari, Sa'id Muhammad Ya'qub: 63
Massey, Doreen: 8
Mehmed V, Sultan: 170
Merewether, C.L.: Dali' Agent, 96
Merewether, William: 32
Messick, Brinkley: 110, 148

269

INDEX

Metcalf, Thomas: 7, 19, 35, 42, 48
Metcalf, Barbara: 7, 19, 35
Mitchell, Timothy: 124
Mitchell, W.J.T.: 75
Morocco: 79
Movement of Arab Nationalists: 7
al-Mu'ayyad: 139; political views of, 151–2
Mughal Empire: 38, 189
Muhammad, Dhu: 134, 146
Muhammad, Imam al-Mahdi: reign of, 30
Muhammad, Imam al-Mu'ayyad: reign of, 29
Muhammad, Prophet: 113, 141, 151, 155, 180; Companions of, 156; descendants of, 12, 65, 112, 138, 153, 173–4
am-Mushin, Ahmad: 173
Muhsin, Imam al-Mutawakkil: 111
mujahid: concept of, 112
Muqbil, Muhammad 'Ali: 66, 68
Muqbil, Muhammad Nasir: 85
Muslim Brotherhood: 167
Mussolini, Benito: 158
al-Mutahhar, Qadi 'Abd al-Karim: 123–4, 149, 189; chronicle of Imam Yahya's reign, 118-19; editor of *al-Iman*, 139
Mutawakkilite Kingdom of Yemen: 140, 159, 161, 165, 167, 195, 197–200; conflict with Aden Protectorate (1918–34), 171; Italian treaty, 157-8; Ministry of Education, 161; Ministry of Transport, 161; Ministry of War, 161; Treasury of, 161

Nadvi, Sayyid Sulaiman: 156
Napier, Charles: 21
Nasir, Shaykh Mansur b.: territory of, 128

Nasser, Gamal Abdel: 201
National Liberation Front (NLF): 7, 202
Nationalism: 3–4, 42, 149; Arab, 105, 166; dynastic, 165; Indian, 10, 37, 201; secular, 201
Nepal: 48
Netherlands: 159
North Atlantic Treaty Organization (NATO): 205

Oman: 106
Onley, James: 10
Orientalism: 20–1; Ottoman, 110, 115
Ottoman Empire: 12, 14–15, 33, 39, 42, 53, 89, 109–10, 117, 119, 121, 132, 149–50, 164, 166, 172, 176, 189; collapse of (1918), 12, 108, 128, 136, 139, 149, 171; government of, 53–4, 61, 72, 97, 101, 150, 170; military of, 86, 102, 108, 111, 116, 122–4; occupation of Yemen (1872–1918), 7, 11, 22, 51, 76, 78, 87, 92, 108, 111, 127, 135, 140, 177, 184; Sublime Porte, 23, 87, 91, 116; Tanzimat, 7, 11–12, 15, 107, 109–13, 115, 135, 198; territory of, 7, 51, 65, 76, 82, 109, 111
Outram, James: 52, 71; background of, 21

Palestine: British mandate of, 138
Pan-Arabism: 201
Pan-Asianism: 13
Pan-Islamism: 7, 13, 149; Sunni, 143
Pandey, Gyan: 9
Pasha, Ahmad Mukhtar: 108
Pasha, Ahmad Zaki: 157
Pasha, Hasan Tahsin: 115

INDEX

Pasha, Mehmed Ali: 124
Peel Commission (1859): recommendations of, 47
Pathan: territory of, 97
People's Democratic Republic of Yemen: 7; establishment of (1967), 74
Phillips, Wendell: 197
Playfair, Robert: 28
Prideaux, William Francis: 26
Print culture: 138-9
Public sphere: 13, 15, 139, 150, 151, 166

Qasim, Imam al-Mansur Husayn b.: reign of, 28–9
Qasimi dynasty: 46, 70, 117; statecraft model of, 120–1
al-Qassab, Kamil: 156
al-Qu'ayti, Sultan 'Awad b. 'Umar: 39, 41
Qutaybi: 97, 177, 183, 186–8, 190, 199; conflict with 'Alawi, 101; Shaykhs of, 188; territory of, 96
al-Qutaybi, Shaykh Muhammad Salih al-Akhram: 98, 176, 183, 188; family of, 99
al-Qutaybi, Muqbil 'Abdullah: 99

Reform Association (Jam'iyyat al-Islah): 167
Reilly, Bernard: Political Resident of Aden, 194; Governor of Aden, 194
Djibouti: 45, 55, 57–8, 61, 66
Rida, Rashid: 12, 138–9, 150–2, 155–6, 158, 164; critique of nationalism, 149;
Rihani, Ameen: 106, 135, 144
Rija'i: 52; territory of, 51
Royal Geographical Society: members of, 76

Rubi'atayn: 180; territory of, 178
al-Rusi al-Ahnumi, Husayn b. Husayn: 29; *al-Barahin al-Mudi'a fi al-Sira al-Mansuriyya*, 28
Russian Empire: 150; Jadidist movement, 13

Sabahya (Subayhi): 23, 46-7, 50, 52, 54, 59, 60, 62–3, 65, 69, 70–1, 199; firearm trading activity, 61–2; relationship with 'Abdali, 52–3; territory of, 51, 69, 180
Salafism: 12, 15, 139, 141–2, 153
Salam, Fadl b. 'Ali b. Fadl b. Salih b.: 28
Salih, 'Ali 'Abdullah: Aden, 2; President of Yemen, 2
al-Sallal, 'Abdullah: role in removal of Imam al-Badr Muhammad (1962), 202
Sanhan: 122
Satia, Priya: 20, 94
al-Sa'ud, King 'Abd al-'Aziz b.: 131, 138, 150, 155, 156-7, 162; agreement with Standard Oil Company (1933), 165
Saudi Arabia: 116, 162; 'Asir, 163, 165, 195, 205; Hijaz, 156, 165; Mecca, 131, 139, 151, 155–7; Medina, 151, 156; Najran, 163, 165; Ta'if, 133; Treaty of Mecca (1926), 162; *Umm al-Qura*, 164–5
Saudi-Yemeni War (1934): 140, 166–7; Treaty of Ta'if (1934), 165–6
Sayf, Amir Shayif b.: 39, 41, 91, 93, 102
sayyids: 113, 120, 144, 163, 174
al-Shabab al-Mu'minin ('Believing Youth'): support for Sayyid Husayn Badr al-Din al-Huthi, 204
Sha'iri: 92, 180; territory of, 185

271

INDEX

al-Shami, 'Ali b. Husayn: 159
al-Shami, Sayyid Muhammad b. Muhammad: Governor of Dali', 179, 188
Sharaf al-Din, Imam al-Hadi: death of (1890), 111
Sharaf al-Din, Muhammad: Account of military campaign against northern tribes, 135
Sharjabi: territory of, 50
al-Shawkani, Muhammad 'Ali: 117
Shayif, Amir Nasir b.: 102, 169, 176, 179
Shu'aybi: 180
Sikhism: 49
Somalia: 57, 188
Somaliland: 57, 59
Soviet Union (USSR): 155, 159
Standard Oil Company: 165
Stark, Freya: 73-5
Stewart, Major General: Political Resident, 71–2
Sufism: 116
Sumati: 67
Survey of India: 79, 86; members of, 23, 76
Symes, G.S.: Political Resident of Aden, 195
Syria: French mandate of, 138; Great Syrian Revolt (1925–7), 171

Taha, Sayyid Muhammad: 176
Talib, 'Ali b. Abi: 117
al-Tha'alibi, 'Abd al-'Aziz: 155–6, 158
Thailand: borders of, 93
Tihama: 193, 195
Treaty of Da"an (1911): 115–16, 128, 131, 162, 173, 176; personnel involved in, 161; provisions of, 174
Trouillot, Michel-Rolph, 28
Tunisia: Revolution (2010–11), 205

Turkey: 151; abolition of Caliphate (1922–4), 138–40, 155, 171; Ankara, 149; National Assembly, 149

'Ujayl, Ahmad b. Musa: destruction of tomb of, 134, 145
al-'Ulfi, Qadi Muhammad 'Ali: 145–6
United Kingdom (UK): 123, 136, 150, 169, 175–6, 179, 181, 183–4; Colonial Office, 195; concept of 'nine tribes', 13–14, 19–20, 23–5, 30, 32–3, 46–7, 53–4, 70–1, 76, 78, 80–1, 84–5, 87–9, 91, 93–5, 97, 101–2, 132, 152, 154, 172, 177, 181, 184, 199, 201; Criminal Tribes Act (1871), 48; government of, 52, 61, 66, 101; Habitual Criminals Act (1869), 48; India Office, 88–90; Interpretation Act (1889), 10; London, 88, 203; military of, 56, 98–9, 192; navy of, 17, 20; occupation of Aden, 4, 6, 10–11, 14, 17, 19, 24, 42; Royal Air Force (RAF), 71, 195
United States of America (USA): foreign policy of, 203–5; military of, 205
'Usaymat: 130-132
USS *Cole* bombing (2001): 202

Van der Meulen, Daniel: 123, 127
Victoria, Queen: 18, 34; 1858 proclamation of, 10

wadi: 51, 65; concept of, 50; Bayhan, 173, 184; Hardaba, 96, 98; Hayh, 63; Khurayba, 81; Ma'adin, 51, 60, 62–3, 65–7, 180; Ma'baq, 51, 62; Safiyya, 86–8, 90; Sha'b, 62, 180; Taym, 182, 187; Tuban, 31–2, 79–80, 88, 90

INDEX

Wahab, Colonel R.A.: 84–6; head of Anglo-Ottoman Boundary Commission, 86-92; member of Survey of India, 23
Wahhabism: 118
Wahhasha: 51, 63; Julaydi section of, 65
al-Wasi'i, Qadi 'Abd al-Wasi': 156, 170
al-Wazir, 'Abdullah b. Ahmad: 132, 144; family of, 131; military forces commanded by, 134
al-Wazir, 'Ali b. 'Abdullah: 128–9, 144; family of, 131; military forces of, 180
Waziristan: 86
Wedeen, Lisa: 2
Williams, Raymond: 84
Wilson, Woodrow: 'Fourteen Points', 13, 149, 171
Winichakul, Thongchai: 93

Yafi'i: 23, 50, 71
Ya'qub, Shaykh Sa'id Muhammad: 65
Yasin, Sayyid Qadri: 67
Yemen: 8, 110, 118, 139–41, 143–4, 149, 159, 196, 199; Abyan, 30–1; Aden, 5, 30–2, 36, 51–2, 57, 63, 72, 79, 102, 121, 123, 135, 162, 181, 185, 191, 202–3; Arhab, 125; Bayt al-Faqih, 134, 140, 145; borders of, 152; Dammaj, 146; Dhamar, 125, 144; Habur, 131; Hajja, 126, 131, 134; Haraz, 125; Hubaysh, 129; Hudayda, 162, 191; Hujariyya, 30–1, 33, 50–1, 62–3, 128, 130; Ibb, 125, 128; Jabal Jahhaf, 183, 185–6; Jabal Harir, 169; Jabal Radfan, 92, 96, 180-3, 187, 189–90, 192; Jabal Yafi', 173, 175; Jawf, 134; Kawkaban, 126; Khawlan, 134, 173–4; Kuhlan, 126; Lahj, 25, 28, 30–2, 34, 39, 58, 69, 77, 79–80, 85, 98, 176, 180, 190; Luhayya, 148; Ma'rib, 134, 173–4, 197; Mawiya, 85, 193; military of, 123; Mukalla, 39; Mukha, 18, 20, 57, 109, 130, 191; Najran, 131; Ottoman occupation of (1872–1918), 7, 11, 22, 51, 76, 78, 87, 92, 108, 111, 127, 135, 140, 177, 184; Qaflat al-'Adhr, 126; Qa'taba, 178, 182, 192–3; Quz'a, 180; Red Sea coast, 58, 108, 116, 150, 163; Sanaa, 1–2, 5, 16, 22, 78–9, 108, 111, 123, 125–6, 148, 170, 191; Sharaf, 126; Shihara, 126; Shihr, 39; Suda, 126; Ta'izz, 125–6, 128–30, 144–5, 148, 193; 'Udayn, 129; unification of (1990), 1, 3, 5, 204
Yemen Arab Republic: 7; Civil War (1962–70), 5–6; military of, 3
Yemeni Civil War (1994): 3, 202
Yemeni Socialist Party: 203
Youth for Commanding Good and Forbidding Evil (Shabab al-Amr bi-l-Ma'ruf wa-Nahi 'an al-Munkar): 167
Yusuf, Shaykh 'Ali: 151

Zabara, Qadi Muhammad b. Muhammad: 147, 156-7
Zaraniq: 133–4, 137, 193; branches of, 132; Ma'aziba, 132; Sayf al-Islam Ahmad's campaign against, 133-135
Zaydi Imamate: 4–6, 8, 11–12, 14, 25–6, 34, 37, 42, 77, 108, 111–12, 136, 142; legal basis of, 160; military coup against (1962), 2; concept of 'obedience,' 118-20; transformation of, 117-18

EXECUTIVE EDITOR OF THE ANNALS OF COMMUNISM SERIES

Jonathan Brent, Yale University Press

PROJECT MANAGER

Vadim A. Staklo

AMERICAN ADVISORY COMMITTEE

Ivo Banac, Yale University
Zbigniew Brzezinski, Center for Strategic and International Studies
William Chase, University of Pittsburgh
Victor Erlich, Yale University
Friedrich I. Firsov, former head of the Comintern research group at RGASPI
Sheila Fitzpatrick, University of Chicago
Gregory Freeze, Brandeis University
John L. Gaddis, Yale University
J. Arch Getty, University of California, Los Angeles
Jonathan Haslam, Cambridge University

Robert L. Jackson, Yale University
Czeslaw Milosz (deceased), University of California, Berkeley
Norman Naimark, Stanford University
Gen. William Odom, Hudson Institute and Yale University
Daniel Orlovsky, Southern Methodist University
Mark Steinberg, University of Illinois, Urbana-Champaign
Strobe Talbott, Brookings Institution
Mark Von Hagen, Columbia University
Piotr Wandycz, Yale University

RUSSIAN ADVISORY COMMITTEE

K. M. Anderson, director, Russian State Archive of Social and Political History (RGASPI)
N. N. Bolkhovitinov, Russian Academy of Sciences
A. O. Chubaryan, Russian Academy of Sciences
V. P. Danilov, Russian Academy of Sciences
A. A. Fursenko, secretary, Department of History, Russian Academy of Sciences (head of the Russian Editorial Committee)
V. P. Kozlov, director, Rosarkhiv

N. S. Lebedeva, Russian Academy of Sciences
S. V. Mironenko, director, State Archive of the Russian Federation (GARF)
O. V. Naumov, assistant director, RGASPI
E. O. Pivovar, Moscow State University
V. V. Shelokhaev, president, Association ROSSPEN
Ye. A. Tyurina, director, Russian State Archive of the Economy (RGAE)

ANNALS OF COMMUNISM

Each volume in the series Annals of Communism will publish selected and previously inaccessible documents from former Soviet state and party archives in a narrative that develops a particular topic in the history of Soviet and international communism. Separate English and Russian editions will be prepared. Russian and Western scholars work together to prepare the documents for each volume. Documents are chosen not for their support of any single interpretation but for their particular historical importance or their general value in deepening understanding and facilitating discussion. The volumes are designed to be useful to students, scholars, and interested general readers.